Since the late 1970s, the gap between the rich and poor in Britain has widened considerably. It is now recognised that the growth of inequality in the United Kingdom has been faster than that of any comparable industrial country. This is obviously an important issue, and one which after a long period of neglect is attracting increasing attention. Economists and others concerned with social problems linked with rising inequality are making efforts to understand the factors which have contributed to the current situation.

Based on the results of the first major research programme in this area since the Royal Commission of the 1970s, this book examines income and wealth distribution in the United Kingdom over the last two decades. The country's leading specialists in the area tackle the problem from a wide variety of perspectives. Contributions include: the analysis of income distribution; the effects of greater female participation in the labour force; social security reform; and geographical variation at the national and local scale. Understanding the complexity of these, and other, factors is crucial to designing policies which can begin to cope with income inequalities.

New inequalities

New inequalities

The changing distribution of income and wealth in the United Kingdom

Edited by

John Hills

London School of Economics

CAMBRIDGE UNIVERSITY PRESS

CAMBRIDGE
UNIVERSITY PRESS

University Printing House, Cambridge CB2 8BS, United Kingdom

Cambridge University Press is part of the University of Cambridge.

It furthers the University's mission by disseminating knowledge in the pursuit of education, learning and research at the highest international levels of excellence.

www.cambridge.org
Information on this title: www.cambridge.org/9780521553261

© Cambridge University Press 1996

First published 1996

A catalogue record for this publication is available from the British Library

Library of Congress Cataloguing in Publication data
New inequalities: the changing distribution of income and wealth in the UK / edited by John Hills.
     p.   cm.
    Includes bibliographical references.
    ISBN 0 521 55326 1
    1. Income distribution – Great Britain.   2. Income – Great Britain.
    3. Wealth – Great Britain.   I. Hills, John.
    HC260.I5N49   1996   339.2'2'0941 – dc20   95-9285 CIP

ISBN 978-0-521-55326-1 Hardback
ISBN 978-0-521-55698-9 Paperback

'The Joseph Rowntree Foundation has supported this project as part of its programme of research and innovative development projects, which it hopes will be of value to policy makers and practitioners. The facts presented and views expressed in this report, however, are those of the authors and not necessarily those of the Foundation.'

Contents

Figures

Tables

Contributors

A. B. Atkinson is Warden of Nuffield College, Oxford. He was previously Professor of Political Economy at the University of Cambridge and Chairman of the Suntory–Toyota International Centre for Economics and Related Disciplines at the LSE. His research is in the field of public economics and income distribution. Recent publications include: *Public Economics in Action* (Oxford University Press, 1995) and *Incomes and the Welfare State* (Cambridge University Press, 1995).

James Banks is Programme Manager of consumption and saving research at the Institute for Fiscal Studies. Recent publications related to savings behaviour include: 'Life-cycle expenditure allocations and the consumption costs of children', *European Economic Review* (1994) and 'Household saving behavior in the UK', in J. Poterba (ed.), *International Comparisons of Household Saving* (Chicago University Press, 1994, with R. Blundell).

Vani Borooah is Professor of Applied Economics at the University of Ulster. His research interests lie in the areas of income distribution, labour economics and public choice. Recent publications include: 'Trade unions, relative wages and the employment of young workers', *European Journal of Political Economy* (1993, with K. Lee), and 'The Temporarily Versus the Permanently Poor: Measuring Poverty in a Two-Period Context', *Research Paper*, No. 114, University of Melbourne (1994, with J. Creedy).

Gill Court is a Research Fellow at the Institute for Employment Studies. Her current research focuses on employment issues, in particular the labour market for highly qualified people and the changing structure of employment. Recent publications include: 'Missing Subjects: Gender, power and sexuality in merchant banking', *Economic Geography* (1994, with L. McDowell), 'The gender division of labour in a post-Fordist economy', *Environment and Planning A*, 26 (1994, with L. McDowell) and 'The changing graduate labour market', in R. Williams (ed.), *Students, Courses and Jobs: A Conference Report, QSC Conference Papers*.

Frank Cowell is Professor of Economics at the London School of Economics. His research is in the field of inequality and income distribution. Forthcoming publications include: *Measuring Inequality* (2nd edition, Harvester Wheatsheaf, 1995) and *Thinking about Inequality* (Cambridge University Press, 1996).

Ian Crawford is a Senior Research Officer at the Institute for Fiscal Studies, specialising in research into consumer behaviour. Recent publications include the IFS commentary 'VAT on Domestic Energy' and 'The Distributional Aspects of Environmental Taxation', *Scottish Economic Bulletin* (1993).

Andrew Dilnot is Director of the Institute for Fiscal Studies and a leading commentator on government tax and benefit policy. He has recently co-authored a book on the economics of pensions, *Pensions Policy in the UK* (Institute for Fiscal Studies, 1994), and edited the IFS green budget, *Tax Options for 1995*, the annual analysis of the tax issues facing the Chancellor at budget time.

Martin Evans is a Research Officer with the Welfare State Programme at the London School of Economics. His research interests include housing finance and social security systems in Britain and other countries. Recent publications include: 'Beveridge and his assumptive worlds: The incompatibilities of a flawed design', in J. Hills, J. Ditch and H. Glennerster (eds.), *Beveridge and Social Security: An International Retrospective* (1994, with H. Glennerster) and 'Social security in Britain: Needs versus costs', in J. Midgley and M. Tracy (eds.), *Challenges to Social Security: An International Exploration* (1995, with D. Piachaud).

Amanda Gosling is a Research Officer at the Institute for Fiscal Studies and a Ph.D. Student at University College, London. Her recent research has included work on the determination of union status, the effect of unions on the level and the distribution of wages and on wage inequality more generally. Forthcoming publications include: 'British unions in decline: an examination of the 1980s fall in trade union recognition', in *Industrial and Labor Relations Review* (with R. Disney and S. Machin) and 'Trade unions and the dispersion of earnings in British establishments, 1980–90', *Oxford Bulletin of Economics and Statistics* (with S. Machin).

Anne Green is Senior Research Fellow at the Institute for Employment Research, University of Warwick. She is a geographer with particular interests in local labour markets, and the spatial dimensions of economic, social and demographic change. Her recent research includes the development of local environment indicators, analyses of local unemployment trends, and investigation of the location and mobility decisions of dual career households.

Paul Gregg is a Research Fellow at the Centre for Economic Performance, London School of Economics. His current research uses panel data to analyse individuals' experiences in the labour market over time, especially unemployment and low pay, and the vulnerability of firms to cyclical swings in the economy. Recent publications include: 'Signals and cycles: Productivity growth and changes in union status in British companies 1984–1989', *Economic Journal* (1993, with S. Machin and D. Metcalf), and *Work and Welfare: Tackling the Jobs Deficit* (1993, with E. Balls), Commission on Social Justice Report, No. 3.

Chris Hamnett is Professor of Human Geography at Kings College, London. He was previously Professor of Urban Geography at the Open University. His recent publications include: *As Safe as Houses: Housing Inheritance in Britain* (Paul Chapman, 1991, with Peter Williams), *Housing and Labour Markets* (Oxford University Press, 1990, edited with J. Allen), and *A Shrinking World* (Oxford University Press, 1995, edited with J. Allen).

Susan Harkness is a Research Officer at the Centre for Economic Performance, London School of Economics. Her research interests are on women's earnings and labour market position.

John Hills is Reader in Economics and Social Policy at the London School of Economics and Adviser on Income and Wealth to the Joseph Rowntree Foundation. Recent publications include: *The Dynamic of Welfare: The Welfare State and the Life Cycle* (Harvester Wheatsheaf, 1995, edited with J. Falkingham) and *Beveridge and Social Security: An International Retrospective* (Oxford University Press, 1994, edited with J. Ditch and H. Glennerster).

Stephen Jenkins has been a Professor at the ESRC Research Centre for Micro-Social Change, University of Essex, since October 1994. He was formerly Professor of Applied Economics at the University of Wales, Swansea, where his research for chapter 3 was undertaken. His research interests lie in poverty, income inequality and income mobility, and modelling of labour supply and benefit spell durations. Recent publications include: 'Accounting for inequality trends: decomposition analyses for the UK', *Economica* (1994), 'Parametric equivalence scales and scale relativities', *Economic Journal* (1995, with F. Cowell), and 'Earnings discrimination measurement: A distributional approach', *Journal of Econometrics* (1994).

Julie Litchfield is a Research Officer at STICERD, London School of Economics, working principally on income inequality and poverty within the United Kingdom and Latin America. Recent publications include: 'Inequality, mobility and the determinants of income among the rural poor in Chile, 1968–1986', STICERD Development Economics Research Programme, *Discussion Paper*, DERP/53, London School of Economics (1994, with C. D. Scott).

Hamish Low is currently studying for a M.Phil. in economics at Brasenose College, Oxford and worked at the Institute for Fiscal Studies to produce the IFS commentary *The Distribution of Wealth in the UK* (1994).

Stephen Machin is a Reader in Economics at University College, London and a research associate at the Centre for Economic Performance, London School of Economics. He has worked and published widely in areas including trade unions, minimum wages, wage inequality, the position of women in the labour market and various aspects of company performance. Recent publications include: 'Minimum wages, wage dispersion and employment: Evidence From the UK Wages Councils', *Industrial and Labor Relations Review*, 1994, and 'Changes in the relative demand for skills in the UK labour market', in A. Booth and D. Snower (eds.), *Acquiring Skills: Market Failures, their Symptoms and Policy Responses* (1994).

Patrick McGregor is a Senior Lecturer in the School of Public Policy, Economics and Law at the University of Ulster. His current research includes the comparison of income and expenditure measures of economic welfare. Some results of this work were published in 'Is low spending or low income a better indicator of whether or not a household is poor? Some results from the 1985 Family Expenditure Survey', *Journal of Social Policy* (1992, with V. Borooah).

Patricia McKee is Senior Computing Officer in the School of Public Policy, Economics and Law at the University of Ulster. She is currently researching the changing burden of taxation. Her publications include: *Regional Income Inequality and Poverty in the United Kingdom* (Dartmouth, 1991, with V. Borooah and P. McGregor).

Nigel Meager is an Associate Director at the Institute for Employment Studies (formerly the Institute of Manpower Studies). His research interests include the functioning of national, regional and local labour markets, changing patterns of work, labour market policy evaluation, policies towards the self-employed and small business, and issues relating to equal opportunity and labour market disadvantage. Recent publications include:

'From unemployment to self-employment in the European Community', in F. Chittenden (ed.), *Small Firms: Recession and Recovery* (1993) and 'Self-employment policies for the unemployed: The emergence of a new institution and its evaluation', in G. Schmid (ed.), *Labor Market Institutions in Europe* (1994).

Costas Meghir is Professor of Economics at University College, London and Deputy Director of the ESRC research centre at the Institute for Fiscal Studies. His recent research in this field has included work on female labour supply, transitions between work and unemployment and on wage inequality. Recent publications include: 'Estimating labour supply responses using tax reforms' (IFS mimeo, 1994, with R. Blundell and A. Duncan) and 'The evolution of wages in the UK' (IFS mimeo, 1994, with E. Whitehouse).

Janet Moralee is a Research Officer at the Institute for Employment Studies (formerly the Institute of Manpower Studies), currently working on the area of women in the labour market. Recent publications include: 'Women in building' and 'The position of women in the economy and labour market in the East Midlands' (Institute for Employment Studies Report, 1995, with S. Dench, J. Court and D. Frost).

Gwyneth Mulholland is a Research Officer in the School of Public Policy, Economics and Law at the University of Ulster. She is currently researching in the area of the contract and regulatory state.

Mike Noble is a lecturer in the Department of Applied Social Studies, Oxford University. Prior to that he was a social welfare lawyer working in a community work/welfare rights project. His major research interests are in the areas of income maintenance policy and poverty and exclusion. Recent publications include: 'After redundancy', in T. Hayter and D. Harvey (eds.), *The Factory and the City* (Mansell, 1993, with A. Schofield).

Jenny Seavers is an Honorary Research Fellow and Course Tutor at the Open University. She is currently working on issues relating to housing, particularly capital gains and losses made by owner-occupiers, motivations behind home ownership and housing decision–making between couples. Recent publications include: 'Demographic change in shire England, 1961–91' (University of Leicester, *Rural Mobility and Housing Research Paper*, 4, 1992, with G. J. Lewis and P. McDermott) and 'A step on the ladder? Home ownership careers in the south east of England' (Open University South East Programme, *Occasional Paper* No. 14, 1994, with C. Hamnett).

George Smith is a research fellow in the Department of Applied Social

Studies at Oxford University. His main areas of research are in the fields of educational disadvantage, youth employment and training schemes, inner city policy, social security and community development. Recent publications include: 'From social research to educational policy: 10/65 to the Education Reform Act 1988', in C. Crouch and A. Heath (eds.), *Social Research and Social Reform* (Oxford University Press, 1993, with T. Smith), and 'Changing benefits for boarders and hostel dwellers: Unintended consequences?', *Benefits* (April/May 1993, with M. Noble).

Jonathan Wadsworth is a researcher at the Centre for Economic Performance, London School of Economics and the National Institute of Economic and Social Research. He has worked and published on a range of labour market issues.

Jane Waldfogel is an Assistant Professor of Social Policy at the Columbia University School of Social Work in New York. Her recent research includes work on the effects of family status on women's pay, maternity leave and the importance of women's earnings for family well-being. Recent publications include: 'The price of motherhood: Family status and women's pay in a young British cohort' (*Oxford Economic Papers*, forthcoming), 'Another look at the wage effects of children' and 'Women working for less: Family status and women's pay in the US and UK' (Malcolm Wiener Center for Social Policy, *Working Papers*, Harvard University, both 1994).

Acknowledgements

The research on which this book is based was funded by the Joseph Rowntree Foundation, under its Programme on Income and Wealth. The authors are very grateful to the Foundation, not just for this financial support, but also for the help and encouragement provided throughout by Derek Williams and other members of the staff of the Foundation. The projects reported here were greatly helped by a number of Advisory Groups, and the kind advice and suggestions of those involved in them, including Nick Adkin, David Avenall, Susan Balloch, Fran Bennett, Sean Butcher, Alissa Goodman, Gordon Harris, Alex Hirschfield, Sally Holtermann, Paul Johnson, Alan Marsh, David Owen, David Piachaud, Andrew Rees, Bill Silburn, Mark Stewart, Nigel Stuttard, Holly Sutherland, Robert Walker, Steven Webb and Brian Wilson. They also benefited from the reactions and suggestions of the participants in a two-day seminar held at the LSE in February 1994, at which initial findings from most of the projects were presented.

The research projects used a wide range of data sources and survey results in their analysis, including the DSS's *Households Below Average Incomes* dataset, the *Family Expenditure Survey*, the *General Household Survey*, the *Labour Force Survey*, the *Census of Population*, the *British Household Panel Survey*, the *DSS Survey of Retirement and Retirement Plans*, the NOP *Financial Research Survey*, benefit data from Oxford and Oldham, and regional prices data from the Reward Group. The authors and the editor are greatly indebted to all those involved in granting permission to use these data and in arranging for them to be available for analysis, including the Central Statistical Office, Department of Social Security, Controller of Her Majesty's Stationery Office, the ESRC Data Archive, the ESRC Research Centre on Micro-Social Change, the Office of Population Censuses and Surveys, National Opinion Polls, Oxford City Council, Oldham Metropolitan Borough Council, and the Reward Group.

The editor's job was made incomparably easier by the cheerfulness and efficiency with which contributors met deadlines and provided help and advice to other projects within the programme, and by the excellent research support provided by the Suntory–Toyota International Centre for Economics and Related Disciplines, particularly by Stephen Edward, Luba Mumford, Brian Warren and John Wild. The whole exercise would, however, have been impossible without Jane Dickson's calm efficiency and administrative skills, both in the running of the research programme and in preparing this volume for publication.

Note on date conventions
The following usage has been adopted in the text:
1987/88: HBAI data, the two calendar years 1987 and 1988 taken together
1987–88: The financial year starting in April 1987
1987–90: The period 1987 to 1990

John Hills
January 1995

1 Introduction: after the turning point

John Hills

More than 20 years ago the then Labour government established a Royal Commission on the Distribution of Income and Wealth (RCDIW). The final reports of that commission were published in the summer of 1979. The most recent data to which it had access related to 1978 for earnings dispersion, 1977 for the distribution of household income using *Family Expenditure Survey* (FES) data, the financial year 1976–77 for the overall distribution of income based largely on tax records (the 'Blue Book' series), and 1976 for the distribution of wealth.

The picture painted by the Commission's reports was one of substantial inequalities in the distribution of income and wealth, but one where those inequalities had been narrowing. The 'Gini coefficient' inequality index[1] for the distribution of post-tax income between tax units in the Blue Book series had fallen from 36.6 per cent in 1964 to 31.5 per cent in 1975–76 and 1976–77, well below its 1949 level of 35.5 per cent, indicating reduced income inequality (RCDIW, 1979, table 2.3). The ratio between the top and bottom deciles[2] of male full-time gross weekly earnings was 2.36 in 1978 compared to 2.46 in 1970, but up slightly from 2.32 in 1977. For women the ratio had fallen to 2.34 in 1978, its lowest point in the series examined, compared to 2.57 in 1970 (RCDIW, 1979, table 2.16). The inequality of the personal wealth distribution had reduced substantially between the 1920s and the mid-1960s, and narrowed again between the early and mid-1970s (RCDIW, 1979, tables 4.4 and 4.5).

In 1979 the new Conservative government was elected. One of its earliest actions was the abolition of the Royal Commission, reflecting the changed priority towards distributional issues. From official statistics published through the 1980s, it became apparent, however, that major changes were occurring, particularly in the distribution of income. By 1984–85 (the latest year for which the series was published) the Gini coefficient for post-tax income had reached 36.2 (CSO, 1987), up by 3.6 percentage points from its low point in 1975–76 and 1977–78 (allowing for a change in definitions which added about 1.1 percentage points to the coefficient). The

1

annual CSO *Economic Trends* articles analysing the 'distribution and redistribution of income' using the FES showed rising inequality throughout the 1980s, and a new DSS series, also based on the FES, looking at the position of *Households Below Average Income* (HBAI), showed negligible real income growth at the bottom of the distribution after 1979, despite significant rises in average incomes.

In 1992 the Joseph Rowntree Foundation, an independent research foundation, decided to establish a research programme on different aspects of trends in the distribution of income and wealth. A series of research projects started in 1993 and were completed between the summer and autumn of 1994. The results of the research programme informed the work of the *Income and Wealth Inquiry Group*, also established by the Foundation, whose report was published early in 1995. The chapters of this book bring together the results of twelve of those projects, together with a chapter commissioned by the Inquiry Group from Professor Tony Atkinson (a member of the Royal Commission at the time of its abolition). In the descriptions of these chapters below, footnotes give a reference to the more detailed reports which are available on the findings of some of the projects.

1.1 Overall changes in income distribution

The dramatic changes in income distribution explored in much of this book are illustrated in figure 1.1. This shows the Gini coefficient for the distribution of income from three series:

- The CSO *Blue Book* series for the distribution of post-tax income between 'tax units' (married couples or single people) between 1949 and 1984–85 (there is a break in the series when definitions changed)
- The CSO *Economic Trends* FES-based series for the distribution of equivalised disposable income between households (that is, total household disposable income adjusted by a factor reflecting the size and composition of the household) from 1977–93[3]
- The series derived by Goodman and Webb from the Institute for Fiscal Studies (IFS) (in another project within the Rowntree programme) for the distribution of equivalised net household income between *individuals* using FES data using a three-year moving average from 1961–91, and using broadly the same income definitions as the DSS's *Households Below Average Income* analysis (on the 'before housing costs' (BHC) measure).

Because the three series are based on different units of analysis and different income definitions, their *levels* differ. However, for the years where they overlap there is substantial agreement in the *trends* which they

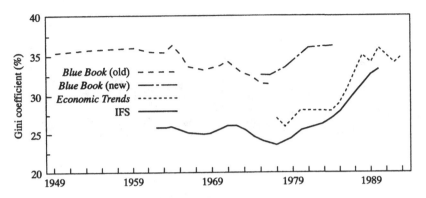

Figure 1.1 Trends in income inequality
Sources: Atkinson and Micklewright (1992, table BI1); CSO (1994, pp. 64–5);
Goodman and Webb (1994, appendix figure 2.2).

show. As figure 1.1 illustrates, there was a marked turning point in the
second half of the 1970s, coinciding – as it happens – with the latest years
for which the Royal Commission had data. Whereas the Blue Book series
was about 4 percentage points lower in 1975–76 and 1976–77 than it had
been in 1949, between 1978 and 1990 the Gini coefficient in the *Economic
Trends* series rose by 10 percentage points, and the IFS series rose by 9.8
percentage points between 1977 and 1990. The latest years of the
Economic Trends series begin to suggest that this rise halted in the early
1990s, but it is too early to judge whether a new turning point has been
reached, or whether the figures simply show a temporary phenomenon.

The implications of the rise in inequality during the 1980s for the real
living standards of different income groups are illustrated by figure 1.2.
This compares (in the bottom panel) the change in living standards by
income group between 1979 and 1991/92 (the average of the two years
1991 and 1992) shown by the latest HBAI analysis (DSS, 1994) with the
comparable changes over the period 1961–79 from the IFS analysis using
the same methodology (Goodman and Webb, 1994). In each case, income
is shown both before deducting housing costs (BHC) and after deducting
them (AHC), the latter definition giving a better measure of the change in
living standards for certain groups, particularly low income tenants in the
1980s when real rents were rising.[4] The changes shown are for the growth
in real incomes at the decile group medians (i.e. at the mid-points of each
tenth of the distribution). The actual people in each tenth of the distribution will not, of course, be the same in each year.

Again, figure 1.2 suggests that what was happening to incomes in the
1980s was very different from what had happened in the previous two

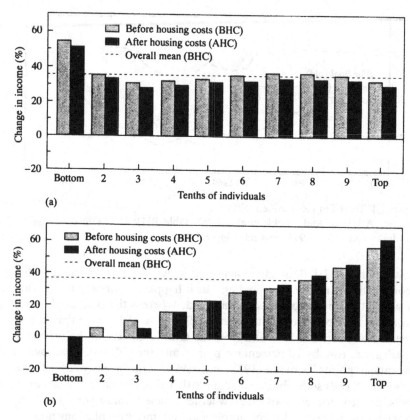

Figure 1.2 Change in real net income, by income group
(a) 1961–79
Source: Goodman and Webb (1994, appendix figure 2.4).
(b) 1979–1991/92
Source: DSS (1994, table A1 and appendix 10).

decades. In the earlier 18-year period shown in the top panel, average incomes rose by 35 per cent (BHC). For no income group was the increase less than 28 per cent, and for the poorest group, incomes rose by over 50 per cent. By contrast, in the 12–13-year period covered by the official DSS series, average incomes rose by 36 per cent – as much over this shorter period as over the previous one – but for the bottom seven-tenths of the distribution, incomes rose more slowly than the average. Right at the bottom, incomes stagnated. Measured after allowing for housing costs, real incomes at the mid-point of the poorest tenth were 17 per cent *lower* in 1991/92 than in 1979. There is some doubt about the accuracy of some of the reported incomes of the self-employed – an issue examined in chapter 9 by Nigel Meager, Gill Court and Janet Moralee – but even excluding the self-employed, real incomes after housing costs fell for the poorest tenth by 9 per cent.

Regardless of the precise figures and definitions, the implication of these figures is clear: since the late 1970s, the living standards of those in the bottom two- or three-tenths of the income distribution have failed to rise significantly, while those at the top of the distribution have risen much more rapidly than the average. The nearer the top an income group lies, the faster its income has risen. The chapters of this book explore this new phenomenon from a variety of angles, looking at the changes in overall income inequality in part I, at different components of income distribution in part II, at geographical/spatial aspects in part III, and at issues connected with wealth distribution – and the links between income and wealth – in part IV.

1.2 The overall income distribution

In chapter 2, Tony Atkinson explores the economics of income distribution from several perspectives. He sets the growth in income inequality in the United Kingdom shown in figure 1.1 in an international context using national studies for other countries, highlighting the difference between the scale of the growth of inequality in the United Kingdom and that in other countries, and shows that rising inequality in the 1980s was *not* a universal phenomenon.

Atkinson argues that economic theory does not at present provide an adequate basis to explain the inequality changes of recent years. The chapter sets out six major reasons why theories of factor incomes (wages, profit and rent) do not provide a theory of personal distribution: heterogeneity of incomes, human capital, diversity of sources, intervening institutions, income from abroad, and the impact of the state budget. Atkinson then goes on to examine in detail three areas. The first is inequality of earnings, including the changing skill differential, deindustrialisation, and the influence of labour market institutions. The second is the impact of rising real interest rates and share prices, discussing the behaviour of companies, pension funds and other intervening institutions. The third is the distributional role of the government budget and public choice explanations. The chapter concludes that the existing literature provides valuable insights but that we lack at present an overall framework to relate the different parts of the income distribution story.

Frank Cowell, Stephen Jenkins and Julie Litchfield present in chapter 3 the revealing results of a new way of analysing empirical information on income distribution, applied to the dataset on which the Department of Social Security's analysis of *Households Below Average Income* between 1979 and 1988/89 is based (DSS, 1992).[5] They use the data for individual households to build up the frequency distribution for incomes in the two years, and show how the richness of the data can be exploited to give a much more detailed picture of the distribution than comes, for instance, from conventional fixed-interval bar charts.

Cowell *et al.*'s analysis shows how the *shape* of the distribution changed over the 1980s. In 1979 the pattern could be summarised roughly as a (rather bumpy) peak of incomes concentrated around a single level, and then a long 'tail' of comparatively few people with relatively high incomes. If all that had happened over the 1980s had been an equal growth in all incomes, the picture for 1988/89 would be of much the same shape, but shifted to the right. In fact what happened was that part of the initial peak stayed in the same place – incomes at the bottom did not grow – but the size of the initial peak became smaller, and the tail of higher incomes became much more substantial. The picture presented suggests that the overall income distribution is, in fact, the product of several sub-distributions, which changed in different ways over the 1980s. The chapter goes on to explore different ways of splitting the population between groups to identify these sub-distributions. Partitioning the population by source of income turns out to be particularly informative.

Chapters 4 and 5 are concerned with different aspects of the link between the incomes of different groups and changes in their living standards. Results like those shown in figure 1.2 are based on the differences in the 'real' incomes for those in each income group using the *same* price index for all income groups: implicitly, they assume that inflation is the same for all households.

In chapter 4 Ian Crawford explores whether inflation has, in fact, been the same for those at the top and bottom of the income distribution, if one allows for the great differences between the kinds of goods which they buy (but not for factors like region – discussed below – or the kinds of shops used).[6] Crawford's results show that there can be quite noticeable differences in inflation rates between the groups from year to year. In some periods – such as the early 1980s – 'inflation' was faster for the poor than the rich. In others – such as the late 1980s – the reverse was true. The exact time period chosen can therefore make a large difference to the results. So, crucially, can the way in which housing is allowed for in calculating 'the cost of living'. Crawford compares the differences between price indices constructed using the way in which the Retail Prices Index (RPI) allows for owner-occupiers' housing costs and those using an alternative measure, the 'user cost of capital' approach. The chapter also looks at the contribution which changes in indirect taxes made to the rise in the cost-of-living for different groups over the 1980s. This brings out the importance of exemptions from VAT for those with low incomes, which protected them from the effects of the rises in VAT rates and slowed the rise in their cost-of-living compared to the average, but also the regressive nature of some of the other indirect tax changes, having the opposite effect.

This analysis is on a national scale, allowing for differences in consumption patterns between rich and poor. In chapter 5, Vani Borooah, Patrick McGregor, Patricia McKee and Gwyneth Mulholland examine the effects of regional differences in prices, using data collected by the Reward Group for prices of the same items in different locations across the United Kingdom.[7] They show both that prices for some commodity groups vary across the United Kingdom, and that many of these differences widened over the 1980s. This has a number of implications. First, as the higher income regions like London and the South East also tend to have a higher cost-of-living, regional income differences are somewhat reduced by allowing for differential costs. Second, inflation was higher in these richer regions over the 1980s than in poorer regions. As high income households are more concentrated in the richer regions, a part of the growth in income inequality of the 1980s illustrated in figure 1.2 would be removed by allowing for regional differences in the cost-of-living. The scale of this effect depends again on the way in which housing is allowed for. If the 'user cost of capital' approach is allowed for (taking into account the rate at which house prices had risen over a 20-year period), the narrowing effect is slightly larger than that produced using the RPI's method for dealing with owners' housing costs.

1.3 Components of income distribution

As Tony Atkinson points out in chapter 2, it is not possible to read straight from changes in the distribution of a single component of income (such as the dispersion of individual earnings) to changes in the overall distribution of income. As figure 1.3 shows,[8] there are several intervening stages between the two. Not only are there other sources of income, such as self-employment, investment income or pensions, but an important role is played by the way in which income from these sources is associated. For instance, investment income may become more equally distributed between those receiving it, but if its receipt becomes more closely correlated with high incomes from other sources, the ultimate result may be a widening of the overall income distribution.

In this context, it is important to note that measures of income like those shown in figure 1.2 or used in the DSS's *Households Below Average*

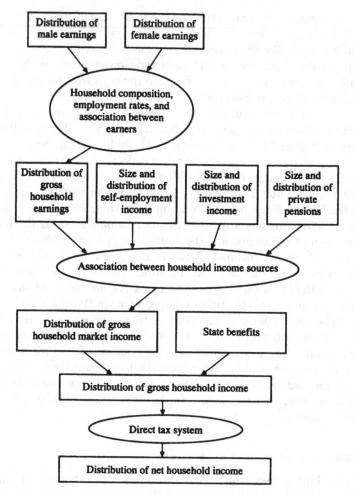

Figure 1.3 Factors affecting distribution of net household income

Income analysis are based on *household* incomes, even if in the analysis each individual is given equal weight. The association between the incomes of household members is therefore of great importance, particularly that between the earnings of partners in a couple: whether high-earning men live with high-earning women, or whether men and women without any earnings at all are in the same households, and changes in these associations, become critical questions (and are explored in chapters 7 and 8).

In chapter 6, Amanda Gosling, Stephen Machin and Costas Meghir concentrate on what happened to the distribution of male hourly earnings between 1966 and 1992, highlighting in particular the period after 1978 when the gaps between high paid and low paid men widened sharply.[9] This followed a period of roughly 90 years during which surveys of earnings suggested that there was considerable stability in earnings differentials (for manual workers, at least). Gosling *et al.* use evidence from the *Family Expenditure Survey* to examine the relationships between earnings differentials and skills groups (as measured by occupational group and, after 1978, number of years of full-time education).

Their analysis explores not only the widening gaps between skill categories, but also those which have occurred *within* skill categories, suggesting that more was going on in the 1980s than simple shifts in the supply and demand for labour in broadly defined categories. While the analysis does for instance, confirm the rising differentials between different skill groups found by other researchers,[10] it shows that this only explains the smaller part of the rise in dispersion. A particular feature of the analysis is the examination of the changing experience of successive cohorts of workers newly entering the labour market. This leads Gosling *et al.* to suggest that the widening gap between older and younger workers seen in cross-sectional data does not necessarily represent a general rise in the premium placed on experience within the labour market. Instead, what may be occurring is a cohort effect, with younger generations of workers at a disadvantage compared to older generations. Particularly for those with low levels of skill or qualifications, this disadvantage, they suggest, may be permanent rather than being remedied by later experience effects.

Chapter 7, by Susan Harkness, Stephen Machin and Jane Waldfogel, concentrates on women's earnings and their contribution to family incomes, using data for couples and single women aged 24–55 from the *General Household Survey* over the period 1979–91.[11] During this period there were major changes in women's labour force participation and in the relative contribution of women's earnings to family incomes. First, the authors report the decline of the male 'breadwinner' – male earnings fell as a share of gross family income for couples aged 24–55 from nearly 73 per cent in 1979–81 to 61 per cent in 1989–91, while the shares from female earnings and from other sources rose. Female earnings are now a much more important part of family incomes and this is the case for many couples, not just for the wives of relatively well paid men. In fact, over the 1980s the share of family income from women's earnings rose most rapidly for the wives of men with low earnings (but not for those with no earnings).

This, Harkness *et al.* argue, has two important implications. First, the growth in female labour force participation in the 1980s had an equalising effect on the distribution of income (within this particular population group).[12] Second, women's earnings cannot be regarded as simply 'pin money' and therefore irrelevant to the incidence of low family incomes: without the contribution of women's earnings, they show, poverty rates for these couples would have been far higher. The chapter also examines the changing labour market position of single women (both with and without children) over the 1980s, examining whether what has been most important has been the rising incidence of lone parenthood (that is, changing family structure) or changes in behaviour within groups, concluding that the latter has been the more important.

Paul Gregg and Jonathan Wadsworth in chapter 8 pick up the theme of rising female participation for couples where the man is earning, but falling participation where he is not, to look more generally at the problem that earners are becoming concentrated in a smaller number of households. This was one of the contributory factors behind the growth in overall income inequality in the 1980s. Quite apart from the effects of rising earnings dispersion overall, household incomes became more unequal because some had two wages coming in, while others had none, and this polarisation between 'work-rich' and 'work-poor' increased over the 1980s.

Gregg and Wadsworth use data from the *Labour Force Survey* between 1975 and 1993 for adults not in full-time education and aged under 60 to explore the reasons behind this shift. They examine first the rise in non-employment for those without an employed partner (either because they are single or because their partner is not employed), and then focus on the way in which this appears to have occurred mainly because of a collapse in their exit rates from non-employment. For instance, far fewer couples who start a year with no earner now end the year with one or two earners than used to be the case. The authors then investigate a number of potential explanations of this phenomenon, although the data allow more by the way of rejection of some explanations than of confirmation of others.

Another striking feature of the 1980s was the large rise in self-employment in the United Kingdom. This is investigated by Nigel Meager, Gill Court and Janet Moralee in chapter 9.[13] This affected the overall distribution of income significantly because families with self-employed members are to be found disproportionately at both the bottom and the top of the income distribution. Jenkins (1995) found that between 1981 and 1986 changes in self-employment incomes were the largest single contributor to overall inequality growth. However, as discussed above, it has been suggested that because some of the self-employed may misreport their incomes to official surveys this may have contributed a spurious component to the growth in the number of people living in households with relatively low incomes.

Meager *et al.* report the results of their investigation of a number of data sources, in particular the new ESRC *British Household Panel Survey*, as well as the 1988 survey of *Retirement and Retirement Plans*. These sources include those where the authors expected under-reporting to be less of a problem than with, say, returns to official surveys which might be seen as linked to taxation. One finding is that data from a variety of sources confirm the existence of a substantial group of the self-employed with low incomes when in work (and also in retirement for some of the formerly self-employed). This group has particular characteristics, and it was the self-employed with these characteristics who were one of the most rapidly growing groups in the 1980s. Using multivariate analysis, the authors investigate whether self-employment has an influence separate from other linked characteristics in determining the odds that someone will be at the top or bottom of the income distribution (which it appears to for the latter, but not the former). They also point to the important implications of the wide dispersion of self-employment incomes, and of the way in which state pensions are not well-adapted for the self-employed, for continued inequality in retirement.

Finally in this part of the book, Martin Evans in chapter 10 examines a further important component of gross incomes, that determined by the benefit system.[14] He looks in particular at the effects of the reforms to means-tested benefits which were implemented in 1988 following the results of the 'Fowler reviews' of the social security system. These reforms were billed as the 'most radical since Beveridge', so they might have been expected to have had a major effect on income distribution. In fact, Evans concludes, their effect was more to move certain kinds of household around within the lower part of the income distribution, rather than to make any significant difference to the numbers with incomes below particular thresholds or poverty lines. The chapter shows various ways in which the reforms succeeded in their objective of making the system simpler to administer, and in which they targeted more resources on some groups rather than others. However, it also raises the question of whether the reforms created gaps in the minimum income safety net which the social security system is supposed to guarantee.

Taken together with other studies of particular aspects of UK income distribution,[15] the findings reported in this part of the book show that it would be a mistake to single out one particular factor as having been responsible for the substantial changes over the 1980s. What was remarkable was that changes in most of the factors determining income distribution were pushing in the same direction.

1.4 Spatial aspects of income and wealth distribution

Chapters 11 and 12 examine whether the growth in income inequality described at a national scale in earlier chapters has been accompanied on the ground by an increasing polarisation between areas, as measured by available indicators of deprivation or affluence. In chapter 11 Anne Green presents findings from her study of the Censuses of 1981 and 1991.[16] The Census does not contain direct information on income levels or people's stock of wealth, but it does contain information on a number of factors which are known from other sources to be correlated to a greater or lesser extent with high or low incomes. Using these indicators, Green presents results by geographical area over the 1980s in Great Britain at two scales, by local authority district, and at ward (neighbourhood) level.

At local authority district scale, Green's findings indicate both continuity and change in which districts are to be found at the top of a variety of 'league tables' by deprivation indicators. Some feature high up the rankings in both years, and feature highly on a variety of rankings. There are, however, districts which substantially improved their position over the 1980s – notably including (on some indicators) areas associated with closures in the steel industry in the early 1980s. For others, their position deteriorated between 1981 and 1991, notably including several Inner London boroughs. In general, the results for indicators of affluence are rather more stable: areas which appeared affluent in 1981 were still so in 1991.

While these results do not indicate any greater distance in 1991 than in 1981 between 'best' and 'worst' areas at this scale, the results analysed at the much finer ward scale do indicate an increase in geographical polarisation over the period. Green's results suggest that what is occurring is more complex than any simple 'North–South divide', with significant changes happening *within* cities and towns, related to the kinds of labour market changes explored in earlier chapters.

This theme is picked up by Michael Noble and George Smith in chapter 12. They present results from their micro-level study of Oxford and Oldham.[17] This is based not only on the use of Census data (this time at the even finer 'enumeration district' level) for 1981 and 1991, but also on the use of computerised and post-coded Housing Benefit records from the two towns. This allows them to build up very detailed maps using the same kinds of indicators of deprivation and affluence used in chapter 11, as well as showing the proportion of the population receiving Income Support at six-monthly intervals.

Their results confirm at a finer scale some of the conclusions reached by Green's national study. First, there is considerable stability over time in which areas within each town are classified as better- or worse-off, but at

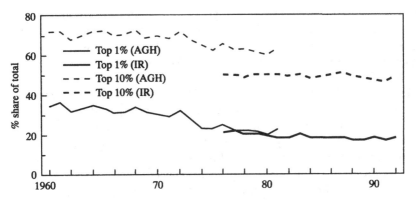

Figure 1.4 Distribution of marketable wealth, 1960–90
Sources: AGH from Atkinson *et al.* (1989, table 1) (GB); IR from Good (1990, table C) and Inland Revenue (1994, table 13.5) (UK).

the same time there is clear evidence of an increasing gap between 'best' and 'worst' areas over time at this scale, with this increased polarisation particularly pronounced in Oldham. The results also suggest the importance of the connection between housing tenure and income in this process. Because council housing tends to take the form of large single-tenure estates, as council tenants have increasingly become concentrated in the lower income groups,[18] so polarisation on the ground has increased.

1.5 Wealth and its links with income

Chapters 13 and 14, the final two chapters, examine aspects of the distribution of people's wealth, in the sense of their *stock* of assets (as opposed to their flow of income), and look in particular at the links between income and wealth levels. Figure 1.4 presents the most recent Inland Revenue figures for the shares of marketable wealth owned by the top 1 per cent and 10 per cent of wealth-holders, as revealed by data on the size of estates, together with earlier trends taken from Atkinson *et al.*'s (1989) study. Figure 1.4 suggests that the distribution of marketable wealth narrowed significantly in the 1960s and early 1970s, but that the long-term trend towards reduced inequality ended in the mid-1970s, since when there has been very little change. Using a wider definition of wealth, including the value of people's accrued rights to occupational and state pensions, inequalities in wealth increased between 1976 and 1992 (Inland Revenue, 1994, table 13.7).

There are, however, limitations to the information which can be drawn from the estate-based wealth distribution series. First, its coverage of the total of marketable wealth is quite high, but it excludes a large proportion of the population who have low (but positive) levels of wealth. Second, because the source of the data is records of estates as assessed for taxes when they are passed on at death, they provide no direct information on the links between income and wealth.

In chapter 13, James Banks, Andrew Dilnot and Hamish Low present the results of analysis of a survey which allows these gaps to be filled, at least in part. They present findings from the *Financial Research Survey*, carried out by National Opinion Polls. This survey asks respondents about both their incomes and the level and types of their financial assets. Banks *et al.* point out that the survey appears to omit the richest wealth-holders, who account for much of the total of marketable wealth, but suggest that their results are broadly representative of the position of the 'bottom 90 per cent' of the population. They also use data from the first wave of the *British Household Panel Survey* to estimate levels of housing wealth, which they combine with the information on financial assets to give a picture of marketable wealth more broadly defined. These surveys allow them to present new findings on the way in which wealth distribution is linked separately to both income and age, in terms of the kinds of asset held and in the overall value of assets, and to examine the shift in asset-holdings between 1987–88 and 1991–92.

Both life-cycle factors and income level are important determinants of people's wealth levels. This is particularly important in the case of net equity in owner-occupied housing, which for many people represents their most important asset. Data from the *British Household Panel Study* on housing assets are explored in more detail in chapter 14, by Chris Hamnett and Jenny Seavers. They describe the two different ways in which the capital values of owner-occupied property can be derived from the survey – original purchase price adjusted for subsequent house price increase on a regional basis, and the owner's own estimate of current market value – and discuss the problems of establishing the value of outstanding mortgages to give reliable estimates of net housing wealth (or housing equity). Hamnett and Seavers's results show that age and income are not the only factors which have strong links with the level of net housing wealth (other factors include socio-economic group, region, and year of purchase), and that it is very important to distinguish between outright owners and mortgagors in analysing these links. The survey also allows examination of the rather different position of those owners who were originally tenants of their house, but have subsequently purchased under schemes such as the Right to Buy.

The chapters in this book shed new light on the substantial distributional changes in the United Kingdom over recent years. The gradual, and uneven, reduction in the inequality of income ended in the late 1970s, and income inequality in the United Kingdom grew rapidly in the 1980s, more than reversing the previous post-war fall. Meanwhile, the inequality of wealth distribution reduced substantially up to the mid-1970s, but has since levelled out. While it is possible that the evidence available at the moment precedes a new turning point or change of trend, as with that surveyed by the Royal Commission of the 1970s, these changes have already had major implications both for the economy and for the social fabric. Understanding the complexity of the factors which have contributed to them is a crucial step on the way to designing policies which could begin to cope with their effects.

Notes

1. The Gini coefficient is one of the most commonly used indices of the inequality of a distribution, taking a value of zero if all the units (individuals, tax units or households) under investigation have the same income (under whatever definition being used), rising to a maximum of one (or 100 per cent) if a single unit has all of the income, and the rest none.
2. 10 per cent of earners have earnings below the bottom decile, and 10 per cent have earnings above the top decile.
3. Incomes are adjusted using the DSS's 'McClements' equivalence scale. Note that the figures for individual years are rounded to integers, and that income definitions vary between years, so that the differences between years are subject to some uncertainty.
4. This is because for tenants receiving Housing Benefit covering all of their rents, a rise in rents causes an increase in Housing Benefit, and hence in BHC incomes, even though their living standards are unchanged. Using AHC incomes removes this problem.
5. See Jenkins and Cowell (1994) and Jenkins (1994) for further results from the study on which this chapter is based, including results for intervening years between 1979 and 1988/89 and extension to 1990/91.
6. See Crawford (1994) for more details of the study reported here.
7. See Borooah et al. (1994) for more discussion of the results described here.
8. Figure 1.3 is a simplified version of an equivalent diagram presented in Gardiner (1993).
9. See Gosling et al. (1994a and 1994b) for more details of the study reported here.
10. See, for instance, Schmitt (1994).
11. See Machin and Waldfogel (1994a) and Harkness et al. (1994) for more details of the study on which this chapter is based.
12. As far as overall income distribution is concerned, the effect is less clear, as the phenomenon also contributed to a rising gap between the incomes of this group and other population groups.

13. See Meager *et al.* (1994) for the full report of the study on which this chapter is based.
14. See Evans *et al.* (1994) and Evans (1994) for more detailed discussion of the results presented here.
15. See the discussion of some of these factors in chapter 2 and in Atkinson (1993a), and see Jenkins (1995) for an overview of changes between 1971 and 1986 and of the relative importance of different components. For aspects related to changes in the taxation system, see Johnson and Webb (1993), Giles and Johnson (1994), and Redmond and Sutherland (forthcoming). For a discussion of the evolution of relative benefit rates, see Hills (1993).
16. See Green (1994) for a full report of the results of the study.
17. See Noble *et al.* (1994) for further details of the study.
18. Hills (1993), figure 49.

Part I

Income distribution

2 Seeking to explain the distribution of income

A. B. Atkinson

Economists sometimes vaguely wonder why economic theory is so unpopular ... Is there anything in this to excite surprise, if we reflect for a moment on the inadequacy of the answer furnished by the theory of distribution, as at present taught, to the questions in which the ordinary person is interested? (Cannan, 1905)

2.1 Introduction

There is little doubt that the distribution of income in the United Kingdom has become more unequal since 1979. Average real incomes have grown significantly, but at the bottom of the scale there has been little or no rise in real income, whereas top incomes have risen a great deal faster than the average. This widening of income differences is a departure from the pattern of previous decades in the United Kingdom which saw a modest reduction in income inequality over the post-war period. Similarly, inequality has increased in the United States. According to the 1994 Economic Report of the President, 'starting some time in the late 1970s, income inequalities widened alarmingly in America' (Council of Economic Advisers, 1994: 25).

What can explain this rise in inequality? Why has the previous trend been reversed? What is the likely future development? The lay person may well expect to find these questions addressed and answered in economic textbooks. The distribution of income is surely central to the understanding of the working of the economy. Yet, as Cannan indicated 90 years ago, the ordinary person will be disappointed. Economic analysis today, as in 1905, has little in the way of conclusive answers regarding the explanation of the distribution of income among citizens.

Indeed, the question has – at least until recently – been remarkably little discussed. Much of what can be found in textbooks under the heading of the 'Theory of Distribution' is concerned with the determinants of payments to factors of production (labour, land and capital): the *factor distribution of income*. The relationship of the factor distribution with the *personal distribution of income* is typically not spelled out. However, statements about the distribution of national income between wages and profits, or about the relative wages of skilled and unskilled workers, do not tell us directly how the share of the top 20 per cent or the bottom 20 per cent is likely to have changed. The factor distribution is certainly part of the story, but it is only part, and the other links in the chain need to receive more attention.

My principal purpose here is to argue that the economic analysis of the distribution of income is in need of further development before we can hope to give a definitive answer to the question in which the ordinary person is interested: why has inequality increased? This does not mean that current economic theory has nothing to contribute. It certainly offers insights into parts of the story, but what is required is for the different elements to be brought together.

The main part of the chapter is concerned with the different stages in comprehending the distribution of income: aggregate factor incomes, differences in earnings and in capital incomes, the role of the corporate sector and of financial institutions, and the distributional impact of the state. The focus is on explaining the recent trend towards increased inequality, since without some understanding of the reasons for the reversal of the historical pattern we cannot form a view as to whether it is likely to continue in the future. At the same time, it is not possible to cover all the links in the chain. In particular, I have relatively little to say here about unemployment, not because I believe it to be unimportant,[1] but because I have written extensively about it elsewhere.

This chapter is concerned with the *theory* of income distribution, but it may be helpful to begin with a brief summary of the evidence to be explained. How far is the trend observed in the United Kingdom and the United States common to all OECD countries?

2.2 The empirical evidence to be explained: trends in income inequality

The empirical evidence concerning the recent trends in income inequality in different OECD countries has been surveyed by Gardiner (1993) and Atkinson *et al.* (1995). Figures 2.1–2.3, drawing on this work, show the degree of income inequality in a range of countries. It should be emphasised that these figures are *not comparable across countries*. One can draw no conclusions from these graphs about the *relative* degree of inequality in different countries. In each case, the figures are drawn from national studies of income inequality which are not designed for purposes of international comparison, and they are not necessarily based on the same concepts of income or method of calculation: for example, the US series,

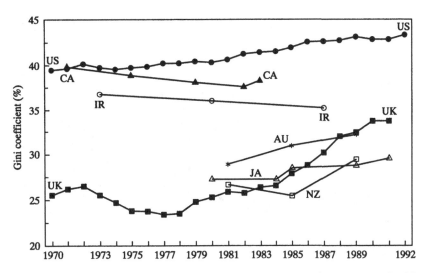

Figure 2.1 Trends in income inequality in the United Kingdom compared with other Anglo–Saxon countries and Japan, 1970–92

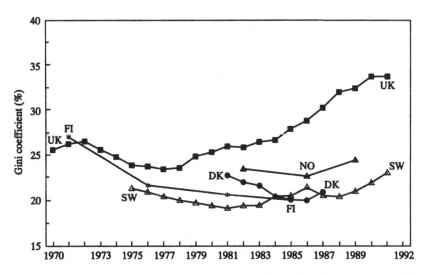

Figure 2.2 Trends in income inequality in the United Kingdom compared with Scandinavia, 1970–92

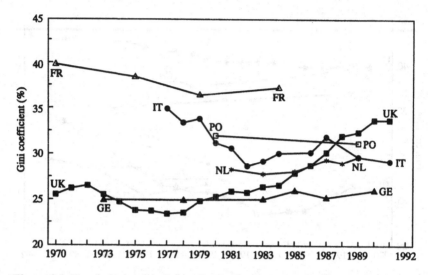

Figure 2.3 Trends in income inequality in the United Kingdom compared with EU countries, 1970–92

unlike those for other countries shown, relates to the distribution of gross income (before taxes) and is not adjusted for household size. I have chosen those series which give a reasonable span of years and which are themselves intended to be consistent over time. They therefore may serve to give an indication of the relative *trends* in different countries, but it should be stressed that complete consistency can never be assured (and in some cases I have linked series or shown series with a break). The data and sources are listed in the appendix on pp. 45–7.

The main features with regard to the United Kingdom and the United States are well known. In the United States, the official figures indicate that an upward trend in inequality was already present in the 1970s – see figure 2.1, which shows the Gini coefficient for the period 1970–92. (The Gini coefficient is an index of inequality, which would take the value of zero if all incomes were identical and would approach 100 per cent if all income were received by one person.) The coefficient increased from 39.4 per cent in 1970 to 43.3 per cent in 1992. Given the fact that the series are not comparable across countries, it is the 4 percentage point increase in the coefficient which should be noted, as should the fact that the difference between the 1980s and the 1970s was one of degree rather than of any sharp change in direction. In the United Kingdom, the timepath is different. Up to 1977, income inequality fell, as measured by the Gini coefficient in figure 2.1. 1979 saw a reversal, and between that year and 1991 the Gini coefficient rose by nearly 9 percentage points, which is more than double the increase over two decades in the United States, and more than double the decline in the United Kingdom from 1949 to 1976 (Atkinson, 1993a, table 1).

The sharp rise in measured inequality in the 1980s in the United Kingdom does indeed stand out in figures 2.1–2.3 (in each case the United Kingdom is shown in bold). Figure 2.1 compares the situation with that in other Anglo–Saxon countries and Japan. In Australia and Japan, the upward trend over the 1980s is not very different from that in the United States in that the Gini coefficient increased by 2–3 percentage points during the decade. The same is true in New Zealand, although the increase in inequality appeared to come after 1985 (see Boston, 1993; Saunders, 1994). In Canada and Ireland, on the other hand, there is no significant upward trend over the period shown.

Turning to mainland Europe, we can see from the comparison with Scandinavia in figure 2.2 that Sweden exhibited the same U-shaped path as the United Kingdom. There was a downward trend until the beginning of the 1980s, followed by a rise in measured inequality. The Gini coefficient increased by some 4 percentage points in 10 years, a rate which places Sweden between the United States and the United Kingdom. In the other three countries, the trend over the first half of the 1980s was different, with a downward trend. There are signs that this has been reversed in the second half of the 1980s, but again nothing matching the rise in inequality observed in the United Kingdom.

The pattern across countries does not therefore appear to be a uniform one, and this is further borne out by figure 2.3, which shows a number of other countries in the European Union (in addition to Denmark and Ireland already covered in figures 2.1 and 2.2). There is an upward trend over the 1980s in the Netherlands, although again of a relatively modest proportion: the Gini coefficient rose by less than 2 percentage points between 1983 and 1989. For France the available data stop in 1984, but the increase between 1979 and 1984 was less than 1 percentage point; that in West Germany over the whole decade was of the same order. In Italy and Portugal there was a slight downward trend in measured income inequality, in the former case accompanied by a marked cyclical pattern (inequality increasing as the economy grew faster – see Brandolini and Sestito, 1993).

One clear conclusion is that the United Kingdom stands out for the sharpness of the rise in recorded income inequality in the second half of the 1980s. This was unparalleled in the countries examined. Among the other OECD countries, it is certainly wrong to think in terms of a world-wide trend towards increased income inequality in the 1980s: the upward trend was exhibited to differing degrees in different countries, and was not to be found at all in some countries. At the same time, those seeking to identify a common pattern for OECD countries other than the United Kingdom and United States could say that continuing progression towards *reduced* inequality was the exception rather than the rule.

2.3 From the factor distribution to the personal distribution of income

The article by Cannan quoted at the start of this chapter pictured the feelings of a young man who, inspired to study economics by concern for the contrasts between rich and poor, attends a series of economics lectures on distribution which deal with the returns to factors of production (the earnings of labour, capital and land) without any attempt to relate them to the personal distribution. Cannan portrays the student going home in a rage, but a more constructive response is to seek to relate the economic theory of production to the personal distribution represented in the statistics just cited.

For the theory of production is potentially of relevance in explaining what we observe. To the degree that countries *are* experiencing similar trends (which we have seen to be open to question), one line of explanation may be found in the changes which they are facing in the world economy. There is a great deal of discussion about the impact of the globalisation of the economy, about the growth of North–South trade in manufactures, about the outsourcing of production, and about the mobility of capital across frontiers. If competition from the South is intensifying, and if production is being transferred overseas, then this has implications for the production in rich countries of manufactured and other traded goods. This may be expected to affect the returns to factors employed, and hence the factor distribution of income. The factor distribution of income may be influenced by other developments which countries face in common, notably technical progress in the form of computerisation and information technology. Labour-saving innovations may be affecting the level of wages. Equally, there has been much discussion of the world-wide rise in real interest rates, which may have affected the cost of capital, and hence the level of investment.

One cannot enter into the debate about these issues without an analysis of the basic economics of production. It is with this that textbook treatments of distribution are typically concerned: the relevant part of Samuelson's first year text is headed 'Wages, rent and profits – the distribution of income' (Samuelson and Nordhaus, 1989). According to the aggregate theory of production, national income is governed by a production function which depends on the available quantities of the factors of production: labour, capital, and land. In mainstream economic theory, this is coupled with the competitive theory of factor pricing, according to which the returns to factors are equal to the value of their marginal contribution to production. This determines the division of total national income between wages (paid to labour), profit (paid to capital) and rent (paid to land).[2] Competitive theory has been criticised, with alternatives proposed, such as the Cambridge theory based on the accumulation of relationships, or the Kaleckian theory based on imperfect competition, but it is these ideas which form the main component of the 'theory of distribution' as it appears in economics texts.

The functional, or factor, distribution of income was of particular concern to classical economists. There is the famous quotation from Ricardo in which he told Malthus that Political Economy should be 'an enquiry into the laws which determine the division of the produce of industry amongst the classes who concur in its formation' (1951: 278). At the time that Ricardo addressed this question, the factor distribution was seen as directly relevant to the personal distribution, in that the different sources were identified with particular classes of people. As Musgrave has described it:

For classical economists, this scheme was doubly attractive. For one thing, it was an analytically convenient grouping, the pricing of various factors being subject to different principles. For another, it was a socially relevant grouping, as the division of society into capitalists, landlords, and workers gave a fair picture of social stratification in the England of the early nineteenth century. (1959: 223)

Today, however, this is scarcely adequate. There are six major reasons why a theory of factor income distribution does not provide a theory of personal distribution.

2.3.1 Heterogeneity of incomes

First is the need to explain the distribution of factor incomes *within* classes, such as the size distribution of wages. Why do Chief Executive Officers receive many times more than teachers? Why do airline pilots get paid more than train drivers? This is particularly relevant in seeking to explain the recent trend in income inequality. In the United Kingdom there is plain evidence of widening differentials in the distribution of wage income: for men, the real earnings of the bottom decile (10 per cent up from the bottom) grew by 11 per cent between 1983 and 1992, compared with 29 per cent for the median, and 51 per cent for the top decile (OECD, 1993: 164). In the United States, differentials have also widened, but since this has taken place around a stagnant level of average wages, the real wages of the low paid have fallen. In other countries, there is evidence of widening dispersion, or that the earlier trend towards reduced differentials has come to an end. A recent OECD study of earnings dispersion concluded that:

While the earlier decade [the 1970s] saw generally decreasing dispersion, the 1980s were marked by increases in twelve of the seventeen countries for which data are available ... The rises were generally small, except in [the United Kingdom and the United States]. (1993: 176)

Why should dispersion have increased, and why did it take place to differing degrees?

2.3.2 Human capital

The investment which people make in themselves in the form of education, training or other activities which raise their productivity represents a determinant of production which has analogous features to investment in physical capital, and needs to be incorporated in the production function. The role of such investment in human capital was certainly recognised by Adam Smith:

A man educated at the expense of much labour and time to any of those employments which require extraordinary dexterity or skill, may be compared to one of those expensive machines. (Smith, 1776, book 1, chapter 10, part I)

It is however in the second half of the twentieth century, with the work of Schultz and Becker, that human capital has received particular attention, a shift which reflects its increased real world importance:

The mode of accumulation in the nineteenth century appears to have been much more heavily directed towards conventional capital formation, while the mode of accumulation in the twentieth century seems to have been much more heavily directed towards human capital accumulation. (Williamson, 1991: 90)

Within economic theory, human capital has been a leading feature of the new growth theory developed in the past decade (Lucas, 1988). Human capital is important not just in influencing the evolution of the general level of wages, with part of the share of wages representing a return to this form of investment, but also in increasing our understanding of wage inequality. As noted by the OECD,

In the 1980s the difference between the earnings of workers with a college or university degree and those with only high school education ... rose in most countries. The contrast between falling differentials in the 1970s and increases in the 1980s was as marked as for the overall dispersion. Particularly large rises were seen in the United Kingdom and the United States. (1993: 170)

Wage differentials in terms of education, or more generally a skilled/unskilled premium, are one of the elements which have been advanced as explanations of rising overall earnings inequality. One important instance is the impact of increased North–South trade, where it has recently been argued by Wood that:

The optimists are right to emphasise the efficiency gains from trade with the South, but they greatly underestimate the adverse side-effects of this trade on income inequality in the North. The pessimists are right that there is a large and enduring distributional problem, but they are wrong about its nature: it is not that capital gains and labour loses, but that skilled labour gains and unskilled labour loses. (1994: 4)

Some of the issues involved in this controversial question are discussed in subsequent sections.

2.3.3 Diversity of sources

Rather than people being identified with a single source of income, they now receive income from a range of sources, so that one individual may be in receipt of wages, interest income, and rent (for example, through owning a house). A worker is not simply reliant on wages. This means that we cannot draw any direct implications for the personal distribution from observations of changes in factor prices. For example, since the 1970s, there has been a significant increase in the real interest rate (the interest rate allowing for the erosion of capital by inflation), but the mechanisms by which higher real interest rates affect the personal income distribution are far from evident. From the newspaper headlines which accompany interest rate changes, one might conclude that the United Kingdom is a nation of borrowers, but there are both gainers and losers. This diversity of sources is in part associated with different stages of the individual life-cycle. In the early stages of adulthood, people may largely depend on wage income, and may borrow to finance housing and other capital purchases, but as they get older they acquire savings which provide an increasing source of income, especially after retirement. Capital income may, on this model, accrue particularly to the elderly, whose total current income may be below average – which is a far remove from the capitalist or rentier envisaged by classical economists. This is reinforced when we consider the further important feature of the existence of intervening institutions which provide transfer income such as pensions.

2.3.4 Intervening institutions

The production model referred to above does not explicitly allow for the existence of institutions such as corporations, financial intermediaries or pension funds, which stand between the production side of the economy and the receipt of household incomes. Corporations modify the links between returns to factors and the incomes received. The company receives profits, part of which are paid out in dividends, but part is retained for further investment. Where companies have a target dividend policy, this may smooth out cyclical fluctuations in profit income (an aspect investigated by Nolan, 1987). Pension funds act as intermediaries. They own shares, real property, and other assets, receiving the income from these assets and paying it out, or accumulating it, on behalf of the members of the pension schemes. The importance of such intermediaries is illustrated by the pattern of ownership of company shares. In the United Kingdom there has been a long-term decline in the proportion of shares belonging directly to individuals. In 1963 individuals owned more than half (54 per cent) of UK ordinary shares; by 1975 this had declined to 37.5 per cent (Hofmann and Lambert, 1993, table 1). In 1992, the proportion was 21.3 per cent, with 34.7 per cent of UK ordinary shares owned by pension funds, and 16.5 per cent by insurance companies (the next largest holding – 12.8 per cent – was by overseas residents).

The existence of intervening institutions has to be taken into account when considering the implications of changes such as those in the level of interest rates, and we have to allow for private transfers as a source of personal income which has no counterpart in national income.

2.3.5 Income from abroad

Individuals and companies receive income from abroad, and make payments abroad. This applies to individual earnings and self-employment, but is particularly important for the corporate sector, where companies operate in many countries and receive profit income from subsidiaries, and for the ownership of foreign securities, whether bonds or equities. In the UK corporate sector, income from abroad net of profits due abroad rose from 6.5 per cent of domestic income in 1979 to 13.8 per cent in 1989 (CSO, 1993, table 3.2). The flows are both ways: as we have just seen, overseas residents own a sizeable fraction of UK ordinary shares.

2.3.6 Impact of the state budget

The gross incomes generated by production are typically modified by taxation, used to finance public spending, including transfers which constitute a fifth source of personal incomes. The state may in part finance spending through borrowing, and the national debt adds to the range of assets which may be held by the personal sector. Interest on the national debt is a source of income which again has no counterpart on the production side. As far as the explanation of income inequality is concerned, the state budget may have moderated the rise in inequality in earnings, and the impact of higher interest rates; moreover, there may have been changes in tax and benefit policy. The fact that different OECD countries have experienced different distributional changes suggests that a role may be played by policy choices.

The elements outlined above are illustrated in figure 2.4, which sets out schematically the links between the factor and personal distributions of income (although it does not distinguish explicitly human capital, and does not show income paid abroad). In what follows, I consider in turn certain parts of the story, each associated with a potential explanation of the rise in income inequality, beginning with the largest source of personal income: that from wages.

The percentages at the top of figure 2.4 show the proportion of gross domestic product (GDP) paid to different factors in the United Kingdom in 1992; the percentages at the bottom show the proportion of disposable household income from different sources (the positive numbers add to some 120 per cent since direct taxes and contributions are deducted in arriving at disposable income). Superficially the numbers at the top and bottom of figure 2.4 may appear similar: for example, the share of wages is virtually the same. However, this is misleading. The household category 'rent, dividends and interest', for instance, is similar in size to the factor share of rent in GDP, but includes dividends paid by companies, income from abroad, and interest paid on the national debt, and excludes rent paid to pension funds or accruing to the state or paid to overseas residents. The household income includes two categories of transfers (31.3 per cent of disposable income) which have no counterpart in national income.

Finally, it should be noted that the factor shares in national income have exhibited little apparent trend in the United Kingdom in recent years – see figure 2.5. There is cyclical variability, and the wage share certainly rose in the mid-1970s (and then fell), but over the 1980s there was no clear-cut trend. The share of nominal profits in GDP, excluding self-employment income, was virtually the same in 1989 as in 1979. There is indeed a

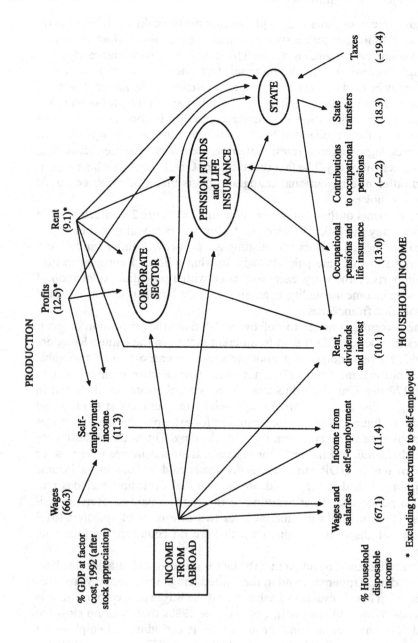

Figure 2.4 Links between factor and personal distributions

PRODUCTION

% GDP at factor cost, 1992 (after stock appreciation)

Wages (66.3)

Self-employment income (11.3)

Profits (12.5)*

Rent (9.1)*

INCOME FROM ABROAD

CORPORATE SECTOR

PENSION FUNDS and LIFE INSURANCE

STATE

Taxes (−19.4)

State transfers (18.3)

Contributions to occupational pensions (−2.2)

Occupational pensions and life insurance (13.0)

Rent, dividends and interest (10.1)

Income from self-employment (11.4)

Wages and salaries (67.1)

HOUSEHOLD INCOME

% Household disposable income

* Excluding part accruing to self-employed

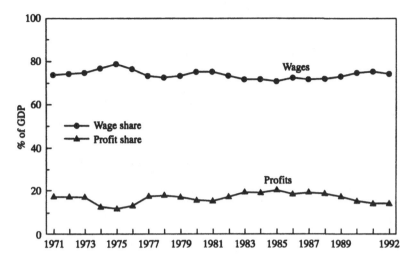

Figure 2.5 Share of wages and profits in GDP in the United Kingdom, 1971–92

striking contrast between the apparent absence of trend in factor shares and the marked rise in inequality in the personal income distribution.

2.4 Wage income: human capital and changing skill differentials

The concept of 'human capital' enjoys wide usage, and its interpretation is equally diverse. At times, it appears to be used a general metaphor; at others, it is given a quite precise meaning, such as years of formal education. Here I illustrate the approach by considering the determinants of the skilled/unskilled differential, where unskilled workers are those who have received no more than the basic, compulsory level of education, whereas skilled workers have additional formal education, apprenticeship or training. (This refers to an advanced country, in that it assumes that everyone receives a basic education.)

The skilled/unskilled differential provides, in the context of aggregate production, a step towards disaggregating total labour. We can envisage total output as being produced using skilled labour, unskilled labour, and capital (leaving aside land). There is some evidence that skilled labour, embodying human capital, and physical capital are complementary inputs, and that both are substitutes for unskilled labour (Fallon and Layard, 1975). This means that the conditions of derived demand for the two types of labour are likely to be different, and that the shares of national income accruing to them may behave in different ways over time.

This disaggregation is in turn relevant to those theories which have

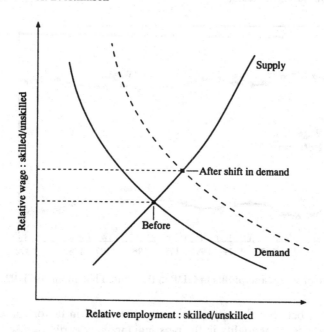

Figure 2.6 Supply and demand for skilled/unskilled labour

sought to relate the rise in earnings inequality to changes in production. Suppose that the labour market can be represented, as in figure 2.6, in terms of the *relative* supplies and demands and relative wages of the two types of labour.[3] There appears to have been a rise in the relative demand, as indicated, since the premium for skilled workers has increased at a time when the relative number of educated workers in employment rose (Levy and Murnane, 1992: 1352n for the United States, and Gregg and Machin, 1994 for the United Kingdom). If that is the case, then the observed change cannot be explained simply in terms of shifting along the demand curve, since we have moved upwards and to the right. There must have been a shift in the demand curve.

2.4.1 Deindustrialisation

Why should the demand for skilled workers, relative to unskilled, have changed? The first such theory considered here focuses on the role of changes in the sectoral mix of output. There has in OECD countries been a marked decline in manufacturing employment and a rise in service sector employment: the share of manufacturing in total employment has fallen from 27.6 per cent in 1969 to 20.8 per cent in 1989 (Wood, 1994: 202).

The *deindustrialisation* explanation for increased earnings inequality is often cited rather casually, and is just as often casually rejected. The precise implications do, however, depend on how the labour market is assumed to operate. One version in effect puts in reverse the Kuznets (1955) theory that income inequality first rises then falls as the economy industrialises. Kuznets considered a two-sector economy in which overall inequality depends on the proportion employed in each sector, on the degree of inequality within sectors, and on the difference between the mean incomes in the two sectors. A rise in the proportion employed in the higher income industrial sector could, on certain assumptions, lead first to rising and then falling overall inequality. Applying the theory now to the post-industrialisation phase, with the two sectors being manufactures and services, it is possible that this could lead to a reversal of the trend towards less inequality.

This version of the deindustrialisation hypothesis has been criticised on the grounds that it cannot explain the increase in earnings inequality *within* sectors (see Levy and Murnane, 1992: 1350). It is here that the difference between skilled and unskilled workers may be important. The structural shift may affect the relative wages of different groups of workers, and hence the earnings dispersion within sectors. If it is the case that the contracting manufacturing sector uses relatively less skilled labour than the expanding service industries, then this generates an increased relative demand, and hence may lead to a fall in the relative wages of unskilled workers. Through this general equilibrium effect, we may observe increased wage dispersion in all sectors.

The above analysis applies where the relative supplies of skilled and unskilled labour are fixed, or the supply curve is vertical. In general, the supply may respond positively to the relative wage rate, as shown in figure 2.6, so that there is a combination of an increased wage differential and an increased number of skilled workers. In the limiting case where entry to skilled occupations is free, and people decide purely on the basis of the pay-off to training, there is only one equilibrium wage differential (the supply curve is horizontal). In this case, we would observe no change in wage differentials, simply an expansion of the number of skilled workers. Government policy to increase the supply of skilled workers would, if effective, have the effect of reducing the wage differential, but the increased number of skilled workers would still affect the personal distribution.[4]

2.4.2 Changes in production methods

A sectoral shift is not the only possible explanation of the decline in demand for unskilled workers. There may be a reduced demand *per unit of output*, as a result of changes in production methods. One mechanism by which this may come about is again international trade. Firms have increasingly in recent years shifted production facilities overseas, with mass production being carried on in low wage countries. Such outsourcing reduces the domestic labour input. If it is the case that research, design, financing, and other head office activities remain in the home country, requiring skilled labour, then the relative demand curve is shifted.

A second mechanism is that of technical change biased towards skilled labour. The precise implications depend on the form of the production function (Bean and Pissarides, 1991): if the elasticity of substitution between skilled and unskilled labour is equal to 1, then no distinction can be drawn between different forms of labour-saving technical progress. In this connection, it seems necessary to take account not just of two types of labour, but also of capital. As suggested earlier, capital may be a substitute for unskilled labour, but complementary with skilled labour. If new techniques are much more automated (capital-intensive), then they may require less unskilled labour per unit of output but more skilled labour. The spread of computers and information technology is an obvious example.

2.4.3 Relating skill differentials to the personal distribution of income

Despite the modern example of information technology, these explanations are reminiscent of those advanced to explain the evolution of the skilled/unskilled wage differential in the past, such as the account by Williamson (1985) of British earnings inequality from the late eighteenth century to the First World War. As described by Feinstein in his critique of Williamson's approach, 'the significant underlying forces are technology, factor supplies, and world market conditions, interacting through factor markets' (1988: 701). The problem, however, is to relate movements in this differential to the observed income distribution. Williamson assumes that this is straightforward: 'the income share of the bottom 40 per cent is clearly determined by the relative behavior of the real earnings of the common unskilled laborer' (Williamson, 1985: 117). In the context of the late twentieth century, one has to recognise that many of those in the bottom 40 per cent are without work income, being retired or unemployed or unable to work on account of sickness or disability. The model can then be extended to allow for those not in work being predominantly at the bottom, followed by the unskilled workers, with skilled workers constituting the upper income group. But this does not seem satisfactory, since one cannot read directly from the distribution of earnings to the distribution of equivalent disposable household incomes.

In moving from the distribution of earnings to the distribution of equivalent disposable household incomes among those in work, we have first to add individual earnings to form family (or household) incomes, then calculate disposable income net of taxes and transfers, and finally adjust for differences in family size. These mediating steps may change the ranking of people, and hence the implications of a rise in the premium earned by skilled workers. This is brought out by a hypothetical (and extreme!) example where all families consist of a skilled worker married to an unskilled worker. In this case, the gains by the skilled worker are offset by the losses to the unskilled worker. There is no change in the overall distribution among families in work, simply a rearrangement within the family (which may of course be important). In reality, skilled workers are more likely to be married to other skilled workers, but the point remains that the ordering according to individual wages is not the same as that by total family earnings. A significant element in this relation is the participation or non-participation of family members in the paid labour force (see Gregg and Wadsworth, chapter 8 in this volume).

The adjustment for family size may also change the ordering from that by wages alone. To take again an extreme example, if all skilled workers earn 60 per cent more than unskilled workers, but have an average of 3.2 equivalent adults in their families, compared with 2.0 for unskilled workers, then there is no inequality in measured equivalent incomes. The family size effect may be moderated by taxes and transfers. The larger family may receive more of its income in the form of transfers, such as child benefit, so that changes in wages have a lesser proportionate effect. This is reinforced to the extent that taxes and transfers are income-related. A progressive income tax means that inequality in disposable incomes increases less than that in gross income. If we take account of means-tested benefits, then the resulting poverty trap (with implicit marginal tax rates of 80 per cent or more) may mean that unskilled workers suffer a negligible reduction in net incomes, with the fall in wages being offset by increased income-tested transfers.

For all of these reasons, one cannot read directly from changes in the skilled/unskilled differential to changes in the personal income distribution. Understanding movements in the differential is an important step in explaining income inequality, but it is only one step.

2.5 Wage income: size distribution and labour market institutions

Analysis of the skilled/unskilled differential is only part of the story in that the rise in earnings dispersion has been observed not just between skill groups but also within groups (see Levy and Murnane, 1992, for evidence for the United States). Our explanation has therefore to go beyond the earnings of representative groups to *individual earnings* (for a recent review, and development of this literature, see von Weizsäcker, 1993).

Explanations of individual earnings have introduced a wide variety of considerations, including the distribution of innate abilities, mental and physical, family background and socialisation, access to formal education, apprenticeships and other training, parental advantage in entry to particular occupations, and trade union membership, in addition to purely stochastic influences. To include all of these, even in a highly schematic way, in a model of the personal distribution of income is highly demanding, and it is not surprising that much of the literature focuses on one or two elements to the exclusion of others. Nonetheless, we can identify the following broad types of explanation:

(a) Where individuals differ according to an innate income-earning characteristic, distributed in some exogenous way across the population (for example, the distribution of mental abilities as measured in an IQ test), and the contribution of the economic theory is then to explain how this pre-specified distribution of IQ is translated into earnings differences

(b) Where individuals receive from their parents or others, a transferable income-earning advantage (such as genetic ability, or access to education, or material wealth), and the economic model is then concerned with the evolution of individual earnings across generations, with whether historical advantages and disadvantages are perpetuated, and with the degree of social mobility

(c) Where individuals are identical *ex ante*, enjoying neither differential innate abilities nor parental endowments, but there is uncertainty regarding outcomes, which may be modelled as a pure random process, where people's earnings are regarded simply as the result of a lottery or, alternatively, people may make choices between careers which *ex ante* look equally promising but there are differences in *ex post* outcomes.

These theories are of interest but do not obviously contribute to explaining the recent rise in earnings inequality. Insofar as the explanation depends on exogenous elements such as the distribution of abilities, it is not evident why these should have changed in the United Kingdom since the late 1970s. Insofar as it depends on inter-generational transmission, there is again no reason to suppose that has changed markedly. For example, changes in education or its quality could be expected to work gradually and to have greatest impact on young workers. It is certainly possible that the variance of *ex post* outcomes has increased, but that statement does not constitute an explanation.

Accounting for the rise in earnings inequality is likely to involve more than the supply side of the labour market, and attention is concentrated here on the demand side. This has been examined earlier in terms of the relative demand for skilled and unskilled workers, and it may not be apparent how it can explain differences in wages *within* these groups. If two people are identically qualified, will not employers pay them the same? In recent years, economists have come to pay more attention to what employers themselves have known for many years – that it may be more profitable to pay higher wages than the market-clearing rate. Low paid workers may not be low cost workers.

Such 'efficiency wage' theories can take a variety of forms (Akerlof and Yellen, 1986). It may be that productivity depends on the wage in that people work harder or more carefully or more imaginatively if they are paid more. Firms may pay wages above the market-clearing rate in order to reduce turnover and hence the costs of training. It may be that employers are unable to monitor continuously the effort put in by workers, so that they can shirk with only a small probability of being caught (and dismissed). By paying a wage premium over and above that available in other jobs, the employer can induce workers to put in effort even with incomplete monitoring.

Where such efficiency wage considerations apply, we may observe two equally qualified workers paid different amounts. Mr A may work in an industry where monitoring is difficult and receive a wage premium over that paid to Mr B in an industry where any shirking is immediately evident. Mr B would prefer Mr A's job, but an offer to work for a smaller premium would not be credible, since the employer would know that he would shirk. It is possible that firms in the same industry may pay different rates, there being two equally profitable ways of producing a given output, one involving higher wages and higher productivity, one lower turnover.[5]

It is conceivable that the increased earnings inequality reflects a structural shift in terms of the role of efficiency wages. Employers may have responded in different ways to increased competition from abroad. Some may have sought to increase work discipline and reduce labour costs via downward pressure on wages. Others have sought to retrain workers and make them stake-holders in the enterprise, thereby increasing their productivity. Both responses may be consistent with profit-maximising behaviour, but they have different implications for wages and the wage distribution. These varied responses may reflect other changes taking place over the 1980s which have removed pressures for wage standardisation. These include:

(1) The privatisation and the breaking up of nationalised industries: in the case of the United States, it has been found that deregulation of the

airline industry was accompanied by an increase in firm-specific differentials for pilots, flight personnel and mechanics, indicating variation in the responses of airlines (Card, 1989)

(2) The decline in trade union membership and diminution of union power: Gosling and Machin (1993) find that the distribution of earnings is more compressed in plants with recognised unions and that, among the semi-skilled, pay dispersion increased between 1980 and 1990 in both union and non-union plants, but that the increase was much larger in the latter

(3) The abolition of minimum wage legislation (Wages Councils): Machin and Manning (1994) suggest that the existence of Wages Council minimum rates was associated with reduced dispersion in those industries covered.

The field of individual earnings determination is characterised by a range of interesting theories (and suggestive empirical findings) which cast light on particular facets of the labour market. What seems at present lacking is an overall framework which can bring together different considerations, such as individual differences in productivity, efficiency wages, trade union bargaining, and industrial structure.

2.6 Capital income

Capital income from personal savings (interest income, dividends, and rent on property) represents only a small part (about 10 per cent) of total household income, but this does not mean that it can be dismissed as unimportant. First of all, it is distributed more unequally than earnings, and may exercise a more than proportionate influence on the evolution of overall income inequality. If all capital income were to go to the top 1 per cent, then adding capital income equal to 10 per cent of total income would raise the Gini coefficient from say 20 per cent to 28 per cent (Atkinson and Micklewright, 1992: 31). Secondly, capital income is important indirectly via the ownership of assets by pension funds and other institutions. One has to remember that capital income (profit plus rent) is around a quarter of national income (excluding that part received by the self-employed).

2.6.1 Rising capital incomes

These considerations are relevant when we consider the implications of rising capital incomes. Since the 1970s the real rate of interest has increased: the medium-term real interest rate was around 2 per cent at the end of the 1970s but 4 per cent at the end of the 1980s (Blanchard, 1993, table A2).[6] This rise in real interest rates may be expected to have benefited those who hold interest-bearing assets and to have disadvantaged those who are borrowers. The position is however complicated by the fact that the distribution of income usually cited is that of *money* income: the adjustment for inflation referred to above is not typically made in the income distribution statistics. There is no correction for the reduction in purchasing power as a result of inflation, so that real interest income is over-stated. More importantly in the present context, money interest income may appear to have fallen, whereas the reduction in the rate of inflation means that real interest rates have risen. It is not clear that the real interest rate rise accounts for the observed rise in inequality.

Capital income takes the form of dividends as well as interest (and rent, which is not discussed). Income from equities has to be seen against a background in which the share of profits in national income in the United Kingdom did not increase significantly (as shown in figure 2.5). If we take the 10-year period 1979–89, then real GDP in the United Kingdom rose by 29 per cent, and real corporate domestic income by little more (35 per cent).[7] Total real corporate income, on the other hand, increased faster (42 per cent) than GDP on account of net income from abroad. At the same time, there was an increase in the proportion of corporate income distributed as dividends. As a result, real dividends increased by 65 per cent (for the FT-Actuaries 500 share index). The rise in real dividends was however surpassed by the increase in real share prices, which was 132 per cent between 1979 and 1989. That the rise in share prices over the 1980s has exceeded that in dividends is reported in other countries: according to Blanchard (1993, table A3), the dividend–price ratio fell in the United States from 5.4 per cent in 1979 to 3.4 per cent in 1989. Unless there has been an increase in the expected real rate of capital gain, this fall in the dividend–price ratio means a lower overall rate of return to holding equities, whereas real interest rates have risen. Various explanations have been advanced to explain this divergence (Blanchard, 1993; Pratten, 1993), which include a correction for historic under-valuation of equities and a reduction in the risk premium required to hold equities.

We have therefore a situation over the 1980s where share values increased faster than dividends, which in turn increased faster than profits. How can these be expected to have affected the personal distribution of income? If we consider first the position of individual shareholders, then they benefit both from increased dividends and from real capital gains. The interpretation of the distributional impact is again complicated, in this case because capital gains, or losses, are not typically recorded in the empirical studies of the personal distribution. The rise in the stock market value of the shares owned by individuals does not show up directly in the

Gini coefficients cited in section 2.2. The same applies to the gains realised as a result of privatisation, including those on the sale to tenants of council houses.

Personal shareholdings are now much smaller than those of pension funds, and similar institutions. These funds benefit from capital gains on shares, and from the rise in real interest rates on their bond-holdings. In the case of defined contribution schemes, these will increase payments out. To some extent these appear in the personal income distribution in the form of higher pensions or annuities; to some extent they will be paid at a later date (and have not therefore yet appeared in the statistics). In the case of defined benefit schemes, there is a rise in the ratio of assets to liabilities. This has typically led to a combination of improved benefits (with the effects just described) and reduced contributions, with employers taking 'contribution holidays'. In the latter case, it is the profitability of the parent employer which has benefited.

From this brief account, it is clear that the impact on the personal income distribution of changes in interest rates, dividends and share values is far from immediately transparent. Not only are the statistics inadequate to measure past changes, but the forecasting of future developments depends on a better understanding of capital market behaviour, including the dividend policy of companies, the relationship between the return on equities and that on bonds, and the responses of pension funds to changing yields.

2.6.2 Interest rates and the national debt

The rise in the real interest rate has important implications for the state. Contrary to much popular belief, the state has a positive net worth (Hills, 1989): the value of its physical plus financial assets (131 per cent of GDP in 1987) exceeds its liabilities (55 per cent of GDP in 1987; liabilities do not include future state pension obligations). The positive net worth of the state does not however mean that it benefits from a rise in interest rates. Much of the assets are in a form which does not generate a cash flow, such as social infrastructure (roads, schools, hospitals) or where the cash return is low or negative (nationalised industries or local authority housing). There may have been changes in the total return to such assets over the 1980s but in the form of variations in asset values rather than cash receipts.

It is therefore the liability side of the state balance sheet where the effects of interest rate changes have been greatest. The impact depends on how the government responds. If, for example, the government seeks to keep constant the ratio of debt to national income, then a rise in real interest rates causes taxes to be raised or public expenditure to be reduced (the key element being the difference between the money interest rate and the money growth rate of national income). The distributional impact then depends on the choices made by governments, to which we now turn.

2.7 Distributional role of the government budget

The state has appeared at several points in the story so far. While some of these, such as the interest on the national debt, involve the government budget, many forms of state intervention are not primarily budgetary in their impact. It is indeed important to stress that the state can affect the distribution of income in many ways apart from the taxes, transfers and spending (on education, health, etc.) of which people naturally think. Minimum wage legislation is an obvious example, as is the privatisation of nationalised enterprises or the sale of council houses. But there are many others, such as the conditions of public procurement, competition policy, the removal of capital controls, company law, rules governing pension funds, and trade union legislation. In this section, I consider the impact of the government budget in the United Kingdom, but these other dimensions need to be borne in mind. It is quite possible that budgetary policy may be necessary to offset distributional changes brought about by decisions in other policy domains.

2.7.1 Impact of taxes and transfers

In considering the impact of the budget, we can in principle distinguish between the *automatic* response of taxes and transfers to changing gross incomes and *active* policy changes in the field of taxes and transfers. For instance, the existence of unemployment insurance provides a degree of protection against loss of work incomes, moderating the rise in inequality which may take place in gross incomes. This is an automatic effect. If on the other hand governments make changes to unemployment insurance, this would come under the heading of active policy response.

The government budget contains a number of automatic mechanisms. To the extent that the receipt of social insurance benefits is correlated with the lack of income from work, these transfers reduce the financial loss. Income-tested benefits perform a similar function, and for those in work the transfer increases if wages fall behind (for those who claim their entitlement). A progressive income tax moderates, by definition (in that disposable income is a declining proportion of gross income), the rise in inequality in gross income. This is true even where the marginal tax rate is constant, provided that the average tax rate rises with income: with a

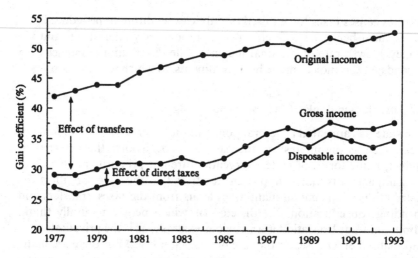

Figure 2.7 Incomes before transfers (original income), after transfers (gross income) and after direct taxes (disposable income), 1977–93

marginal tax rate denoted by MTR, and an overall average tax burden denoted by ATR, the Gini coefficient for net income is $(1-MTR)/(1-ATR)$ times that for gross income. With a marginal tax rate, direct and indirect combined, of 55 per cent (see Kay and King, 1990, table 13.3) and an average tax rate of 40 per cent, the impact of the tax system would be to reduce the Gini coefficient to $(1-0.55)/(1-0.4)$ of its original value, or by 25 per cent.

In fact the actual reduction estimated in the official Central Statistical Office (1994: 65) study of the effects of taxes indicates that the progressive impact is non-existent:

A further, but comparatively smaller, compression of the income distribution occurs at the stage of disposable income, but this is reversed after indirect taxes are taken into account. (CSO, 1994: 37)

As is illustrated by figure 2.7, the major recorded redistribution in the UK budget is that associated with cash transfers.

Figure 2.7 shows how the indicators of redistribution have varied in the United Kingdom over the period since 1977, combining automatic and discretionary changes. The timing is of particular interest. The Gini coefficient for original income (not including transfers) increased from around 44 per cent in the 1970s to 50 per cent in the 1980s, reaching this value around the middle of the decade and not then rising so rapidly. The rise in the Gini coefficient for gross income, which includes transfers, was less rapid up to the mid-1980s: the rise from 1979 to 1985 was 2 percentage points compared with a rise of 5 percentage points for original incomes. At first sight, at least, the welfare state appears to have moderated the rise in pre-transfer incomes. After 1985 the situation reverses: the Gini coefficient for original incomes rose by 1 percentage point from 1985 to 1989 but that for gross income (including transfers) increased by 4 percentage points.[8] The rise for disposable income was still larger (5 percentage points).

The fact that the redistributive impact of transfers and direct taxes appears to have fallen since the mid-1980s is circumstantial evidence that discretionary policy changes have contributed to the rise in income inequality. There are *a priori* grounds to support such a conclusion. Johnson and Webb (1993) have calculated that application of the 1979 tax and benefit system to the 1988 distribution of household incomes would have reduced the Gini coefficient by about 3 percentage points.[9] The effect of indexing social security benefits to prices rather than to net average earnings is examined in Atkinson (1993a), which shows that it could account for a sizeable increase in inequality. Atkinson and Micklewright (1989) list 17 distinct changes in unemployment insurance between 1979 and 1988, the majority of which reduced the level or coverage of benefit.

2.7.2 Public choice explanations

To the extent that the rise in income inequality has been the result of discretionary policy choices, we have to push our analysis a stage further and ask what it is that determines these policy choices. As public choice economists have emphasised, the government's actions cannot be treated as purely exogenous.

Suppose that we take the example of benefit uprating. Over the postwar period there came to be a general consensus that the level of pensions and other benefits should be increased along with rising standards of living. However this changed in the 1980s, and the level of the basic pension fell from 32 per cent of net average male earnings in 1983 to 22 per cent in 1993. What caused this change in the direction of policy? Did it reflect a change in social judgements? Have our concepts of equity changed, becoming less relative and more absolute, so that purely inflation-proofing of benefits is now regarded as an acceptable target? Is it that the cost of providing pensions has increased, so that the electorate has modified its view of what can be afforded? Or is it a reflection of changing priorities on the part of the government, able to pursue their own agenda without electoral restraint?

Similar questions may be asked about unemployment insurance. Why was the response in the 1980s to higher unemployment to make the benefit system less generous to the unemployed? One answer is that there has been a change in the model of unemployment on which the government bases its decisions, with it now apparently believing in the largely voluntary nature of unemployment. But has there also been a decline in altruism? Has *ex ante* electoral support for the policy of providing an income guarantee given way to *ex post* self-interest? One can see how this might have happened if people had voted for the welfare state for motives of insurance, but once the recession arrived, the majority found that they were not at risk, and so ceased to give as much weight to the risk of unemployment (Atkinson, 1990).

This is speculation. The main point to be made is that the explanation of trends in the income distribution requires an analysis of public decisions. Explaining the distribution of income requires an explanation of government behaviour.

2.8 Conclusions

This chapter has attempted the ambitious task of reviewing the economic theory of income distribution, and is probably better described as a prospectus for an as-yet-unwritten book than as a self-contained essay. Indeed, the principal theme has been the limitations of existing theory in answering the question: why has income inequality increased? The literature provides valuable insights, but we lack at present an overall framework to relate the different parts of the picture. Most importantly, we need to link the theory of factor prices – the mainstay of economics textbooks – with the personal distribution of income. This in turn requires the study of intervening institutions such as companies or pension funds and of the 'entitlement rules' (Brandolini, 1992) which govern flows in the economy. It means incorporating public choice models of government behaviour.

This is a challenging programme, but without further progress one can only have limited confidence in policy recommendations. The best designed policy may be thwarted by the reactions of individuals, or by the corporate sector, or by the operation of the labour or capital markets. It is not sensible to make proposals for new policy directions without understanding why governments have made the choices they did in the past.

Appendix: statistical data

Table 2A.1 *Income distribution in the United Kingdom, other Anglo–Saxon countries and Japan: Gini coefficients from 1970*

Year	AU	CA	IR	JA	NZ	UK	US
1970						25.5	39.4
1971		39.8				26.2	39.6
1972						26.5	40.1
1973			36.7			25.5	39.7
1974						24.7	39.5
1975		38.8				23.8	39.7
1976						23.7	39.8
1977						23.4	40.2
1978						23.5	40.2
1979		38.0				24.8	40.4
1980			36.0	27.3		25.3	40.3
1981	28.9				26.7	25.9	40.6
1982		37.5				25.8	41.2
1983		38.2				26.4	41.4
1984				27.3		26.6	41.5
1985	30.9			28.5	25.5	27.9	41.9
1986						28.8	42.5
1987			35.2			30.2	42.6
1988						32.0	42.7
1989	32.2			28.7	29.5	32.4	43.1
1990						33.7	42.8
1991				29.6		33.7	42.8
1992							43.3

Note:
* Coefficient obtained by linear interpolation of the Lorenz curve constructed from decile shares.

Sources:

Australia (AU)	Saunders (1994, table 7)
Canada (CA)	Wolfson (1986, table 3)
Ireland (IR)	Callan and Nolan (1993, table 4)
Japan (JA)*	Supplied by Management and Coordination Agency, see Atkinson, Rainwater and Smeeding (1995, chapter 5)
New Zealand (NZ)	Saunders (1994, table 7)
United Kingdom (UK)	Goodman and Webb (1994, p. A2 (BHC))
United States (US)	US Department of Commerce (1993, table B-3, p. B-6).

Table 2.A2 *Income distribution in mainland European countries: Gini coefficients from 1970*

Year	BE	DK	FI	FR	GE	IT
1970				39.8		
1971			27.0			
1972						
1973					25.4	
1974						
1975				38.4		
1976			21.6			
1977						34.9
1978					25.4	33.4
1979				36.4		33.8
1980						31.2
1981		22.7	20.6			30.6
1982		22.0				28.7
1983		21.6			25.5/	29.2
					25.0	
1984		20.5		37.2		30.1
1985	22.5	20.1	20.0		26.0	
1986		20.0				30.2
1987		20.9			25.2	31.9
1988	23.4					
1989						29.7
1990					26.0	
1991						29.2
1992	23.7					

Sources:

Belgium (BE)	Cantillon *et al.* (1994, table 30)
Denmark (DK)	Hansen (1993, table 3.4)
Finland (FI)	Uusitalo (1989, table 5.4)
France (FR)	Canceill and Villeneuve (1990, p 71)
West Germany (GE)	Hauser and Becker (1993, table 7)
Italy (IT)	Brandolini and Sestito (1993, table 2a).

Table 2.A2 *continued*

Year	NL	NO	PO	SW
1970				
1971				
1972				
1973				
1974				
1975				21.3
1976				20.9
1977				20.4
1978				20.0
1979				19.7
1980			32.0	19.4
1981	28.3			19.1
1982		23.4		19.4
1983	27.8			19.4
1984				20.4
1985	28.1			20.5
1986		22.6		21.4
1987	29.4			20.5
1988	29.0			20.4
1989	29.6	24.4	31.2	21.0
1990				21.9/
				23.5
1991				24.7
1992				

Sources:
Netherlands (NL) Data supplied by Central Bureau of Statistics, see Atkinson,
                  Rainwater and Smeeding (1995, chapter 4)
Norway (NO)   Epland (1992, table 4)
Portugal (PO)   Rodrigues (1993, table 3)
Sweden (SW)   Gustafsson and Palmer (1993, annex).

Notes

1. There are strong grounds for believing (Atkinson, 1993a) that the rise in income inequality in the United Kingdom between the 1970s and the 1980s was associated with a fall in the proportion of families with income from work, although this did not continue beyond the mid-1980s and other considerations were responsible for the continuing rise in inequality beyond that date.
2. For a brief summary, see, for example, Craven (1979) or Atkinson (1983, chapter 9).
3. This is an over-simplification in a number of respects. In particular, figure 2.6 ignores the cost of capital, which may be important in view of the differences in substitutability referred to in the preceding paragraph.
4. Any increase in the average wage has the effect of reducing the *relative* position of those remaining unskilled workers. The slope of the Lorenz curve depends on this relative wage (the unskilled wage divided by average income), and hence moves outward in the direction of greater inequality.
5. There is evidence of considerable inter-plant differentials for workers of similar skill levels – see Mayhew (1977) for the United Kingdom, and Davis and Haltiwanger (1991) for the United States.
6. The real rate of interest is the money rate of interest *less* the rate of inflation, here based on the consumer price index.
7. The sources of the figures quoted in this paragraph are CSO (1993, tables 1.4 and 3.2) and Pratten (1993, table A1). It should be noted that the corporate sector includes public corporations, as well as companies and financial institutions, but not pension funds or life assurance funds.
8. The figures are subject to sampling error, and have been rounded to the nearest whole percentage point, so that these conclusions should be treated with caution.
9. It should be noted that they apply the tax and benefit structure for 1979 *uprated to take account of price inflation*; the results could well be different if they were uprated in line with average incomes.

3 The changing shape of the UK income distribution: kernel density estimates

Frank A. Cowell, Stephen P. Jenkins and Julie A. Litchfield

3.1 Introduction

There has recently been considerable popular and professional interest about what may have happened to the UK income distribution during the 1980s. Explaining what happened is predicated on establishing what the changes actually were and how different groups were affected, and yet there is a variety of ways in which the facts about the changing shape of the distribution could be persuasively summarised. Broad-brush overviews are tempting but they are likely to miss a lot of economically important features which fill out the picture of what really happened in the United Kingdom during the 1980s. There are several ways of making the picture richer. One could just provide many more numbers – lots of data for income classes and population groups, an array of statistics on dispersion – but in this chapter we argue the merits of an alternative, complementary, approach. We analyse in greater detail than hitherto the changes in the shape of the income distribution using graphical methods, and show how this analysis can be informative about the causes of the secular changes in income distribution in recent times.

The motivation for our alternative approach is to let the facts speak for themselves as far as possible. Of course, we should recognise that perception of what the relevant facts are depends upon the presentation method – but we argue that our approach, based on kernel density estimation methods (explained shortly), provides a succinct and informative summary of the details of the changes in ways that are easily understood. They are also consistent with the story that emerges from numerical approaches to the evidence about the UK income distribution. Moreover the methods are usefully suggestive about hypotheses to explore for explanation. We demonstrate this by comparing income density estimates for the population as a whole with the estimates for a range of economically important population subgroups.

The data used in this chapter are those that form the basis of the

Households Below Average Income (HBAI) report (DSS, 1992). The data refer to 1979, 1981, 1987 and 1988/89 (information pooled for 1988 and 1989) and notwithstanding the HBAI label, cover the incomes of the whole population, rich and poor.[1] HBAI data are derived from the *Family Expenditure Survey* (FES) and cover approximately 7000 households per year (about 18,000 persons). Two measures of individual living standards are provided in the HBAI: real income before the deduction of housing costs ('net income BHC'), and real income after the deduction of housing costs ('net income AHC'). The distinction between the two raises several theoretical and practical issues which go beyond the scope of this chapter. Neither concept is ideal and it is likely that in the special circumstances of the United Kingdom income AHC is more appropriate as a measure of economic status for some groups and income BHC for others.[2] For the sake of brevity and consistency we focus on income BHC here. To account for inflation, all incomes are expressed in April 1992 prices; to account for differences in household composition, money incomes are deflated by the McClements equivalence scale. To derive personal distributions, each household's net income is weighted by the number of persons in that household.

As it happens the broad-brush picture of what happened in the 1980s is straightforward and compelling. There was some growth in real income levels on average, reflecting a combination of income growth especially for the richest and income falls for the very poorest, so inequality grew substantially. However, to give depth and perspective to this simple caricature of events we want to focus on trends in a number of specific distributional features and to do so succinctly using a single approach. The distributional features are:

• *Income levels* and changes in the location of the distribution as a whole
• *Income inequality* and changes in the spread of the distribution
• *Clumping and polarisation* and changes in patterns of clustering at various points along the income scale.

Collectively, these three features describe what we refer to as the 'shape' of the income distribution. We summarise them using pictures of the income frequency *density function*.

The density function is the fundamental statistical concept underlying the empirical frequency distribution – the presentational device used to considerable effect in the HBAI Report (DSS, 1992: 21–2). The empirical distribution presented there shows, for each particular dataset, what proportion of the income receiving units fell into each of a set of £5-a-week income brackets. The density function can be thought of as the theoretical analogue of the frequency distribution; it characterises the income distribution by focusing on the question: 'what is the concentration of the

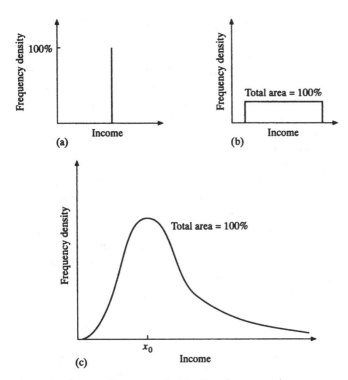

Figure 3.1 Income frequency density function examples
(a) Perfect equality
(b) A uniform density
(c) A 'typical' frequency density function. Source: Lambert (1993, figure 2.3).

population at different points of the income scale?' In doing so it captures the essential characteristics of distributional 'shape'. This point can be illustrated by the three hypothetical examples shown in figure 3.1.

First, at one extreme, if there were perfect equality (figure 3.1a) then the 'true' picture of income would be one where everyone is concentrated at one particular income value, as in figure 3.1a. Second, if there were an absolutely uniform spread of the population over the income range from the poorest of the poor to the richest of the rich – and hence significant inequality – the picture would look like figure 3.1b. Figure 3.1c presents an in-between shape which is often described as being 'typical' (though we shall question the appropriateness of this description later in the chapter). The area under the density function between two income levels is the proportion of the population with incomes within that income range; the total area enclosed by the function equals 1 (100 per cent of the population).

Changes in distributional location and clumping can be straightforwardly examined using the density function. General increases in incomes shift the density concentration along to the right. Changes in income clumping and polarisation are revealed by shifts in the 'bumps' of income concentration at different points along the income scale.

Obviously examples like figures 3.1a and 3.1b are not realistic descriptions of the UK income distribution, but then what is? To obtain a realistic description we need to make intelligent use of the data: this might be nothing fancier than a free-hand sketch of the curve that seems to be traced out by the empirical distributions such as those presented in the DSS charts. This technique effectively regards the observed frequency distribution of income as the basis for an estimate of the 'true' underlying density function, but when we try to make this more precise we run into difficulties. The problem is that the income distribution is quite a complex animal, and it is not immediately obvious how the data should be used to capture it: by contrast to other types of models in economics, simple theoretical reasoning is unlikely to yield sufficient prior information about its shape. However the density function can be estimated by adopting a parametric or non-parametric approach.

The parametric approach requires that one specifies a particular functional form which appears to be a good way of capturing the essential characteristics of the shape of the distribution.[3] One then estimates the parameters of the functional form for each set of observations and describes the changing pattern of income distribution in terms of the changes in the estimated parameters. Whilst this approach has merits, it suffers from two obvious problems. First there is the difficulty of finding a particular formula that will act as a satisfactory template for the kind of distributions that one wishes to describe and that will be reasonably tractable. Second there is the lack of transparency to a non-specialist audience of the two-stage approach if it is used to provide evidence of the shape of the distribution.

The non-parametric approach can be thought of as a formalisation of the free-hand approach to sketching in a curve to fit an empirical frequency distribution. We use a technique known as *kernel density estimation* to implement this systematised curve sketching and to estimate the density functions that characterise the income distribution. The idea underlying this procedure is that one slides a viewing window over the data, and the estimate of the density depends on the number of observations that happen to fall within the window as it passes along the income scale. As we explain below and in the appendix on pp. 69–71, the approach is statistically more sophisticated and more revealing than the simple histogram method used in HBAI Reports (DSS, 1992, 1993a), in Jenkins and Cowell (1993), and elsewhere.

But why should we use kernel density estimation and the corresponding graphical presentations to analyse the distribution rather than using numerical approaches? If we were to use a range of inequality and poverty indices, as we and others have done before, this would require judgements about which index or which poverty line to use, and this might affect the conclusions drawn. Moreover we would lose, as we shall show, some very interesting details of the patterns of change. An index focuses on just one specific feature: for example, inequality indices are designed to pick up changes in dispersion but not trends in income levels or income clumping. Of course different types of indices can be used to pick up these features, but the analysis loses its simplicity as the number and types of indices proliferates. There are other ways too of summarising distributions besides the income frequency density function, such as Pen's Parades (the cumulative distribution function turned on its side), or Lorenz curves. Our case for using the density function is simply that it provides the most revealing perspective for our current purposes. We stress that we provide information which complements rather than replaces that which emerges from other approaches. Note, moreover, that these other graphs and indices can be systematically derived from the density estimates, which can be seen as a fundamental building block in distributional analysis.

To see the advantages of using kernel density estimation methods let us look first at one of the main alternatives.

3.2 A first look at the overall income distribution: histograms

As we noted, histograms are one of the standard methods for representing income distribution functions graphically. To construct the simplest version of these – a 'fixed-bin histogram' – an income range is divided into a fixed number of intervals ('bins') of equal width and vertical bars are drawn in each interval with heights proportional to the relative frequencies of each income (equal bar areas correspond to equal proportions of the sample in question). We now illustrate some of the problems arising with histograms using data for the 1988/89 income distribution: see figures 3.2a–3.2f. The histogram in figure 3.2f is defined in exactly the same way as the histogram presented in the HBAI report (DSS, 1992: 21).

Although all the histograms are derived in the way we have described, it is clear that they could be used to support a number of different views about what the shape of the income distribution really is. Our examples draw attention to several problems. First, and most obviously, histograms

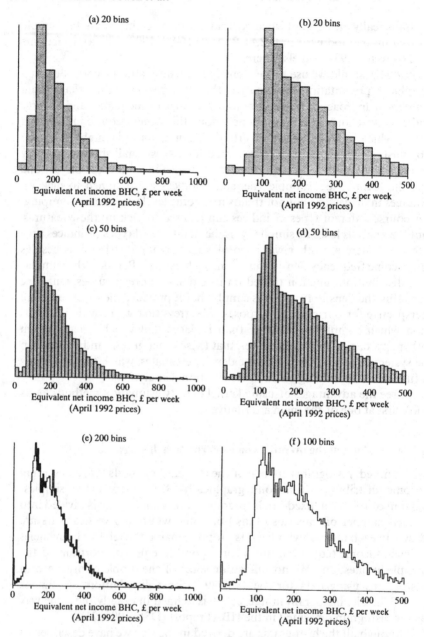

Figure 3.2 Histograms of the 1988/89 income distribution

are inherently 'lumpy' so that one finds discontinuities in the estimated distribution at the edge of each bin (the vertical jumps in figures 3.2a–3.2f) which may not be an appropriate property to impute to the true picture of the distribution. But there are a number of other, less obvious, problems with using the histogram approach.

Second, the number of bins used is relatively arbitrary. There is a crude trade-off between having a small number of bins with little detail from each (as in figures 3.2a–3.2d), and a large number of bins that picks up so many microscopic irregularities that the picture becomes confusing (as in figures 3.2e and 3.2f). To change the metaphor, as the number of bins increases, the 'noise' increases as well, and in the complex pattern which emerges, it is difficult to distinguish which are genuine features and which are noise. For example the histograms in figures 3.2a and 3.2b suggest that there is a single major concentration of incomes between £100 and £120 per week. By contrast the histograms in figures 3.2e and 3.2f suggest two modes in the middle income ranges and a minor mode at £0 per week, but the data are very noisy.

Third, the bin width is the same regardless of the number of incomes in the interval. To reflect the amount of information available, there are advantages to using narrower bin widths in dense parts of the distribution (the middle) and wider ones in the more sparse parts (the tails), but again such adjustments are relatively arbitrary.[4]

Fourth, apart from the problem of the bin width being fixed, the picture may also be sensitive to the income point at which we start drawing the bins. For example, one might get quite a different picture if the boundaries £0, £10, £20, £30, ... were replaced with the boundaries -£4, £6, £16, £26, ... or another set of £10 per week income brackets.

Fifth, truncating the sample distribution above some income level is another way of handling the long sparse upper tail and potential outliers, but this introduces further problems of its own (besides that of ignoring the richest incomes). For example, it is clear from comparisons of the pictures on the left and right hand sides of figure 3.2 (truncation points of £1000 and £500 respectively) that different choices trade off greater levels of detail and loss of some information altogether.

Taken together the histograms in figure 3.2 suggest that the 1988/89 income distribution is right-skewed, with most incomes concentrated between £100 and £250 per week, and that there is a long upper tail, but further inferences about details of the picture are unclear or unreliable. Reliably distinguishing detailed changes in distributional shape is even more complicated.[5]

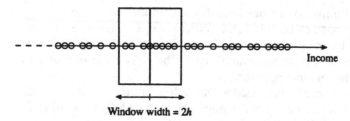

Window width = 2*h*

Figure 3.3 Estimating the density at each income level, using the sample observations (o) found within the 'window' about that income

3.3 A better view of the income distribution: kernel density estimates

We now investigate these hypotheses using methods which go towards handling the problems outlined above, and thus helping provide clearer and more robust conclusions about what actually happened to incomes.

As we suggested earlier, better results can be achieved using the kernel estimation method, which has something in common with the idea of fitting a density function by eye. The idea is as follows. Imagine all the income observations arranged in order on a line: in the light of figure 3.2 we expect these to be relatively sparse in the income ranges corresponding to the very rich and the very poor, and to be packed thickly in the middle income ranges. To estimate what the density of the observations is at some target income £*x*, we imagine a 'window' superimposed on the data (for example £*x*−£5 to £*x*+£5): see figure 3.3.

We then aggregate the information within the window to give the estimate of density at the 'crosshairs' positioned on the target income £*x*. Next we slide the window along and estimate the density at a new point picked out by the crosshairs in the window. The crudest way of doing the aggregation each time would be to make a simple count of all the observations that appear in the window (which is very similar to the histogram method described above, and suffers from the same drawbacks). A more sophisticated approach is to give greater weight to those observations that lie close to the crosshairs, and this is the essence of the kernel density estimation procedure that we use. (The 'kernel' refers to the rule used to assign weights to observations in the window – see the appendix, p. 71 for further details.)

The simple version of the procedure presented in this section assumes that the window always has the same width, wherever we position the crosshairs (and whichever year we are examining). Obviously this window width needs to be carefully chosen – rather than the arbitrary ±£5 used for the sake of example – since it will control the degree of smoothing in the procedure. The importance of choosing an appropriate window width is

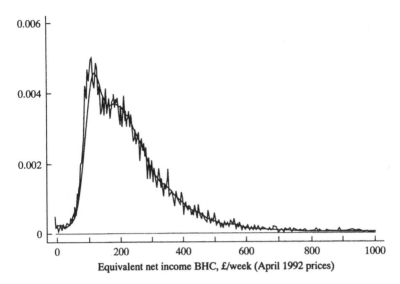

Figure 3.4 Fixed window width kernel density estimates for 1988/89 income distribution ($h = 1, 10$)

demonstrated by figure 3.4, which shows 1988/89 income frequency density estimates. Clearly, using a window half-width of £1 leads to 'noisy' estimates and under-smooths the data (cf. figure 3.2e). By contrast a half-width of £10 implies a relatively smooth curve in which several features are manifest. In particular, we now see that there is a double mode in the middle income ranges, though the extent of clustering at each mode is not the same. (We examine the genesis of this feature in detail below.) There also appears to be a small but significant income cluster near £0 and a non-negligible concentration of incomes above £500 per week (the upper truncation point in the DSS, 1992, histograms).

Changes between 1979 and 1988/89 are summarised using a fixed window-width kernel in figure 3.5a. Obviously there has been a sea-change in the shape of the income distribution over the 1980s. In part, this change can be characterised as a large increase in inequality, which has been documented elsewhere.[6] This feature is evident from the increased dispersion displayed by the estimated density functions: we see a big shift in the density towards upper income ranges, combined with an increase in density at the very bottom of the distribution. In other words, there were relatively more people at very low incomes and relatively more at higher levels.

However the picture of change also reveals some novel features which have not been widely commented upon. Chief amongst these is the clear characterisation of the change in clumping patterns in the middle income

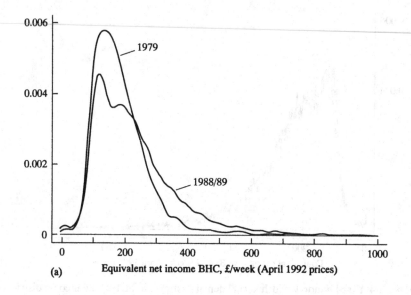

(a)   Equivalent net income BHC, £/week (April 1992 prices)

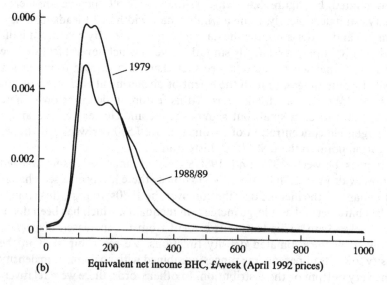

(b)   Equivalent net income BHC, £/week (April 1992 prices)

Figure 3.5 Income distribution, 1979 and 1988/89
(a) Fixed window width kernel estimates ($h = 10$)
(b) Adaptive kernel estimates
(c) Adaptive kernel estimates of the relative income distribution

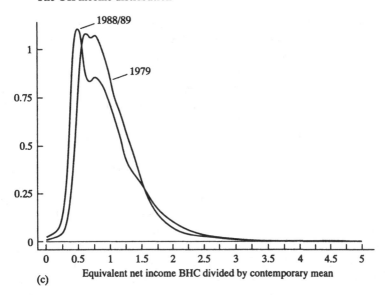

(c)   Equivalent net income BHC divided by contemporary mean

Figure 3.5 (*cont.*)

ranges.[7] The income frequency density function in the 1980s is like a mountain which has been subjected to substantial erosion from one direction, shifting much of the rock at the peak down to the right, and so building up the slope on that side substantially and a second smaller peak also. By contrast to this landslip, there has been only a small trickle down the other side of the mountain. Our estimates for 1981 and 1987 (not shown here) indicate that the erosion at the peak of the density mountain largely took place between 1981 and 1987, rather than in the late 1980s.

Arguably, however, the inferences about the very tails of the distribution are not reliable because of the sparseness of the data at these points. As the crosshairs are passed over this part of the income range, very few observations fall within the fixed-size window; the density estimate may thus be unduly influenced by individual observations. Let us therefore see what happens if we allow the width of the window to be adapted in response to the sparseness of the data over which it is being passed: look at figure 3.5b.[8]

With the improved estimation method, some interesting matters of detail emerge. For example, compared to figure 3.5a, there is no longer such a noticeable bump of income clustering at £0 – though it remains the case that there was a greater concentration in 1988/89 at very low real incomes than there was a decade earlier. The increase in concentration at very high incomes remains clear, too, and so does the asymmetry of the erosion process. Interestingly, the estimates now reveal that the 1979 density mountain had twin peaks, and it is tempting to link each of these with the corresponding peaks in 1988/89; we return to this shortly.

For another perspective, we also present pictures of the distribution of 'relative income', i.e. income deflated by contemporary mean income. Controlling for changes in overall living standard levels in this rough way, we get a more focused view of how (relative) inequality changed. Figure 3.5c shows even more starkly than figure 3.5b that the large increase in inequality during the 1980s arose from a shift in density towards low relative incomes combined with a shift towards higher relative incomes.

Figures 3.5b and 3.5c can also be used to comment on changes in the extent of poverty. Recall that the area under the density function between two income levels is the proportion of the population with incomes between those levels. In particular, the area between zero and some low income threshold is the proportion of the population poor (the so-called Headcount Ratio). Although we would usually examine the areas directly, by integrating our estimated densities – i.e. derive the income frequency distribution function – some conclusions can be drawn without doing this. Figure 3.5c can be used for comparisons of relative poverty. Because the relative income density function for 1988/89 lies everywhere above that for 1979 at every income level up to about 60 per cent of contemporary average income, the Headcount Ratio was higher in 1989 than 1979 – for all poverty lines in the range 0–60 per cent of the contemporary average at least.[9] Figure 3.5b is relevant for comparisons of absolute poverty (poverty line fixed in real income terms), and indicates that conclusions in this case will be much more dependent on the choice of the low income threshold level.

The pictures shown so far give an important clue to the understanding of the nature of the change in the overall UK income distribution during the period. They suggest that the aggregate income distribution is the mixing of two or more separate underlying income distributions, each of which may have responded differently to the events of the 1980s, or may even have been driven by separate economic and social forces. This is not the place to advance a variety of competing hypotheses about the determinants of the income distribution, but considerable insight on the problem can be obtained by looking at the changes in the income distributions and relative numbers of certain economically important subgroups of the population.[10]

3.4 Changes in the income distribution for population subgroups

Which subgroups should we focus on? Previous research on the UK income distribution suggests several candidate partitions, especially employment status, age and household composition: see *inter alia* Atkinson (1993a), Jenkins (1995), and Johnson and Webb (1993). We investigate income changes using three partitions which are defined in the following way:[11]

- *Elderly/non-elderly*, based on whether the head of the person's household (HoH) is aged 60+ years or not
- *SB recipient/non-recipient*, based on whether the benefit unit of the head of the person's household receives Supplementary Benefit (or Income Support after the 1988 benefit changes) or not – a good indicator of the household head's (full-time) work status
- *Has children/childless*, based on whether the person's household contains any dependent children or not.

As it happens, our choices were constrained in several respects: by the availability of suitable variables in the HBAI datasets, by the need to keep the number of subgroups per partition relatively small, and for computational reasons.[12] Nevertheless there is good reason to suppose that this elementary partition of UK residents picks up, albeit crudely, some of the essential distinguishing features which have marked out different types of individuals, families and households for different types of economic fortune during the 1980s; the classification corresponds to some of the crucial income determinants in British society of the period. So this fairly small set of variables should enable a relatively good description of the income distribution changes which took place.

Our first investigation of the relationship between subgroup changes and aggregate changes uses the partition by age: see figure 3.6. In this figure and in all similar ones below, the number in parentheses next to a curve is the number of persons in the relevant subgroup as a proportion of all persons.

Clearly the distributions for persons in elderly and non-elderly households are quite different. Amongst elderly households, there is a distinct concentration of incomes around one income level – corresponding to state retirement pension and benefit levels. Very few people have incomes below this level, but there is a significant spread above it – which may reflect the incomes for pensioners with private incomes and those still working (see below). How has the shape of the distribution changed during the 1980s? Interestingly, the modal income remained much the same, but there was a change in income clumping. Notice the distinct fall in the height of the peak of the density mountain and shift in mass towards upper–middle income ranges. It is this change which explains the increase in average income from £153 per week in 1979 to £191 in 1988/89.[13]

For non-elderly households the distribution changed in some similar ways: e.g. there was also a shift in income concentration from around the

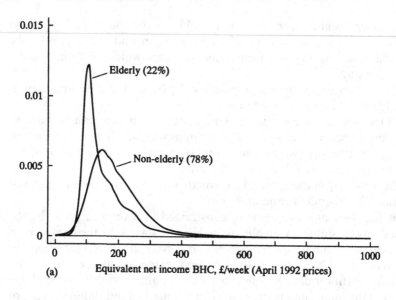

(a)   Equivalent net income BHC, £/week (April 1992 prices)

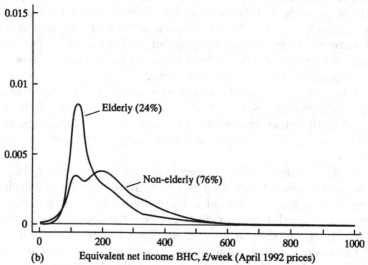

(b)   Equivalent net income BHC, £/week (April 1992 prices)

Figure 3.6 Income distributions for elderly and non-elderly households
(a) 1979
(b) 1988/89

mode towards the upper–middle income ranges (average income rose from £194 to £250 per week). However, by contrast, there was a distinct double mode in the 1988/89 income distribution, with the lower mode at much the same income level as the mode for elderly households. The bi-modality, and the echoing of the aggregate picture in figure 3.5b, suggests that a characteristic other than age, e.g. benefit recipiency status, is better for identifying the economically important component distributions underlying the aggregate changes.[14]

The finding that age may not be an important variable for explaining income distribution changes during the 1980s is consistent with Jenkins's (1995) conclusions derived using inequality index decomposition methods. On the other hand the conclusion apparently differs from that of Marron and Schmitz (1992) who, like us, use kernel density estimation methods. They show a bi-modal UK income distribution, for which the height of the lower mode increased between 1968 and 1983 and the height of the second decreased. This is explained in terms of the differently shaped uni-modal income distributions for pensioners and non-pensioners and the growth in relative numbers of the former, poorer, group. The explanation for our different results is straightforward: Marron and Schmitz's income definition does not make any adjustment for differences in household composition using equivalence scales, and they use household distributions rather than personal distributions. As a result their distributions are differently shaped from ours. However, if one is interested in the distribution of income as an indicator of the distribution of personal economic well-being, and if there is significant heterogeneity of household types, then our approach is the more appropriate one because it makes an appropriate adjustment to the valuation of households' incomes and the weighting of households' representation in the distribution as the demographic structure of the population changes.[15]

Let us now check in more detail our hypothesis that changes during the 1980s can be usefully explained by distinguishing changes for benefit recipients and others: see figures 3.7 and 3.8, which give the pictures separately for non-elderly and elderly households respectively.

Figure 3.7 demonstrates that the bi-modal shape of the distribution for the non-elderly population shown in figure 3.6 in fact reflects the mixing of two income distributions with very different shapes. Amongst SB-recipient households, incomes are tightly concentrated around an income level of about £100 per week, and this pattern changed little during the 1980s.[16] The distribution amongst non-recipient households is much more widely dispersed along the income scale, and this spread increased significantly during the 1980s. (In some ways the subgroup income distribution shapes seem to be moving towards the caricature representations in figures 3.1a and 3.1b.)

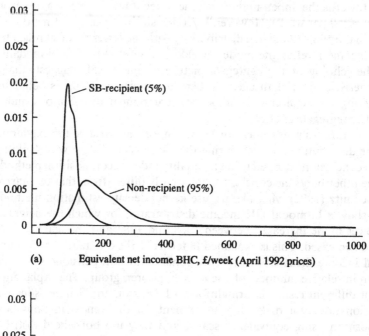

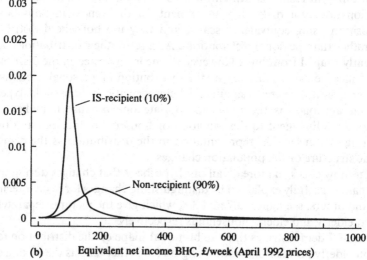

Figure 3.7 Income distributions for non-elderly households, by benefit receipt
(a) 1979
(b) 1988/89

The reasons for the emergence of the twin-peaked distribution for non-elderly households during the 1980s are now apparent. There was a shift in density concentration towards higher income levels amongst working households combined with an increase in the relative numbers of SB-recipient households. (The proportion of persons in the latter group doubled between 1979 and 1988/89, from about 5 per cent to just over 10 per cent.)

Figure 3.8 suggests that the story is different in several respects for elderly households – as one might expect given the lower incidence of full-time work and greater importance of retirement pensions amongst this group. The density for SB-non-recipient households maintained its relatively smooth uni-modal shape (and shifted rightwards). By contrast, the density functions for SB-recipient household take on some rather intriguing shapes and in future work it would be interesting to explore the factors corresponding with the various clumps (e.g. tenure status). Note however that the number of elderly SB-recipient households was relatively small in 1979 – one fifth of all elderly households – and this proportion halved by 1988/89. The density function for all elderly households thus increasingly reflected that for SB non-recipients.

Let us now see how making a distinction between childless and other households modifies the story for non-elderly households. Not much, it seems: look at figure 3.9. The distribution amongst SB-recipient households is very similar regardless of the presence of children. For the childless subgroup there was some shift in density towards higher incomes during the 1980s, but this had little impact on the shape of the distribution for all non-elderly households (even in 1988/89 the subgroup comprises only 2 per cent of the group). There is a more obvious distinction between the shapes of the two distributions for working households, and yet the picture does not appear to have changed dramatically during the 1980s: childless households remained generally better-off than households with children, and their incomes remained more unequal.[17] The density functions for both groups were squashed down and to the right. What probably had a greater influence than the income changes *per se* was the change in relative size of the groups. In 1979 childless working households comprised just under 30 per cent of all non-elderly households, but just over 34 per cent in 1989. The proportion for working households with children fell from 66 per cent to 55 per cent.

3.5 Concluding comments

The UK income distribution during the 1980s does not have the standard textbook uni-modal shape. Rather it has an intriguing bi-modal character,

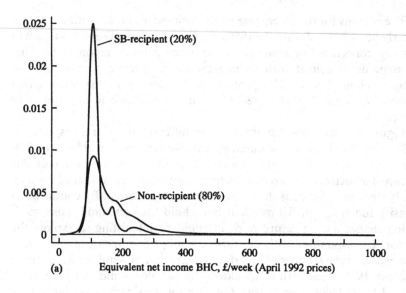

(a)   Equivalent net income BHC, £/week (April 1992 prices)

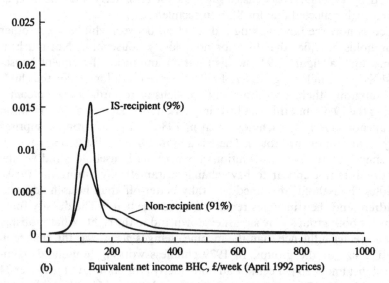

(b)   Equivalent net income BHC, £/week (April 1992 prices)

Figure 3.8 Income distributions for elderly households, by benefit receipt
(a) 1979
(b) 1988/89

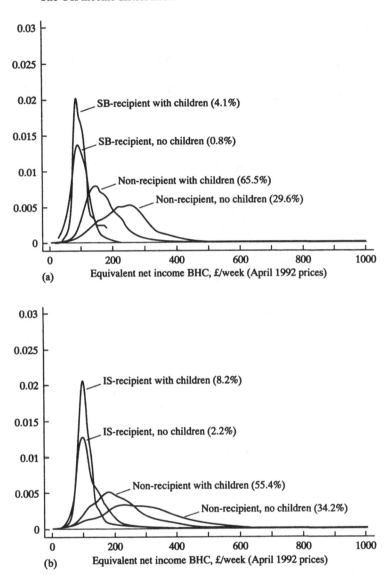

Figure 3.9 Income distributions for non-elderly households, by benefit receipt and presence of dependent children
(a) 1979
(b) 1988/89

the nature of which changed substantially in the decade after 1979. Our approach has shed some new light upon some features of the period that are already becoming well known – the patterns of general increase in income levels and in inequality – but, more importantly, the density estimation approach has also revealed some novel features that are potentially very significant. These are the distinct changes in the patterns of income clumping.

These changes echo a phenomenon that has generated considerable discussion in the United States, but which has not been given much attention in the United Kingdom, namely the 'disappearing middle class', which is one of a variety of labels that has been attached to the kind of income distribution polarisation similar to the picture that has emerged in this chapter. We should emphasise that in principle this phenomenon is something which is quite distinct from changes in inequality (or in income levels): one could easily imagine cases where, for example, society was becoming more unequal but less polarised. This provides a challenge for our thinking about how we assess income distributions. The measurement tools which economists have developed focus almost exclusively on changes in income levels and dispersion.[18]

Our subgroup breakdowns are usefully suggestive about the clumping changes. It appears that the driving forces behind the aggregate shape changes are the shift in density to higher income levels for working households, combined with relatively few changes in the distribution for non-working households, and the increase in the relative size of the latter subgroup. In sum, the aggregate changes appear to reflect a greater stratification between two subgroups, one relatively rich, one relatively poor.[19]

As a measure of how our findings contrast with other summaries of the shape of the income distribution, consider what Jan Pen wrote two decades ago. First he described a picture of a smooth uni-modal distribution (like figure 3.1c), and then commented that:

One of the first things that catches the eye about this [income frequency density] curve is that it has one peak. That seems self-evident, but it is not so. Some mass phenomena are so distributed that we see two peaks ... The fact that we find a single-peaked curve in Western Europe and the United States already suggests to some extent that there are no strictly segregated groups of income recipients and that the well-known split into workers and capitalists does not dominate the picture either. (1971: 61–2)

Is the wheel turning full circle? In that the clumping pattern in the United Kingdom during the late 1980s appears to broadly correspond to the way in which individuals receive their income, there is a *prima facie* connection between changes in economic organisation during the period and the apparent polarisation. We have a (re)introduction of the phenomenon that was familiar to classical economists whereby the distribution of income was described primarily in terms of people's economic function. See Atkinson (chapter 2 in this volume) for further development of this theme.

Appendix: kernel density estimation – an overview

For many of the summary statistics that are of interest to students of the income distribution there are methods of using sample data with a two-fold advantage: the methods are fairly obvious in their application and are also statistically appropriate. For example, if the sample has been carefully drawn then the sample mean is likely to be a good estimate of the population mean; the same applies to most inequality measures and to quantiles and income shares (the ordinates of Pen's Parade and the Lorenz curve respectively).

The density function is rather different. Suppose we have a sample of n observations on income ($y_1...y_n$), what may we infer about $f(y)$, the density of the distribution at some arbitrary income value y? A simple frequency count is unlikely to be useful. An alternative approach is to assume that each sample observation gives some evidence of the underlying density within a 'window' around the value y. Then we can estimate $f(y)$ by specifying an appropriate kernel function K, which itself has the properties of a density function, and a window half-width (or 'band width') h, and computing the function

$$f|(y) = \frac{1}{nh} \sum_{i=1}^{n} K(z),$$

where $z := (y-y_i)/h$.

The simple histogram is an example of this device. Specify a set of 'bins' into which the sample observations are to be dumped, in other words a set of income intervals, none of which overlap, but which completely cover the income range; denote the income value that forms the left hand end of each bin by b_j. All the sample income observations that lie on or the right of b_j and to the left of b_{j+1} contribute to the height of the rectangle above the horizontal line segment in bin j (i.e. the interval $[b_j, b_{j+1})$). In the case where all the bins are of uniform width, so that $h = b_{j+1} - b_j$, we would have

$$K(z) = \begin{cases} 1, & \text{if } b_j \leq y_i < b_{j+1} \text{ and } b_j \leq y < b_{j+1}; \\ 0, & \text{otherwise.} \end{cases}$$

However, this is an extreme way of taking into account the influence of a sample observation in the immediate neighbourhood of y on the

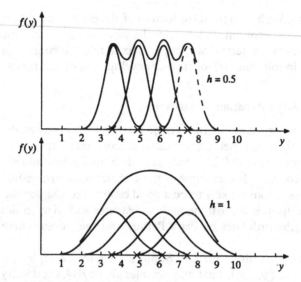

Figure 3A.1 Density estimation with a Normal kernel

estimated density at that income value: in effect, one is saying that each observation has full, uniform, influence within a window of width $2h$ and nil effect outside. It is perhaps more useful to allow the impact of each neighbouring observation to be gradually tapered: the greater the distance from y, the less the impact. This means considering a kernel function that is less drastic than the simple histogram. For example, K is often taken to be the Normal density so that

$$K(z) = \frac{1}{\sqrt{2\pi}} \exp(-z^2/2).$$

One alternative is the Epanechnikov kernel function, defined as

$$K(z) = \begin{cases} 3(1-z^2/5)/4\sqrt{5}, & \text{if } |z| < \sqrt{5}; \\ 0, & \text{otherwise.} \end{cases}$$

The effect of using the Normal kernel is illustrated in figure 3.A1 for the case where there are just four income observations. The top part of figure 3.A1 illustrates the use of a narrow band width, and the bottom part the case of a fairly wide window: the kernel density for each of the observations $y_1...y_4$ is illustrated by the four adjacent lower curves: the uppermost curve depicts the resultant density estimate for all four observations.

There is a variety of methods for specifying the kernel function and also for specifying the band width (for example, so as to make the width of the window adjustable to the sparseness or otherwise of the data). Kernel density estimation methods are discussed extensively by Silverman (1986), and at a more introductory level by Fox (1990).

All the estimates presented in this chapter were derived using STATA kernel density estimation programs written by Salgado-Ugarte *et al.* (1993) and modified by Jenkins, e.g. to handle weighted data. Cross-checking was done using Cowell's *C* program SMOOTHIE. Some preliminary estimates were derived in GAUSS using NP-REG. (Our thanks to Alan Duncan and Andrew Jones for providing their program.) The fixed kernel estimates in section 3.3 are based on calculations at 500 equally-spaced points across the sample income range (truncated above at £1000 per week) and use the Epanechnikov kernel function. Otherwise we use adaptive kernel density estimates evaluated at each sample income point. The preliminary estimates used to calculate local 'window factors', and hence window widths varying with data sparseness, are based on a Normal kernel function where the band width for each year varies and is calculated 'automatically' using the formula given by Silverman (1986: 48).

Density estimation is computationally-intensive and computing time is related to the number of observations. To make things manageable we aggregated the HBAI data – arranged with the 'person' as the unit of observation (a household of size s appears s times in the data) – so that each household appeared once, and modified the grossing up weight accordingly. This reduced the number of dataset observations substantially. However this procedure also constrained the list of variables which could be used to partition the sample in section 3.4: we had to use variables with a value common to all members of the same household. This ruled out our use in the present chapter of, for example, the HBAI economic status variable – this refers to the economic status of an individual's benefit unit. See Jenkins (1994) for density estimates using this variable and several others.

Table 3.A1 *Percentages of persons in population subgroups, by year*

Population subgroup		1979	1981	1987	1988/89
Household with dependent children?	yes	55.9	54.7	50.0	49.4
	no	44.1	45.3	50.0	50.6
Household head aged 60+ years?	yes	22.1	23.4	23.9	23.9
	no	77.9	76.6	76.1	76.1
Household head's benefit unit receives SB/IS?[a]	yes	8.2	10.4	12.7	10.1
	no	91.9	89.6	87.3	89.9
Subgroup with household head aged 60+ years					
Household head's benefit unit receives SB/IS?	yes	19.6	19.4	11.1	9.2
	no	80.4	80.6	88.9	90.8
Subgroup with household head aged <60 years					
Household head's benefit unit receives SB/IS?	yes	4.9	7.6	13.2	10.4
	no	95.1	92.4	86.9	89.6
Household with children and household head's benefit unit receives SB/IS		4.1	6.6	10.5	8.2
Household without children and household head's benefit unit receives SB/IS		0.8	1.0	2.6	2.2
Household with children and household head's benefit unit does not receive SB/IS		65.5	62.7	53.5	55.4
Household without children and household head's benefit unit does not receive SB/IS		29.6	29.7	33.3	34.2
		100.0	100.0	100.0	100.0

Note:
[a] 'SB/IS': Supplementary Benefit/Income Support.
Source: authors' calculations from the HBAI datasets.

Table 3.A2 *Mean income[a], by population subgroup and year*

Population subgroup		1979	1981	1987	1988/89
All persons		185	184	221	236
Household with dependent children?	yes	173	167	201	218
	no	200	204	242	253
Head of household aged 60+ years?	yes	153	158	183	191
	no	194	191	233	250
Household head's benefit unit receives SB/IS?[b]	yes	110	112	117	119
	no	192	192	236	249
Subgroup with household head aged 60+ years					
Household head's benefit unit receives SB/IS?	yes	118	122	128	135
	no	161	167	190	197
Subgroup with household head aged <60 years					
Household head's benefit unit receives SB/IS?	yes	101	104	114	114
	no	199	199	251	266
Household with children and household head's benefit unit receives SB/IS		100	101	112	112
Household without children and household head's benefit unit receives SB/IS		102	120	125	124
Household with children and household head's benefit unit does not receive SB/IS		179	174	220	234
Household without children and household head's benefit unit does not receive SB/IS		245	251	302	317

Notes:

[a] Income = equivalent net household income (£ per week, April 1992 prices).

[b] 'SB/IS': Supplementary Benefit/Income Support.

Source: authors' calculations from the HBAI datasets.

74   Frank A. Cowell *et al.*

Notes

Thanks are due to the Analytical Services Division, Department of Social Security, for supplying the HBAI micro-data, and to the Joseph Rowntree Foundation which has supported this project as part of its Income and Wealth Programme. The facts presented and views expressed in this chapter are those of the authors and not necessarily those of the DSS or the JRF.

1. See DSS (1992) and Jenkins and Cowell (1993, 1994) for a detailed description of the derivation of the data and variable definitions. After we completed this chapter, the DSS (1993a) released another HBAI report with information for 1979, 1988/89, and 1990/91. The 'old' HBAI dataset provides a more detailed coverage of trends during the 1980s, which suits our aims in this chapter. We are using the 'new' dataset in current work (see e.g. Jenkins, 1994).
2. For further discussion, see Johnson and Webb (1992).
3. See Cowell (1995) for an overview.
4. An additional complication arising when comparing distributions from different years is that a fixed band width (e.g. £5 as in figure 3.2), corresponds to a different fraction of the income range in each year.
5. Cf. figure 3 in Jenkins and Cowell (1993) which provides histograms like figures 3.2e and 3.2f for each of 1979, 1981, 1987, and 1988/89 (but with upper income truncation at £800 per week).
6. See, e.g. Atkinson (1993a), Coulter *et al.* (1994), Jenkins (1994, 1995), and Jenkins and Cowell (1995).
7. There are more formal statistical methods available for investigating the numbers of density modes than our informal 'eyeball' methods: see, e.g. Silverman (1981). We hope to use these in future work.
8. See the appendix, pp. 69–71 for a more details of the definition and derivation of the adaptive kernel estimates.
9. The range must extend beyond 60 per cent of the average because Headcount Ratios depend on comparisons of areas, not density function intersections *per se.* See Jenkins and Cowell (1993, 1994) for HBAI poverty comparisons using empirical cumulative distribution functions.
10. Note that the aggregate income density at each income level equals the weighted sum of the subgroup densities, where the weights are the subgroup population shares.
11. Later on, we also define subgroups using combinations of these definitions. The numbers in each subgroup are summarised in appendix table 3A.1.
12. See the appendix, p. 71 for elaboration.
13. Average incomes for population subgroups are summarised in appendix table 3A.2.
14. Note that the non-elderly distribution receives a much larger weight than the elderly one in the aggregation process. To derive the aggregate density, add together at each income level roughly three quarters of the density function height for the non-elderly subgroup and roughly one quarter of the density function height for the elderly subgroup (the subgroup shares changed little during the 1980s).

15. Mookherjee and Shorrocks (1982) find, using inequality index decompositions, that changes in age structure are important for explaining income distribution changes in the 1970s. However they, too, use unadjusted household income distributions. See Jenkins (1995) for further discussion.

16. According to the 1989 DSS Tax-Benefit Model Tables, the net income BHC for a childless married couple receiving Income Support in April 1989 was £79.10. This corresponds to an equivalent net income BHC in April 1992 prices of just over £100, which is close to the modal income we observe. SB/IS scale rates kept pace with price inflation during the 1970s and 1980s – which explains why the mode changed little in real terms – but scale rates fell relative to average earnings, which helps explain the polarisation. See Barr and Coulter (1991, figures 7.6 and 7.7) for a summary of changes in SB levels between 1973 and 1987.

17. For numerical summaries also showing this, see Coulter *et al.* (1994) and Jenkins (1994).

18. For a notable exception, see Wolfson (1994), who defines polarisation in terms of divergence about the median of the distribution. For reference, the medians in our data are £167 in 1979, and £202 in 1988/89 (income = equivalent net income BHC).

19. This conclusion is confirmed by Jenkins (1994), whose findings are based on kernel estimates of frequency density functions for 1979 and 1990/91 for persons classified into three groups according to family economic status (one or more full-time self-employed, one or more full-time employee, no full-time earner).

4 UK household cost-of-living indices, 1979–92

Ian Crawford

4.1 Introduction

The only circumstance under which one can speak accurately about *the* cost-of-living index is one in which household expenditure patterns do not vary. If relative prices move and households consume goods and services in different proportions, then each household will have its own unique cost-of-living index. This chapter concerns the pattern and extent of these variations in the cost-of-living between different types of household.

To illustrate this, consider the data on a typical necessity: domestic fuels. Figure 4.1 shows the Engel curve[1] for domestic fuel drawn non-parametrically using UK data from the 1992 Family Expenditure Survey (FES). The fuel share of total spending declines as the logarithm of total expenditure increases. This downward-sloping Engel curve is typical of goods that are usually thought of as necessities; poorer households with lower total expenditure spend a greater proportion of that total on necessities like fuel and food than do richer households.[2]

Figure 4.2 shows the price of domestic fuels relative to the all-item retail price index from 1978 to 1992. Figures 4.1 and 4.2 are sufficient to show the existence of systematic differences between the cost-of-living of different households. The relative price movements illustrated will have a greater effect on the cost-of-living of households which consume more fuel than others. Banks, Blundell and Lewbel (1994) show that Engel curves are neither flat nor always linear for a range of commodities using UK FES data.

There has been a number of studies[3] which have analysed inter-household differences in the cost-of-living and in inflation since the Second World War. The general picture of relative inflation is presented in table 4.1. As can be seen, the post-war period can be divided into fairly well defined phases in which increases in the relative prices of necessities pushed up the cost-of-living of poorer households faster than that of richer households.

76

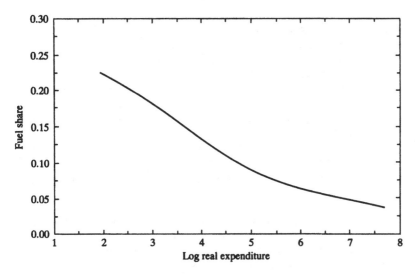

Figure 4.1 Engel Curve for domestic energy, FES, 1992

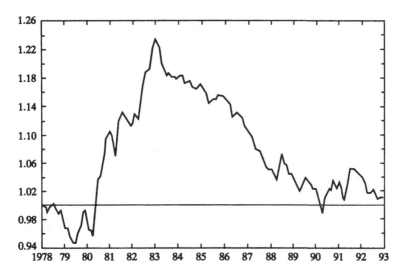

Figure 4.2 Relative price of domestic fuel, United Kingdom, 1978–92

The plan of this chapter is as follows. Section 4.2 presents a discussion of the properties of some alternative cost-of-living indices, the method and the data to be used in the study. Section 4.3 focuses on patterns of non-housing inflation for different income groups and demographic groups. Section 4.4 looks at the influence of indirect tax reforms over the

Table 4.1 *The post-war experience in the United Kingdom, 1939–1980s*

1939–45	The prices of basic commodities were kept low favouring poorer households. The prices of luxuries were much increased (where they were available)
1945–61	Relative price of necessities rose fast, introducing a substantial anti-poor bias
1961–66	Prices of luxuries caught up somewhat The anti-poor bias was reduced
1966–71	The bias against the poor disappeared altogether by the beginning of the 1970s
1970s	Prices of necessities rose despite food subsidies; later, with membership of the Common Market, dismantling of food subsidies and the oil crisis, the cost of necessities rose Inflation hit poorer households hardest once more
Early 1980s	Some evidence of anti-poor bias once more

period on non-housing inflation. Section 4.5 examines the results of the inclusion of housing costs in the analysis. Two possible methods of calculating housing costs are discussed and alternative all-item cost-of-living indices are calculated using both measures. Section 4.6 draws some conclusions.

4.2 Calculating household cost-of-living indices

Cost-of-living indices measure the cost of reaching a given standard of living under different economic circumstances. Under changing prices, the true cost-of-living index is the relative (minimum) cost of attaining a reference-level living standard at each set of prices. Traditionally in economics, the standard of living is measured by the goodness (utility) consisting in consumption.[4] This is typically proxied by income or total expenditure.

Calculation of true cost-of-living indices requires that the cost function (describing the minimum cost of attaining a given standard of living/utility level) is known. The usual way of obtaining the cost function is by estimating a system of demand equations, and applying the normal theorems of duality. Banks, Blundell and Lewbel (1994) utilise this method in a five-good demand system based on UK FES data. However, this approach is arduous and is only practicable for a low number of very broadly defined goods. Furthermore, using broad definitions of expenditure groups incurs the cost of discarding information on variations in spending patterns within these groups. As a result, economists have attempted to devise measures that avoid the need for explicit estimation of welfare and behavioural responses to price changes.

Two of the most commonly used indices are the Laspeyres and Paasche. These indices take base- and end-period expenditure weights respectively. However, the only circumstance under which the Laspeyres and Paasche indices will be equal to the appropriate true indices is one in which household preferences exhibit no substitution effects, i.e. household consumption patterns do not respond to relative price changes. Empirical studies usually find ample evidence of substitution effects.[5]

A useful alternative to the Laspeyres and Paasche indices is one proposed by Törnqvist (1936), which Diewert (1976) shows to be equivalent to the true index under a relatively more plausible model of household consumption behaviour which allows for substitution effects. The Törnqvist index is therefore based upon a preferred model of household behaviour, and although it still avoids the need to estimate substitution effects, it does not suffer the substitution bias inherent in the Paasche and Laspeyres indices.[6] It also has the advantage that the model of preferences underlying it is fairly general[7] and performs relatively well in applied work on demand analysis.[8]

The method adopted here is to calculate chained series of pairwise Törnqvist indices for each commodity. This will mean that each link in the chain refers to a different reference welfare level. Nevertheless, Diewert (1978) shows that these indices differentially approximate each other as well as the true index provided that variations in prices and expenditures between each period are small. He argues that this provides a strong justification for minimising period-to-period variations in prices and quantities by means of frequent rebasing and by chaining annual indices.

The indices calculated in this chapter use information on price movements from the 74 sub-indices of the Retail Price Index (RPI) for the period 1978–92, and corresponding household expenditure data from the FES for the same period. Because the price data are collected from national sources, there is no regional variation and as a result this chapter ignores regional issues.[9] Differences in cost-of-living indices between population groups are thus generated entirely by differences in their spending patterns, scaled by relative price movements. In the following sections, cost-of-living indices for specific population groups are calculated and compared to the all-household 'headline' measure.

4.3 Non-housing measures

There are several ways of illustrating group cost-of-living indices. Most previous studies (Fry and Pashardes, 1986; Bradshaw and Godfrey, 1983,

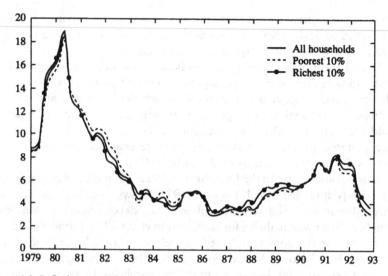

Figure 4.3 Inflation rates, by income group, per cent, 1979–92

for example) present cost-of-living levels. However, most of the policy-relevant issues are to do with annual changes in the level, i.e. inflation. Benefit uprating, for example, is designed to compensate households for year-to-year changes in their cost of living rather than the levels. Figure 4.3 illustrates the annual change (inflation) in the Törnqvist[10] cost-of-living indices (exclusive of housing) for all households and for those in the top and bottom income decile groups from 1979 to 1992.

Non-housing inflation rates for households at the top and bottom of the income distribution follow the average closely. In general, the all-households average rate lies between the other two but the ranking changes; there are periods when poorer households are facing a higher rate of inflation and richer households a lower rate than the average, and there are also periods when this is reversed. Figure 4.4 emphasises the between-group differences by plotting the difference in inflation rates from the average at each point. The all-households average index is therefore normalised to zero and the differences for each income group are traced around it. For example, in early 1982 when the average all-households inflation measure is around 8 per cent (see figure 4.3), figure 4.4 shows that the richest 10 per cent of households saw their cost of living increasing at a rate approximately 0.8 percentage points lower than average (i.e. at around 7.2 per cent), while the cost of living of the poorest 10 per cent was increasing at a rate approximately 0.8 percentage points faster than average (i.e. at around 8.8 per cent). The difference in

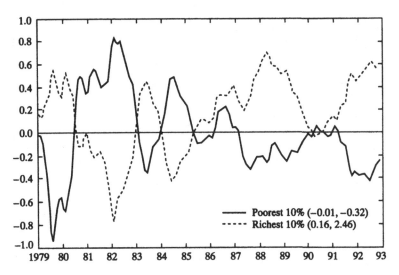

Figure 4.4 Difference in inflation rates, by income group, percentage points, 1979–92

inflation rates between the richest and poorest households was thus about 1.6 percentage points at this time.

Figure 4.4 shows the cycling nature of the indices more clearly than figure 4.3. The first number in parentheses in the legend for richer households is the average difference from the all-households index for the whole period. This says that, on average, inflation for richer households was 0.16 percentage points higher than the average for all households between 1979 and the end of 1992. The second number in parentheses shows the difference in the *level* of the cost-of-living index at the end of the period expressed as a percentage of the all-households average index *level*. This shows that, at the end of the period, the cost-of-living of richer households had grown by 2.46 percentage points more than the average, and follows directly from their higher-than-average inflation rate. The corresponding numbers for poorer households show that, on average, their inflation rate was 0.01 percentage points lower than the average, and that by the end of the period their cost-of-living had grown by 0.32 percentage points less than the average.

The overall downward effect on relative inflation for poorer households is largely a product of falls in the relative price of necessities such as food and clothing and (since the early 1980s) domestic fuels (which form a relatively large part of their total spending), and increases in the prices of many luxuries such as eating out, entertainment and other services (which form a relatively small part). Figures 4.5 and 4.6 illustrate these trends in

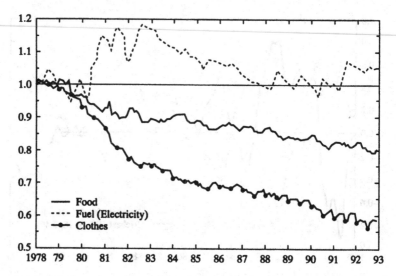

Figure 4.5 Relative price of necessities: food, fuel (electricity)[a] and clothing, 1978–92

a Poorer households' fuel consumption consists predominantly of electricity. See Baker and Crawford (1993).

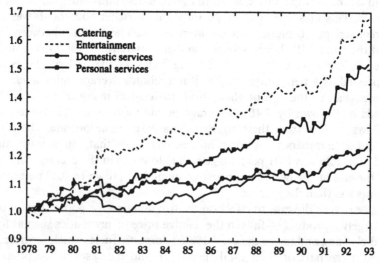

Figure 4.6 Relative price of luxuries: catering, entertainment and services, 1978–92

Table 4.2 *Proportion of total non-housing expenditure allocated across goods, FES, 1978 and 1992*

Group	Year	All	Poorest 10 per cent	Richest 10 per cent
Food	1978	0.24	0.34	0.16
	1992	0.17	0.23	0.10
Catering	1978	0.04	0.03	0.05
	1992	0.04	0.03	0.05
Alcohol	1978	0.06	0.04	0.06
	1992	0.05	0.05	0.04
Tobacco	1978	0.04	0.06	0.02
	1992	0.02	0.05	0.01
Fuel	1978	0.07	0.10	0.05
	1992	0.06	0.09	0.04
Durables	1978	0.07	0.05	0.10
	1992	0.07	0.05	0.08
Clothes	1978	0.10	0.08	0.10
	1992	0.07	0.08	0.06
Motoring	1978	0.13	0.09	0.16
	1992	0.15	0.11	0.15
Fares	1978	0.03	0.03	0.03
	1992	0.04	0.04	0.03
Entertainment	1978	0.05	0.03	0.08
	1992	0.11	0.05	0.22
Other	1978	0.17	0.15	0.18
	1992	0.21	0.21	0.23

relative prices, and table 4.2 reports the average expenditure shares for each group at the beginning and end of the period.

Table 4.2 shows that the average share of spending allocated to necessities (food, fuel, clothing) for all households has fallen from 0.41 to 0.30 over the sample period. The downward-sloping Engel curve relationship for necessities is apparent at both ends of the period. Richer households spend less on necessities than average (0.31 falling to 0.20), and poorer households spend more (0.52 falling to 0.40). The corresponding share increases have been in luxury goods such as entertainment and the 'other' category, which is mostly services. One of the largest differences between the two groups over time is spending on entertainment, which has grown much faster among richer households. The expenditure patterns shown in table 4.2, coupled with the relative price movements illustrated in figures 4.5 and 4.6, largely explain why the *non-housing* cost of living of richer

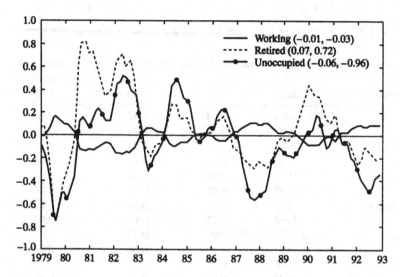

Figure 4.7 Difference in inflation rates, by employment status of head, percentage points, 1979–92

households increased by more over this period than that of poorer households did.

Figure 4.7 illustrates the difference from the all-households' inflation index by employment status of the head of household. Employment status and income are closely related, and therefore it is not surprising that the cycles of the retired and unoccupied groups are similar to those of the poorer households in figure 4.4. The main differences lie in the period 1989–90 when inflation for these groups was above the average to a greater extent than it was for the poorer households shown in figure 4.4. As with the poorer households, the average difference for the unoccupied group is negative (–0.06 percentage points), as is the difference in cost-of-living growth levels at the end of the period (–0.96 percentage points). However, longer periods above the average for retired households in the early 1980s and in 1989–90 mean that the retired households have done, on average, slightly worse with a positive average difference over the period (+0.07 percentage points) and corresponding higher cost-of-living growth level at the end (+0.72 percentage points).

Taking the poorest 10 per cent of the population and calculating changes in their average cost of living gave figure 4.4. Variations in income and total expenditure are naturally small within the group and consequently differences in spending patterns due to households' positions along the Engel curve are also small. However, differences in household demographics within this section of the population may imply differences between Engel curves defined on these characteristics. There are, for example, poor households with children and poor households without children, poor young households and poor old households. These other factors will contribute to within-group variations in budget shares which may also be well determined.

A major demographic characteristic which influences households' expenditure patterns is the presence of children. However, the differences in relative inflation rates for households with and without children are small, no more than ±0.2 percentage points at the most in the very early 1980s. The presence of children makes a household take on some of the spending characteristics of poorer households (adults forgo spending on luxuries like entertainment for more spending on necessities like food and clothing). This sort of spending pattern reduces the incidence of inflation over the period on households which consume these goods. The presence of children within a household results in an average inflation rate which is ' 0.07 percentage points below the population average over the period, and a cost-of-living growth of 1 percentage point below the average at the end. Households without children, like richer households, are able to spend more on luxuries and over the period had a higher-than-average inflation rate.

Households in the bottom decile group with children have experienced an average rate of inflation over the period 0.04 percentage points less than the decile group average (0.05 percentage points less than the all-house-holds average). Poor households without children, with a little more money to spend on luxuries, had an average rate of inflation which was 0.05 percentage points above the decile group average (0.04 percentage points above the population average).

The general result which emerges from this analysis of non-housing inflation is that, because the price of luxuries has risen faster than the price of necessities over the period, households that allocate a higher propor-tion of total non-housing expenditure to necessities (either as a result of low household income or additional non-earning household members) have experienced a lower-than-average increase in their cost-of-living.

Nevertheless, it should be noted that conclusions based on the data pre-sented in this chapter are heavily dependent upon the period from which the data are drawn. This is demonstrated by previous studies such as Bradshaw and Godfrey (1983) and Fry and Pashardes (1986) which find an anti-poor bias in price increases based on observations over shorter time periods.

4.4 Indirect taxation

Since 1979, there have been various reforms to the structure and rates of VAT and excise duties. This section removes the influence of tax changes from the cost-of-living indices presented in section 4.3. The widening of the VAT base in April 1994 to include domestic fuels does not fall within the period of this study although its implications for households across the income distribution are obvious from section 4.3.[11]

In the United Kingdom, VAT is a broadly progressive tax, in the sense that richer households pay more VAT as a proportion of total spending.[12] This progressivity is entirely due to the base upon which VAT is levied and the spending patterns shown in table 4.2. During the period 1979–92, food, domestic fuels, passenger transport and children's clothing, *inter alia*, were zero-rated for VAT (i.e. entirely untaxed). Given that these types of goods are more important elements of total expenditure for poorer households, zero-rating means that the burden of VAT falls most heavily on better-off households.

The incidence of excise duties is more mixed. The main dutiable goods are tobacco, alcohol and petrol. In general, petrol expenditure is higher for richer than for poorer households because of wider car-ownership amongst wealthier households. As a result, petrol excise duties are progressive when looked at across the whole population.[13] Tobacco duties, however, are regressive. Table 4.2 shows that poorer households spend proportionately more than richer households on tobacco. This is due to higher rates of smoking in the bottom income decile group rather than higher consumption by smoking households. Patterns of alcohol consumption and the incidence of duties, however, are more complex.

The Engel curve for alcohol is quadratic and has an upside-down U shape. Alcohol expenditure therefore has the characteristic of a luxury for poorer households (the upward-sloping portion of the curve), and of a necessity for richer households (the downward-sloping portion of the curve).[14] Within the alcohol commodity group, there are further differences, with richer households spending more on wines and spirits than poorer households, with a general shift from beer to wines and spirits over the period across all households. Because of their higher alcohol expenditure shares, the overall incidence of alcohol taxation is upon poorer households. A shift in the balance of alcohol taxation away from wines and spirits also impacts more upon poorer households.

To illustrate the effects of indirect tax changes on the cost-of-living of different income groups, price increases due to VAT and excise duty changes have been removed from the price indices from 1978 onward and the cost-of-living indices recalculated.[15] Figures 4.8 and 4.9 show the

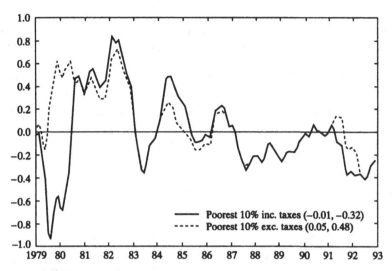

Figure 4.8 Difference in inflation rates for the poorest 10 per cent, with and without taxes, percentage points, 1979–92

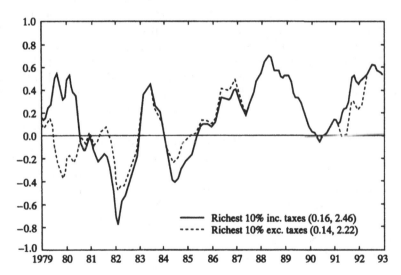

Figure 4.9 Difference in inflation rates for the richest 10 per cent, with and without taxes, percentage points, 1979–92

differences from the average inflation index for the poorest and richest households. The solid lines correspond to the lines in figure 4.4; however, here the indices are calculated using the Laspeyres formulation and not the Törnqvist.

The problem with the Törnqvist index in this application lies in the use of the end-period weight. The end-period weight depends on the end-period price vector, so when the counter-factual tax-exclusive price series is used, the correct end-period weights are not observed. Instead, only the base-period weights are observed and therefore the Laspeyres index is calculated.

The first major difference between the taxed and untaxed series occurs in mid-1979. This corresponds to the VAT reforms in Sir Geoffrey Howe's first Budget. The amalgamation of the two VAT rates to a single, higher, 15 per cent rate caused the faster increase in the cost-of-living of richer households and the slower-than-average increase for poorer households illustrated. One year later, the effects of the VAT increase drop out of the inflation rates for both groups, and return the tax-inclusive series to close to the tax-exclusive path.

Increases in excise duties, particularly on beer and cigarettes, and later the cut in wine duties are shown to push up inflation for poorer households between mid-1980 and 1987. The next period was one in which most excise duties were simply uprated in line with inflation in each Budget. The final feature of note comes with the increase in the VAT rate to 17.5 per cent in 1991 by Norman Lamont. Just as it did in 1979, the VAT increase pushed up cost-of-living inflation for richer households faster than for poorer households. Again, the effects only last one year.

Overall, the effects of indirect taxes have been to slow cost-of-living inflation for poorer households relative to the average. In the absence of VAT and indirect taxes, the poorest 10 per cent of households in the income distribution would have had an average increase in their cost of living which was 0.05 percentage points higher than average instead of 0.01 percentage points lower. Richer households' cost-of-living increases would have remained higher than average due to increases in the relative price of luxuries, but by a lesser amount (0.14 percentage points per year rather than 0.16 percentage points).

4.5 Housing

Housing costs form one of the largest components of total household expenditure. Not only are the weights relatively large, but the contribution of mortgage payments in particular has been quite volatile. These factors together make the cost-of-living indices extremely sensitive to fluctuations in mortgage interest rates; on average, a 1 per cent increase in mortgage interest rates raises the RPI by 0.5 per cent. There is no reason to suppose that this increase in living costs would be distributed evenly across the population. Instead, it will impact on home-owners, with some rents possibly increasing after some time-lag. These different effects across tenure groups may add substantially to the differences in the non-housing cost of living for different population groups illustrated in section 4.3.

The treatment of shelter costs for home-owners is practically and conceptually difficult. At present, shelter costs for home-owners are represented in the RPI by nominal mortgage interest payments. Essentially, the current approach is to multiply the average outstanding mortgage debt (calculated as a weighted average of the value of mortgages taken out over the previous 25 years) by the current interest rate.

The use of the interest charge measures current expenditure by the household, but does not reflect the *price* of the shelter service which the house provides. In the same way as the price of a new consumer durable is unaffected by the monthly payments made to the finance company when it is bought on hire-purchase, there is a clear and obvious distinction between the *price* of shelter services and the *borrowing costs* of the household.[16] Mortgage costs go up and down with interest rates and fall to zero at the end of the term, but this is not related to the price of the flow of shelter services which the house provides.

While the current approach entails a high degree of sensitivity to interest rate changes, large variations in house prices hardly affect the RPI at all due to the 25-year moving average. Current expenditure on shelter by incumbent home-owners will be unaffected, but if the price of shelter services is the imputed rent then this should rise with house prices. In the United Kingdom, however, the imputed rent approach is difficult to apply because the house rental market is heavily influenced by the provision of public housing. The use of imputed rents in the RPI was abandoned in 1975.

There is a particular problem with the measurement of shelter costs for outright owners (households which own their homes outright). These households do not make mortgage payments and so the use of mortgage interest payments for them would give a zero cost. Nevertheless, there must be some cost to owner-occupation; after all, the capital invested in the house may be more profitably invested elsewhere. Furthermore, these households own an asset which is slowly deteriorating physically and technologically. It is also an asset with a capital value which fluctuates. The concept of the user-cost approach is an alternative designed to deal with this.

If a household were to borrow in order to buy a house at the beginning

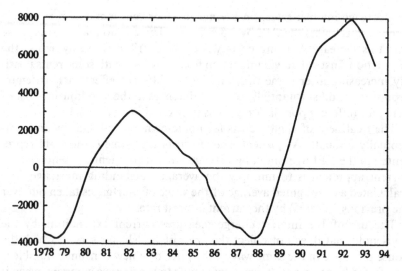

Figure 4.10 Nominal user cost of shelter, £ per annum, 1978–93

of the year, and sell it at the end, the costs to the household would be given by:

$$uc_t = \left[m_t(1+r_t^m) + (1-m_t)r_t^e + d_t - E\left\{ \frac{P_{t+1}^h - P_t^h}{P_t^h} \right\} \right] P_t^h$$

where m_t is the ratio of the amount borrowed to the purchase price, r_t^m is the tax-adjusted mortgage interest rate, r_t^e is the interest rate on alternative investments, d_t is the depreciation rate and transactions costs, P_t^h is the purchase price of the house and the final term in the square brackets reflects the expected capital gain (or loss) made on the house over the year. Dougherty and van Order (1982) show that in a competitive market, user costs equal imputed rents.

Under some, not particularly uncommon, circumstances (rapid house-price inflation and relatively low real interest rates), the expected capital gain on housing can outweigh the cost of borrowing and as a result the user cost can be negative. This is illustrated in figure 4.10, which shows the user cost of shelter in the United Kingdom from 1978.[17]

The house-price increases in the mid- to late 1980s show up clearly as the expected capital gains on housing sent the user cost negative at less than -£3500 p.a. at its lowest point. This simply reflects the fact that, at the time, housing represented a good investment, the returns to which substantially outweighed the costs. The house-price falls at the beginning of the 1990s and the high interest rates at the time combine to push the user

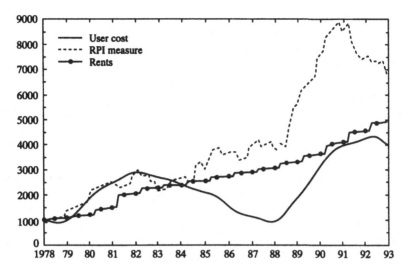

Figure 4.11 Shelter costs: rents, mortgage payments, RPI method and the user cost, 1978 = 100

cost up to a peak of around £8000 p.a. The beginnings of the recovery in the housing market and the recent falls in interest rates pull the index down again at the end of the period.

Figure 4.11 shows the user-cost index, the mortgage payment index used in the RPI and the price series for rents. The fact that the influence of house-price movements on the RPI measure is negligible is illustrated quite clearly as the RPI measure continues to rise gently in the mid-1980s when expected capital gains cause the user cost to fall. The RPI measure also peaks earlier than the user cost when interest rates first start to fall. Because the lowest point in the house-price cycle was not reached for a few months after interest rates fell, the user-cost measure continues to rise, although at a slower rate. The pattern of steps in the rents series is due to the influence of annual changes in rents charged on public housing.

The issue of the appropriate weight for the user-cost series is difficult to resolve. The concept of a user cost is notional. The cost is incurred by the household but accrued rather than actually paid. Mortgagors, for example, accrue capital gains and losses but only pay their monthly mortgage bills. The usual weight applied to changes in the price of a good is the expenditure share, where expenditure is price multiplied by quantity. In the case of housing, the implicit quantity is one. The expenditure is therefore the current price. This implies that the weight to apply to the user-cost price series is the average nominal user cost itself.

One problem with this is that the size of the weight is both large and extremely volatile, as can be seen from figure 4.10. In 1978, for example, average total weekly non-housing expenditure was £68. The average weekly user cost was around -£70. In 1992, the average weekly user cost was around £150, while average total non-housing expenditure was £224. At other times (early 1980s, 1985 and 1989), the user cost was zero. Annual increases in the user-cost series reached around 100 per cent in early 1979 and in 1988, while they were negative at other times. Including the user-cost price series with the nominal user-cost weight would result in an unacceptably volatile index which was completely dominated by shelter costs. It is also difficult to know how to deal with a negative weight. The approach adopted here is a compromise aimed at focusing on the different effects of the two price series. The weight used under the user-cost approach is mortgage payments for households with mortgages, and average mortgage payments for households that own their houses outright. This has the benefit of using similar weights to those used under the RPI method for mortgagors, but also gives a positive weight to owner-occupiers owning outright. Section 4.5.1 presents results based on housing-inclusive cost-of-living indices calculated using the RPI method. Section 4.5.2 discusses and compares the effects of using the user-cost approach.

4.5.1 The mortgage interest approach

Figure 4.12 shows the Törnqvist all-households' average inflation rate calculated with and without housing costs using the mortgage interest payment method used in construction of the RPI.

The effects of rents and mortgage payments are clear, particularly in the late 1980s when increases in interest rates pushed inflation in the all-items index above inflation in the non-housing index. The differential effects on renters versus mortgagors are shown in figure 4.13.

The first major point of departure is 1981 when local authority rents were increased sharply[18] as grants from central government were cut, and in the following year mortgage interest rates fell. The main differences, however, are apparent from 1988 onward as increases in interest rates pushed the cost-of-living of home-owners up faster while rents lagged. The interest rate cuts which enter the index from early 1990 had the reverse effect, cutting the rate of increase for home-owners relative to the average and allowing the cost-of-living for renters to catch up with the average as rents rose more sharply and interest rate cuts for home-buyers pulled the average down. By the end of the period, the average cost-of-living for households with mortgages rose 1.07 per cent more than the all-households average on this measure of shelter costs.

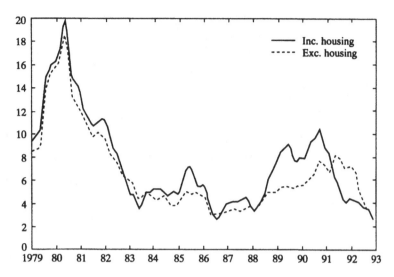

Figure 4.12 Annual increase in cost-of-living, with and without housing costs: all-households, RPI shelter-costs measure, per cent, 1979–92

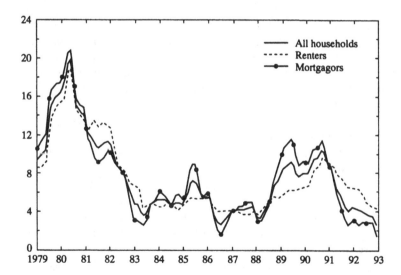

Figure 4.13 Inflation rates by tenure, RPI shelter-costs measure, per cent, 1979–92

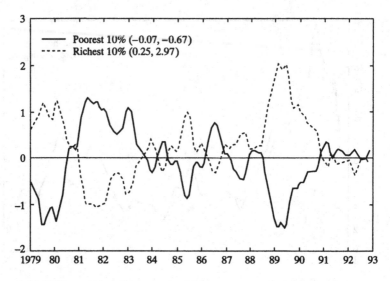

Figure 4.14 Difference in inflation rates, by income group, RPI shelter-costs measure, percentage points, 1979–92

Figure 4.14 shows the difference in cost-of-living inflation for households in the top and bottom 10 per cent of the income distribution.[19] To a large extent, the differences are driven by variations in tenure types between the two groups. The increase in the cost-of-living for poorer households in early 1981 corresponds to the timing of the rent increase. Similarly, the fall in the mid- to late 1980s coincides with the increases in mortgage rates which are shown to impact on the richer households, most of whom are home-owners.

Compared with figure 4.4, the inclusion of housing costs appears to amplify the cycles in the indices. Adding housing costs increases the average difference for poorer households from –0.01 to –0.07 percentage points and the final difference in growth levels from 0.32 per cent to 0.67 per cent less than the population mean. This is because increases in housing-costs inflation generally coincide with non-housing inflation. The 1981 rent increases, for example, coincided with a period of higher-than-average non-housing inflation for poorer households. Mortgage inflation at the end of the 1980s coincided with a period of higher-than-average inflation for the richer households. Only at the end of the sample period, in the 1990s, do the housing and non-housing effects appear to cancel each other out as rents rise once more relative to mortgages while non-housing inflation for the poorest 10 per cent fell.

Figure 4.15 shows the difference in inflation rates for three broad date-

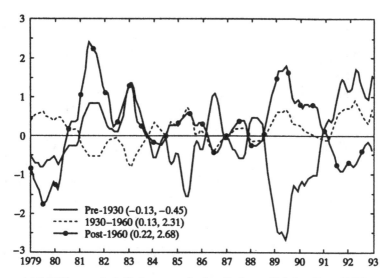

Figure 4.15 Difference in inflation rates, by head's date-of-birth cohort, RPI shelter-costs measure, percentage points, 1979–92

of-birth cohorts: households in which the head was born before 1930 (i.e. those where the head was aged 50 or more at the start of the period and over 63 at the end), those in which the head was born after 1930 but before 1960, and those in which the head was born after 1960 (i.e. households in which the head was under 19 at the beginning and under 32 at the end).

The path for the youngest cohort is similar to that for renters and poorer households until about 1983. They seemed to be particularly hard hit in early 1981 by the combined effects of the rent increase and other, non-housing inflation. During the mid-1980s, this cohort appears to take on some of the characteristics of richer home-owners, possibly as a result of the right to buy council houses and as part of the general shift towards owner-occupation. This turns out to be unfortunate since they then enter the period of high interest rates with more members who are mortgagors. The average difference from the all-households inflation rate is therefore quite high at 0.22 percentage points above average and consequently their cost-of-living level at the end has grown 2.68 per cent more than average. There therefore appears to be quite a strong cohort-specific effect in which an ill-timed move into owner-occupation increased the cost of living of younger households. In contrast to those born after 1960, the eldest house-holds did relatively well, finishing the period with a cost-of-living which had grown 0.45 per cent slower than average.

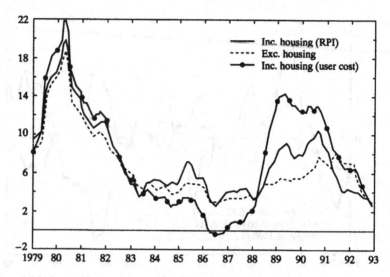

Figure 4.16 Annual increase in cost-of-living, with and without housing costs: all-households, user-cost measure and RPI shelter-costs measure, per cent, 1979–92

4.5.2 The user-cost approach

Figure 4.16 shows Törnqvist average inflation rates calculated exclusive and inclusive of housing costs, with shelter costs measured by the user-cost method as well as the RPI mortgage interest payments method. Because the user-cost and mortgage interest payment indices start off similarly, the differences from figure 4.3 in the timepath of the all-items index up to the early 1980s are slight. From that point onwards, however, they are quite striking. As the expected capital gains on housing impact upon the shelter-costs index during the mid-1980s, the user-cost method gives an average all-items inflation index which goes negative in 1986. Increased interest rates and capital losses at the end of the 1980s combine to push the all-items user cost measure well above the RPI measure.

Figure 4.17 shows the effects of this pattern by tenure type. As expected, home-owners do relatively well during the housing boom, enjoying falls in their cost of living. Home-owners who own their houses outright in particular did very well in this period as their shelter costs reflect the capital gains without the mortgage costs. This, however, had the consequence that they were more exposed to the capital losses in the next few years. This gave outright owners an inflation rate which was 1.56 percentage points higher than average over the whole period, but by the end of 1992 their

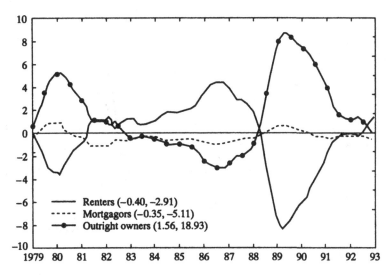

Figure 4.17 Difference in inflation rates, by tenure, user-cost measure, per cent, 1979–92

cost-of-living had grown by nearly 19 percentage points more than average. This was due to their exposure to capital losses on their homes in the late 1980s.

Section 4.5.1 picked up the relationship between the proportion of mortgage payers and income bracket – households on higher incomes were more likely to be paying a mortgage, and the size of mortgage was likely to be greater than that of less well-off households. The mortgage interest payments method, therefore, fails to pick up the large number of usually older households in the bottom income decile group which own their homes outright.[20] The user cost of housing does apply to these households because they experience capital gains and losses on the value of their homes. Figure 4.18 shows the difference for average inflation for the poorest and richest 10 per cent of the population.[21] As expected, because of the number of outright owners in the bottom decile group, this is quite different from the corresponding figure using the RPI measure (figure 4.14). Now, the inflation in the bottom decile group is 0.75 percentage points higher than average over the period, leaving the bottom decile group with a cost-of-living which has risen 9.19 percentage points more than the average by the end of the period.

Figure 4.19 shows the cohort differences corresponding to figure 4.15. The pattern here is again markedly different. The oldest households now do worst, with an average inflation rate 0.88 percentage points higher than

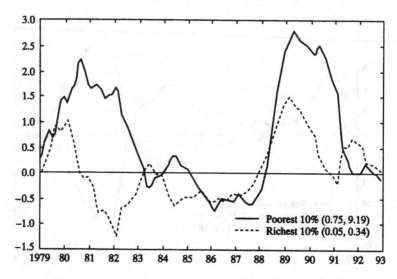

Figure 4.18 Difference in inflation rates, by income group, user-cost measure, percentage points, 1979–92

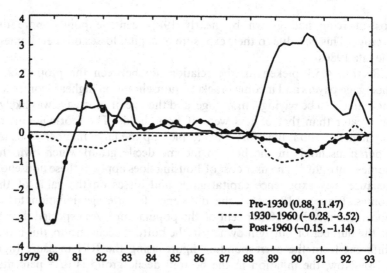

Figure 4.19 Difference in inflation rates, by head's date-of-birth cohort, user-cost measure, percentage points, 1979–92

average and a cost-of-living growth at the end of the period which is 11.47 per cent faster than average. This is clearly due to what happens after 1987. The reason for the large hump in inflation for the eldest cohort is probably the treatment of households that own their houses outright. These sorts of households were therefore exposed to the capital losses on their homes which the user-cost measure includes, and this completely alters the picture to one where the cohort-specific effect falls not on the young but on the old.

4.6 Conclusions

Several criticisms can be made of the approach adopted in this chapter. First, differences in spending patterns could be a function of differences in prices which we do not observe in these data. Apart from the regional aspect, which is not examined (see chapter 5 in this volume), price differences could also be correlated with the household characteristics which are examined. For example, poorer households without private transport may be forced to buy goods at the corner shop rather than the edge-of-town superstore. The prices they face may be higher than those paid by richer households. However, this only matters if the rates of change in these different sets of prices are different over time, or if households switch between the two sets of prices.

Secondly, the issue of quality changes has not been addressed. Quality improvements in goods and services over the period may mean that more utility is now derived from consumption of some goods than was formerly the case. This means that cost-of-living indices like those calculated here may over-estimate cost increases because they do not adjust for quality improvements. A counter-argument may be that consumers become harder to please as quality improves over time. Higher quality would then be needed to elicit the same level of welfare in 1992 than in 1979. It is not possible to address the issue of quality with these data.

This chapter does not resolve the issue of the treatment of housing costs. The sensitivity of the results to different measures of shelter costs is illustrated, but further work is required to develop truly sensible treatment of shelter costs with an appropriate weight. This would provide enough material for a long study in its own right.

It is important to reiterate that these results are entirely dependent upon the period studied. A different period would have given different results. The run of data from 1979 to 1992 does, however, nest two other papers (Bradshaw and Godfrey, 1983; Fry and Pashardes, 1986) and shows that their results, like those here, do not apply more widely than over the period from which they draw their data.

The object of this chapter has been to examine the extent and pattern of differences in the cost-of-living for subgroups of the population. The main result is that differences in the overall growth in cost-of-living at the end of the period studied are small. However, relative inflation rates for different households cycle over the period and there are several periods in which inflation rates differ widely between the top and bottom of the income distribution and between demographic groups.

The fall in the relative price of necessities and the corresponding increase in the price of luxuries over the period and the difference in expenditure patterns between rich and poor households have meant that the cost-of-living has increased faster for richer households than it has for poorer households. The progressive nature of indirect taxes between 1979 and 1992 has been shown to have contributed to this effect. This means that the real income of poorer households is slightly higher at the moment, and the real income of richer households is slightly lower at the moment, than standard income statistics suggest, and this marginally narrows the increase in real income inequality. However, this does not imply that it is good to be poor. The differences are small and the welfare effects of low income massively outweigh the effects of a slightly lower-than-average increase in their cost-of-living.[22] Given that these differences between groups are small, the obvious question is whether they matter when uprating benefits, etc. Benefit uprating is designed to compensate poor households for year-to-year increases in the cost-of-living. On average, cost-of-living increases in line with the average index over the period would have been broadly accurate (in fact, they have been overly generous by a very small amount). This should not be taken to imply, however, that there is no need for the government to use an index more representative of the cost-of-living of poorer households to uprate benefits. This chapter has demonstrated that households in receipt of benefits have had both periods of higher-than-average and periods of lower-than-average increases in living costs in the order of around ±2 per cent. These periods can last up to one or two years. Benefit uprating on the basis of average increases has therefore over-compensated them for increases in their cost-of-living at some times and under-compensated them at other times. These period-to-period errors matter if there are liquidity constraints and households cannot, for example, borrow in order to smooth their consumption. There almost certainly are such constraints, and this means that using the 'wrong' index imposes costs on poorer households even if the overall increase is more or less right when viewed over a longer period.

Notes

The author would like to thank James Banks, Richard Blundell, Andrew Dilnot, Alissa Goodman, Terence Gorman, John Hills, Pat McGregor, Judith Payne, Marysia Walsh, Steve Webb, two anonymous referees and seminar participants at the London School of Economics and the Institute for Fiscal Studies. Finance for this research, provided by the Joseph Rowntree Foundation under the Income and Wealth Programme and the ESRC Research Centre for the Micro Economic Analysis of Fiscal Policy at IFS, is gratefully acknowledged. Material from the Family Expenditure Survey, made available by the Central Statistical Office through the ESRC Data Archive, at the University of Essex, has been used by permission of the Controller of Her Majesty's Stationery Office. All errors are the sole responsibility of the author.

1. The proportion of the total household budget allocated to fuel against log total expenditure.
2. Luxuries are usually characterised by upward-sloping Engel curves, necessities by downward-sloping Engel curves.
3. Allen (1958), Brittain (1960), Tipping (1970), Muellbauer (1977), Piachaud (1978), Bradshaw and Godfrey (1983), Fry and Pashardes (1986).
4. Sen (1985) argues persuasively against the usual approach of thinking about the standard of living as utility, income and wealth, suggesting a wider interpretation in which living standards are conceived of in terms of human functionings and capabilities. Sen may be right, but it is difficult to see how to implement his ideas with existing data.
5. Blundell et al. (1994), for example, find evidence of large own- and cross-price substitution effects in UK FES data.
6. For a proof of this see Diewert (1978).
7. Christensen et al. (1975).
8. Deaton and Muellbauer (1980a), Blundell et al. (1994).
9. See Borooah et al., chapter 5 in this volume.
10. The final year has been calculated as a Laspeyres index.
11. See Crawford et al. (1993).
12. The analysis of tax incidence depends upon the chosen proxy for living standards: either expenditure or income. Using income gives a different (less progressive) picture from expenditure because richer households spend a smaller proportion of their incomes than poorer households. However, since indirect taxes are applied to expenditures it seems natural to use expenditure as the appropriate proxy here. Further, welfare is usually seen as inhering in consumption (for which expenditure is a better proxy) rather than income: money itself is useless except to the extent to which it can be turned into goods and services.
13. Amongst car-owners, however, petrol duties are regressive and fall particularly hard on poorer rural households for which car-ownership, and therefore petrol expenditure, are more of a necessity. See Baker and Crawford (1993).
14. Banks, Blundell and Lewbel (1994).

15. It is assumed that indirect taxes have been passed on in full to consumers.
16. See Robinson and Skinner (1989).
17. User costs were calculated using average monthly house-price data supplied by the Department of the Environment. Expected capital gains were estimated non-parametrically. Essentially, this process applied a 12-month weighted moving average around each data point. In principle, a period of more than 12 months can be used but this would have either required house price data for the future (which is not available), or that the period of the study to be cut down. Following the Bank of England's treatment of user costs in its housing-adjusted retail price index, depreciation was set at 0.5 per cent, transactions costs at 2 per cent and average proportion of the price borrowed at 65 per cent. The mortgage interest rate is from table 7.1L in *Financial Statistics* (HMSO). The opportunity cost calculations are based on the Treasury Bill yield from table 38 in *Economic Trends* (HMSO).
18. See figure 4.12.
19. Before housing costs (BHC), measure: see Goodman and Webb (1994).
20. In 1991–92, in the bottom income decile group (BHC measure), 24 per cent of households own their homes outright and 28 per cent have a mortgage (DSS, 1994).
21. This uses the same definition of income as that used in figure 4.15. It may be appropriate to extend the definition to include the capital gains and losses on housing. Figure 4.18, however, allows the comparison between the two measures using exactly the same population groups as in figure 4.15.
22. See Stoker (1986).

5 Cost-of-living differences between the regions of the United Kingdom

Vani K. Borooah, Patrick P. L. McGregor, Patricia M.
McKee and Gwyneth E. Mulholland

5.1 Introduction

Are some regions of the United Kingdom 'cheaper' than others, in the sense that a given basket of commodities can be bought in them for a smaller outlay of money? Moreover, are such differences, if indeed they do exist, persistent over time? This chapter attempts to provide answers to these questions. If both were answered in the affirmative, then a policy of paying nationally determined unemployment benefits might have, depending upon their region of residence, significantly different consequences for the real incomes of the unemployed and so affect their participation in the labour market. Despite the importance of these questions there is no regional component to the Retail Prices Index (RPI), which is the main, and most prominent, measure of price movements in the United Kingdom.

In attempting to shed some light on this area of darkness, this study used regional price data provided by the Reward Group. These data were used in conjunction with weights derived from the Family Expenditure Survey (FES) to construct regional retail price indices.[1] Both the data and the construction of the weights are described in section 5.2. Differences in regional housing costs might be expected to play an important part in determining cost-of-living differences between regions, and so section 5.3 is devoted to a discussion of the many problems associated with their measurement. Section 5.4 brings together material from sections 5.2 and 5.3 to paint a portrait of regional variations in the cost-of-living in the United Kingdom and is followed by a discussion of some possible applications of the analysis. Finally, section 5.6 presents some conclusions.

5.2 Regional relative cost indices: non-housing items

The primary source of regional price data used in this study was the Reward Group. This Group undertakes a six-monthly survey of the

Table 5.1 *Reward commodity quotations*

RPI category	Reward quotations	National prices	FES categories
Food and catering	39	—	39
Alcoholic drink	4	—	4
Tobacco	2	—	2
Fuel and light	3	—	3
Household goods	9	2	11
Household services	3	3	7
Clothing and footwear	—	5	5
Personal goods and services	7	1	8
Motoring and travel	15	1	7
Leisure goods	6	2	8
Leisure services	4	1	6
Housing:			
Repairs and maintenance	3	—	3
Rents, rates, water charges, etc.	1	—	1
Owner-occupiers:			
Mortgage payments	—	—	—
Rates	6	—	1
	102	15	105

cost-of-living throughout the United Kingdom and the Irish Republic, involving it in the collection of price data covering all the main sections of household expenditure. Specific items are chosen as price indicators and their prices are collected from one or two shops in particular towns within a region. In total, 211 prices are collected in each of approximately 104 towns and these are supplemented by 18 regional prices covering car insurance, electricity and gas, and by national prices for items whose prices do not vary across the regions.[2] For gas, electricity, houses, rates, cars and car insurance the Reward price quotations relate to eight specified 'lifestyles'. We calculated a weighted average of these figures using the FES to determine their relative importance. Reward collects about one sixth of the quotations contained in the RPI for the month that it compiles its index.

The raw price data amounted to 102 quotations from Reward, supplemented by 15 national prices. Consolidating lifestyles yielded 105 separate quotations, details of which are shown in table 5.1. The construction of regional price indices from this raw price data was carried out in two stages. First, regional group indices were constructed, where the groups were as defined by the current RPI.[3] Each group price index was a weighted average of the price ratios of the individual commodities in it with the weights being the commodity budget shares.[4] Since there are many more commodities in the FES than commodity price quotations in Reward, the expenditure weight contained not only the specified commodity but also those which were considered to be closely related to it.

The second step was to aggregate the regional commodity-group price indices into cost-of-living indices. Although every attempt was made to follow RPI procedures in this it proved impossible in respect of two items. First, pensioner households are treated separately by the RPI and a 'pensioner price index' is calculated for this group. However, the small number of pensioners in the FES sample means that the RPI has to pool data for three years in order to produce pensioner price indices. In order to achieve a comparable level of precision, a similar procedure at a regional level would have led to constant weights being employed over 1979–90. Thus the regional price indices of this study relate to an aggregate of pensioner and non-pensioner households.[5] Second, the FES expenditure figures are known to be under-recorded for some categories – soft drinks, confectionery, alcoholic drink and tobacco products – and these are accordingly adjusted using trade and Customs and Excise data. Such a procedure was not feasible and consequently, the weights used are *unadjusted* FES weights.

A major concern with this procedure was sample size which varied in 1989, for example, between 1241 for the South East and 275 in East Anglia (which had the smallest sample in Britain; in Northern Ireland it was 122). The issue of small sample size was addressed by pooling data across different years[6] with the magnitude of the percentage standard error,[7] associated with the individual commodities, being used to determine the commodities for which data needed to be pooled. If this exceeded 20 per cent for three of the 12 years for which data were analysed, then a three-year moving average of expenditure on those commodities (suitably adjusted for price changes) was employed. Two subsets of the commodity groups may be distinguished; that comprising food and catering, alcoholic drink, tobacco, fuel and clothing contained relatively few items that required pooling. The subset comprising the remaining groups (house maintenance, household goods and services, personal goods and services, motoring and travel, and leisure goods and services) contained several that required pooling, particularly expensive goods that are infrequently purchased. The effectiveness of pooling varied over time and region; if we consider the standard error for colour TV sets in 1985, this declined from 22.2 per cent to 12.7 per cent in the South East with pooling. In East Anglia the decline, from 32.5 per cent to 26.6 per cent was more modest.[8]

Following the RPI approach, chained Laspeyres indices were calcu-

Table 5.2 *Dispersion of group price indices*

	Root mean square about the mean (%)	Root mean square about the RPI (%)
Tobacco	1.18	1.49
Household services	0.88	1.69
Clothing and footwear	0.17	1.76
Food and catering	1.58	1.92
Leisure services	2.26	2.87
Household goods	2.32	3.00
Motoring and travel	1.59	3.54
Personal goods and services	2.57	3.55
Fuel and light	3.58	5.01
Leisure goods	2.66	5.20
Alcoholic drink	4.26	6.64
Housing – repairs	5.65	8.05

lated, for each region, for each of the main non-housing groups.[9] Table 5.2 shows the dispersion for each group, across the regions, over 1979–90, first with respect to the mean value of the index (RMSM) and then with respect to the appropriate sub-index of the RPI (RMSRPI).[10] The groups with high dispersion were alcoholic drink, fuel and light and housing repairs, both about the mean (greater than 3 per cent) and about the RPI (greater than 4 per cent). With alcohol and housing repairs, the RPI generally lay above the regional indices while for travel it was below. The remaining groups[11] showed moderate amounts of dispersion, both about the mean and the RPI, with the exception of leisure goods.[12]

A comparison of the regional price indices for the different commodity groups with the corresponding group sub-indices of the RPI established that the former satisfactorily tracked the latter.[13] After this assessment, the central question of the relative (to the United Kingdom) cost of regions was addressed. The relative cost of region r ($r = 1 \ldots 12$), at time t, ($t = 1979 \ldots 1990$), was measured by the Törnqvist index.[14] The assumption that regional differences in price are transient is not generally valid, and this is evident from figure 5.1 where the outlying cases of the group relative cost indices are graphed (the remaining cases showed no systematic differences).

For four of the 12 commodity groups (tobacco, household services, leisure goods and clothing) the regional cost indices moved so closely that no distinctive pattern could be discerned (the clothing price index was obtained entirely from national prices and the household services price index had half its price quotations emanating from national sources). The two price quotations for tobacco were both for branded

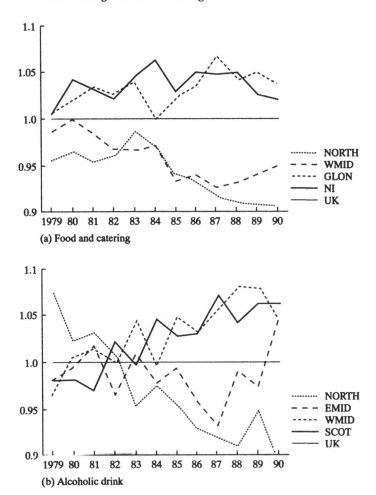

Figure 5.1 Regional relative costs, by commodity group: the outlying cases

cigarette packets; hence it would appear that the retailers had limited opportunity to vary cigarette prices. The graph for housing repairs is not displayed due to the low number of price quotations; the difficulties in deriving relative prices for motoring and travel (see n. 16) led also to the exclusion of its graph.

Northern Ireland was the region most frequently found at the extremes of such relative cost comparisons. It was above average in the cost of: food, housing repairs, fuel[15] and travel[16] and below average in the cost of leisure services. Greater London had relatively high costs for: food, fuel, personal goods and services, and leisure services while Scotland had relatively high costs for housing repairs and household goods but relatively low costs for

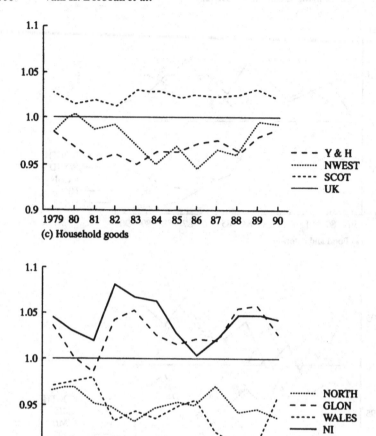

Figure 5.1 (*cont.*)

fuel and leisure services.[17] In general, the frequency with which particular regions appeared at the extremes of the relative cost values suggested that the assumption of cost uniformity across the regions of the United Kingdom was only valid for the area comprising the central regions of Britain; such an assumption was not applicable to Greater London, Scotland, Northern Ireland and the North.

5.3 Regional relative cost indices: housing

The calculation of the RPI in 1990 assigned 18.5 per cent of the total weight to housing cost and, of this, nearly 40 per cent was assigned to

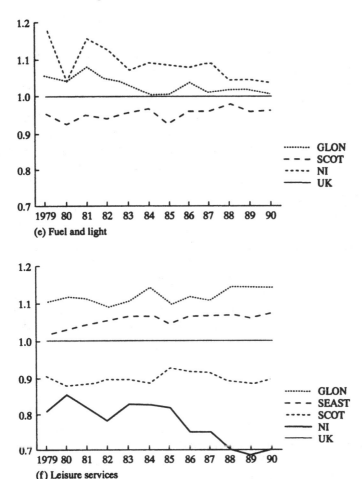

(e) Fuel and light

(f) Leisure services

Figure 5.1 (*cont.*)

mortgage interest payments (MIP). The translation of the RPI methodology to the regional level[18] forms the substance of the early part of this section. This is followed by an examination of the issues of capital gains and the user cost of housing which are ignored by the RPI's methodology and, arguably, constitute a major deficiency.

As opposed to the cost of owner-occupation, rent differentials across the UK regions are easy to measure and, over 1979–90, were both well defined and persistent. Rents in Scotland and Northern Ireland were relatively low, while being relatively high in Greater London, the South East and East and West Midlands. Since 1987, rents in the remaining regions, with the exception of Wales, have converged on the UK average.

5.3.1 Index of mortgage interest payments

The basis for estimating MIP is provided by estimates of average mortgage debt of mortgage holders (AMDMH) which requires data on the distribution of mortgages by vintage, and average house prices.[19] To compute the age distribution of mortgages the methodology outlined in annex 2 of the RPI Advisory Committee (1986) was applied to the regional data.[20] Part of mortgage debt was eligible for tax relief and part was not; the values of MIP were calculated by multiplying the eligible and non-eligible parts of AMDMH by, respectively, the net and gross rates of interest[21] and summing the amounts so obtained. The MIP calculated from AMDMH related to mortgage-holders; in order to narrow the focus to owner-occupiers, the MIP values were scaled down by 0.6. Lastly, in order to obtain an average across *all* households the resulting figure was multiplied by the proportion of housing stock made up of owner-occupiers.[22] A chained index of MIP was calculated for the United Kingdom with the distribution of mortgage vintages held constant for each link. The discrepancy between this and the corresponding RPI series was under 0.005 except for 1985 and 1986 when our index was 0.106 above and 0.090 below the RPI one respectively (the 1989 difference was 0.027).

5.3.2 The user cost of capital

The user cost of housing (UC) measures the opportunity cost of home-ownership by considering the rate of return that an owner's investment in housing might be expected to command,[23] if it was invested in a financial asset with similar risk characteristics. It thus depends upon the cost of finance, the alternative rate of return on housing equity, depreciation and the anticipated capital gain:

$$UC_t = [m_t\, r_t^m + (1 - m_t)\, r_t^e + d_t - E(\Delta P_t / P_t)] P_t \qquad (1)$$

where

P_t = current house price

m_t = mortgage as a proportion of P_t

r_t^m = (after tax) mortgage interest rate

r_t^e = (after tax) rate of return on equities

d_t = depreciation, insurance and discounted annual transactions costs expressed as a proportion of P_t

$E[\Delta P_t / P_t]$ = one-period expectation of the proportionate capital gain, where $\Delta P_t = P_{t+1} - P_t$.

In terms of the empirical implementation of the user-cost concept, however, several alternative approaches are available (see Robinson and Skinner, 1989). This study considers two such approaches: the Bank of England's (1993) Housing Adjusted Retail Prices (HARP) index; and the windfall income approach of Fry and Pashardes (1986).

User-cost and the HARP index

The HARP index may be derived from (1) by setting:

$$r^e = r^m \text{ and } E(\Delta P_t / P_t) = r^b - r^i$$

where r^b is the rate of return on 20-year government bonds, with r^i the rate on an indexed bond of similar characteristics (assumed constant at 3 per cent); if $r^b = r^m$ then the user cost is:

$$UCHARP_t = [r^i + d_t] P_t = 0.047 * P_t,$$

where d_t (after taking account of repairs and transactions items) is assumed to be 1.7 per cent.

As it is derived above, UCHARP is driven by the *level* of house prices and not by their rate of change. House-price inflation can be introduced at the regional level by assuming

$$E(\Delta P_t / P_t) = r^b - r^i + g_r$$

where $g_r = (\Delta P_t / P_t)_r - (\Delta P_t / P_t)_{UK}$ is the difference in the percentage rate of house-price change between region r and the United Kingdom. Consequently, the proportional rate of change of UCHARP, in region r, is a function of the rates of change of UK house prices and the regional differential.[24] The HARP index essentially assumes that the anticipated rate of change of house prices is the same as the anticipated overall inflation rate as indicated by the bond market. The modification introduced above is to assume that regional differences in anticipated house-price inflation are based on historic differentials. While it is clearly preferable to include a forward-looking component into the expectation (such as employing a 12-month moving average as used by Crawford in chapter 4 in this volume), the lack of monthly data precluded this. In addition, the result would be less comparable with the Bank of England's index than the approach outlined above; as is evident by comparing table 5.3 to figure 4.11, the results are sensitive to the method of construction.

The average rates of house price inflation, over time periods of 10 and 20 years, were estimated for each region by regressing log P_t on a time dummy. As might be expected, the changes based upon the 10-year interval were less stable than those based upon the 20-year interval. The former fluctuated between 14.6 per cent per year for the 10-year period

preceding 1980 to 11.3 per cent per year for the 10-year period prior to
1989. The latter rose steadily from 10.1 per cent per year, for the 20-year
period prior to 1979, to 12.9 per cent per year for the 20-year period
prior to 1989.

Capital gains as windfall income

Fry and Pashardes (1986) observed that because capital gains
were often so large, user-cost as defined in (1) could often be negative. To
avoid this problem, they regarded capital gains on housing (CG) as windfall income which was not to be entered as a component of housing cost
but rather to be deducted from total expenditure. Their aggregate price
index, P_{FP} was thus defined as:

$$P_{FP} = \frac{\sum P_r q_{UK} - CG_r}{\sum P_{UK} q_{UK} - CG_{UK}}$$

(2)

where CG_r = (Average Capital Gains in region r) × (Number of owner-
occupiers in UK) and the preceding terms are aggregate consumption in
the United Kingdom valued at the region's and UK prices. The associated
price index for owner-occupied housing was

$$[m_t r_t^m + d_t] P_t,$$

which is essentially the mortgage interest payments of owner-occupiers
plus a depreciation charge.[25] To implement the Fry–Pashardes method,
capital gains were calculated by regression.

Table 5.3 shows the nominal expenditures implied by the various measures of housing costs. Mortgage interest payments were usually between
one third and one half of the user-cost measure, though movements in the
former tended to be sharper. Capital gains were usually larger than mortgage interest payments, though the force of this statement was considerably weakened when depreciation was added to MIP. In spite of the fact
that the levels of the different components of housing cost were markedly
different, their rates of growth since 1979 were similar.[26] However, such
similarities masked quite dramatic regional differences.

In order to highlight such regional differences, the 12 regions were
grouped into two relatively homogeneous entities comprising: the South
(Greater London, South East, South West and East Anglia); and the
North (North, Yorkshire, and Humberside, North West and Wales). The
remaining regions: East and West Midlands, Scotland and Northern
Ireland were less homogeneous and were considered as a third group.
Figures 5.2, 5.3 and 5.4 show for 1979–90 movements in the housing-cost
measures for, respectively, the regions of the South, the North and the

Table 5.3 *Measures of UK owner-occupier housing cost, £/week*

Year	Mortgage interest payment	User cost – HARP (20 years)	Capital gains	Fry– Pashardes
1979	4.47	15.08	5.98	9.86
1980	6.83	18.80	9.20	13.54
1981	7.93	21.16	11.58	15.49
1982	9.45	21.98	9.87	17.30
1983	7.26	23.58	6.74	15.68
1984	9.10	26.06	7.14	18.41
1985	11.52	28.45	9.79	21.68
1986	12.60	31.72	11.92	23.93
1987	13.71	36.56	14.78	26.77
1988	13.09	44.41	20.39	28.95
1989	20.27	54.62	28.26	39.78
1990	26.80	59.40	32.39	48.01

residual group and table 5.4 shows the 1979 and 1990 levels of housing cost. Given the broad agreement between MIP and the user cost of capital calculated on a 20-year interval (UCHARP20), it would appear that, on these measures, relative to the United Kingdom, housing costs were higher in Greater London and the South East but were at UK levels in East Anglia and the South West. However, when user costs were calculated on a 10-year interval (UCHARP10), the greater short-term capital gains for regions of the South meant that, by 1990, housing costs in the South, on this measure, were lower than the average for the United Kingdom. Figure 5.2 shows the dramatic surge in capital gains for Greater London and the South East relative to the rest of the United Kingdom after 1984. Over the period 1979–90 the percentage increase in capital gains for the regions in the South amounted to the highest in the United Kingdom.

Clearly, the period over which capital gains is calculated plays a crucial role in determining housing costs as measured by user costs. The differential rate of regional house-price inflation relative to the United Kingdom was much more marked when capital gains were calculated over a 10-, rather than a 20-, year interval; the similarity of the latter to the MIP case has led us to use it almost exclusively, since to do otherwise would mean that regional cost-of-living differences were being driven virtually entirely by the method of construction of the housing element, and any link with the accepted measure of changes in the price level would be lost.

The housing cost calculations for the North (figure 5.3) showed it to be the mirror image of the South, with the caveat that housing costs in the

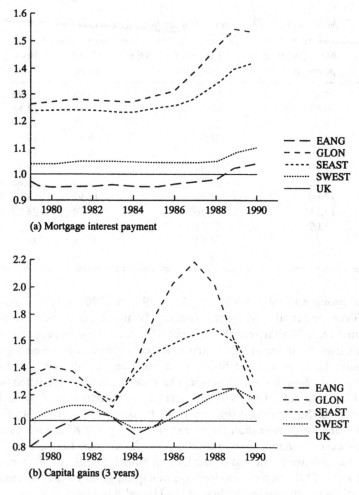

(a) Mortgage interest payment

(b) Capital gains (3 years)

Figure 5.2 Relative housing cost of owner-occupation: south

regions of the North moved more closely together than in the regions of the South. Measured by both MIP and by UCHARP20, the North emerged as a low housing-cost area; in 1990, MIP in the North, at £18.50 per week, was less than half the figure for Greater London and for the South East, though the weekly user cost in the North of £49 was closer to the weekly user cost of £72 in the two southern regions. The percentage change in these two measures over the period 1979–90, for the North, was also below the UK average. However, with user costs measured on a 10-year interval, the North–South position was reversed, with the weekly user

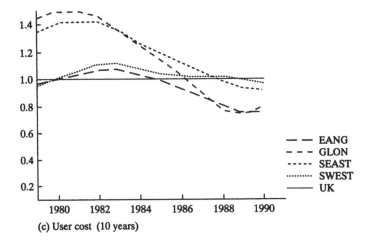

(c) User cost (10 years)

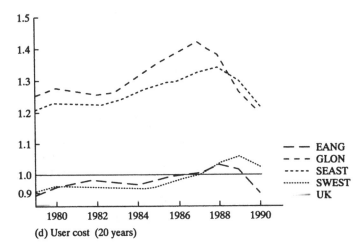

(d) User cost (20 years)

Figure 5.2 (*cont.*)

cost (UCHARP10), in 1990, of all four northern regions being greater than Greater London and the South East.

Turning to the residual group, the regions of the Midlands displayed a consistent pattern with housing costs in the West Midlands being higher than in the East Midlands (see table 5.4). In both regions, housing costs were below the UK average as measured by MIP; as measured by the two user-cost calculations, housing costs in the West Midlands lay slightly above, and in the East Midlands slightly below, the UK average. Scotland and Northern Ireland shared a similar pattern with housing cost move-

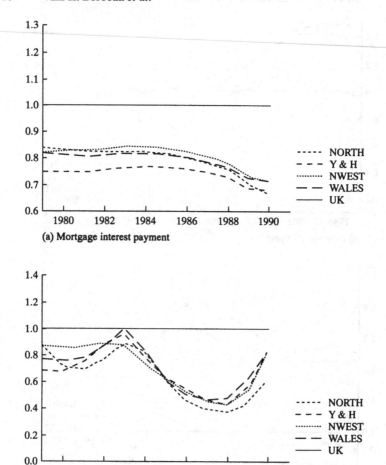

Figure 5.3 Relative housing cost of owner-occupation: north

ments in Scotland being a more muted version of such movements in Northern Ireland.

5.4 Regional cost-of-living differences?

The non-housing, and housing, cost indices discussed, respectively, in sections 5.2 and 5.3 were combined in order to arrive at an aggregate relative cost index for the regions of the United Kingdom, the results of which are reported in this section. With housing cost excluded, the indices for the 12

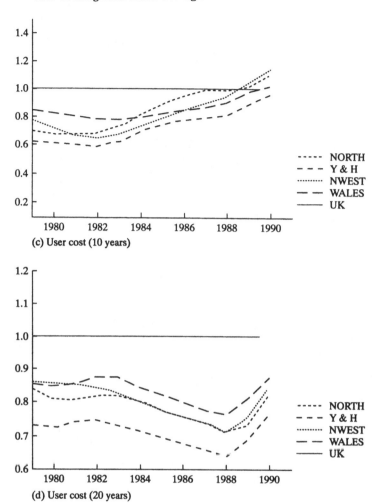

(c) User cost (10 years)

(d) User cost (20 years)

Figure 5.3 (*cont.*)

commodity groups were combined to form a Relative Cost excluding Housing index and movements in it are shown, for the different regions, in figure 5.5. On this analysis, the regions could be considered in terms of four broad groups.

The first group comprised Greater London, the South East and the East Midlands. Here there was a gradual increase in the relative cost of the regions, averaging 1.5 per cent for Greater London. Interestingly, when separate cost functions were distinguished for households in different ranges, the relative cost index for households above median income

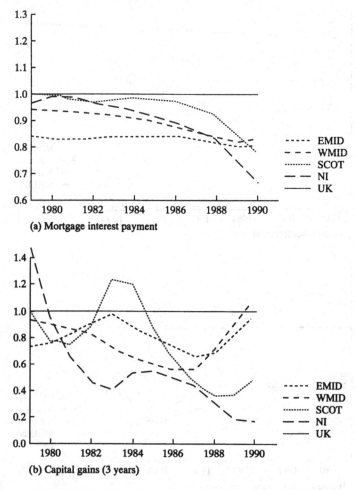

Figure 5.4 Relative housing cost of owner-occupation: other

lay above that for households below median income for all the regions in this group. In other words, in this group of regions the less well-off were relatively less disadvantaged when compared to those below median income in the United Kingdom as a whole, than was the case with the better-off.

The second group consisted of the South West, North West and Yorkshire and Humberside. For this group the relative cost did not change over time and the relative cost index for above median income households was generally greater than that for households with income below the median. The third group, comprising the West Midlands, East Anglia and Scotland, presented a picture of gradually declining relative costs over

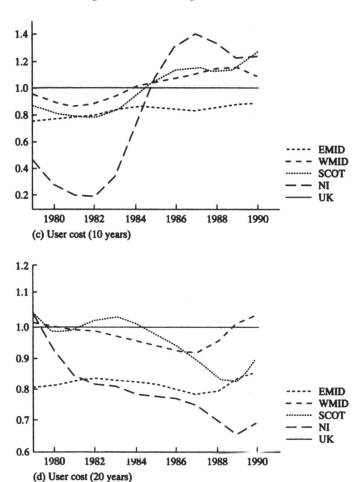

(c) User cost (10 years)

(d) User cost (20 years)

Figure 5.4 (cont.)

1979–90. Only in Scotland was there a pronounced difference between the relative cost of above and below median income households, with the former lying below the latter throughout 1979–90. This decline in relative costs was more marked for the fourth group comprising the North, Wales and Northern Ireland. Each of the regions in this group experienced a fall of more than 2 per cent in relative costs, with the relative decline being more for above median income households.[27]

The inclusion of housing cost into the aggregate relative cost index involves, as discussed in section 5.3, on housing, a choice between different measures of the cost of owner-occupation. Movements, over 1979–90, in the values of the relative cost index for each region, under the MIP and

Table 5.4 *Weekly housing costs of owner-occupiers, 1979 and 1990*

	North	Yorks and Humb	NWest	EMid	WMid	EAng	GLon	SEast	SWest	Wales	Scot	NI	UK
Owner-occupiers (%)													
1979	46	55	59	57	56	58	49	62	63	59	35	53	55
1990	60	66	68	71	68	70	62	75	74	72	51	66	67
Mortgage interest payments (£)													
1979	3.80	3.40	3.61	3.89	4.25	4.49	5.54	5.64	4.76	3.67	4.66	4.43	4.47
1990	17.95	17.91	18.38	21.57	22.08	28.41	40.99	38.16	29.52	19.13	22.16	18.24	26.80
% Increase	11.3	12.1	11.7	12.4	11.4	13.4	14.8	14.0	13.0	11.8	11.3	9.9	12.9
User cost (20 years, £)													
1979	12.64	11.07	13.01	12.20	15.31	14.09	18.91	18.27	14.27	12.91	15.70	15.78	15.08
1990	49.26	45.68	50.92	51.00	61.71	55.94	71.22	72.55	60.94	51.92	53.69	41.36	59.40
% Increase	10.8	11.0	10.5	11.7	11.5	12.1	12.0	12.3	12.6	11.0	9.8	8.3	11.7
User cost (10 years, £)													
1979	10.62	9.44	11.66	11.45	14.45	14.70	21.80	20.34	14.31	12.83	13.18	7.05	15.08
1990	65.92	57.17	68.11	52.90	64.82	44.34	47.13	54.26	57.68	60.87	75.58	73.88	59.40
% Increase	16.6	16.0	16.1	13.0	14.2	8.6	4.4	7.3	11.4	13.5	16.1	29.8	11.7
Capital gains over 3 years (£)													
1979	29.40	23.32	29.81	24.66	31.62	27.10	45.44	41.47	33.46	25.98	34.09	50.29	33.74
1990	108.77	142.32	140.51	168.34	189.63	184.28	202.36	226.72	200.89	144.12	85.84	29.00	172.49
% Increase	6.0	9.2	7.0	12.2	11.5	15.0	14.7	14.6	13.4	8.8	3.4	-3.1	12.2

Note:
% increase calculated by regression.

UCHARP20 measures, are shown in figure 5.6; the mean values of these indices over the same period are shown in table 5.5. When mortgage interest payments were used as the measure of housing costs, the movement in relative costs was similar to that when housing was excluded, though some differences could usefully be noted. When housing cost was included in the aggregate index, Greater London and the South East increased their mean relative cost index value to 1.052 and 1.020, from 1.023 and 1.005 respectively. On the other hand, the inclusion of housing led Northern Ireland to experience a fall in relative cost of a magnitude comparable to London's increase. In between these extremes, all the other regions (except West Midlands which showed a small rise) experienced small falls in their relative cost.[28] Thus, one effect of including housing cost, via MIP, in the aggregate relative cost index was to increase the prominence of regions at the extremes of the cost spectrum.

When housing costs were measured by user cost with capital gains estimated over 20 years, the declining cost group of regions now included Yorkshire and Humberside and the North West but excluded the East Midlands and East Anglia. However, Greater London and the South East remained regions of increasing relative cost. If estimated over a three-year period, capital gains dominate the aggregate relative cost index[29] with Greater London, the South East, East Anglia and the South West becoming regions with low relative costs. At the other extreme, Northern Ireland, with a relative cost index of 1.89 in 1989, was, on the same treatment of housing cost, almost twice as expensive as the UK average.

5.5 Applications of the analysis

A study of regional variations in the cost-of-living has several applications, of which three are discussed in this section. First, there is the adjustment of social security benefit levels to take account of regional differences in prices. Secondly, conclusions about the relative deprivation or prosperity of regions, as measured by real disposable income, could also be susceptible to change in the face of regional variations in the cost-of-living. Lastly, conclusions about the number of persons living in poverty could also alter when regional cost-of-living variations are allowed for.

The nominal value of non-housing social security benefits in the United Kingdom is the same regardless of the region of residence of the recipients. However, the translation of such benefits into real income depends critically upon relative (non-housing) cost differences between regions (shown in column (1) of table 5.5); ignoring such differences would mean that the real income implications of social security benefits would be different for different regions.

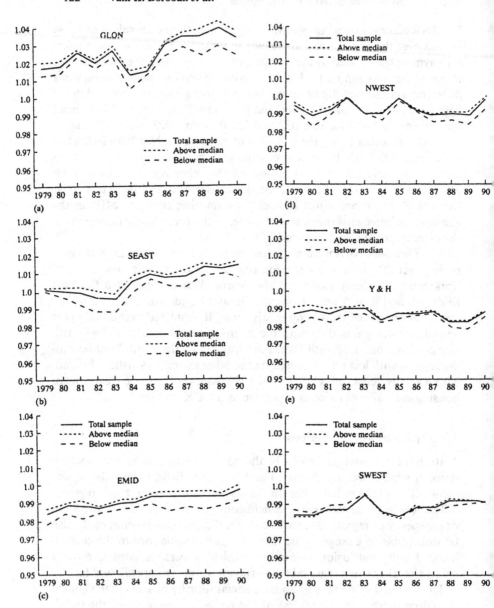

Figure 5.5 Aggregate relative cost (excluding housing), by region
(a)–(c) Group 1: increasing relative cost
(d)–(f) Group 2: constant relative cost

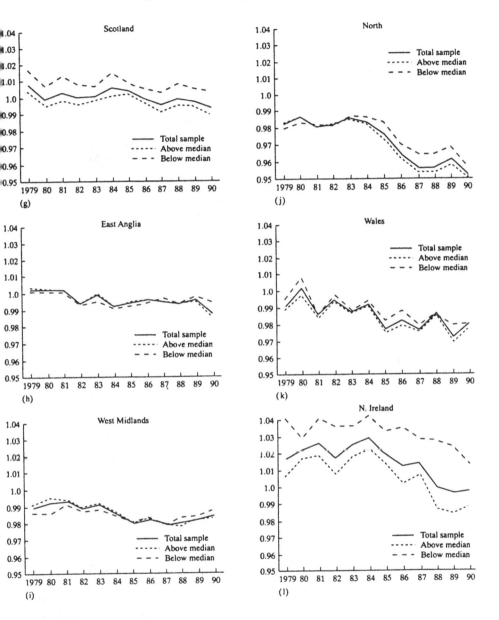

(g)–(l) Group 3: decreasing relative cost

Figure 5.5 (*cont.*)

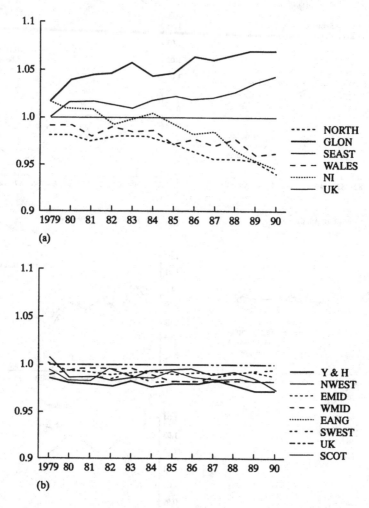

Figure 5.6 Aggregate relative cost (including housing), by region
(a)–(b) Mortgage interest payment

To examine the effect of regional cost-of-living variations on magnitudes of relative regional prosperity, regional estimates of *per capita* personal disposable income (PDI) were adjusted for regional differences in price levels and expressed as a percentage of the corresponding UK values. In the absence of any regional price adjustment, the North's *per capita* PDI was 91.5 per cent of that of the United Kingdom's. However, when regional cost differences were accounted for, with housing cost being measured by MIP, this figure rose to 94.5 per cent; when UCHARP20 was

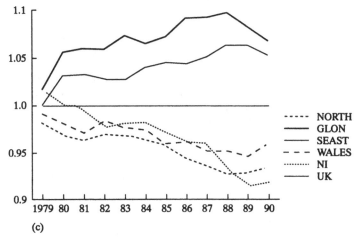

(c)

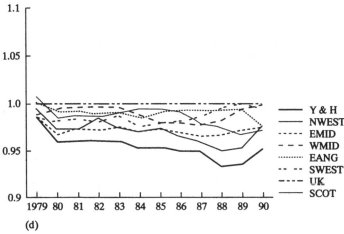

(d)

(c)–(d) User cost (20 years)

Figure 5.6 (*cont.*)

used to measure housing cost, this figure rose to 96 per cent. By way of contrast, the corresponding figures for Greater London were 125.4, 119.2, and 117.2 per cent. Details for all the regions are shown in table 5.6.

The effects on calculated poverty rates (as measured by the Head Count Ratio) of adjusting for regional price differences are shown in table 5.7. The poverty line for a household was defined as its Supplementary Benefit Entitlement (SBE) and then, respectively, as 140 and 120 per cent of its SBE.[30] Table 5.7 shows the proportion below various poverty lines in each

Table 5.5 *Mean values of the relative cost indices*

	Housing cost measured by			
	Excluding housing (1)	Mortgage interest payments (2)	User cost (20 years) (3)	Fry–Pashardes index (4)
North	0.972	0.968	0.953	1.153
Wales	0.985	0.978	0.967	1.114
WMid	0.986	0.988	0.989	1.055
Yorks and Humb	0.987	0.979	0.955	1.130
SWest	0.988	0.987	0.986	0.919
EMid	0.991	0.987	0.972	1.068
NWest	0.993	0.987	0.970	1.135
EAng	0.996	0.991	0.991	0.945
Scot	1.000	0.990	0.986	1.178
SEast	1.005	1.020	1.040	0.823
NI	1.014	0.988	0.968	1.258
GLon	1.026	1.052	1.069	0.826

Table 5.6 *Average regional PDI, 1979–90, as percentage of the UK average*

		Adjusted by the relative cost index, measure of housing costs:	
	Relative personal disposable income	Mortgage interest payments	User cost (20 years)
NI	85.5	86.6	88.5
Wales	88.1	90.1	91.2
North	91.5	94.5	96.0
WMid	91.9	93.1	92.9
NWest	93.6	94.8	96.4
Yorks and Humb	93.6	95.6	98.0
Scot	94.9	95.9	96.3
EMid	95.7	97.0	98.4
EAng	96.6	97.5	97.5
SWest	98.9	100.2	100.3
SEast	107.6	105.4	103.4
GLon	125.4	119.2	117.2

Table 5.7 *Regional poverty: Head Count ratios,* * 1984–85

| | Poverty line (as multiples of Supplementary Benefit entitlement) | | | | | |
| | 1.0 | | 1.2 | | 1.4 | |
	Unadjusted	Adjusted	Unadjusted	Adjusted	Unadjusted	Adjusted
SEast	5.2	5.4	10.4	10.8	18.3	18.5
EAng	5.3	5.3	11.7	10.8	19.5	19.5
SWest	6.3	5.8	10.5	9.6	17.8	17.5
GLon	6.6	7.3	13.0	13.3	18.7	19.1
EMid	6.8	6.8	13.7	13.2	23.3	22.5
NI	9.2	10.5	17.7	18.5	26.2	28.2
Scot	9.2	9.6	15.9	16.3	25.5	25.9
WMid	9.4	9.3	17.6	16.2	28.4	27.0
Wales	11.5	11.4	18.1	17.3	25.1	24.7
Yorks and Humb	12.1	11.2	21.8	20.4	30.8	29.6
NWest	14.4	14.0	21.7	21.7	29.4	29.1
North	16.9	16.4	25.3	23.9	36.0	35.2

Note:
* The Head Count ratio is the number of poor expressed as a proportion of total population.

region for the period 1984/85, together with the proportion when regional household expenditure[31] is deflated by the Relative Cost excluding Housing index. Adjusting for regional prices reduces the Head Count Ratio, for all three poverty lines, in the North and in Yorkshire and Humberside, but increases it in the South East, in Scotland and in Northern Ireland. With the poverty line defined at SBE levels, adjusting for price left only three regions (the North, North West and South West) with the same rank as before adjustment.

5.6 Conclusions

This chapter began by asking if there were differences in the cost-of-living between the regions of the United Kingdom. In terms of the individual commodity groups, the answer, not unlike the curate's egg, is 'yes' – in parts, namely alcoholic drink, fuel and housing repairs, which varied considerably between regions. In so far as an area of homogeneous prices could be said to exist, it was the area that can broadly be termed 'central Britain', but excluding Greater London. There was considerable diversity in prices between regions lying outside this area.

In terms of aggregate costs (but with housing excluded), Greater London, the South East and East Midlands showed, over 1979–90, a gradual rise in relative cost and the adverse effect of this rise was greater for the better-off (i.e. households with above median income) as opposed to the less well-off. The increased expensiveness of these regions was mirrored by a decline in aggregate relative cost in the North, Wales, and Northern Ireland and also by the fact that, in these regions, it was the better-off who benefited relatively the most. For the remaining regions, aggregate non-housing relative cost was either stable or showed a slight decline. In terms of levels, aggregate non-housing cost in Northern Ireland was, on average, 3.3 per cent above that of the United Kingdom, while Greater London cost was 2.5 per cent higher. At the other extreme, aggregate non-housing cost in the North was 2.5 per cent lower than the UK level. These figures, incidentally, provide an indication of the adjustments to the nominal value of benefits that would have to be made in order to ensure regional uniformity in terms of the real values of benefits.

On both the mortgage interest payments and user-cost measures of owner-occupier housing cost, Greater London and the South East were, in terms of aggregate cost, relatively expensive regions, with the differential, over 1979–90, varying between 20 and 50 per cent above the UK level.[32] The North, the North West, Wales and Yorkshire and Humberside consistently had lower aggregate cost than the United Kingdom, while aggregate cost in Scotland and Northern Ireland declined over 1979–90. The remaining regions tended to have stable aggregate costs at, or near, the UK level. When user cost was computed incorporating estimates of capital gains calculated over shorter periods, the regional picture was much less stable.

The inclusion of housing cost into total cost did not significantly alter the regional pattern of relative cost, but it did serve to attenuate this pattern. The relative expensiveness of Greater London and the South East, over 1979–90, increased when housing cost was included; conversely, the inclusion of housing cost meant that Northern Ireland changed from being slightly more, to slightly less expensive than the UK average.

The principal application of the results contained in this chapter is the deflation of the nominal values of regional personal disposable income. While no major changes in rank occurred through regional price adjustment, the relative dispersion across regions was considerably reduced. The range of relative nominal *per capita* disposable income was 39.9 per cent over the regions between 1979 and 1990, but with adjustment for price differences this was reduced to 32.6 per cent when housing costs were measured by mortgage interest payments and to 28.7 per cent using user cost.

Notes

The authors are grateful to the Reward Group for providing the regional price data and thanks are due to Steve Flather, the Managing Director of the Group, for his assistance and advice in using and interpreting the data. Material from the Family Expenditure Survey, made available by the Central Statistical Office through the ESRC Data Archive at the University of Essex, has been used by permission of the Controller of Her Majesty's Stationery Office. Thanks are also due to Margaret Dolling of the CSO, Ian Crawford of the IFS and Daren Pain of the Bank of England for giving us the benefit of their expertise. An earlier version of this chapter was presented at a conference on Income and Wealth in the United Kingdom, organised by the Joseph Rowntree Foundation at the LSE, and we are grateful to participants at this conference for their comments. Needless to say, we alone are responsible for any shortcomings of this work.

1. For a discussion of the FES see Kemsley *et al.* (1980). For a discussion of the theory underlying cost-of-living indices see Deaton and Muellbauer (1980b), Forsyth and Fowler (1981) and Diewert (1990). For the construction of the RPI, see National Audit Office (1990), CSO (1991) and Cornish and Waterson (1992).
2. For example, newspapers. The group does not attempt to get a clothing quotation and instead takes the RPI index as a uniform price across all regions. In addition, this study assumed national uniformity in prices, as measured by the RPI, for furniture, pet food, postage, telephones, fees, etc., personal services, car maintenance, records, newspapers and licences.
3. With the modifications that food was combined with catering and that motoring was combined with travel.
4. The Reward price data were based upon surveys carried out in January. In

order to ensure that the weights derived from the FES were consistent with this, the expenditure data for each calendar year were split in two, and the half years on either side of 1 January were combined. Unfortunately this led to 1979 being represented by only half the usual sample size.

5. However, like the RPI, this study excludes the 4 per cent of households with the highest incomes.

6. Which is also how the RPI addresses sample size problems.

7. Defined as $100\,(S/\bar{X}\,\sqrt{N})$ where S is the sample standard deviation of expenditure on the commodity, $\bar{X}$ the mean and N the sample size.

8. A much fuller discussion of the position is developed in a paper with the same title as this chapter which has been published as no. 34 in the series *Ulster Papers in Public Policy and Management*, available from the School of Public Policy, Economics and Law at the University of Ulster at Jordanstown.

9. Defined as

$$\frac{\sum P_{t+1}\,q_t}{\sum P_t\,q_t}.$$

10. The measure of dispersion employed for the group indices is the root mean square about the mean, RMSM. If x_{jt} is the index for region j at time t then

$$RMSM = \sqrt{\frac{1}{121}\sum_{t=1}^{11}\sum_{j=1}^{12}(x_{jt}-\bar{x}_t)^2}.$$

In order to gauge the dispersion about the RPI, the statistic RMSRPI, which replaces the mean by the annual RPI, was used.

11. Since only national prices were used for clothing the only point of note is that the RMSM was non-zero due to different regional weights being used. The discrepancy between the regional indices and the RPI, as measured by the RMSRPI, was due to the fact that RPI weights were 18 months out of date while the weights for the regional indices were current weights.

12. The 12 group indices were combined to form an aggregate index for each region. Except for 1987, the aggregate regional indices tracked the RPI well; the major discrepancies were in household goods, motoring and travel, and leisure goods. The RMSM and the RSMRPI were, respectively, 0.74 and 1.09 per cent. The difference in weights used in the aggregate index compared to the corresponding RPI case were, in 1989, −38 for alcohol, −27 for housing, −12 for tobacco, +11 for travel and +51 for leisure services (due to our wider definition). The remaining group differences were in single figures.

13. In general, the comparisons were satisfactory. Details are available, on request, from the authors.

14. The Törnqvist index, P_T, is defined by

$$\log P_T = \sum_{j=1}^{N}\tfrac{1}{2}(S_{rj} + S_{ukj})\log(P_{rj}/P_{ukj})$$

where S_{rj} is the share of the jth commodity in the total expenditure of consumers in region r. Its desirable properties were established by Diewert (1976).

15. Since Northern Ireland has a limited gas market, instead of using the Reward quotations for bottled gas, the expenditures recorded for gas were allocated equally to coal and electricity. In computing the relative cost index for Northern Ireland, the UK price index was similarly adjusted.

16. The travel index depends entirely on car transport. Bus and rail fare quotations were included in the Reward data and were used in calculating the regional counterpart of the RPI. However, they could not be used for the relative cost index since they were based on different journeys. For example, the Scottish rail fare was about five times the London one.

17. Quality issues are important in considering leisure services. The Reward quotations for football match, golf and cinema might consist of quite different commodities. For example, a soccer match in Belfast would be considered by some to be qualitatively different from a Premier League game in Manchester.

18. The other components of housing cost (rents, rates, water charges, repair/maintenance charges and DIY charges) can be treated like any other commodity.

19. The average mortgage debt of mortgage-holders (AMDMH) is defined as:

$$AMDMH(t_1,t_2) = \sum_{j=1}^{25} DIST(t_1 - j)\, AVPR(t_2 - j)\, ADV(t_2 - j)\, MB(j)$$

where

$DIST\,(t_1 - j)$ is the proportion of all mortgage-holders whose mortgage was contracted j years ago from t_1

$AVPR(t_2 - j)$ is the average house price j years ago from t_2

$ADV(t_2 - j)$ is the proportion the mortgage comprises of the price of the house – taken as 65 per cent constant

$MB(j)$ is the mortgage balance on a standard 25-year mortgage taken out j years ago, that is

$$MB(j) = \left(1 - \frac{1}{(1 + i)^{25-j}}\right)\Bigg/\left(1 - \frac{1}{(1 + i)^{25}}\right)$$

where i is the interest rate, assumed constant and equal to 0.09.
The paper referenced in n. 8 gives a more detailed account of the procedure.

20. The RPI computes DIST from the FES using the number of years that an owner-occupier head of household has lived at the present address (var A131) as a proxy for mortgage duration. This procedure could not be used at the regional level since there were too few observations.

21. Data on the gross interest rate for 1979–87 were provided by the CSO and table 13.12 of *Financial Statistics* was the source for 1988–90. The basic tax rate was obtained from *Inland Revenue Statistics* supplemented by CSO data.

22. Obtained from *Housing and Construction Statistics*.

23. Dougherty and van Order (1982) show that with perfectly competitive markets

we get the same index of capital costs from the standpoint of a household expressing its preferences over time or a landlord renting the unit (to himself).

24. $$\frac{d\,UCHARP_r}{UCHARP_r} = \frac{-g_r}{(r^i + d_t - g_r)}\left[\frac{dg_r}{g_r} + \frac{dP_t}{P_t}\right].$$

25. Fry and Pashardes (1986) measure m_t by 'annual average debt outstanding to building societies per borrower, expressed as a percentage of average house prices' (p. 63). However, since the relevant entity is the cost of financing equity held in the housing stock it would be more accurate to use average debt per owner-occupier.

26. Being 12.9, 12.2 and 17.7 per cent per year for MIP, Capital Gains and User Cost (HARP) respectively.

27. Within a region households above and below median income cannot be directly compared since both the standard of living and prices differ. If we cast the comparison into a framework where there is only a single household, then the relative cost (Törnqvist) index measures the price index at a level of utility between that of a region and that of the United Kingdom. The distance between a region's less well-off and the less well-off in the United Kingdom as a whole would be less than that between a region's better- and worse-off.

28. With Scotland being the only region, other than Northern Ireland, to experience a percentage point fall in relative costs between 1979 and 1990.

29. A relative Törnqvist index for this case was not possible.

30. Borooah *et al.* (1991) provide an extensive analysis of poverty using SBE-based poverty lines. See Ruggles (1990) for alternative definitions of poverty lines.

31. See McGregor and Borooah (1992) for a discussion of low expenditure versus low income as indicators of poverty.

32. The two caveats to this general statement are that first, the turning points of the UCHARP20 series preceded those on the MIP series and secondly, the level of expenditure on housing (and thus its weight in the aggregate cost index) when measured by UCHARP20 was more than twice the level as measured by MIP.

Part II

Components of income

6 What has happened to the wages of men since 1966?

Amanda Gosling, Stephen Machin and Costas Meghir

6.1 Introduction

The gap between rich and poor has increased dramatically over the last 20 years and the incomes of the bottom 10 per cent were no higher in 1991 than in 1967 (see Goodman and Webb, 1994). Wages are an important part of household income and the trends in the dispersion of wages mirror very closely the trends in the dispersion of income. Knowing the reasons for the changing structure of the wage distribution is thus crucial to an understanding of the trends in overall household income.

This chapter uses 27 years of data from the Family Expenditure Surveys over the period 1966–92 to describe and explain changes in the structure of male wages. We look at the evolution of wage differentials within and across different groups of workers and relate the changing wage structure to the changes in the structure of supply and demand. The analysis of the growth of women's wages over time is complicated because some women withdraw from the labour market at various points in their life-cycle to have children or work in the home and it is likely that the timing of this move will be affected by wages. Thus we may see growth of wages with age for women, simply because those women who leave the labour market to have children have lower wages and not because the wages of any particular group of women are rising. Likewise we exclude young (aged under 23) and older (aged over 59) men from the analysis.

The structure of this chapter is as follows. Section 6.2 describes the changes that have been taking place in the wage structure in the United Kingdom in recent years. Section 6.3 discusses the issues and possible reasons for the observed widening of differentials. Section 6.4 reports empirical evidence based on data from the Family Expenditure Survey (FES) which examines and tests these arguments in more detail. Finally, section 6.5 discusses the policy implications of the research and offers some concluding remarks.

135

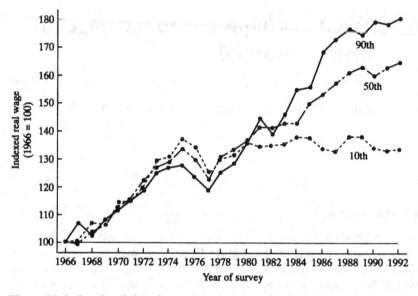

Figure 6.1 Indexed male hourly earnings, by percentile, 1966–92

6.2 Changes in the wage distribution, 1966–92

To illustrate the magnitude of changes in the UK wage structure, figure 6.1 plots indexed real hourly wages (1966 = 100) for different parts of the distribution. All men in the sample between the ages of 23 and 59 inclusive who worked at least one hour in the past week are included. Four distinct stages in the evolution of the UK wage structure emerge:

(1) A period (1966–72) when there was real wage growth throughout the distribution coupled with no change in the wage structure

(2) A short period (1972–75) when relative differentials were falling and all wages were growing in real terms; for example in 1974, the 10th percentile wage was 40 per cent higher than it was in 1966 and the 90th percentile wage was only 25 per cent higher

(3) The period following this when the social contract was at its toughest and where all wages were falling

(4) A long sustained period (1978–92) when growth rates diverged across the distribution; over these 15 years, the 10th percentile wage did not change, never recovering the wages received in 1975, while the median grew by 35 per cent and the 90th percentile by over 50 per cent.

To draw out the relative differences, figure 6.2 plots the ratios of the 90th percentile to the median and the median to the 10th percentile between 1966 and 1992. Looking first at the top line, the 90/50 ratio, a

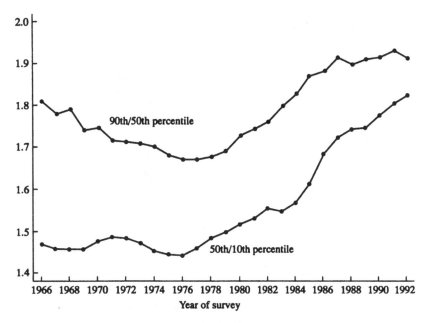

Figure 6.2 Dispersion of male wages, 1966–92

bowl-shaped relationship emerges, with differentials falling until the mid-1970s and then rising dramatically and overtaking the 1966 level by 1984. Apart from the period 1970–76 when pay differentials between the top and the bottom were compressed, there was no real change in the 50/10 ratio until after the incomes policy period of the mid-to-late 1970s, after which the ratio rose steadily. Over the whole period, median wages increased from being 47 per cent more than the 10th percentile in 1966 to being over 80 per cent more by 1992. Thus, since the mid-1970s, the real wages of low paid workers have fallen successively further and further behind the rest. This appears to be the most dominant trend in the distribution of wages over this time period.

To put the recent UK experience in context, it is interesting to look at what has happened over a longer time period. Whilst there is no consistent time series of data on wage dispersion over the last century, the data that exist (on male manual full-time weekly earnings) suggest that the gap between the highest and the lowest paid is now larger than at any time this century. Moreover, the size of the changes over the last 15 or so years is unprecedented. Table 6.1 shows this quite clearly.

To highlight the potential role that changes in the structure of earnings may have played in shaping the changes in the distribution of household

Table 6.1 *Wage dispersion of full-time male
manual workers, 1886–1990*

	50th/10th differential	90th/50th differential
1886	1.458	1.431
1906	1.504	1.568
1938	1.447	1.399
1970	1.486	1.475
1976	1.425	1.449
1982	1.464	1.526
1988	1.556	1.565
1990	1.570	1.591

*Sources: New Earnings Survey; British Labour
Statistics: Historical Abstract 1886–1968*, table 79.

income, we can compare the trends discussed above with trends in the overall distribution of income. Data on the distribution of income is usually defined at family level and then 'equivalised' (normalised by household size and presence of children) to control for different family size. This means that the two trends are not directly comparable. Nevertheless, figure 6.3 plots the 90/10 percentile ratio of hourly earnings with that of equivalised household income.[1] As can be seen, the two series are very similar. Both household income and hourly real wages of men were less dispersed in the middle of the 1970s than either the 1960s or the 1980s. According to these data, wage dispersion has been rising steadily since 1976 and income dispersion since 1977.

The two series diverge slightly after the mid-1980s, when the 90/10 hourly wage differential does not widen as fast as that of income. One reason for this is that the distribution of employment income across households is not only a function of the wage that different people are offered but also the distribution of employment and hours worked across households. Chapters 8 and 7 by Gregg and Wadsworth and by Harkness *et al.* in this volume discuss the increase in dispersion of hours worked across households. It is likely, however, that both the stagnation of wage levels at the bottom of the distribution and the growth in unemployment have similar underlying economic causes. Other factors which may have been important in explaining the rise in income inequality, discussed in Atkinson (chapter 2 in this volume) and Goodman and Webb (1994) are changes in taxes, increases in returns to investment income and the growth of self-employment.

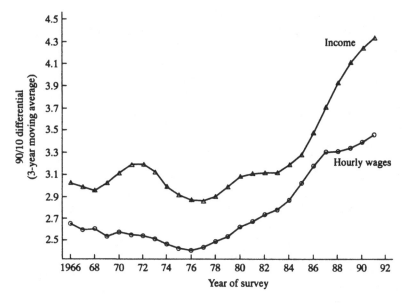

Figure 6.3 Income and wage dispersion, 1966–91

6.3 Changes in the UK labour market, 1966–92

This increase in wage inequality has prompted a large body of research both in the United States and the United Kingdom.[2] Changes in the structure of wages have been related to several factors, including changes in the structure of the demand for labour, changes in the composition of skills among the workforce and in the influence of pay-setting institutions.

The increased integration of international product and capital markets (globalisation) has been suggested as a reason why the demand for unskilled workers in developed economies such as the United Kingdom and the United States should have fallen (Murphy and Welch, 1992). Investment is now more mobile and thus more likely to move in response to cross-country differences in unit wage costs. Similarly, in order to maintain their competitive position, firms which face international competition are under more pressure to keep their unit wage costs down. Skilled workers are thus at more of a premium than before and there are fewer unskilled jobs at any given wage.

It has also been suggested (see Bound and Johnson, 1992 or *et al.*, 1994 for the United States; Van Reenen, 1993 or Machin, 1994 for the United Kingdom) that technological change has increased the relative productivity of skilled versus unskilled workers. Examples of this are the rapid influx of computers into many workplaces and the introduction of machines to do assembly tasks previously done by unskilled or semi-skilled workers in sectors like the automobile industry. This seems to have created an increase in the demand for skilled workers to run these machines and an increase in the proportion of workers needed for administrative and supervisory roles. This stands in direct contrast to technological changes implemented earlier this century and during the industrial revolution, which tended to reduce the need for skilled labour.

There is also considerable evidence that important compositional changes have occurred in the UK labour market. In 1969, for example, 39 per cent of the total workforce worked in manufacturing, whilst by 1990 this had fallen to 23 per cent. In 1969 the private service sector employed 49 per cent of the workforce, whilst by 1990 it employed 70 per cent.[3] It is likely that the return to skill is higher in these new types of employment where jobs are more heterogeneous. It may also be likely that the increase in female participation, itself perhaps a consequence of the decline in the relative earning power of unskilled married or cohabiting men (Harkness *et al.*, chapter 7 in this volume) has increased the numbers competing for unskilled jobs, although what evidence there is suggests that the increase in participation has come from educated women (see, for example, Gregg and Wadsworth, chapter 8 in this volume).

Other authors (e.g. Freeman and Katz, 1994) have stressed the importance of labour market institutions, particularly trade unions and minimum wage setting mechanisms, in shaping the way that labour markets have responded to these changes in the structure of supply and demand. In this light, Freeman and Katz (1994) and Gregg and Machin (1994) cite evidence showing that the United Kingdom and the United States are alone in experiencing such a widening of wage differentials in the 1980s (with the United States still having a much higher level). While earnings differentials in most countries became more compressed in the 1970s, and the 1980s saw rises in a number of countries, the increases in dispersion of the 1980s are much smaller elsewhere than in the United States or the United Kingdom. It is clear that the recent rise in earnings dispersion is not a global phenomenon. This is illustrated in table 6.2 which reports the 90/10 male earnings ratio of several countries.

The first point to make is that the fall in demand for unskilled labour may result in both falls in employment and declines in the relative wages of the less skilled. In this light, one important difference between the experience of the United States and that of Europe over recent years is that the United States has not experienced such large and persistent levels of unemployment. In the United Kingdom inactivity rates of men of working age doubled from 7 to 14 per cent from 1973 to 1991.[4] Moreover, real wages at or below the median have been falling steadily in the United

Table 6.2 *Cross-country evidence on male 90/10 earnings ratio, early 1970s–early 1990s*

Country	Early 1970s	Late 1970s/ early 1980s	Late 1980s/ early 1990s
United Kingdom	2.48 (1973)	2.41 (1979)	3.39 (1991)
United States	4.71 (1975)	4.48 (1980)	5.58 (1989)
Canada	—	3.60 (1981)	3.94 (1990)
France	3.22 (1973)	3.25 (1980)	3.42 (1991)
Sweden	2.06 (1973)	1.97 (1981)	2.16 (1991)
Norway	—	2.05 (1979)	1.97 (1991)

Source: Gregg and Machin (1994).

States over the last 20 years. By contrast, in the United Kingdom real wages at the 10th percentile have been flat since the late 1970s. In many states in America, there is no universal benefit available to able bodied unemployed men without children and benefit is instead restricted to those who have worked, if only for a few weeks, over the past year. The collapse in demand for unskilled workers, then, seems more likely to affect their wages rather than their employment.

Secondly, the ability of the workforce to respond to the increasing demand for skilled labour by upgrading their skills is likely to depend on their educational background and their opportunities for training. The education and training systems then become very important. It has been argued that not only are UK workers less skilled on average than those in the rest of Europe, but that they also lack the general skills obtained from basic education that are necessary for further training (see Finegold and Soskice, 1988).

There have been significant changes in public policy toward education in the last century. The minimum school leaving age was raised from 14 to 15 in 1948 and again to 16 in 1973. The 1960s and 1970s saw the expansion of further and higher education after the Robbins Report. It is evident that the level of wages among particular age groups is likely to be affected by the returns to and the distribution of education (Becker, 1975). How the variance of wages is then affected by education policies will depend on what is happening to the structure of demand. In the face of increasing relative demand for educated workers, we should expect policies such as those described above to mitigate the increased educational premia.

Even if there had been no changes in the structure of demand in the United Kingdom, we should expect the dispersion of wages to rise given the recent moves away from national- and industry-level wage-setting and from the overall decline in union presence. There have been important changes in government policy towards pay over the last three decades. Up until 1978, there were explicit controls over wage increases through incomes policies. These will compress pay differentials if they contain a flat rate element as in the 1975–77 period of the social contract, a maximum level of pay increase as in the £250 limit imposed during 1972–73, or any preferential arrangement for lower paid workers. Moreover, they constrained the growth of relative pay differentials even when all workers received the same rate of pay increase. For the last 15 years, there has been no such centrally imposed restraint.[5]

Since 1980, two institutional arrangements that held up the wages of low paid workers have been removed or weakened. Although Wages Councils (committees made up of employers and worker representatives to set industry-level minimum wages) were not abolished until 1993, the number of inspectors was reduced and young workers were taken out of the net in 1986 (see Machin and Manning, 1994). The 'fair wages resolution' was abolished in 1980. This not only protected the wages of public sector workers in low paid occupations but also workers in any organisation contracted to do work for central or local government. The effect of the abolition on low wages is thus magnified given the recent trend towards subcontracting of many local government tasks such as cleaning.

The actual mechanism by which pay is set are also important. There is evidence that the variance of wages is smaller when pay is set at an industry or national level and/or between unions and firms than when it is set unilaterally by the employer. Gosling and Machin (1995) for Britain or Freeman (1980, 1982, 1993) and Card (1991) for the United States show that trade unions are associated with lower levels of wage dispersion. Between 1980 and 1990, there was a large drop in union presence in the United Kingdom: the percentage of the workforce belonging to a trade union fell from 58 per cent to 42 per cent over this time period (see Waddington, 1992); the proportion of workplaces with recognised unions fell from 64 per cent in 1980 to 53 per cent by 1990 (see Millward *et al.*, 1992; Disney *et al.*, 1995). Moreover, even in the union sector, national- or industry-level pay agreements all but disappeared over the 1980s and pay is now more likely to be set within the firm or the workplace.

6.4 Evidence on the changing structure of supply and demand

We have thus summarised the main reasons why we should expect the shape of the earnings distribution to have changed. We now present some preliminary evidence from our data on shifts in composition and raw returns to skill. The FES gives us three measures of skill: occupation, education and potential experience (age now minus age left full-time education). Unfortunately we have only information on years of schooling from 1978 and the definition of skill changed fundamentally in 1987 so it is not comparable across years. We thus only look at skill differentials before 1987 and educational differentials after 1977.

6.4.1 Composition

In the absence of any other off-setting factors, we should expect that an increase in the relative demand for skills should result in an increase in the skilled proportions of the workforce as some workers upgrade their skills and those that cannot are dislodged from the workforce.

The top panel of table 6.3 shows the percentage of workers in six broad occupational categories in three years 1968, 1978 and 1986. It shows a steady increase in the proportion of workers in the higher grade non-manual occupations (professional and managerial workers) from 25 per cent of the workforce in 1968 to over a third in 1986 and a decline in the proportion in the low grade semi-skilled and unskilled occupations from 25 per cent to under 15 per cent. Overall the proportion employed in manual occupations has fallen.

The bottom panel shows how workers in later years are more educated then their predecessors. In 1978, for example, only 11 per cent of workers had some form of post-school education; by 1992, this proportion had increased to over 18 per cent. Changes in the minimum school leaving age have resulted in declines in the proportions leaving school at or before 16. In 1978, for example, over 25 per cent of the workforce left school at or before 14; this dropped to just under 3 per cent by 1992. There have also been increases in the numbers staying on past the minimum school leaving age.

These compositional changes could have taken place because workers were becoming more skilled, perhaps in response to changes in demand, or because less qualified workers could no longer find work. We cannot evaluate the relative importance of these effects by occupation as very few out of work men in our sample report an occupation. For education, however, it is possible to decompose the changes into those driven by the changing characteristics of the sample as a whole and those driven by differential employment rates. Doing this for the change in the proportion of the workforce that left school at 16 (which declined from 79 per cent in 1978 to 66 per cent by 1992) generates the results described in table 6.4. As can be seen almost a quarter is due to the fact that a greater proportion of those who left school at 16 do not work.

Table 6.3 *Skill composition, 1968–92, per cent*

Occupation	1968	Year: 1978	1986
Professional	13.48	15.94	18.54
Managerial	10.62	14.44	16.61
Clerical	9.38	6.97	7.48
All non-manual	33.48	37.35	42.63
Skilled	38.60	39.85	40.15
Semi-skilled	18.09	18.34	13.31
Unskilled	9.83	4.45	4.36
All manual	66.52	62.64	57.82

Age left full-time education	1978	Year: 1986	1992
14 or less	26.71	9.87	2.81
15	35.29	30.89	27.66
16	16.50	28.56	34.78
All 16 or under	78.50	69.32	65.25
17 or 18	10.26	14.42	16.32
Over 18	11.24	16.25	18.43
All over 16	21.50	30.68	34.75

Table 6.4 *Decomposing the proportions in the low education group*

	Change attributable to	% of total change
Changing characteristics of the sample	–0.105	–78.42
Different employment rates	–0.033	–24.91
Interaction terms	0.004	3.32
Total change 1978–92	–0.14	100

Note:
See appendix, p. 156, for the derivation of this formula.

6.4.2 Occupational and educational differentials, 1968–92

There are various ways of presenting the growth in wages across skill groups. Plotting the level of wages over time is misleading if you are interested in proportionate changes, as an increase of £5 over two years means a smaller percentage increase for those on higher wages but corresponds to the same slope. For that reason economists usually use logs,[6] but this often makes it difficult to interpret. ln(£5) is inherently more meaningful than 1.609 even though they are both the same number. One way of getting round this problem is to use a log scale. The graphs are constructed in logs but the labels are transformed back into levels. This is why 4 and 5 on figure 6.4a are further apart than 9 and 10.

Figure 6.4a and figure 6.4b show real wage growth over the 1970s and 1980s by skill level. Figure 6.4a plots the median wage over time for five occupational groups and figure 6.4b does the same for three education groups: those leaving school at or before 16, those leaving at 17 or 18 and those leaving after 18. It is clear that differential growth rates across occupations and education levels do reflect the differential growth rates across the wage distribution, with growth rates being higher for the lower skilled and the bottom of the wage distribution during the late 1960s and 1970s and higher for those at the top during the 1980s.

Taking the unskilled and semi-skilled first, it is clear that most of the growth in real wages occurred in the late 1960s and early 1970s. Median hourly wages increased from about £3.90 in 1968 to just under £5 an hour in 1975 (all figures at 1994 prices). After the falls of the incomes policy period, wages of unskilled workers never recovered this high as growth rates after 1978 are approximately zero. The wage profile of skilled workers follows a similar trend, although skilled wages have risen significantly over the 1980s from just under £5 to just under £6 an hour. The wages of clerical workers rose at a steady rate throughout the period.

This picture reverses when one considers the wages of managerial workers which increased during the late 1960s and early 1970s, fell from 1973–77 and then rose dramatically after that, increasing by almost a third over the period in real terms. Likewise the wages of professional workers increased faster during the 1980s and were comparatively flat during the 1970s.

Median wages of those who have had some form of post-18 education (see figure 6.4b), rose by a third over this period from £7.50 an hour in 1978 to over £10.00 an hour in 1992. Median wages of those workers who left school at or before 16 rose by only 10 per cent from about £5.50 an hour to £6.00 an hour. Thus while there has been wage growth across all education groups since 1978, it is clear that the workers who have done best are those who left full-time education after 18.

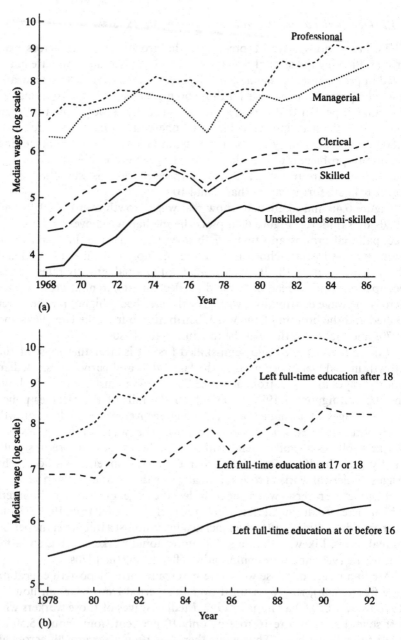

Figure 6.4 Wage growth, £/hour, 1994 prices, 1968–92
(a) By occupation
(b) By education

Figure 6.5a and figure 6.5b show that there has been a U-shaped relationship between skill differentials over time and that the increase in occupational differentials after 1978 is mirrored by the concurrent increase in the educational premia. Thus in 1978, median wages of workers who left school after 18 were 40 per cent higher than those who left school at or before 16. By 1992 this differential had increased to over 60 per cent. Similarly the percentage differential between managerial and unskilled workers fell from 70 per cent in 1968 to 40 per cent in the mid-1970s and then rose back to the level of 1968 by 1986.

As we only observe education after 1978 and occupation before 1987, we cannot use data from the FES to see whether the compression in occupational differentials in the 1970s was accompanied by a similar fall in educational differences or whether occupational differences continued to rise after 1986. Research using other datasets does, however, suggest that this has been the case (see Chennells and Van Reenen, 1994; Schmitt, 1994). Moreover there does not seem to be any systematic change in the relationship between education and occupation during the nine years when we have data on both skill definitions.

The data on educational and occupational differentials and on the skill composition of the workforce would seem to suggest that there has been an increase in the relative demand for skills proxied by these very broad categories. The graphs in figure 6.6 show, however, that there has been a similar rise in differentials within the lower skilled occupations and the lower education groups.

Figure 6.6a demonstrates that dispersion is highest within the heterogeneous managerial category. The 90/10 differential within this group fluctuates about the level of 3.2 from 1968 to 1986. This means that the top 10 per cent of male wage earners in this category earn more than 3.2 times the bottom 10 per cent. Similarly dispersion measured by the 90/10 ratio amongst professional workers fluctuates around 2.6 over the period. Looking at the lower skilled occupations, we see that wage inequality within these groups rises after the mid-1970s, so that by 1986 dispersion within these groups was very close to that found within the professional category of workers. Similarly wage dispersion amongst those workers leaving school at or before 16 (see figure 6.6b), rises constantly over this period.

If all the increase in wage inequality could be explained by changes in the pattern of demand and supply for these broad skill categories then we would expect there to be no sustained changes in dispersion within each group. The fact that we do observe increases in dispersion amongst these groups suggests that the changes in the labour market involve more than simple shifts of demand and supply between these categories.

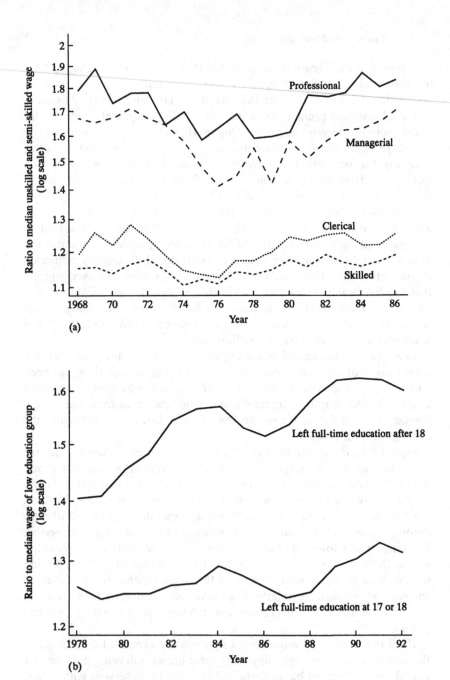

Figure 6.5 Occupational and educational differentials
(a) Occupational differentials, 1968–86
(b) Educational differentials, 1978–92

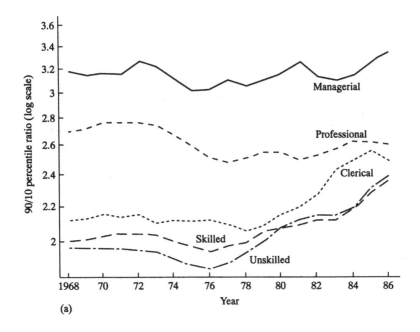

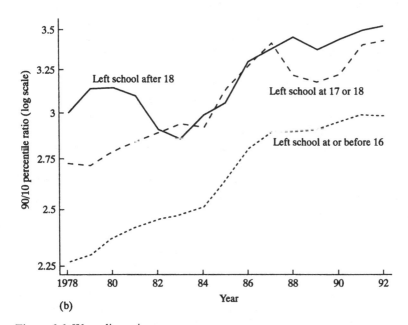

Figure 6.6 Wage dispersion
(a) Within occupations, 1968–86
(b) Within educational group, 1978–92

6.4.3 The returns to experience

We next look at how the level and the growth of wages differs across age groups. If the return to experience is rising, we would expect to see an increase in the difference between the wages of young and older workers. This has been stressed by researchers looking at the United States as one of the driving forces behind the rise in wage inequality (see Bushinsky, 1994; Juhn *et al.*, 1993). We shall discuss in more detail below the interpretation of this growing gap, but we will first present evidence from our data on how it has changed both before and after controlling for education.

Figure 6.7a and figure 6.7b show how the gap between old and young workers measured by the ratio of median wages has changed over the last 27 years. Looking at the graph which does not control for education (figure 6.7a), the first thing to notice is the small size of the gap between young and older workers in the beginning of the period. In 1966, the median wages of 40 year olds was only 38 per cent more than the median wage of 23 year olds. This gives little evidence for the presence of any returns to experience during the late 1960s and early 1970s. By 1992 the wage gap between young and old workers increased to over 25 per cent so that the median wage of 40 year old men is now 65 per cent more than the median wage of 23 year olds. If the only factor determining the size of this gap were the returns to experience then we could not only say that these had increased dramatically but that they were almost non-existent during the late 1960s and early 1970s.

Human capital models of wage growth (Becker, 1975; Mincer, 1974) predict that workers with more education will experience faster earnings growth as they accumulate more experience that those workers with less education. Figure 6.7b shows that the gap between old and young workers is indeed higher for workers who stayed on in full-time education to a later age. It cannot be the case that the increase in the proportion in the workforce who have stayed on at school post-16 can explain the overall increase in the gap between old and young workers, however, as this gap rises fast amongst workers who left school at or before 16.

6.4.4 Interpreting the wage gap between young and old workers

The growing gap between the wages of young and older workers does not necessarily mean that the returns to experience have risen. First, the wage gap between young and old workers is not only a result of the fact that older workers have more experience. It is conceivable that there are 'cohort' effects on wages. An example of this might be the long-run effect of the 1979–82 recession on the wage and employment opportunities of

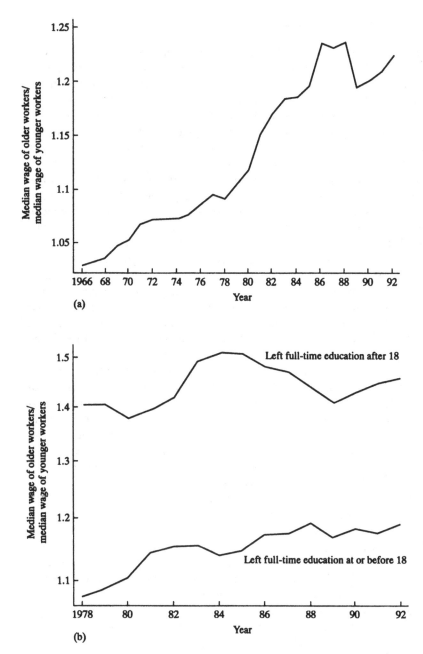

Figure 6.7 Growing difference between the wages of younger (23–28) and older (over 28) workers
(a) 1966–92
(b) 1978–92, by education group

those workers who had recently entered the labour market. Similarly cross-generational differences in the quality of education may be reflected in wages. Second, if the returns to experience are higher for those workers with more education, then it is perhaps likely that these workers too will be also affected by increases in the returns to experience. This does not happen, as the cross-sectional age earnings profile for workers who left school after 16 shows no sustained trend, unlike the profile for the low education group (see figure 6.7b).

There are two ways of measuring the returns to experience. You can look at the difference between old and young people at any point in time, or you can measure the wage growth over time for a given birth cohort. Both these need to be interpreted with care. The former includes not only the effect of experience on wages, but also any of the 'cohort' effects discussed above. A large gap in wages between old and young workers does not necessarily mean that the wages of younger workers will increase as they age. Similarly the growth in wages experienced by a particular individual over time is not only a pay-off to the skills acquired in the labour market over time but also the effect of changes in aggregate productivity, the business cycle and so on. Thus more structure is required to estimate the returns to experience. If these returns are constant across generations, i.e. a year's work increases wages by the same percentage amount for a 40 year old in 1947 and in 1959, the data will reveal this with an absence of cohort age interactions. This restriction can be expressed formally in a statistical model of the wage distribution; this is explained in some detail in Gosling *et al.* (1994b). It is important to note that if rejected the implication may be that returns to experience have changed, but other interpretations are not excluded. For example, it could mean that macroeconomic events have differing effects across generations.

In Gosling *et al.* (1994b) we test whether the returns to experience have changed, once one controls for the possibility of permanent (i.e. irrespective of age) differences in wages across generations, our definition of cohort effects. We find no evidence that the returns to experience have changed, and that the increasing difference between younger and older workers over time is entirely attributable to cohort effects. Moreover, we only find evidence of any returns to experience for workers who left school after 16 and those at the top of the wage distribution. There is thus nothing to suggest that the low wages of some of the new entrants into the labour market will increase as they accumulate more labour market experience.

Figure 6.8a and figure 6.8b suggest that there are important cross-generational differences in the dispersion as well as the level of wages. Figure 6.8a shows that the 90/10 percentile ratio has risen amongst men of similar experience levels and figure 6.8b suggests that this is even the case within

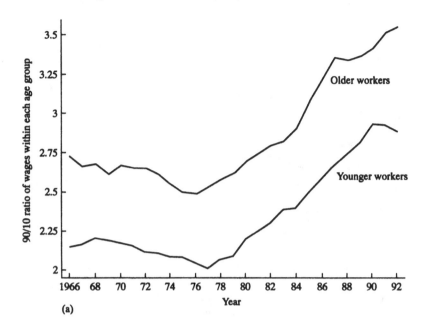

(a)

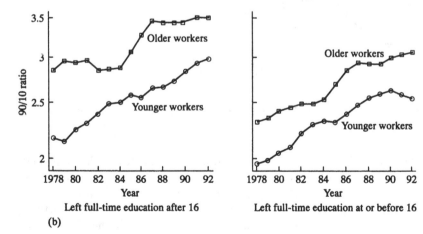

Left full-time education after 16   Left full-time education at or before 16

(b)

Figure 6.8 Within-age group dispersion
(a) 1966–92
(b) 1978–92, by education group

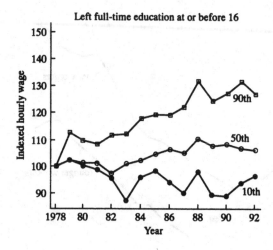

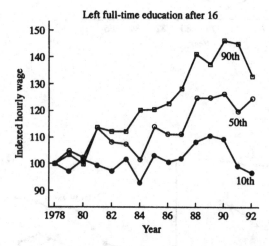

Figure 6.9 Wage growth across generations of 23–28 year olds, 1978–92, by education group

education and experience groups. In the mid-1970s, for example, the highest paid 10 per cent of workers between the ages of 23 and 28 earned about twice the lowest paid 10 per cent; in 1992 this gap had risen to almost 3 times.

Figure 6.9 shows what this rise in dispersion means for the growth of wages across generations of workers at different points in the distribution. These plots indexed real hourly earnings for workers between 20 and 28 at the 10th percentile, the 90th percentile and the median for those who left school at or before 16 and those who left after 16.

Many young workers who left school at or before 16, as the upper panel of figure 6.9 shows, receive lower wages than they would have done in the past. The bottom 10 per cent, for example, have hourly wages over 5 per cent lower than they would have done in 1978. Again the highest paid amongst this group are doing much better than they would have done in the past. The lower panel shows that the 10th percentile wage of 23–28 year olds with some post-compulsory education is the same in 1992 as it was in 1978. The median wage is 20 per cent higher, however at the 90th percentile wage is over 40 per cent higher. Thus while most young workers who have stayed on later at school receive higher wages than they would have done in the past, this is not so for all of them.

6.5 Concluding remarks

In the United Kingdom wage inequality has risen at an unprecedented rate since the late 1970s. At the same time there has been no growth of wages at the bottom of the distribution. This is important because there is a link between low pay, the incentive to work due to high replacement rates and hence poverty. In this chapter we document, using micro-data from the FES, the key facts underpinning this rise and consider what factors may have been behind the observed increase.

It is clear that the dispersion of real hourly wages for men in work was fairly flat between 1966 and 1972, that the distribution became more compressed between 1972 and 1977, after which there was a very sharp rise. During this later period the real wages of the 10th percentile of the earnings distribution displayed zero growth, the median grew by 35 per cent and the 90th percentile grew by well over 50 per cent.

The increasing gap between the wages of skilled versus unskilled men suggests that the demand for skill has increased, either because of changes in technology or changes in the structure of product markets, and that the supply of skilled labour has not changed fast enough to compensate. This may because of failures in the education and training system which prevent unskilled workers obtaining, at least in the short run, the skills that the labour market demands. It is likely that policies that encourage children to stay on at school and more people to go into adult and further education are needed to reduce these skills shortages and to improve opportunities for workers at the bottom of the distribution.

Further examination reveals that, whilst the return to education and skill increased during the 1980s, this cannot explain all the increase in wage dispersion. Wage inequality has risen fastest among workers with low levels of education and skill. Similarly the wages of younger, new entrants to the labour force in the 1980s declined very markedly as compared to older cohorts and dispersion has risen fast amongst young workers with low levels of education.

Thus the unobserved components determining wages seem to have become more important during the 1980s. This leads us to focus attention on why young entrants are facing more dispersed opportunities and on how the components of unobserved skill are determined. An important factor here may well be the greater dispersion of pre- and early labour market opportunities, such as the quality of education and the availability of training at the start of a career, as well as the fact that an increasing number of young children are brought up in inner city areas with increasing levels of unemployment and poverty.

Appendix: decomposing the change in the proportion of workers in the low education group

Definitions:

n_t = the number of men in the sample in group i at time t

N_t = the number of men in the sample at time t

u_t = the unemployment rate of group i and time t

U_t = the unemployment rate at time t

P_t = the proportion of those who work that are in group i at time t.

Thus the proportion P_t at any point in time can be written:

$$P_t = \frac{n_t}{N_t} \times \frac{(1-u)_t}{(1-U)_t}$$

and the change in P_t can therefore be expressed as:

$$\Delta P_t = \Delta \frac{n_t}{N_t} \times \frac{(1-u_t)}{(1-U_t)} + \frac{n_t}{N_t} \times \Delta \frac{(1-u_t)}{(1-U_t)} + 2 \times \Delta \frac{n_t}{N_t} \times \Delta \frac{(1-u_t)}{(1-U_t)}$$

where:

$$\Delta \frac{n_t}{N_t} \times \frac{(1-u_t)}{(1-U_t)}$$

is the change attributable to changing characteristics of the sample and

$$\frac{n_t}{N_t} \times \Delta \frac{(1-u_t)}{(1-U_t)}$$

to the changing difference in unemployment rates across groups in the sample and

$$2 \times \Delta \frac{n_t}{N_t} \times \Delta \frac{(1-u_t)}{(1-U_t)}$$

is the interaction term.

Notes

Material for the Family Expenditure Survey, made available by the Central Statistical Office through the ESRC Data Archive at the University of Essex, has been used by permission of the Controller of Her Majesty's Stationery Office. The authors would like to thank the Joseph Rowntree Foundation for finance, Alissa Goodman and Steven Webb for help with the FES data, and Orazio Attanasio, Richard Blundell, Lorraine Dearden, Zvi Griliches, Paul Johnson, John Hills, Tom MaCurdy, Andrew Oswald, Judith Payne, John Pencavel, Mark Stewart, John Van Reenen, Steven Webb, Edward Whitehouse, an anonymous referee, participants in seminars at Keele, Warwick and an ESRC conference on wages and members of the Joseph Rowntree Foundation Programme on Income and Wealth for helpful comments and suggestions. This is a revised version of a paper that also appeared in *Fiscal Studies* (November 1994).

1. See Goodman and Webb (1994) for details of how these figures were computed.
2. For the US work, see the collection of papers in the *Quarterly Journal of Economics* (February 1992) or the surveys by Levy and Murnane (1992) or Freeman and Katz (1994), among many others, and for the United Kingdom see Gregg and Machin (1994) or Schmitt (1994).
3. Source: *Employment Gazette.*
4. Source: OECD, *Employment Outlook.*
5. See Clegg (1979) for a detailed discussion or Goodman and Webb (1994) for a summary of the different incomes policies in force.
6. As $\ln(x/y) = \ln(x) - \ln(y)$.

7 Women's pay and family incomes in Britain, 1979–91

Susan Harkness, Stephen Machin and Jane Waldfogel

7.1 Overview

One of the most striking trends in Britain over the past 10–15 years is the sharp rise in the labour force participation of women. Despite women's increased participation, other aspects of their labour force activity remain unchanged. Women still tend to be clustered in female-dominated occupations and, compared to men, they are still disproportionately likely to be working part-time, and to be low paid.

At the same time, Britain has seen a dramatic rise in the poverty rate and a sharp increase in family income inequality (see Goodman and Webb, 1994). There is now no doubt that, since the mid-1970s, the rich have become richer, and the poor have become poorer. But what has been in doubt is what, if any, relationship exists between women's work patterns and pay on the one hand and family poverty and inequality on the other. One school of thought suggests that, since many women work part-time and are married to male earners, their earnings are essentially 'pin money' and their low pay is of little consequence. An alternative view would be that since many women are married to low earners, or are living on their own, their earnings are an important component of family income and hence their low pay has important consequences for family poverty and family income inequality.

In this chapter we assess these alternative perspectives by investigating the links between trends in women's earnings and in family incomes over the period 1979–91. The structure of the chapter is as follows. Section 7.2 describes the importance of women's pay for family income in married and cohabiting couple families and documents how the share of women's earnings in family income has changed over time. This section also explores the links between women's pay and poverty and details the relationship between changes in women's earnings and the rise in family income inequality among married and cohabiting couple families. Section 7.3 analyses the importance of women's pay for single woman families. Section 7.4 then brings together the two groups analysed in sections 7.2

and 7.3. It considers what has happened to the aggregate share of female earnings in family income by looking at the relative importance of changing family composition versus changes within single or married/cohabiting couple groups. Section 7.5 concludes by summarising the key findings and drawing out the implications for policy.

7.2 The importance of women's pay in family income: married/cohabiting women

We use up to 13 years of data (1979–91) from the General Household Survey (GHS) to examine the relative fortunes of women aged 24–55 in different kinds of families. Our focus in this section is on married and cohabiting couple families (of whom there are some 2000–2800 in each year of the GHS); in section 7.3 we also look at single woman families (of whom there are approximately 1000 in each year of the GHS).[1]

7.2.1 Descriptive data on married/cohabiting families

Table 7.1 reports summary statistics for two sub-periods, 1979–81 and 1989–91, for all married and cohabiting couple families in our GHS samples and illustrates big within-family changes over the period 1979–91. Average real monthly income amongst couples aged 24–55 rose from £1387 in 1979–81 to £2019 by 1989–91, reflecting an increase of 47 per cent as compared to the 1979–81 level (equivalised income rose by 38 per cent, from £1116 to £1540). The average real monthly earnings of husbands/male cohabiters rose much more slowly over the period, from £1030 to £1271, or by 23 per cent. Average real monthly earnings of wives/female cohabiters, on the other hand, grew much faster, from £238 to £457, corresponding to a 92 per cent increase.[2]

The monthly earnings differences mainly reflect the divergent trends in participation for husbands and wives (the importance of changes in labour market activity for within-family income changes will be demonstrated even more forcefully below). As table 7.1 makes clear, male employment rates fell by just under 4 percentage points (from 93.4 per cent to 89.6 per cent) while female employment rates rose by almost 16 percentage points (from 55.2 per cent to 71.0 per cent).

Reflecting this, a picture of important changes in family structure related to labour market activity thus emerges. The incidence of dual earner families rises from 53 to 67 per cent, and the traditional male breadwinner family falls sharply from 40 to 23 per cent. Similarly, there is a rise in no-earner families (from 4.5 to 6.4 per cent) and of single female-earner families (from 2.1 to 4.0 per cent).

Table 7.1 *Sample characteristics of married and cohabiting couple families,
1979–91[a]*

	1979–81	1989–91	Change
Total monthly income	1387	2019	+£632
Equivalised income	1116	1540	+£424
Male monthly earnings	1030	1271	+£241
Female monthly earnings	238	457	+£219
Monthly non-labour income	119	290	+£171
Percentage of men in employment	93.4	89.6	–3.8%
Percentage of women in employment	55.2	71.0	+15.8%
Percentage of women full-time (if employed)	42.4	48.7	+6.3%
Percentage with both man and woman employed	53.1	67.0	+13.9%
Percentage, man employed, woman not employed	40.3	22.6	–17.7%
Percentage, woman employed, man not employed	2.1	4.0	+1.9%
Percentage with neither employed	4.5	6.4	+1.9%
Total number of families	7799	7534	

Notes:
[a] Source for all tables in this chapter is the General Household Survey. Sample
includes married or cohabiting couple families where the woman is age 24–55
and the man is age 24–55. All income and earnings figures are expressed in 1991
pounds, using the monthly RPI deflator. Employed is defined as having income
from earnings during the past month (even if the person was inactive or
unemployed during the week of the survey).

Figure 7.1 shows the large shifts in labour market activity (even
amongst this specific group of the population) that have occurred between
1979 and 1991. First, non-participation (i.e. zero earnings) of women has
become much less frequent as more women have entered the labour
market. Second, non-participation by men has become more frequent.[3]
Third, 'no-earner' families (where both the male and female earnings are
zero) and 'dual-earner' families have become much more common. The
increased frequency of no-earner families has also been documented
recently by Gregg and Wadsworth (chapter 8 in this volume), who argue
that this is a consequence of the fact that there are more unemployed men,
whose wives/partners typically have low participation rates.[4]

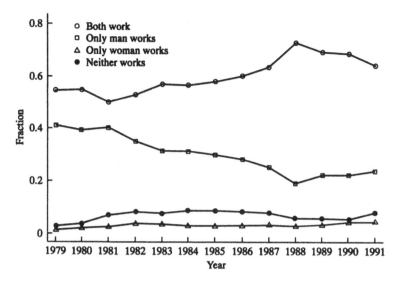

Figure 7.1 Changes in the labour force activity of men and women in married/cohabiting families, based on 1979–91 General Household Survey data

7.2.2 Shares of labour market earnings of men and women in family income

Given these large changes in the relative labour market status of married and cohabiting men and women between 1979 and 1991, it is important to investigate what has happened to the relative shares of male and female earnings in total family income. To do so, we first define family income as

$$Y = E_M + E_F + Y_N \tag{1}$$

where Y is family income, E_i is labour market earnings for individual i ($i = M$, F for males and females) and Y_N is non-labour income.

Next, we define relative family income (income relative to the average) as

$$y = \alpha_M \cdot e_M + \alpha_F \cdot e_F + (1 - \alpha_M - \alpha_F) \cdot y_N \tag{2}$$

where y ($= Y / \overline{Y}$) is relative income, α_i ($= \overline{E}_i / \overline{Y}$) is the average share of component i in average income, e_i ($= E_i / \overline{E}_i$) is the relative earnings of group i and y_N ($= Y_N / \overline{Y}_N$) is relative non-labour income (bars denote sample means).

Figure 7.2 shows what has happened to the average shares of the components of family income (the α) from 1979–91.[5] The most striking feature of this graph is the large drop in the share of men's earnings in total family

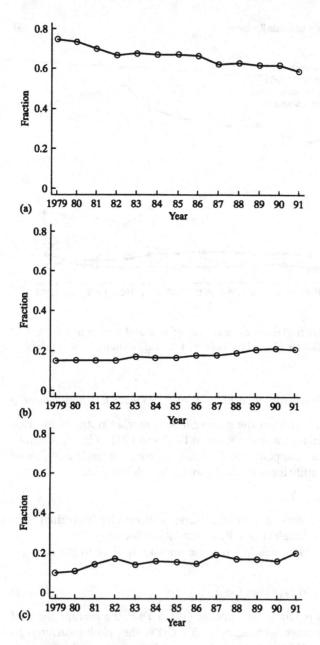

Figure 7.2 Mean earnings shares of men and women in married/cohabiting families in total family income
(a) Male share
(b) Female share
(c) Non-labour share

Table 7.2 *Shares of earnings and non-labour income in total family income, married and cohabiting couple families, 1979–91*

All married and cohabiting couples	1979–81	1989–91	Change
Total monthly income	1387	2019	+£632
Mean female earnings share	0.153	0.208	+0.055
Mean male earnings share	0.729	0.611	−0.118
Mean non-labour income share	0.118	0.181	+0.063
Total number of families	7799	7534	

Married and cohabiting couples where both the man and woman work	1979–81	1989–91	Change
Total monthly income	1560	2252	+£692
Mean female earnings share	0.266	0.279	+0.013
Mean male earnings share	0.685	0.625	−0.060
Mean non-labour income share	0.050	0.096	+0.046
Total number of families	4142	5045	

Married and cohabiting couples where only man works	1979–81	1989–91	Change
Total monthly income	1287	1874	+£587
Mean female earnings share	0.000	0.000	0.000
Mean male earnings share	0.906	0.852	−0.054
Mean non-labour income share	0.094	0.148	+0.054
Total number of families	3142	1705	

Married and cohabiting couples where only woman works	1979–81	1989–91	Change
Total monthly income	1149	834	−£315
Mean female earnings share	0.521	0.523	+0.002
Mean male earnings share	0.000	0.000	0.000
Mean non-labour income share	0.479	0.477	−0.002
Total number of families	305	592	

income from 1979 to 1991. This dramatic drop in the male share is paralleled by rises in both the share of wives' earnings and in the share of non-labour income.

These changes are drawn out in more detail in table 7.2, which again concentrates on comparing the two sub-periods, 1979–81 and 1989–91. The top panel of table 7.2 documents the large fall in the male share from

Table 7.3 *Decomposition of the rise in importance of female share in total family income, married and cohabiting couple families, 1979–81 to 1989–91*

	1979–81	1989–91	Change in female share	Change within group	Change between group
Married and cohabiting couples (four groups[a])	0.153	0.208	0.055	0.007 (12%)	0.048 (88%)

Notes:
[a] Decomposition of changes within married/cohabiting couples based on changes within and between four family types: dual-earner households, male breadwinner families, female breadwinner families, and households with no earners.

nearly 73 per cent in 1979–81 to 61 per cent by 1989–91, while the female share rose from 15 per cent to nearly 21 per cent over the same time period. There are, however, important differences in the evolution of the female share by family groups defined by labour market status of both partners. It is of considerable interest that the female share remained constant amongst the dual-earner families.

Table 7.3 considers the trend in the female share in more detail and performs a formal decomposition of the rise in the female share into within- and between-group factors. As suggested by the preceding discussion the bulk (88 per cent) of the rise in the female share occurs between-groups. When one bears in mind that between-group changes correspond to changes in the employment status of the members of the family, it is the rise in labour force participation of women coupled with the falling participation of men that is responsible for the rise in the female share.

7.2.3 The distribution of male and female shares

Figure 7.3 graphs the distribution of male and female shares (in 11 share bands) for two sub-periods, 1979–81 and 1989–91. In addition to the increased frequency of zero shares for men, there is also a noticeable leftward shift of the distribution for those in work. This decline in male shares, as we saw above, reflects relative wage and employment declines. The shift in female shares is less dramatic (as the change in male shares is accounted for by the sum of the change in female shares and the change in

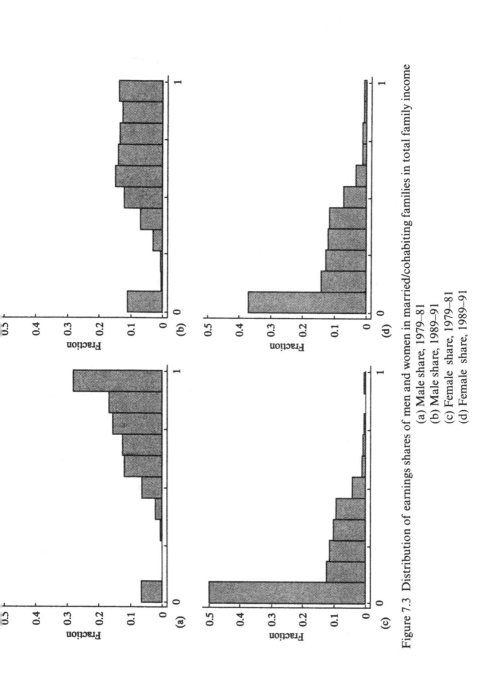

Figure 7.3 Distribution of earnings shares of men and women in married/cohabiting families in total family income

(a) Male share, 1979–81
(b) Male share, 1989–91
(c) Female share, 1979–81
(d) Female share, 1989–91

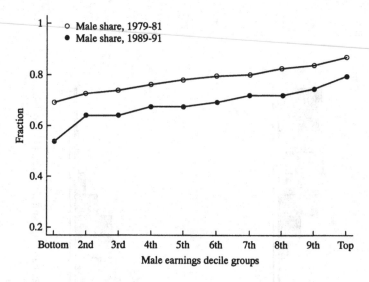

Figure 7.4 Male earning shares, by male earnings decile groups

non-labour shares), but nonetheless the distribution of female shares shows important changes, with the major shift being the reduced concentration of female shares at zero.

7.2.4 The distribution of male and female shares and participation by male earnings

To consider further how these changes in shares varied across families, we analysed trends in some of the variables of interest by male earnings decile groups. This permits us to examine whether the declining labour market position of relatively low paid men is being compensated for by their wives, or whether it is the wives of relatively rich husbands who are increasing their shares in family income. This has important implications for the impact of changing shares on poverty and family income inequality, which we address below.

Our analysis by male earnings decile groups, shown in figure 7.4, demonstrates that the male share rises as expected as one moves to the higher decile groups, but what we are interested in here is how the male share has changed over time. Among married and cohabiting couples, we find that the male share falls over time in all decile groups, but the magnitude of the fall is more marked at the bottom end of the male earnings distribution.

The share of female earnings also displays an interesting pattern, as

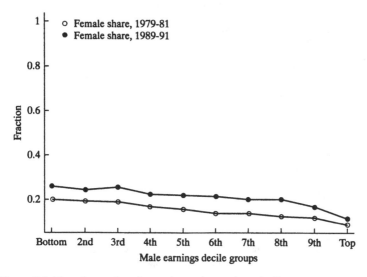

Figure 7.5 Female earning shares, by male earnings decile groups

shown in figure 7.5, rising at all points of the male earnings distribution. The female share rises by more in the lower and middle decile groups of the male distribution.[6] As we will see below, this is important for it implies that, via non-neutral increases in female shares lower down the male distribution, these changes in female earnings have tended to reduce overall family poverty and inequality.

Comparing the pattern of changes in shares of the components of family income, it is clear that the largest shifts have occurred through *changes* in the labour market behaviour of men and women. It appears to be the increased participation by wives (rather than increased earnings among those women who participate) coupled with the deterioration of the relative labour market position of lower earnings husbands that is important.[7]

7.2.5 The relationship between women's pay and poverty

One way to clarify the relationship between women's earnings and poverty is to investigate the importance of women's earnings at different points of the family income distribution. This allows us to examine directly the question of whether wives' or partners' earnings constitute a larger share in poorer or richer families, as well as the question of how this has changed over time.

Analysing the female share by decile groups of the family income

Figure 7.6 Female employment rates, by family income decile groups

distribution confirms the links between women's pay and poverty suggested above (see Harkness *et al.*, 1994). We find that, with the notable exception of the 'no-earner' families, it is in the poorest families that women have increased their share the most. This suggests that economic necessity has been a critical motivating factor in increasing wives' labour force participation over the period. Contrary to some popular perceptions, the wives who entered the labour market in increasing numbers in the 1980s came predominantly from lower or middle income, not higher income, families. This is illustrated in figure 7.6. Note that the increase in participation is greatest in the second through fifth decile groups of the family income distribution, with smaller increases at the top decile groups. As a result, although female participation continues to be higher in the top decile groups, the gap in employment between these decile groups and the lower ones is narrowing. Note also that female participation increased the least in the bottom decile group, again reflecting the non-participation of wives of unemployed men.

Another way to assess the relationship between women's pay and poverty is to estimate how many families would be in poverty if it were not for the income from the woman's work. That is, we can compare the actual percentage of families in poverty with the predicted percentage that would be in poverty without the woman's earnings.[8]

This comparison of actual and predicted poverty rates is shown in table

Table 7.4 *Impact of wives' earnings on family poverty,[a] 1979–81 to 1989–91*

1979–81	Actual % in poverty	Predicted % in poverty without female earnings	Predicted % increase in poverty
All married and cohabiting couple families	3.58	5.28	1.70
Dual-earner families	0.00	0.63	0.63
Families where the man only works	0.60	0.60	0.00
Families where the woman only works	14.72	80.37	65.65

1989–91	Actual % in poverty	Predicted % in poverty without female earnings	Predicted % increase in poverty
All married and cohabiting couple families	7.91	12.26	4.35
Dual-earner families	0.56	4.44	3.88
Families where the man only works	5.28	5.28	0.00
Families where the woman only works	30.82	74.10	43.28

Notes:
[a] Poverty rates are defined as the percentage of families with real equivalent income of less than half of average real equivalised income.

7.4. Table 7.4 shows that poverty rates among married and cohabiting couple families have risen sharply since 1979 and would have risen even more if it had not been for women's earnings. Comparing the sub-period 1979–81 to 1989–91, the actual poverty rate for married and cohabiting couple families climbed from 3.6 per cent to 7.9 per cent. In 1989–91 the poverty rate would have reached as much as 12.3 per cent (or over one half higher than the actual 1989–91 level) without women's earnings. Clearly, then, women's pay is playing a vital role in keeping some low income families out of poverty and the poverty-alleviating role of women's earnings seems more marked by 1989–91.

7.2.6 The relationship between women's pay and family income inequality

Looking at the importance of women's pay across decile groups of male earnings and across decile groups of family income, we have seen that the largest increase in the female share has occurred in the lowest income deciles, with the exception of the no-earner families. This suggests that changes in women's earnings are unlikely to have contributed to the widening of the family income distribution; on the contrary, it appears that they might have had an equalising effect.

We have considered this possibility in more detail in Machin and Waldfogel (1994a) where we consider how the various components of family income, including women's pay, affect inequality across families, using a simple decomposition of the variance of family incomes, $V(y)$, defined as[9]

$$V(y) = \alpha_M^2 \cdot V(e_M) + \alpha_F^2 \cdot V(e_F) + (1 - \alpha_M - \alpha_F)^2 \cdot V(y_N) \qquad (3)$$
$$+ 2.\alpha_M.\alpha_F.\text{cov}(e_M, e_F) + 2.\alpha_M.(1 - \alpha_M - \alpha_F).\text{cov}(e_M, y_F)$$
$$+ 2.\alpha_F.(1 - \alpha_M - \alpha_F).\text{cov}(e_F, y_N).$$

Note that as y is the relative income of families ($= Y/\bar{Y}$) then $V(y) = V(Y) / \bar{Y}^2$ which is the squared coefficient of variation of family income, a frequently utilised measure of dispersion or inequality. In the same way $V(e_M)$, $V(e_F)$ and $V(y_N)$ are the squared coefficients of variations of male earnings, female earnings and non-labour income respectively. So $V(y)$ decomposes neatly into components related to the shares and dispersion of the components of income, and their inter-correlations via the covariance terms.

In table 7.5 we report the squared coefficient of variation of family income and its components for 1979–81 and 1989–91. The inequality of family incomes increased sharply over this period, as the squared coefficient of variation rose from 0.236 to 0.424.[10] There was also a dramatic increase in the inequality of husbands' earnings, but, interestingly, the dispersion of wives' earnings among all couples fell by over 20 per cent (from 1.685 to 1.325) over the same period. This is due to increased participation rates as the squared coefficient of variation rises for working women, as depicted in the bottom panels of the table.

A simple way to assess the impact of wives' earnings on overall income inequality (see, for example, Cancian *et al.*, 1993a, 1993b) is to evaluate the inequality of income if wives' earnings were set to zero. If we define family income with wives' earnings netted out as Y_1 then the importance of women's earnings can be defined in terms of the change in an index of inequality when wives' earnings are, respectively, included and excluded.

Table 7.5 *Changes in the inequality of family income and its components, 1979–81 to 1989–91*

	1979–81	Number of families	1989–91	Number of families
1. All couples				
$V(y)^a$	0.236	7799	0.424	7534
$V(e_M)$	0.332	7799	0.643	7534
$V(e_F)$	1.685	7799	1.325	7534
$V(y_N)$	2.833	7799	3.142	7534
2. Wife works				
$V(y)$	0.145	4305	0.249	5350
$V(e_M)$	0.221	4305	0.341	5350
$V(e_F)$	0.482	4305	0.651	5350
$V(y_N)$	2.008	4305	3.090	5350
3. Both work full-time				
$V(y)$	0.130	1810	0.190	2501
$V(e_M)$	0.267	1810	0.293	2501
$V(e_F)$	0.152	1810	0.263	2501
$V(y_N)$	2.573	1810	2.766	2501

Notes:
[a] $V(.)$ denotes the squared coefficient of variation (i.e. the variance of a variable defined in relative terms); e_M = male earnings/family income; e_F = female earnings/family income; y_N = non-labour income/family income.

That is, one can assess the magnitude and sign of $[V(y) - V(y_1)]/V(y)$, where y_1 is relative income $Y_1/\bar{Y}$, to ascertain the importance of wives' earnings.[11]

Table 7.6 reports the squared coefficient of variation with and without women's earnings. It is clear that inequality is always higher without wives' earnings. This strongly suggests that wives' earnings have had an equalising impact. Note also that this equalising impact is more marked by 1989–91.[12]

7.3 The importance of women's pay in single woman families

Single woman families are those with an adult woman who may or may not have dependent children and who has no male partner present. We disaggregate these families into those with dependent children and those without, as their characteristics (e.g. labour force participation, sources of

172   Susan Harkness *et al.*

Table 7.6 *Impact of wives' earnings on family income inequality, 1979–81 to 1989–91*

	1979–81	1989–91
1. All couples		
$V(y)$	0.236	0.424
$V(y_1)$	0.279	0.568
$[V(y) - V(y_1)] / V(y)$	–0.182	–0.340
2. Wife at work		
$V(y)$	0.145	0.249
$V(y_1)$	0.188	0.339
$[V(y) - V(y_1)] / V(y)$	–0.297	–0.361
3. Both work full-time		
$V(y)$	0.130	0.190
$V(y_1)$	0.231	0.298
$[V(y) - V(y_1)] / V(y)$	–0.777	–0.568

income, etc.) depend to a great extent on the presence or absence of children.[13]

Table 7.7 shows sample characteristics for the single woman families. For those with children, average real monthly earnings are very low, and rise only modestly (from £548 in 1979–81 to £590 in 1989–91). Equivalent real income actually falls (from £568 to £528). Average earnings for women with children are also barely changed. For those without children, average real monthly income is higher and rises at a much faster rate (from £718 to £1058, or from £1049 to £1132 in equivalent terms). Labour market earnings also rise over this time period for this group.

7.3.1 Labour market participation

Table 7.7 also draws out interesting participation changes. It is noteworthy that the percentage of single mothers in employment falls slightly over the period, from 50.1 per cent to 48.0 per cent, in striking contrast with the trend among other groups of women (particularly married and cohabiting women, as we saw earlier). This is consistent with the well documented fall in participation of lone mothers (see, for example, Bradshaw and Millar, 1991). Equally striking is the sharp fall in full-time participation among lone mothers, from 49 per cent of those in work to only 41 per cent, again in contrast with the trend among married and cohabiting women. It is possible that this shift to part-time work among lone mothers is a response to

Table 7.7 *Sample characteristics of single woman families, 1979–91*

Single woman families with dependent children	1979–81	1989–91	Change
Total monthly income	548	590	+£42
Equivalised income	568	528	– £40
Female monthly earnings	221	240	+£19
Monthly non-labour income	327	350	+£23
Percentage in employment	50.1	48.0	–2.1%
Percentage full-time	48.9	41.0	–7.9%
Total number of families	1067	1249	
Single woman families with no dependent children	1979–81	1989–91	Change
Total monthly income	718	1058	+£340
Equivalised income	1049	1132	+£83
Female monthly earnings	558	739	+£181
Monthly non-labour income	160	319	+£159
Percentage in employment	77.6	79.5	+1.9%
Percentage full-time	87.6	86.9	–0.7%
Total number of families	1853	2275	

cutbacks in publicly funded child care over the 1980s,[14] increased part-time opportunities in the labour market, and/or new incentives in the benefit system. What is very clear is that lone parents did considerably worse than other women over the 1980s.

Table 7.8 shows changes in female shares and non-labour shares over the four sub-periods. (These shares together make up total family income since by definition there is no male present in these families.) Among those with children, the female share has fallen by 3 percentage points, from 30 per cent to 27 per cent; this reflects the fall in participation and hours noted above. Even among those without children, the female share has fallen slightly over time, from 68 per cent to 65 per cent, as alternative sources of income have grown.

7.3.2 Poverty among single woman families

Table 7.9 considers poverty rates among single woman families. Not surprisingly, they are much higher than for married/cohabiting families and show a sharp rise, from 19 per cent to 40 per cent of these families, between 1979–81 and 1989–91. Even amongst working women there is a

Table 7.8 *Shares of female earnings and non-labour income in total family income, single woman families, 1979–91*

Single woman families with dependent children	1979–81	1989–91	Change
Total monthly income	548	591	+£43
Female share	0.299	0.269	–0.030
Non-labour income share	0.701	0.731	+0.030
Total number of families	1067	1249	
Single woman families with no dependent children	1979–81	1989–91	Change
Total monthly income	718	1058	+£340
Female share	0.681	0.651	–0.030
Non-labour income share	0.319	0.349	+0.030
Total number of families	1853	2275	

rise in the poverty rate over this time period. The poverty rate is highest, and shows a very sharp increase, amongst single mothers (for those in work the poverty rate rises from 8 per cent to 41 per cent; for those not in work it rises from 50 per cent to 90 per cent). These trends seem to reflect an increase in both the working poor and the overall aggregate rise in poverty that occurred in Britain over the 1980s.

When one considers the importance of labour market earnings in the same way as before it is very clear that they are very important in keeping single women out of poverty income levels. This is naturally something of a tautology as working single women are the only earners in these families, but nevertheless does testify to the fact that labour market activity is important, and becoming increasingly important, for women. These results also highlight the differing experiences of single women as compared to those in married/cohabiting families over the 1980s.

7.4 The impact of changes within family groups versus changes in family structure

Combining our married and cohabiting couple samples with our single woman family samples allows us to explore the extent to which the aggregate rise in the female share amongst all families over the period 1979–91 has been due to the impact of changes within family groups or changes in family structure.

Table 7.9 *Impact of earnings on family poverty, 1979–81 to 1989–91[a]*

1979–81	Actual % in poverty	Predicted % in poverty without female earnings	Predicted % increase in poverty
All single women families	18.70	73.87	65.17
All single women families: Woman works	3.65	85.34	81.69
All single women families: Woman does not work	50.00	50.00	0.00
Single women with children	29.15	64.10	34.95
Single women with children: Woman works	8.43	78.28	69.85
Single women with children: Woman does not work	49.91	49.91	0.00
Single women, no children	12.68	79.49	66.81
Single women, no children: Woman works	1.88	87.97	86.09
Single women, no children: Woman does not work	50.12	50.12	0.00

1989–91	Actual % in poverty	Predicted % in poverty without female earnings	Predicted % increase in poverty
All single women families	40.27	85.39	45.12
All single women families: Woman works	19.73	85.76	66.03
All single women families: Woman does not work	84.59	84.59	0.00
Single women with children	66.37	90.31	23.94
Single women with children: Woman works	40.57	90.48	49.91
Single women with children: Woman does not work	90.15	90.15	0.00
Single women, no children	25.93	82.68	56.75
Single women, no children: Woman works	12.82	84.19	71.37
Single women, no children: Woman does not work	76.82	76.82	0.00

Notes:
[a] Poverty rates are defined as the percentage of families with real equivalent income of less than half of average real equivalised income.

Table 7.10 *Changing family structure and changes within families, 1979–81 to 1989–91*

Family structure changes	Family type as a percentage of total sample in 1979–81	Family type as a percentage of total sample in 1989–91
Married or cohabiting, with dependent children	54.2	39.7
Married or cohabiting, no dependent children	18.6	28.4
Single woman families, with dependent children	10.0	11.3
Single woman families, no dependent children	17.3	20.6
Within-family changes	Female share as a percentage of total family income in 1979–81	Female share as a percentage of total family income in 1989–91
Married or cohabiting, with dependent children	0.107	0.160
Married or cohabiting, no dependent children	0.287	0.276
Single woman families, with dependent children	0.299	0.269
Single woman families, no dependent children	0.681	0.651

Table 7.10 summarises these two types of changes. We would expect that both within-family changes (most notably the rise in the female share in married couple families with children) and family structure changes (especially the decline in the proportion of families that are married couples with children) might have contributed to the overall increase in female share over the period, and it is useful to determine how much each set of factors contributes. As such we report some simple decompositions of the aggregate female share in table 7.11.

The first decomposition presented in table 7.11 simply considers the extent to which the aggregate rise in female shares occurred mainly within or between the single woman and married/cohabiting women groups. It suggests that both within-family changes and changes in family structure played a role, but that the former was of more importance. Overall, the female share increased by 4.7 percentage points from 1979–81 to 1989–91.

Table 7.11 *Decomposition of the rise in importance of female share in total family income, married and cohabiting couple families and single woman families, 1979–81 to 1989–91*

	1979–81	1989–91	Change in female share	Change within group	Change between group
Married and Single (two groups)[a]	0.259	0.306	0.047	0.031 (65%)	0.017 (35%)
Married and Single (four groups)[b]	0.259	0.306	0.047	0.013 (28%)	0.034 (72%)

Notes:
[a] Decomposition based on changes between and within married/cohabiting families and single woman families.
[b] Decomposition based on changes between and within married/cohabiting families and single woman families with and without children.

Of this, 1.7 percentage points, or 35 per cent, is accounted for by the increase in female share due to changes in family structure. The remaining 3.1 percentage points, or 65 per cent, is accounted for by the changes in female share within families.

The second decomposition considers the importance of the presence of dependent children and considers a within/between decomposition with four family groups defined as married/cohabiting or single with and without dependent children. Here, it is evident that, given that women's labour force activity is conditional on the presence of dependent children, the between-group component is more important (accounting for 72 per cent of the aggregate rise in female shares). This is of interest as it strengthens the earlier findings that stressed the importance of changes in labour market activity of women.

7.5 Conclusions

In this chapter, we have evaluated the importance of women's pay for family incomes, poverty and inequality among married and cohabiting couples and single woman families. Using the General Household Survey to track women's earnings and their family incomes from 1979 to 1991, we assess the importance of the contributions of women's earnings to their families' well-being.

We have three principal findings to report with regard to married and cohabiting women. First, the share of men's earnings in total family income fell dramatically in our period of study, as there was a marked decline of 'male breadwinner' families, and the share of women's earnings rose sharply. Hence, women's earnings now form an increasingly large component of total family income. This increased share is almost entirely a consequence of changes in labour market activity of men and women. Second, women's pay, despite being low, plays a critical role in preventing poverty; for example, among married and cohabiting couple families, the poverty rate in 1991 would have been up to 50 per cent higher if it had not been for women's earnings. Third, and perhaps most surprising, the changes in women's earnings have exerted an equalising influence on the income distribution of married and cohabiting couple families; family income inequality among this portion of the population would have risen even more over the period studied here if women, particularly those married to low-earning men, had not increased their contributions to family budgets.

We also separately examine the situation of single woman families and find that, although their earnings have traditionally been more important than married women's, single women's earnings have become less important over time. The experience of single woman families, especially those with dependent children, has been very different from those with married or cohabiting partners and has been reflected in a sharp increase in poverty and a rise of the in-work poor.

Combining our samples of married and cohabiting couple families and of single woman families allowed us to decompose the change in the importance of the female share into that component due to changes within families and that component due to changing family structure. We find that, although both components had an impact over the period 1979–91, the dominant factor was the change in shares within families. Of these within-group changes it seems that changes in the labour market activity of men and women were of vital importance in married/cohabiting families.

The single most fundamental policy implication of our research is that women's earnings, and hence policies that affect them, do matter to their families' well-being. Even married women who are working part-time are not working for pin-money; rather they are bringing home one fifth of their families' income, while married women working full-time are bringing home a substantial two fifths. Nor is there any indication here that the rising importance of women's earnings is a temporary or aberrant phenomenon. Rather, it appears to be deeply grounded in both demographic changes (e.g. the fall in the percentage of married and cohabiting couple families with children) and social changes (e.g. the rising labour force participation of women, particularly those who are married or cohabiting with children) that are unlikely to be suddenly halted or reversed. This means that it would be foolhardy indeed to base future policy affecting women's pay on the assumption that low pay for women does not really matter.

Our results point to the conclusion that we can no longer assume that husbands are 'male breadwinners' and that wives are working for 'pin-money'. To the extent that these assumptions underlie our welfare and labour market policies, a thoughtful review and overhaul of both appear to be long overdue. Good starting points would be a reappraisal of policy in the areas of minimum wages, pay and benefits for part-time work, and 'family-friendly' initiatives to allow working mothers to better manage the balance between work and family responsibilities.

Notes

The Joseph Rowntree Foundation provided funding for this research as part of its Income and Wealth Programme, but the conclusions and opinions expressed here are those of the authors alone. Material from the General Household Survey, made available by The Office of Population Censuses and Surveys through the ESRC Data Archive at the University of Essex, has been used by permission of the Controller of Her Majesty's Stationery Office.

1. A family is defined as a couple, or a single woman, and any dependent children. Any other adults in the household, and their income, are excluded. Total income is defined as total gross family income, which is reported in the survey, for all years except 1983–86, when the total family income question was not asked. This results in an under-count of total income (and of non-labour income) for 1983–86 and is the reason why we (mainly) focus on two sub-periods in our analysis.

2. Note that one cannot define an hourly wage on a consistent basis between the two time periods as hours are only given excluding overtime hours after 1983 (and the weekly wage in those years contains overtime payments).

3. Recent work on male labour force inactivity (e.g. Schmitt and Wadsworth, 1993) shows that male non-participants are much more likely to possess below average labour market skills. Further investigation of our data confirms this. Holding constant age and region, men with a degree are some 8 per cent less likely to be out of a job than those with no educational qualifications in 1979–80 and some 17 per cent less likely in 1989–90. Also, we found the mean imputed wages of non-participants to be 7 per cent below those of participants in 1979–80 and 17 per cent below by 1989–90.

4. See also Dilnot and Kell (1989), Pudney and Thomas (1993).

5. One should not place too much emphasis on the year-to-year variations since, as noted above, the income definition is not consistent through the entire time period (with 1983–86 inclusive being defined as the sum of the separate

components, rather than the total family income variable that is defined in all other years).

6. It is important to note that we are comparing women's share (and participation, below) across male earnings decile groups, not across female earnings or education groups. Thus, this finding of greater share increases in the lower and middle deciles is not inconsistent with the fact that participation and earnings gains over the period were greatest for women with the highest labour market skills.

7. A similar pattern is seen if groups are defined using the distribution of male monthly earnings or earnings after controlling for age, education (non-overtime), hours and region.

8. We define families in poverty as those with equivalent income less than 50 per cent of the mean. One should also note that this rather rough comparison rests on the assumption that other sources of income (e.g. men's earnings or state benefits) would not change in the absence of women's earnings and as such provides an upper bound estimate on how much poverty might increase if not for women's earnings. We present more experiments where we let the labour supply of husbands respond to the setting of women's earnings to zero in Harkness *et al.* (1994).

9. See also Layard and Zabalza (1979) and Smith (1979), who use similar variance decompositions.

10. Other measures of inequality (e.g. based on differentials between various percentiles) clearly draw out the same pattern.

11. As on p. 168 in the section on poverty, this assumes that husbands would not alter their hours if their wives' earnings fell to zero and, as such, provides an upper bound of the potential impact of wives' earnings.

12. Machin and Waldfogel (1994a) report the full covariance matrix described in (3) as well as a more detailed decomposition and make it clear that, in 1979–80, the overwhelmingly important determinant of the inequality of family income was the inequality of male earnings and that the main factor underpinning the rise in income inequality was the rise in male earnings inequality.

13. It is important to note that sample sizes in the GHS are fairly small (less than 1000 single woman families in a typical year) and there is quite a bit of year-to-year variation in the data. For this reason, in much of our analysis we use pooled sub-period samples (see Harkness *et al.*, 1994).

14. As a result of a shift away from direct public provision of child care, local authorities provided fewer day nursery places and fewer childminder places in 1991 than they had in the early 1980s (Department of Health, 1991).

8   More work in fewer households?

Paul Gregg and Jonathan Wadsworth

8.1 Introduction

Britain has experienced two deep recessions in the last 15 years. In the intervening period it also enjoyed one of the longest spells of continuous employment growth this century. By 1990 the level of employment, among the population of working age, had recovered to virtually the same as that prevailing in the mid-1970s. Yet over the same period, between 1975 and 1990, the number of claims for benefits by people under pension age, excluding double counting for multiple-benefit claims, increased by around 1.7 million.[1] In the subsequent recession the number of claims rose by a similar amount again. The Department of Social Security has forecast a continued rise in benefit dependency into the next century. The ability of the state to finance these claims is once again a source of public concern.

As a single claim for means-tested benefit will normally cover the entire household, the number of adults reliant on state support has risen by even more than the growth in the number of claims. This, then, offers a potential explanation of the paradox of rising dependency with growing employment levels, since means-tested benefit is normally limited to where both members of a couple are without work.

Using data drawn mainly from the Labour Force Survey (LFS) this study documents the rise in the number of households without access to earned income and explores why this occurred in periods when aggregate employment was growing. Throughout, we concentrate exclusively on individuals or households aged 60 or less.[2] The evidence suggests that by 1990, twice as many households were out of work compared with 1975, whilst the aggregate employment rate was unchanged. Nearly 15 per cent of the working age population were resident in jobless households in 1993. This represents some 19 per cent of all households.

The difference in non-employment patterns at aggregate and household levels is caused by a change in the distribution of work across households.

20 years ago, many households contained a mixture of adults in and out of work. Since then, the proportion of partially employed households has fallen by around one third. Thus the distribution of work has 'hollowed out' and by implication the distribution of household income widened, with a simultaneous rise in both the number of fully employed (work-rich) and non-employed (work-poor) households.

Section 8.3 explores whether this growing concentration of employment is due to changes in the size of households. Moves toward more single adult households with traditionally low rates of employment would provide a simple explanation for this increase in dispersion. Our analysis suggests this accounts for less than 20 per cent of the observed change. The rest is due to the increasing concentration of work within household size groups. A growing number of multiple-earner households has been accompanied by increasing numbers of single and multiple-adult households with no work.

A dynamic approach offers more insight into the explanations for these aggregate trends than reliance on static cross-sections. Section 8.4 analyses household flows between employed and non-employed states. Most of the rise in household non-employment is caused by a collapse in exit rates from non-employment, rather than an increased risk of becoming non-employed. Between the late 1970s and 1990, the probability of workless households having at least one working member a year later fell from 60 per cent to around 25 per cent. This implies that the duration of a typical spell without any work rose by around 50 per cent. Given the loss of earned income, simple labour supply theory predicts greater efforts to secure work by other household members (the added worker effect). This increased duration is therefore surprising over a period in which both real earnings and aggregate employment probabilities have been rising. Furthermore, the transition rates imply a long-run steady state dispersion of work across households substantially wider than that currently observed.

Section 8.5 examines the determinants of individual probabilities of moving into work according to personal and family characteristics. Entry rates for jobless individuals in households with another member already working rose from 16 per cent in 1979 to 24 per cent in 1993. Meanwhile, entry rates for single adult households or those where both adults were out of work fell (from 18 per cent to 11 per cent and 25 per cent to 12 per cent, respectively). Workless households may have characteristics which employers find unsuitable, and the jobs on offer may have attributes that workless households find unsuitable. The characteristics of individuals in workless families that we can observe, however, offer no further explanation of the changing fortunes across household types. The changing nature of work has seen full-time employee engagements fall from two thirds to

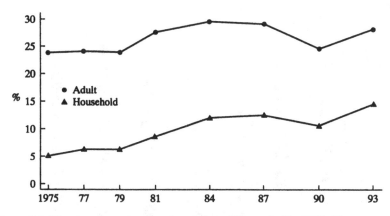

Figure 8.1 Non-employment rates for adults and households, 1975–93

one half of those available. Full-time openings were disproportionately taken by those in workless households and part-time disproportionately by those in working households. The changing nature of work explains about one quarter of the changing fortunes of workless households.

However, after allowing for this, men and women in workless families have increasingly been losing out in the fight for the full- or part-time opportunities available. The limitations of the annual transition data in the LFS leave the reasons behind these developments obscure. Section 8.6 draws some conclusions and implications for the near future.

8.2 The simultaneous rise of workless and two income families

After nine years of continuous growth, the employment rate in 1990 had recovered to near that prevailing in the mid-1970s. Figure 8.1 (top line) shows the adult non-employment rate (percentage of adults of working age not in work) for the period 1975–93. Between 1979 and 1984, non-employment rose by around 5.5 percentage points. Yet the 1975–90 differential fell back to just 0.5 points. This recovery holds even when growth in multiple job-holding by individuals (which has been modest) or the total number of hours are taken into consideration.

Over the same period, the numbers of individual claims for benefits associated with an absence of work rose by around 1.7 million. As often more than one adult is dependent on such claims, this under-estimates the growth of dependency relative to a stable amount of employment. Atkinson (1993b) shows that the proportion of the population dependent on means-tested benefits alone grew from under 5 per cent to 7.5 per cent between the late 1970s and 1990 and had reached 9.5 per cent by 1992.

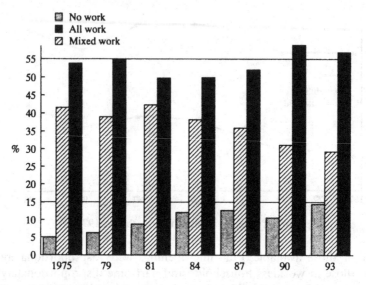

Figure 8.2 Distribution of work across households, 1975–93

The resolution of the paradox is possibly settled by the bottom line in figure 8.1 which plots household non-employment rates (the proportion of individuals living in households with no one in work). This also rose in the early 1980s but, significantly, did not fall during the late 1980s' recovery. It now stands at a historical high of 14 per cent.

Figure 8.2 gives the distribution of work by household type. Over the sample period, there was a dramatic shift away from households with a mixture of working and non-working members and a corresponding polarisation of employment into fully employed (work-rich) and workless (work-poor) households. This process began before the early 1980s' recession. By 1990, the proportion of individuals in households with all members in employment was 10 per cent greater than in 1975. Even after the 1990/92 recession it remained above the level at the previous GDP peak of 1979. The number of individuals in jobless households tripled to 14 per cent over the whole period. This implies that by 1993 some 19 per cent of all working age households were jobless.[3]

A growing proportion of households with no access to earned income is consistent with the growth in recipients of Income Support and related benefits documented by Atkinson (1993b).[4] This separation of work across households is also likely to be a significant factor in the growth in poverty and income inequality in Britain where, according to Gardiner (1994), the income of the poorest fifth of households has

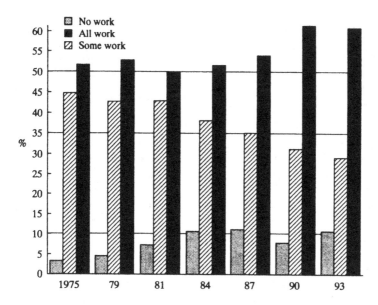

Figure 8.3 Distribution of work in two adult households, 1975–93

fallen by 10 per cent since 1979 and that of the richest fifth risen by around 45 per cent.

8.3 The distribution of work between and within household size types

Separation of work could be caused by changes in household composition. A shift towards smaller sized units (e.g. more single parents) will automatically widen the employment distribution in favour of non- and fully-employed households. Figure 8.3 and table 8.1 (top panel) show the changing pattern of household size, with a steady rise in the proportion of single adult households after 1981. The main variation is in three or more person households, rising in the early 1980s and falling sharply after 1985. This probably reflects the baby boom generation reaching adulthood and leaving home. The two adult household remains the dominant form throughout. The growth in single adult households reflects a trend toward setting up home away from parents prior to marriage and, of course, rising rates of family breakdown.[5] The stock of jobless two adult households triples over the sample period.

The contribution of changing family composition in the rising stock of non-employment can be isolated by decomposing the rise in the household non-employment rate into that attributable to changes in non-employment

Table 8.1 *Household composition and employment, 1975–93*

	1975	1979	1985	1990	1993
Share in total					
Single adult	7.8	8.8	9.3	10.8	13.7
Two adult	63.7	62.4	59.0	59.5	61.5
(of which:					
No work	2.0	2.5	6.2	4.3	6.3
Men only work	27.4	25.3	19.0	15.2	13.6
Women only work	1.4	1.2	2.4	2.9	3.8
Both work)	32.9	33.2	31.4	37.1	37.8
Three+ adult	28.5	28.8	31.8	29.7	24.8
	100	100	100	100	100
Non-employment rate					
Total	0.039	0.062	0.112	0.104	0.144
Single adult	0.216	0.276	0.418	0.380	0.415
Two adult	0.032	0.045	0.112	0.078	0.107
Three+ adult	0.007	0.009	0.034	0.028	0.044

rates within household types and that due to changes in the shares of different household types in the population. The majority (6.4 points) of the rise of the work-poor family is explained by changes in the distribution of work within specific household types.[6] Of the 8.2 percentage point rise between 1979 and 1993, only 1.4 percentage points (or 17 per cent) can be attributed to changing shares of household size groups.

Table 8.1 also shows the rapid growth in the proportion of workless single households. This pattern is common to men and women and all other family sizes. Figure 8.3 shows the pattern for two adult families. The most striking feature is the rise in the proportion of dual earners after 1981. By 1993, there were nearly 10 per cent more dual earning two adult families than in 1979. The collapse of the single earning couple was accompanied by a more than doubling of the two adult non-employment rate from 3 per cent in 1975 to 8 per cent in 1990 (and a further rise to 11 per cent in 1993).

Table 8.1 indicates that only 2 per cent of two adult households were supported solely by a woman in 1975. By 1993 this figure had risen to 6 per cent.[7] Conversely, in households where women did not work, the proportion with no employed adult rose sharply. By 1993, 32 per cent of two adult families where the woman was not in work contained no other employed member, up from 7 per cent in 1975.

Table 8.2 *Two adult household composition and employment status,*
1975–93

% women employed by household type	1975	1979	1985	1990	1993
Man employed	54.6	56.7	62.4	70.7	73.9
Man non-employed	38.6	33.9	28.3	38.7	38.1

Table 8.2 shows that in 1975, 45 per cent of all two adult households were supported by a sole male earner. By 1993 this figure had fallen to 26 per cent. The number of men out of work has risen with no off-setting rise in the incidence of employment of their co-occupant. The 1993 and 1975 proportions in table 8.2 are almost identical. The increasing number of women in employment has primarily occurred in households where their partner is in work. In 1975, 55 per cent of women with employed partners were in work compared with 40 per cent of women with non-employed partners. By 1993, 75 per cent of women with employed partners were also in work, but the proportion of working women in households with unemployed partners remained unchanged at 40 per cent.[8] Hence, the entry of women and exit of men from work has occurred in different households.

8.4 Within-household types: flow analysis

While the rise in the work-poor household is consistent with increasing benefit claims and fluctuating employment levels, it does not explain why this change in work patterns has occurred. A deeper insight into the causes can be gained by examining the inflow and outflow rates associated with the changes in these stocks. It is well known (e.g. Pissarides, 1986) that growth in unemployment occurs primarily because of declining exit rates following rather more temporary increases in entry probabilities. Hence duration of unemployment increases.[9] Tables 8.3a and 8.3b conduct a similar exercise for households using the wider definition of non-employment.[10]

Tables 8.3a and 8.3b use retrospective LFS data concerning individual labour force status one year earlier. By comparing current and retrospective status, the probability of moving between states can be estimated as Flow/Stock, where Flow is the number of households observed changing employment status. It is possible that intervening transitions have occurred, but the figures are nevertheless indicative of changing patterns of employment or non-employment persistence for households.

Table 8.3a *Annual transition probabilities, by household status: one adult households*

	Destination state	
Origin state	Non-employed	Employed
1979		
Non-employed	0.836	0.164
Employed	0.068	0.932
1985		
Non-employed	0.875	0.125
Employed	0.086	0.914
1990		
Non-employed	0.892	0.108
Employed	0.080	0.920
1993		
Non-employed	0.883	0.117
Employed	0.105	0.895

Table 8.3b *Annual transition probabilities, by household status: two adult households*

	Destination state		
Origin state	Non-employed	One-employed	Both employed
1979			
Non-employed	0.406	0.529	0.064
One employed	0.038	0.814	0.148
Both employed	0.006	0.111	0.882
1985			
Non-employed	0.786	0.168	0.045
One employed	0.061	0.758	0.182
Both employed	0.009	0.106	0.885
1990			
Non-employed	0.725	0.225	0.050
One employed	0.054	0.742	0.204
Both employed	0.009	0.107	0.884
1993			
Non-employed	0.759	0.195	0.046
One employed	0.083	0.699	0.218
Both employed	0.012	0.118	0.871

The transition matrices in table 8.3a show a fall in the annual exit probabilities for a non-employed single adult household from 16 per cent in 1979 to around 12 per cent in the 1990s. At the same time, the entry rate into non-employment rose from 7 to 9 per cent in 1985 and again to 11 per cent in 1993. Table 8.3b shows a marked decline in exit from non-employment for two adult households. In 1979, 60 per cent of workless households had at least one earner a year later. By 1993 this had fallen to just 25 per cent. This collapse in the outflow probability has occurred for both exits into one or two income states. The intermediate, partially-employed state has become increasingly unstable, with higher exit rates to both non-employment and dual income status. The stock of two-earner households is highly stable in all periods. The key feature is the difference between the transition probabilities in 1979 and the three later periods, despite the similarity in aggregate employment growth, approximately 250,000, in 1979, 1985 and 1990 (1993 was a period of employment contraction).

The transition rates can also be used to predict the equilibrium distribution of work within household groups, highlighting the eventual distribution of employment if the transition matrix were left unchanged and the economy given time to adjust. A shift in transition probabilities implies a different long-run equilibrium stock. Transition rates may be unstable across the economic cycle but the difference between 1979 and the three later periods looks sufficiently persistent to make this exercise valid. Table 8.4 gives the predicted equilibrium labour force proportions associated with the transition matrices and the current distribution in brackets. In 1979 and 1985 the predicted distribution looks broadly similar to that observed. The predictions for 1993 show marked differences between the actual and equilibrium distributions, suggesting pressure for a continued separation of work in the 1990s.[11]

The transition rates can also be used to examine whether changes in outflow or inflow rates determine the changes in the stock. In equilibrium, inflows into each state equal outflows, hence the household non-employment rate can be rewritten as the inflow rate multiplied by the average duration which approximates to:

$$\text{Stock/Population} = \text{Inflows/Population} * 1/(\text{Outflows/Stock})$$

The second term is just the inverse of the outflow rate, whilst the first term is the inflow rate from the employed state (Inflows/Employed) multiplied by the employed household share, Employed/Population. Between 1979 and 1993 the inflow rate rose from 4.9 per cent to 5.5 per cent (only a 13 per cent rise) for single households. Thus most of the increase in the shock was caused by changes in outflow rates. The predicted jobless duration

Table 8.4 *Steady state distribution of work, by household status, 1979–93*

	1979	1985	1993
Single adult			
Non-employed	0.293 (0.275)	0.408 (0.383)	0.473
(0.396)			
Employed	0.707 (0.725)	0.592 (0.617)	0.527 (0.604)
Two adult			
Non-employed	0.032 (0.041)	0.116 (0.101)	0.133
(0.097)			
One employed	0.420 (0.428)	0.325 (0.363)	0.306 (0.284)
Both employed	0.547 (0.532)	0.559 (0.536)	0.561 (0.619)

Note:
Current distribution in brackets.

rose from 6.1–8.7 per cent (a rise of 42 per cent). For two person households, the inflow rate rose from 1.9 per cent to 3.2 per cent (or by 70 per cent) between 1979 and 1993, whilst the predicted duration rose from 1.7 years to 4.2 years (or by 146 per cent). Hence in both groups, the collapse in the outflow rate accounts for two thirds (in two adult households) to three quarters (in single adult households) of the rise in the stock of workless households. This implies substantial increases in jobless durations for work-poor families. These extended durations without access to earned income must imply severe financial hardship.[12]

It is still unclear why jobless households are losing the ability to enter work. Table 8.5 examines individuals' transition rates disaggregated by sex and the employment status of the co-occupant.[13] In 1979, employment inflows were broadly similar for single adults and those with working partners. Two adult households without work were more likely to obtain work one year later. Single men had a much lower exit rate into work than married men and variation among women was slight.

Of central importance here are the changes over time. Between 1979 and 1993 the transition rates for jobless single adults and those in households with non-working co-occupants fell dramatically, but rose for jobless adults with working partners. The bulk of the 21 percentage point shift in relative transition rates between households with working and non-working partners occurred between 1979 and 1985, stabilised until 1990 and diverged again between 1990 and 1993. The rate of entry into non-employment according to the employment status of the partner is also given. Again, the 1979 differences are small but by 1985 there are trends toward higher rates of job loss for those without a working co-occupant.

Table 8.5 *Annual individual transition rates from and into non-employment, by household status, 1979–93*

	Outflow rate from non-employment				Inflow rate into non-employment			
	1979	1985	1990	1993	1979	1985	1990	1993
Total								
All persons	0.235	0.185	0.216	0.183	0.053	0.068	0.055	0.073
Single person household	0.176	0.105	0.128	0.110	0.067	0.086	0.074	0.098
Co-occupant in work	0.158	0.189	0.229	0.235	0.060	0.063	0.049	0.057
Co-occupant not working	0.253	0.121	0.158	0.124	0.043	0.071	0.061	0.095
Men								
All men	0.436	0.217	0.281	0.221	0.034	0.057	0.043	0.071
Single person household	0.198	0.105	0.155	0.138	0.064	0.084	0.066	0.094
Co-occupant in work	0.398	0.293	0.339	0.328	0.023	0.035	0.025	0.047
Co-occupant not working	0.362	0.161	0.202	0.164	0.037	0.061	0.053	0.085
Women								
All women	0.179	0.167	0.192	0.163	0.082	0.086	0.072	0.076
Single person household	0.163	0.104	0.117	0.098	0.072	0.088	0.082	0.101
Co-occupant in work	0.142	0.174	0.215	0.213	0.098	0.091	0.071	0.067
Co-occupant not working	0.150	0.081	0.120	0.086	0.131	0.145	0.118	0.134

Larger changes occur between 1990 and 1993, which may reflect a period of employment contraction. There has been a remarkable separation in the employment entry rate according to whether other household members work. This is unrelated to aggregate rates of transition into work, which are broadly constant over the periods chosen, and is not, then, a cyclical phenomenon. Simple labour supply theory suggests that members of a workless household would be expected to make greater efforts to secure employment than those in working families because of lower household income – the added worker effect.[14] No such trend is observed for Britain, where other factors off-set these income effects.

8.5 Competing explanations and evidence

There are three prime contending explanations for the growing divergence in transition rates. We need to explain why workless families are less likely to enter work, and the relative movements over time. There have been a number of papers which have looked at the labour supply decision of women with non-working partners, either at one point in time or over a short panel of unemployed men (Dilnot and Kell, 1989; Davies *et al.*, 1992; Pudney and Thomas, 1993 are recent examples). The traditional labour supply approach is to assume individual utility maximisation across income and non-work time taking the employment status of the partner as given, ignoring the fact that labour supply is potentially a joint household decision.[15] This literature places differing emphases on the three factors discussed below.

8.5.1 Within-family considerations

Women married to unemployed men have lower employment rates than those married to men in work. After controlling for other characteristics, studies have found a residual unexplained element to this lower employment rate. This effect has been described by Pudney and Thomas (1993) as 'complementary leisure time'. Couples enjoy being out of work together more than when the man alone is unemployed. Yet Clark and Oswald (1994) demonstrate that unemployment has a profound disutility compared with employment. Using the same data source, our own calculation for *couples* produces the following household distress ranking (out of 12) – both working 2.86; man only 3.14; woman only 4.76; no work 4.24. Thus disutility is highest for households where women only are in work. The mean is statistically different from the first two groupings but not the no-work households.[16] Whilst men are less distressed in no-work households the opposite holds for women. Leisure, on this basis, is not complementary.

McKee and Bell (1985) stress the role of male status within the family. Men lose self-esteem if the woman enters work. This explanation only applies to women and implies an asymmetry across men and women which is not apparent in the other explanations. Both the 'macho male' and the complementary leisure time arguments would predict a difference between workless couples and single workless adults. So we can look for variations across men and women and between couples and single adults to assess this reasoning.

Table 8.5 gives transition rates by gender across household types. Male transitions into work have fallen for all groups. By 1993, transition rates for men in two adult households with a non-working partner had fallen by 20 percentage points since 1979, compared with a 6 percentage point decline for single men and a 7 point fall where the co-occupant works.[17] For women the same patterns emerge, with small falls for single women or those with non-working partners, as opposed to a rise for those with working partners. These swings have occurred against a background of a profound demand shift between men and women.

This common experience of men and women without working partners, if not explained by other factors, would tend to go against the importance of male status within the family (or 'macho male') argument. It is also unclear why single people should have lower exit rates in general than couples in this framework. Furthermore complementary leisure would have difficulty in explaining the change over the period. The decline in entry rates into work for men *and* women in workless couples would require a rise in the desire for complementary leisure time over the period. This seems implausible when benefit levels relative to potential earnings have declined progressively over this period. Whilst this argument might explain some of the cross-section evidence of lower participation of women married to non-working men, we believe it can explain little of the emerging pattern of access to work across households in the 1980s.

8.5.2 Common characteristics

The second explanation relates to changes in the composition of the non-employed population. Male non-employment rates have risen sharply whilst employment amongst women has increased.[18] As dramatic, are differences across education groups. Between 1979 and 1990, the decline in employment rates for men with intermediate qualifications is half that of the least educated and for degree holders almost half again. The largest rise in employment amongst women has occurred amongst the most

Table 8.6 *Two adult household employment and non-employment, by education, 1979-90*

	Total		No work		All work	
	1979	1990	1979	1990	1979	1990
Composition						
Low, low			0.077	0.171	0.485	0.465
Low, intermediate			0.028	0.082	0.541	0.606
Int., int.			0.017	0.030	0.591	0.693
Degree, low			0.015	0.041	0.467	0.587
Degree, int.			0.007	0.018	0.568	0.718
Degree, degree			0.010	0.007	0.633	0.724
Household shares						
Low, low	0.41	0.23	0.716	0.519	0.377	0.177
Low, intermediate	0.29	0.31	0.187	0.328	0.300	0.305
Int., int.	0.19	0.30	0.073	0.118	0.269	0.341
Degree, low	0.03	0.02	0.008	0.011	0.022	0.020
Degree, int.	0.06	0.09	0.010	0.020	0.063	0.101
Degree, degree	0.03	0.05	0.006	0.005	0.030	0.056
Correlation						
Education	0.403	0.431				
Age	0.835	0.907				
Employment	0.082	0.261				
Hours worked (if employed)	-0.012	-0.038				

Note:
Hours worked applies to dual earner households only.

highly educated. If rising female employment and falling male employment do not occur in the same households, it may be because household members have similar education levels. The observed rise in household non-employment is then a coincidence of members experiencing common adverse trends in the labour market.

The most obvious common characteristics are educational attainment, age, region of residence and presence of dependent children. Table 8.6 divides two adult households into six categories according to whether the individual is a degree holder, has low-level qualifications and an intermediate group.[19] The middle panel gives population shares of each of these categories for two adult families. The mode moves away from both partners being low skilled toward both having intermediate qualifications. The top

Table 8.7 *Annual individual employment inflow differentials, by household status, 1979–93*

Status one year ago	1979	1985	1990	1993	Δ1993–79
Unadjusted					
Two adult, one working v. one adult not working	–0.023	0.095	0.126	0.165	0.188
Two adult one working v. two adult none working	–0.073	0.076	0.080	0.143	0.216
With Added Worker and Gender Control					
Two adult, one working v. one adult not working	0.079	0.172	0.184	0.217	0.138
Two adult one working v. two adult none working	0.061	0.171	0.144	0.206	0.145
With all controls					
Two adult, one working v. one not working	0.033	0.124	0.136	0.186	0.153
Two adult one working v. two adult none working	0.030	0.131	0.104	0.177	0.147

panel looks at household work patterns for these education groups. In 1990, over half of jobless households had both members with low qualifications, compared to 18 per cent of those with both members working.

The single-earner household has declined across all education groups. The non-employed household rate rose from 8 to 17 per cent for those with low-level qualifications. Smaller rises were apparent across all other education categories except two degree holders. The contrast with two-earner households is stark. This rose for all groups except where both adults had low qualifications. The concentration of non-employment on households with only low qualifications is consistent with the common characteristics hypothesis. The separation into work-rich/work-poor households is, however, common to all education groupings.

The bottom panel of table 8.6 gives within-household correlation coefficients for key characteristics. The correlations mostly strengthen over the period, more than ever where household members have similar attributes. The exception is hours worked which reflects growth in joint full-time/part-time working.

Table 8.7 gives predicted difference in transition rates between household types before and after including controls for personal and environmental characteristics. The first panel gives predicted difference in transition rates into employment of single adults (row 1) and those in no-earner households (row 2) relative to those with an earner present. In 1979 those with working partners were less likely to enter work (by 2 percentage points relative to single adults and 7 points relative to non-working couples). By 1993 the position is reversed. The swings involved are 19 percentage points for single adults and 21 points for those in non-earning households. As the average transition rate is only around 20 per cent per annum, these relative swings are as large as the average transition rate.

The second panel allows for gender differences and attachment to the labour market. The latter variables are self-assessed evaluations of status one year ago – active job search, sick or retired, looking after family or the home, student and a residual 'other' category. These variables identify any added worker effect implicit in a greater desire for work by members of workless households. Once added worker effects are included, gender plays no additional role.

Inclusion of these variables increases the gap in predicted transition rates between those in working and workless households. Non-employed adults with working partners were less likely to search for work. This should mean that they were also less likely to enter work. Correcting for lower search effort leads to a 6 percentage point differential (8 percentage points compared with single adults), in favour of one worker households in 1979. By 1993, this effect raises the predicted difference in transition rates to over 20 per cent. Hence, the search adjusted differential in favour of those with working partners is larger than the unadjusted gap. However, the swing from 1979 to 1993 is reduced by about one third (about a quarter relative to single adults). The added worker effect for those in workless households has thus diminished. This is because the penalty attached to looking after family or home has decreased and more of those in workless households are reported sick.

Information on children in the household is not available in 1979 so the third panel shows the impact of individual characteristics controlling for education, age and region. Comparison of the final column of table 8.7 shows that the net effect of these controls does not reduce the swing between the transition rates for those with working partners and those with non-working partners or no partner. The controls do, however, explain part of the lower transition rate in any one year. The key factor is education, which suggests more highly educated workers have a higher transition rate and are under-represented in workless households. This effect has not increased through the 1980s.[20] Thus individual characteristics can explain the probability of a transition in any one year (pseudo R^2 rises from 0.044 to 0.20) but not the growing differential in favour of those with an earner in the household.

8.5.3 Employment trends and the social security system

The third explanation is that labour market opportunities differ according to the employment status of other household members. The presence of an earner in the household changes the financial incentives facing the job seeker and can also act as a mechanism for identifying vacancies.[21] The presence of earned income will generally prevent receipt of means-tested benefits in almost all cases. Incentives to take certain forms of work are therefore likely to vary according to whether there is an income in the household, especially where weekly wages are low. The welfare state was designed around the premise that the family required one full-time job (implicitly for the man) to lift them off benefit and provide positive incentives to move into work. As the variation in hourly wages was low and part-time working rare, nearly all vacancies fulfilled these requirements. Low weekly incomes, above a minimum disregard, face punitive rates of benefit withdrawal and taxes levied. With more than one person dependent on the claim (e.g. spouses or children) this problem becomes more acute.

Atkinson (1993b) reports that a single person (no children) faces a replacement rate of 80 per cent at around 75 per cent of median weekly earnings for a couple with two children, at about 50 per cent for a couple without children and somewhere below 40 per cent for a single adult. Part-time work typically has half the hours of a full-time job (around 18 per week) and is also paid at well below median hourly rates of pay. Hence a part-time job offers around one third of median weekly earnings, where even single adults would face replacement rates of over 80 per cent and other groups substantially more.

Uncertain earnings may also be problematic. The process of assessing claims when moves into and out of work are made or earnings change is slow (Family Credit normally takes around 3 months). Hence the limited, uncertain nature of self-employment or temporary jobs may make transitions into these employment forms more risky or financially difficult when there is no second income in the household (Jenkins and Millar, 1989). Dilnot and Kell (1989) provide more details of the disincentive effects of the benefit system for women married to unemployed men, although a similar picture emerges for men trying to enter part-time work.

Table 8.8 outlines the changing pattern of employment in Britain. The proportion of full-time employees fell from 77 per cent to 67 per cent between 1979 and 1993. Self-employment grew strongly up to 1990 and then fell back a little, whilst part-time employment has grown slowly throughout the period.[22] Temporary working was not identified in the LFS until 1984, but did not grow until after 1990 and represents only around 5

Table 8.8 *Employment, by type of work, 1979–93*

	Share of total employment			
	1979	1985	1990	1993
Stock				
Full-time self-employment	0.064	0.094	0.114	0.103
Full-time employees	0.770	0.706	0.678	0.672
Part-time	0.167	0.199	0.209	0.226
Inflow[a]				
Full-time self-employment	0.032	0.059	0.060	0.077
Full-time employees	0.663	0.561	0.519	0.500
Part-time	0.304	0.380	0.421	0.425

Note:
[a] Flows calculated from annual inflows into respective states of individuals not in employment one year prior to sampling.

per cent of all employment. These trends do not appear to represent a major transformation of opportunities available to the non-employed. However, temporary, part-time jobs and self-employment all have shorter durations than full-time permanent jobs (9 months, 3 years and 7 years for full-time employees or self-employment).[23]

The quarterly LFS panel (for 1992–93) indicates that only 20 per cent of those entering a new job from non-employment made a move into full-time permanent employment as an employee. Nearly half of all engagements were part-time and the rest were full-time but temporary or in full-time self-employment (see Gregg and Wadsworth, 1994b). The bottom panel of table 8.8 gives the proportion of inflows into work since 1979. Reliance on annual transitions misses short-duration jobs, but the trend is clear. The effects of differential turnover and growth in untypical forms of employment have a magnified impact on new engagements relative to changes in the stock of these jobs. A 1 percentage point increase in the share of part-time employment in the stock implies a 2 percentage point rise in the share of new engagements. A 1 percentage point increase in the stock of self-employment implies a 2 point rise in the share of new engagements. For temporary jobs, this ratio rises to 1:4. Thus, the observed 6 percentage point rise in the stock of part-time employment and the 4 percentage point rise in the stock of self-employment imply that the

Table 8.9 *Employment, by type of work and household status, 1979–93*

	Share of total			
	1979	1985	1990	1993
Single adult				
Employee	0.609	0.452	0.470	0.429
Self-employed	0.041	0.052	0.066	0.057
Part-time	0.074	0.086	0.111	0.113
Non-employed	0.276	0.409	0.353	0.401
Two adult				
Two × full-time	0.242	0.221	0.268	0.260
Two × part-time	0.002	0.003	0.006	0.007
Two × self-employed	0.008	0.012	0.015	0.014
Two × non-employed	0.045	0.109	0.066	0.100
One full-time, one part-time	0.229	0.215	0.239	0.235
One full-time, one self-employed	0.023	0.036	0.057	0.053
One full-time, one non-employed	0.364	0.289	0.219	0.208
One self-employed, one part-time	0.025	0.040	0.056	0.051
One self-employed, one non-employed	0.040	0.050	0.053	0.039
One part-time, one non-employed	0.013	0.024	0.021	0.036

share of full-time permanent jobs in new engagements has fallen by 16 percentage points or by around 25 per cent since 1979.

Table 8.9 shows that reliance on part-time employment alone by households is rare. Only 11 per cent of single adults rely on part-time employment, yet part time work constitutes 25 per cent of all jobs. Similarly, only 4 per cent of two adult households rely on a single part-time worker. A part-time job is usually supported by a full-time income. However, the prevalence of part-time employment as the prime income source has risen over the period. Households with two full-time posts (employee or self-employment) also grew (from 27 per cent of all households in 1979 to 40 per cent in 1993). The decline of the single full-time job within households (one or two person) is marked.

Table 8.10 disaggregates the aggregate non-employment outflow rate by type of employment entered. In 1979, the bulk of transitions into work by single adults (75 per cent) and those with non-working partners (80 per cent) were into full-time employment, whereas most jobs taken by those with working partners were part-time (60 per cent). Since 1979, male entry rates into full-time work have fallen across all household groups, most strongly for those with non-working partners. Entry rates into full-time

Table 8.10 *Annual individual employment inflow differentials, by household status and type of employment entered, 1979–93*

Status one year ago	Total				Men				Women			
	1979	1985	1990	1993	1979	1985	1990	1993	1979	1985	1990	1993
All moves												
All	0.235	0.181	0.216	0.183	0.436	0.214	0.281	0.221	0.179	0.163	0.192	0.163
Single adult	0.176	0.102	0.128	0.111	0.198	0.102	0.155	0.138	0.646	0.102	0.116	0.098
Two adult, partner in work	0.158	0.185	0.229	0.235	0.398	0.282	0.340	0.328	0.142	0.171	0.215	0.213
Two adult, partner not in work	0.253	0.120	0.159	0.124	0.363	0.160	0.202	0.164	0.150	0.080	0.122	0.086
Full-time												
All	0.163	0.100	0.112	0.091	0.407	0.168	0.222	0.152	0.095	0.064	0.071	0.059
Single adult	0.129	0.057	0.062	0.054	0.172	0.075	0.117	0.090	0.104	0.040	0.039	0.037
Two adult, partner in work	0.061	0.059	0.073	0.090	0.355	0.212	0.250	0.227	0.041	0.036	0.050	0.057
Two adult, partner not in work	0.206	0.076	0.095	0.067	0.327	0.114	0.142	0.096	0.091	0.038	0.053	0.040
Part-time												
All	0.067	0.070	0.091	0.078	0.011	0.025	0.030	0.035	0.083	0.094	0.114	0.100
Single adult	0.042	0.037	0.056	0.048	0.017	0.018	0.020	0.027	0.057	0.057	0.071	0.058
Two adult, partner in work	0.094	0.117	0.116	0.131	0.013	0.030	0.045	0.043	0.097	0.130	0.158	0.152
Two adult, partner not in work	0.032	0.032	0.045	0.037	0.006	0.017	0.027	0.030	0.057	0.038	0.061	0.044

work for women were always lower and have also fallen somewhat since 1979, with the exception of women with working partners. Male transitions into part-time work are small relative to those into full-time work. There is also a higher likelihood of men with working partners taking part-time work. For women, there is a persistent differential in favour of those with working partners entering part-time work.

Accession rates into full-time work declined during the 1980/81 recession and *never* recovered during the 1980s' boom. Those groups most dependent on full-time work were thus likely to suffer lower transition rates back into work than other groups. This holds for men and women with non-working partners. Likewise, the increasing number of part-time opportunities suits households best placed to take such work. Transition rates into full-time jobs have fallen by around one third (or by 5 or 6 percentage points) since 1979. If this decline was evenly distributed across household groups, it would have reduced exit rates for those with non-working partners by 7 percentage points, for single adults by 4 points and for those with working partners by just 2 points. Similarly, transition rates into part-time work have risen by around one fifth in 1990 and 1993 relative to 1979. Such a rise would produce increases in the exit rates for single persons and those with non-working households of less than 1 percentage point, whereas for those with working partners it is nearly 2 percentage points. Changing employment composition can therefore explain around 5 to 6 points of the 21 point swing away from those in non-working households toward those with working partners. It can also explain 3 points of the 15 point swing away from single person households. Although there is a marked gender difference in the incidence of full- and part-time work, the changing pattern of access to part- and full-time employment within the male and female workforces is striking.

This explanation alone thus appears incomplete. The declining flow into full-time work is more pronounced for those with non-working partners. Further, among women the increase in the propensity to take part-time work is most marked for those with working partners. Men are increasingly taking part-time work, with a narrow differential in favour of those with working partners.

There may have been a decline in full-time engagements suitable for men with non-working partners because these men have lower skills. This is in effect a combination of two of the explanations outlined above. Table 8.11 repeats table 8.9 for transitions into each separate employment type. Introducing added worker controls raises the unexplained differential in the transition rates into full-time employment across household types, as before. However, this can explain none of the emerging gap over the 1980s. The other controls make a small difference to the differential across

Table 8.11 *Annual individual employment inflow differentials and transitions into each employment type, by household status, 1979–93*

Status one year ago	1979	1985	1990	1993	Δ1993–79
Full-time					
Unadjusted					
Two adult, one working v. one adult not working	−0.066	−0.011	0.024	0.043	0.109
Two adult, one working v. two adult none working	−0.091	−0.029	−0.018	0.023	0.114
With added worker and gender controls					
Two adult, one working v. one adult not working	0.017	0.073	0.092	0.123	0.106
Two adult, one working v. two adult none working	0.004	0.063	0.042	0.108	0.104
With all controls					
Two adult, one working v. one adult not working	−0.007	0.042	0.063	0.111	0.118
Two adult, one working v. two adult none working	−0.014	0.041	0.016	0.092	0.106
Part-time					
Unadjusted					
Two adult, one working v. one adult not working	0.066	0.100	0.104	0.106	0.040
Two adult, one working v. two adult none working	0.088	0.153	0.131	0.139	0.051
With added worker and gender controls					
Two adult, one working v. one adult not working	0.043	0.089	0.090	0.101	0.058
Two adult, one working v. two adult none working	0.043	0.118	0.107	0.114	0.071
With all controls					
Two adult, one working v. one adult not working	0.026	0.071	0.064	0.083	0.057
Two adult, one working v. two adult none working	0.034	0.108	0.083	0.099	0.065

Self-employed
Unadjusted

Two adult, one working v. one adult not working	-0.003	0.001	0.002	0.006	0.009
Two adult, one working v. two adult none working	-0.007	-0.005	-0.004	-0.003	0.004
With added worker and gender controls					
Two adult, one working v. one adult not working	0.002	0.012	0.004	0.012	0.010
Two adult, one working v. one adult not working	0.003	0.003	0.000	0.006	0.003
With all controls					
Two adult, one woring v. one adult not working	0.001	0.007	0.006	0.009	0.008
Two adult, one working v. two adult none working	0.002	0.000	0.000	0.003	0.001

household types but, as before, not to its growth over the period. The irrelevance of the added worker controls suggests that the effect observed in table 8.10 represents the switch in availability from full-time to part-time work. The decline in the penalty attached to 'looking after the home' appears to be related to the relative abundance of part-time work in later years. The added worker controls increase the swing toward those in households with a working member. Detailed analysis reveals this is due to the growing importance of jobs with very low hours (below 20 per week). Such jobs have an even higher differential in favour of those with working partners.

The substantial shift toward part-time work explains around one quarter of the relative deterioration of transition rates into work of those with no working household member. The bulk of the emerging differential is occurring *within* full or part-time working and therefore, for the moment, remains unexplained.

8.6 Conclusions and future implications

UK employment moved cyclically in the 1980s and 1990s, but benefit dependency grew secularly. This chapter has identified a profound change in the distribution of work across households. The number of households without a working member rose sharply in the recession of the early 1980s but nearly all the subsequent recovery in employment occurred in households with one person already in work, leaving on balance many more multi-income households and twice as many workless households. By 1993, 14 per cent of individuals were resident in households with no work. Britain has become characterised by work-rich and work-poor families. This explains why individual (un)employment can be stable when family-based benefit claims are rising and illuminates one of the principal reasons for the observed widening in household income inequality in Britain.

Only around one sixth of this development can be attributed to changes in family composition toward more single adult households. This is largely attributable to generational effects of household formation and more frequent marriage and family break-up. The key factor behind the growth of the work-poor household is that the exit rate from non-employment into work fell substantially for households without earned income after 1979 and never recovered. This decline implies much longer durations without earned income. The similar swing for men and women, with or without partners, suggests that explanations relying on jobless men stopping their wives from working or that couples are happier being unemployed together are inappropriate.

Explanations which centre on common characteristics of household members associated with lower transition rates and on changing composition of employment toward more part-time jobs seem to offer more fruitful avenues for exploration. However, whilst individual characteristics can explain some of the observed difference in transition rates across household types at any one time they cannot explain the emerging household gap over the last 15 years. Full-time engagements are disproportionately taken by those in workless families and part-time by those with a working member. The collapse in the number of full-time and the rise in part-time engagements explains around one quarter of the relative deterioration in the position of workless families.

Even after allowing for this, men and women in workless families have increasingly been losing out in the fight for the full- or part-time opportunities available. It is probable that unobserved characteristics of the jobs, the individuals involved or changes in the benefit system can explain the remaining elements but it is, as yet, unclear in what proportions.

The differences in transition rates according to the presence of a working household member suggest that any employment growth that occurs during the current recovery will have a muted impact on the numbers of work-poor households and thus on dependency on benefits and household income inequality. This is because new jobs will be disproportionately taken by people in households where someone is already in work. Furthermore, this effect is likely to be stronger than during the 1980s recovery, as the differential in favour of those with working partners has substantially increased.

Notes

LFS data used with permission of OPCS and made available by the Office of Population Censuses and Surveys through the ESRC Data Archive at the University of Essex, has been used by permission of the Controller of Her Majesty's Stationery Office. The authors would like to thank the generous support of the Joseph Rowntree Foundation. The usual disclaimers apply.
1. See DSS (1993b).
2. Age 60 is the upper limit for information relating to educational qualifications in the early years of the LFS. If households contain any individual older than 60 they are also dropped from our analysis. This cut-off also reduces the incidence of early retirement (amongst men) which may otherwise obscure the analysis of access to work. Those in full-time education are also excluded.
3. Since two or more jobless individuals may be resident in the same household, the household non-employment rate is given by N_i*1/n_i where N_i is the non-employment rate for individuals resident in household type i and n_i is the number of occupants in household type i. The chapter concentrates on the

individual measure N_i, since we are concerned with differences in individual transition rates across household types.

4. Some benefits, of course, do not preclude there being another working person in a household, e.g. Unemployment Benefit and non-means-tested Invalidity and Sickness benefits.

5. Youths living at their parents' home are not included as single households. The LFS does identify them as separate family units. Thus single adult households are no younger than the other household types. The mean ages of single, two and three+ adult households in 1993 were 39, 38 and 37 respectively.

6. Using

$$\Delta N = \sum_j (\Delta s_j)\, n_{jt0} + \sum_j (\Delta n_j)\, s_{jt0} - \sum_j \Delta s_j\, n_{ij}$$

where n_{jt0} and s_{jt0} are the base year non-employment rates and shares respectively. The first term represents the between-group variation, the change in non-employment attributable to changes in the proportion of the various household size groups in the population, whilst the second term captures the within-group variation, changes in non-employment occurring within each sub-group. The third term is an interaction of these two effects.

7. These numbers are arrived at by dividing the percentage of women only workers by the percentage of two adult households in table 8.1.

8. These findings are consistent with earlier single cross-section studies. Martin and Roberts (1984), for example, report figures of 62 per cent (employed) and 33 per cent (non-employed) from the 1982 Women and Employment Survey.

9. Schmitt and Wadsworth (1993) demonstrate this for unemployment, non-employment and economic inactivity.

10. Students are excluded from the sample.

11. If L_t is the distribution of labour force states at time t, then

$$L_t = P * L_{t-1}$$

where P is a matrix of transition probabilities which determine the likelihood of moving from one part of the distribution to another. Since

$$L_{t+j} = (P * P *... P) * L_t = P_j L_t$$

then as $j \to \infty$ the long-run distribution of labour force states can be determined. This requires a constant transition matrix P which is unlikely, but the difference between 1979 and the three later periods shown is stark and the differing long-run implications are therefore of interest. The calculations exclude households where the economic state one year ago is unobserved. This produces slight adjustments to the numbers in table 8.1.

12. This implies that in 1979 a two adult household has typically had no work for 18 months. By 1985 (or 1993), this had risen to around 54 months. These annual estimates may omit multiple transitions and hence the estimated durations will be an upper bound on the true figures. See Boskin and Nold (1975) for an analysis of benefit dependency and turnover in the United States using longitudinal data.

13. Most co-occupants are married partners, but other arrangements for two adults being in the same household are not excluded.
14. These predictions do not always carry over to a household labour supply model, see Ashworth and Ulph (1981). Lundberg (1985) has evidence of a small added worker effect for the United States.
15. See Ashworth and Ulph (1981) for a household labour supply study in which a rise in male hours of work is found to induce a rise in female labour supply because leisure is an inferior good.
16. The first wave of the British Household Panel survey sampled 2635 couples of working age of which 1547 were both in work, 189 had women only workers, 559 men only and 340 no work at all.

	Mean distress level		
	Total	Men	Women
Both work	2.86	1.26	1.59
Men only	3.14	1.15	1.99
Women only	4.76	3.02	1.75
No work	4.24	2.21	2.03

17. Converted into predicted jobless durations, these falls for single men look dramatic relative to those for men with working partners.
18. See Schmitt and Wadsworth (1993).
19. Any vocational qualifications are included in this latter group.
20. The presence of children reduces the transition rate of women but does not explain differential transition rates across households if included in the later years.
21. Friends and relatives are a frequent source of information in job search and often one of the most successful, see Gregg and Wadsworth (1994b).
22. Part-time self-employment is included as part-time working in table 8.8, as we feel that part-time status is crucial for income determination.
23. These estimates are derived from the four waves of the quarterly panel of the LFS in 1992 and are based on the reciprocal of the average exit rate from employment.

9 Self-employment and the distribution of income

Nigel Meager, Gill Court and Janet Moralee

9.1 Introduction

Self-employment in the United Kingdom grew extremely rapidly during the 1980s, in comparison both with historical experience, and with what was happening in other industrialised economies.[1] Self-employment almost doubled over the period 1979–89, such that by the end of this period one in eight of those in work was self-employed. There is no simple or single explanation for this development, and the extreme heterogeneity of the self-employed as a group makes it unlikely that one model or theoretical framework can account for aggregate trends in self-employment.[2] The definitions of self-employment are various, but most encompass a wide spectrum, from independent 'entrepreneurs' and traditional small business owner-proprietors at one extreme, to relatively unskilled construction and service sector workers at the other. The latter are often highly dependent on large organisations for their livelihoods, and their 'self-employment', in many cases, differs from dependent or wage employment in name only.

Recent research, drawing on the European Labour Force Surveys (Meager, 1993) shows that UK self-employment has not only grown rapidly, but has become highly 'dynamic', with higher rates of inflow and outflow than in most other European countries. This implies that for a given stock of self-employment in the United Kingdom, a larger proportion of the working population experiences spells of self-employment during their working lives than is the case in other countries. Experience of self-employment may, therefore, have become even more widespread within the working population than the total self-employment figures themselves suggest.

9.2 Impact on income levels and distribution

This rapid growth in self-employment, whatever its underlying causes, raises a number of questions for social and economic welfare in general, and for income levels, poverty and the social security system in particular (see also Brown, 1992). The aim of the research reported in this chapter is to address some of these questions through an extensive review of existing research evidence on the incomes of the self-employed, and through new secondary analysis of a number of existing datasets. In this chapter we present a brief overview of some of the study's findings.

At its simplest, the following issues were addressed in the research:

- What are the likely implications for income levels and distribution of having (a lot) more self-employed in the United Kingdom's working population? If the levels and distribution of income of the self-employed differ from those of employees, then, *ceteris paribus*, a growing share of self-employment will change the distribution of earned income.
- If, as well as increasing in size, the composition of self-employment has been changing, what are the likely implications of these changes for income levels and distribution? If the 'new' self-employed differ from their predecessors in terms of their personal characteristics or the types of self-employed activities they undertake, then again we can expect some changes in the distribution of earned income.
- What effect do spells of self-employment during an individual's working life have on income prospects in later life (the latter being influenced not only by earnings levels *per se*, but also by savings propensities, pensions and social benefit entitlements)?

Existing evidence on the recent trends in, and the changing composition of, UK self-employment (reviewed and augmented in Meager *et al.*, 1994), provides important background information on the above issues, and suggests a number of hypotheses concerning the relationship between self-employment trends and the distribution of income, which were explored in the research. Evidence from the Labour Force Survey (LFS) (and its counterparts in other European countries) is particularly relevant, and is worth summarising briefly.

In particular, the evidence shows that not only has UK self-employment been growing faster than elsewhere, and (because of high rates of inflow and outflow) affecting a larger share of the working population than in many other EU countries, but there have also been some important changes in the composition of the self-employed. New entrants to self-employment in the 1980s were more likely than the existing self-employed to be young, and to be female. The rate of entry to self-employment from unemployment was also high (by international standards), and grew strongly during the 1980s. Previous research (see, for example, Burrows, 1991) suggests that the self-employed have traditionally been disproportionately drawn from families with traditions of self-employment. In so far as this pattern is breaking down, with different types of people entering self-employment than previously, a key question is whether such new entrants have the attitudes, experience and socialisation relevant to success in self-employment, to the same extent as their predecessors. This may affect both earnings potential while self-employed and the likelihood of making adequate provision for old age. More generally, there is a further important question concerning the extent to which some of these 'newer' categories of self-employed (women, younger people, the ex-unemployed) are likely to possess the human and financial capital associated with 'success' and high earnings potential in self-employment.

Further, it is possible that the changing personal characteristics of the 'new' self-employed may be reinforced in their effects by the characteristics of the activities into which many of them enter. In particular, growing self-employment in a number of relatively low value added service sector activities (some personal and business services), which tend to have low barriers to entry but crowded markets and low survival rates, may also have important implications for the earnings potential of many of the new self-employed.

Many of these shifts in the profile of the self-employed during the 1980s (in terms of personal characteristics and business activities) are most clearly embodied[3] among groups such as participants in the government Enterprise Allowance Scheme (EAS),[4] which subsidised the unemployed to enter self-employment (in its peak year, 1987–88, the EAS had over 100,000 participants). Crucially for the present discussion, however, a key finding of survey evaluations of EAS participants (Owens, 1989) is the extremely low earnings levels of a high proportion of this group of self-employed.

There is, therefore, clear evidence of growing self-employment in the 1980s having been associated with important changes in the composition of self-employment. Given the nature of these changes, and the types of activities and individuals increasingly involved, there are good reasons to believe that these changes were not neutral in their effects on income levels and distribution. There is a strong *prima facie* case to suggest that some of these changes may have contributed to an expansion of that part of the self-employed population which is found towards the lower end of the distribution of earned incomes. The core of the study reported here, therefore, was to examine the evidence available from previous research on the income levels of the self-employed, and to carry out new analysis of a number of existing data sources.

9.3 The incomes of the self-employed: previous evidence

Evidence on the incomes of the self-employed in the United Kingdom from previous research has not been extensive, and has been bedevilled by the problem of under-reporting. There is, nevertheless a range of recent studies[5] which throw light on the income levels of the self-employed, including work conducted as part of the Rowntree Income and Wealth Programme. These studies, reviewed in Meager *et al.* (1994), use a variety of methods and definitions, are all subject to the problem of under-reporting of self-employment incomes, and reveal at best a partial picture. There are, nevertheless, some striking consistencies between their findings. Especially notable are the following:

• Without exception, the studies show greater income dispersion among the self-employed than among comparable groups of employees
• In particular, distributions of self-employed incomes display larger 'tails' than do employee distributions – that is, the self-employed contain larger proportions not only of very high earners, but also of very low earners than do their employee counterparts.

As far as changes over time are concerned, the evidence is limited, but recent research (see Jenkins, 1994; Goodman and Webb, 1994), suggests not only that the self-employed income distribution is more dispersed than the employee distribution, but also that this dispersion increased strongly during the 1980s. There is also a suggestion (consistent with the changing composition of self-employment shown by the LFS, discussed above) that this increase in inequality arose more from changes at the bottom of the distribution among the 'poor' self-employed than at the top.

The previous research, therefore, is consistent with the hypothesis that, on the basis of the static income distributions, an increase in the proportion of the workforce self-employed, with no change in its composition, would tend to increase the inequality of the overall earned income distribution, with higher proportions of very high and very low earners. Given that the composition of the self-employed has also been changing in important ways, however, the evidence is also consistent with the hypothesis that this changing composition has further added to the inequality of the self-employed income distribution, particularly through an increase in the group of relatively poor self-employed.

9.4 New evidence from the British Household Panel Survey

In this section we present some findings[6] on self-employed and employee incomes from a new data source, the first wave of the British Household Panel Survey (BHPS). This is an annual household panel survey of 10,000 individuals, drawn from a nationally representative sample of households in Great Britain. The first wave was conducted in Autumn 1991. The questionnaire[7] included detailed information on individual and household finances, including both labour and non-labour incomes (for reasons of space, we concentrate here on an analysis of labour incomes; Meager *et al.*, 1994, present detailed findings from the BHPS on the other sources of income of the self-employed).

The BHPS has the advantage of providing a sample of self-employed whose characteristics are broadly representative of national patterns (as revealed, for example, in the LFS), and there are reasons to suggest that under-reporting of self-employed incomes may be less of an problem in the BHPS than in surveys with a more obvious link to government activity such as the Inland Revenue's Survey of Personal Incomes, or the General Household and Family Expenditure Surveys (GHS and FES) which have been widely used to examine self-employment incomes in the past. There is, nevertheless, a relatively high level of missing data on self-employed incomes in the BHPS, but this appears to be mainly the result of lack of information rather than deliberate withholding of the information (see Meager *et al.*, 1994, for more detailed discussion). We do, however (see below), test the sensitivity of some of our findings to the possibility of under-reporting.

9.4.1 Labour incomes of the self-employed and employees

The trend toward rising self-employment means that self-employed incomes have an increasing influence on overall income distribution in the United Kingdom. We noted above evidence from previous studies of the greater dispersion of incomes among the self-employed and rising inequality within the self-employed income distribution. In this section we take up this theme and look in some detail at how the (labour) incomes of the self-employed differ from those of their employee counterparts (note that throughout the chapter we are concerned with individual labour incomes, and not with the family/household incomes which are analysed in some of the other chapters in this volume – see, for example, Cowell, Jenkins and Litchfield in chapter 3).

We compare self-employed and employee incomes using two approaches. First, we look at the labour income distribution of the self-employed and compare it with that of employees. This highlights differences between the two groups and provides some indication of how a growing share of self-employment in total employment will affect overall labour income distribution.

The second approach examines the distribution of overall labour income (i.e. employees and the self-employed combined) and locates the self-employed within it. Here we are especially interested in the characteristics of individuals in the tails of the income distribution, and whether they are self-employed or employees.

9.4.2 Labour incomes: the self-employed and employees compared

Table 9.1 provides information on the monthly net labour income of the self-employed and employees, along with their respective income distributions. The first point to note is that both mean and median self-employed labour incomes are slightly higher than those of their employed counterparts. On average, the self-employed as a group are better off than employees.

The shape of the two distributions is also different. Self-employed incomes are more dispersed, with the gap between the bottom 10 per cent and top 10 per cent being higher than for employees. This is clearly illustrated by the ratio of labour income at the 90th percentile to that at the 10th percentile. For employees, the ratio is 6.56, but the ratio almost doubles among the self-employed, with labour income at the 90th percentile rising to 12.55 times that at the 10th percentile.

The labour income distribution of employees and the self-employed is shown in full in figure 9.1. It clearly demonstrates the more dispersed range of incomes among the self-employed, with a higher proportion falling into the upper and lower ranges of the distribution than is the case for employees.

The results reinforce the previous research findings, namely that the distribution of earned income is more dispersed than is the case for employees. A second aspect of table 9.1 concerns the level of labour income in different parts of the two distributions (self-employed and employees). It shows that the level of labour income among the self-employed is lower than for employees at the bottom end of the distribution (the lowest decile and lowest quartile groups) but higher towards the top. The difference is especially marked in the decile groups. In the lowest decile group the ratio of self-employed to employee labour income is 0.70 (i.e. self-employed incomes are almost a third lower than those of employees). By contrast, in the highest decile group, the ratio of self-employed to employee incomes is 1.33 (i.e. self-employed incomes are a third higher than those of employees).

Gender These overall patterns disguise very different situations for men and women (figures 9.2 and 9.3).[8] Among self-employed men, relatively few individuals are on very low incomes (less than £100 net a month). For women, on the other hand, a substantial proportion of the total (over a fifth) earn less than £100 a month and the shape of the distribution is different; it curves downwards from the lowest income range (£0–100) whereas that for men rises (with income) to a peak before falling off in a long 'tail' toward the upper end of the distribution.[9] The difference between the two distributions is indicated by the difference in the 90/10

Table 9.1 *Usual monthly net labour income of employees and the self-employed, by gender, £*

	Mean	Standard deviation	Median	Lowest decile	Lowest quartile	Highest quartile	Highest decile	90:10 ratio	No. cases
Total	728.3	742.6	634.0	186.0	390.0	931.0	1297.4	6.98	5007
Employees	714.7	725.9	632.0	190.7	398.0	921.6	1250.0	6.56	4556
Self-employed	869.1	885.5	652.0	132.8	312.1	1093.9	1666.3	12.55	441
Self-employed: employee ratio	1.22	—	1.03	0.70	0.78	1.19	1.33	—	—
Men	917.3	908.2	804.0	380.7	589.0	1100.0	1474.8	3.87	2698
Employees	906.6	906.8	810.0	422.5	600.0	1100.0	1440.5	3.41	2358
Self-employed	991.2	915.5	744.0	243.0	486.7	1214.4	1871.3	7.70	340
Self-employed: employee ratio	1.09	—	0.92	0.58	0.81	1.10	1.30	—	—
Women	507.4	376.4	442.0	138.0	251.0	660.0	944.0	6.84	2309
Employees	509.6	361.0	450.0	144.0	263.7	666.3	941.3	6.54	2208
Self-employed	459.6	624.3	243.0	42.6	123.7	505.9	1125.1	26.41	101
Self-employed: employee ratio	0.90	—	0.54	0.30	0.47	0.76	1.20	—	—

Source: BHPS 1991 (weighted data).

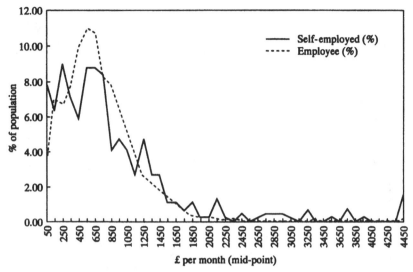

Figure 9.1 Monthly net labour income of employees and the self-employed: all

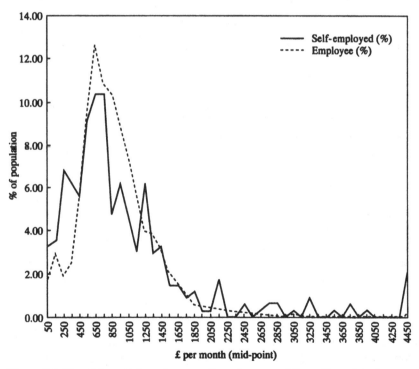

Figure 9.2 Monthly net labour income of employees and the self-employed: men

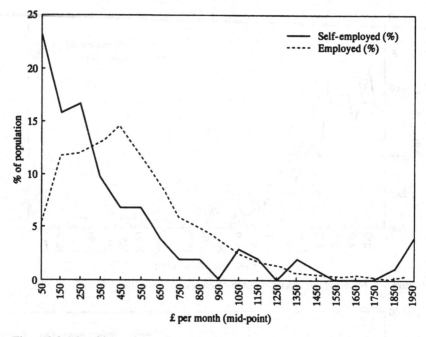

Figure 9.3 Monthly net labour income of employees and the self-employed: women

ratios; the ratio for self-employed men is 7.7, considerably lower than that for women (26.4). Part of the reason for this particularly dispersed pattern among women is that there is a group of self-employed women on very low incomes; small sample sizes may affect the results here, but even at the lowest quartile women's net labour income is £123.70 a month compared to £486.70 for men.

Self-employed men and women also display different income patterns in relation to their employed counterparts. Among men, self-employed mean labour income is higher than for employees but median income is lower. This differs from the pattern for women, amongst whom both median and mean self-employed incomes are lower than those of employees. This suggests that while there is a substantial group of self-employed men with high incomes relative to those of employees, this is less true for women.

Hourly net labour income The reason for the different patterns amongst self-employed men and women is clearly related to the greater propensity for women to work part-time. Overall, 42 per cent of self-employed women work part-time, compared with just 10 per cent of men.

As might be expected, however, even once this difference has been taken into account men's earnings remain higher than those of women: the median net hourly labour income for self-employed men is £3.91, compared to £2.89 for women (table 9.2).

The pattern for self-employed women also differs from that of women employees. This cannot be explained by different propensities to work part-time between the two groups, which are not statistically significant,[10] and even once these differences have been taken into account, self-employed women have lower median hourly net earnings than women employees (£2.89 and £3.35 respectively).

Table 9.2 also shows the effect on other points in the income distribution of taking hours worked into account. For all the self-employed relative to employees, the effect is to increase the difference between the two groups in the extremes of the distribution: the lowest decile of self-employed hourly labour income is about half that of the employee equivalent, whereas for monthly labour income it is a third less. This indicates that there is a group of the self-employed on very low incomes which cannot be explained by the number of hours they work.

In other respects, however, the hourly earnings distribution is similar to that for monthly earnings: self-employed incomes are lower at the bottom end of the distribution (the lowest decile and quartile groups) than the employee equivalent, and higher at the top end of the distribution (the highest decile and quartile groups). In addition, while the 90/10 ratios of the two groups both decline relative to those in the monthly distribution, the self-employed 90/10 ratio remains higher than that for employees.

Amongst men, the net hourly labour income distribution is very similar to its monthly counterpart. The main difference is that for the self-employed the 90/10 ratio increases to 9.87 (compared with 7.70 in the monthly distribution), indicating that hourly incomes are more dispersed than monthly incomes. Amongst women, taking hours worked into account has little effect on the position of the self-employed relative to employees at the lower part of their respective distributions; the main changes take place towards the upper end of the distributions. Self-employed hourly incomes at both the highest quartile and decile are higher than the equivalent figures for employees, whereas in the monthly distribution self-employed incomes are greater only in the highest decile group. In addition, taking the number of hours worked into account reduces the dispersion among both the self-employed and employees, although a substantial difference remains: the 90/10 ratios are 13.27 and 2.73 respectively (compared with 26.41 and 6.54 respectively for monthly earnings).

These results show that taking the number of hours worked into account reduces the level of dispersion, as measured by the 90/10 ratio, in both the

Table 9.2 *Usual hourly net labour income of employees and the self-employed, by gender, £*

	Mean	Standard deviation	Median	Lowest decile	Lowest quartile	Highest quartile	Highest decile	90:10 ratio	No. cases
Total									
Employees	4.30	3.55	3.75	2.25	2.87	5.08	6.75	3.00	4459
Self-employed	5.14	5.43	3.75	1.14	2.01	5.82	11.38	9.97	433
Self-employed: employee ratio	1.20	—	1.00	0.51	0.70	1.15	1.69	—	—
Men									
Employees	4.83	4.56	4.18	2.40	3.16	5.74	7.56	3.15	2296
Self-employed	5.42	5.68	3.91	1.22	2.36	6.09	12.08	9.87	335
Self-employed: employee ratio	1.12	—	0.94	0.51	0.75	1.06	1.60	—	—
Women									
Employees	3.74	1.81	3.35	2.12	2.70	4.41	5.79	2.73	2163
Self-employed	4.18	4.36	2.89	0.64	1.50	5.29	8.49	13.27	98
Self-employed: employee ratio	1.12	—	0.86	0.30	0.56	1.20	1.47	—	—

Source: BHPS 1991 (weighted data).

Table 9.3 *Gini coefficients, by employment status and gender*

	Employee	Self-employed
All	0.35	0.47
Men	0.29	0.42
Women	0.39	0.57

Source: BHPS 1991 (weighted data).

self-employed and employee income distributions (the only exception being self-employed men), but it does not affect the broad patterns identified in the analysis of monthly incomes. Income dispersion among the self-employed remains higher than is the case for employees, and self-employed incomes at the bottom part of the distribution are lower, and those towards the top higher, than the equivalents for employees. The analysis also confirms that there is a group of self-employed on very low incomes.

Summary inequality measure The above analysis shows that the self-employed have a more unequal distribution of labour income than is the case among employees. This is confirmed by a summary measure of inequality, the Gini coefficient. Like all such measures, it suffers from a number of limitations (Cowell, 1995). In particular, it gives greater weight to differences at the middle of the income distribution than at the tails. In the present context, however, this has the advantage that we are particularly interested in the tails of the distribution and to use the Gini coefficient (which under-weights these parts of the distribution in comparisons), is therefore to exercise caution in drawing any conclusions about whether the self-employment distributions exhibit greater inequality than employee ones.

Table 9.3 presents the Gini coefficients for employees and the self-employed and for these two groups by gender. It shows that for men, women, and both sexes together the self-employed labour income distribution is more unequal than the employee equivalent. Income inequality among women generally is higher than that for men, but inequality among self-employed women is particularly marked.

9.4.3 *Labour incomes: the self-employed in the overall labour income distribution*

The data discussed so far show that employee and self-employed income distributions differ in key respects, and this will clearly affect the relative location of the two groups within the overall labour income distribution. The following analysis examines the composition of various parts of the overall labour income distribution (i.e. the self-employed and employees combined) in terms of the job characteristics of those within them. In this way, we can locate the self-employed within this overall distribution.

We focus on the 'tails' of the income distribution and the characteristics of those in the 'poorer' and 'richer' groups. The 'poor' are defined using two alternative definitions: those with incomes in the lowest decile or lowest quartile groups of the *whole sample* labour income distribution (less than £186 and £390 net per month respectively). The 'rich' are defined in a similar way: those with incomes in the highest decile or highest quartile groups (above £931 and £1297.40 net per month).

Table 9.4 shows that relative to all those providing income data, the self-employed are over-represented in the tails of the distribution, especially the decile groups. They account for 8.8 per cent of all individuals in the distribution but for 12.2 per cent of those in the lowest and 15.2 per cent in the highest decile group. This is consistent with the comparison of employee and self-employed income distributions above. It also has important implications for the overall labour income distribution: if self-employment accounts for an increasing share of all those in employment and is characterised by a more dispersed income distribution, the impact of increasing self-employment will be to increase overall labour income inequality.

This shows that the self-employed are more likely to be at the extremes of the overall income distribution than is the case for employees. This may not, of course, be due their self-employed status *per se*, but could reflect other personal characteristics which distinguish them from employees. In order to examine in more detail the role of self-employed status itself in determining location within the overall labour income distribution we have sought to hold key factors constant. Of prime importance are gender, full-time or part-time status, and type of activity.

Gender One of the main determinants of labour income levels is gender: while women account for 46 per cent of those with labour incomes they represent 75 per cent of those in the bottom and just 13 per cent of those in the top decile groups. Gender is, therefore, evidently one of the factors we need to hold constant when assessing the evidence for a distinct self-employment effect explaining the location of the self-employed within the overall labour income distribution. In fact, since women have generally lower incomes than men and their representation among the self-employed is lower than for employees, we would expect the self-employed to have higher incomes than their employee counterparts. That this is not case is

Table 9.4 *Composition, per cent, of labour income distribution tails, by employment status*

% of employees/self-employed in highest/lowest decile and quartile groups of distribution of usual net monthly labour income (whole sample)

	Lowest decile group (<£186.00)	Lowest quartile group (<£390.00)	Highest quartile group (>£931.00)	Highest decile group (>£1297.40)	Whole sample
Employees	87.8	89.4	89.3	84.8	91.2
Self-employed	12.2	10.6	10.7	15.2	8.8
N (=100%)	507	1255	1254	500	5007

Source: BHPS 1991 (weighted data).

itself a strong indication that gender composition alone does not account for differences in incomes between employees and the self-employed. The data in tables 9.5 and 9.6 repeat the analysis of table 9.4 above, separately for men and women. Looking at men first, table 9.5 shows that self-employed men are over-represented in both the lowest and highest decile groups and in the lowest quartile group. This indicates that the position of the self-employed in the overall labour income distribution cannot simply be attributed to the group's gender composition. Even though, relative to women, men are under-represented at the lower end of the overall income distribution, a higher proportion of self-employed men fall into the lowest decile and quartile groups than would be expected given their share of the whole sample.

Among women (table 9.6) a clear pattern also emerges, with self-employed women accounting for a higher proportion of those in the extremes of the distribution, the lowest and highest decile groups, than in both the whole sample and the quartile groups. Thus, while women as a group are over-represented at the lower end of the labour income distribution, self-employed women are particularly likely to be among both the better-off and the less well-off.

Full-time and part-time work   The number of hours an individual works is also clearly related to their labour income. A second dimension of the analysis was, therefore, to look at the proportion of employees and self-employed within the groups of full-time and part-time workers separately (table 9.7). Relative to their share of all full-time work, the full-time self-employed are over-represented at the lower part of the overall labour income distribution, accounting for 8.8 per cent of all full-time workers providing information on incomes, but for 39 per cent of those in the bottom decile group. This is consistent with Goodman and Webb's (1994) results showing that the full-time self-employed accounted for a growing share of those in the bottom income decile group in the 1980s. For part-time workers the opposite is the case and the self-employed are over-represented at the upper end of the income distribution relative to their overall share of part-time work. This may reflect the high earning capacity of some sections of the self-employed, for example, those engaged in consultancy work, who are able to combine good incomes with part-time hours.

Industry   A third aspect of self-employment which bears on an individual's earning propensity is the sector or activity in which that person is self-employed. Table 9.8 looks at the sectoral composition of the self-employed in the tails of the overall labour income distribution in

Table 9.5 Composition, per cent, of labour income distribution tails, by employment status: men

% in highest/lowest decile and quartile groups of distribution of usual net monthly income (whole sample)

	Lowest decile group (<£186.00)	Lowest quartile group (<£390.00)	Highest quartile group (>£931.00)	Highest decile group (>£1297.40)	Whole sample
Employees	82.0	75.7	88.0	84.3	87.4
Self-employed	18.0	24.3	12.0	15.7	12.6
N (=100%)	128	277	1012	438	2698

Source: BHPS 1991 (weighted data).

Table 9.6 *Composition, per cent, of labour income distribution tails, by employment status: women*

% in highest/lowest decile and quartile groups of distribution of usual net monthly labour income (whole sample)

	Lowest decile group (<£186.00)	Lowest quartile group (<£390.00)	Highest quartile group (>£931.00)	Highest decile group (>£1297.40)	Whole sample
Employees	89.8	93.9	94.8	87.9	95.6
Self-employed	10.2	6.7	5.2	12.1	4.4
N (=100%)	379	979	242	62	2309

Source: BHPS 1991 (weighted data).

Table 9.7 *Composition of the labour income distribution, by full-time and part-time work, net monthly earnings, £*

% of full-time and part-time workers and employees and self-employed in highest/lowest decile and quartile groups of the usual net monthly labour income distribution (whole sample)

	Lowest decile group (<£186.00)	Lowest quartile group (<£390.00)	Highest quartile group (>£931.00)	Highest decile group (>£1297.40)	Whole sample
Full-time	12.8	28.6	97.2	96.4	78.4
Part-time	87.2	71.4	2.8	3.6	21.6
N (=100%)	501	1235	1241	490	4955
Full-time					
employees	61.3	79.7	90.2	85.6	91.2
Self-employed	38.7	20.3	9.8	14.4	8.8
N (=100%)	64	353	1207	472	3883
Part-time					
employees	91.5	93.4	62.2	72.1	91.5
Self-employed	8.5	6.6	37.8	27.9	8.5
N (=100%)	437	882	34	18	1072

Source: BHPS 1991 (weighted data).

Table 9.8 *Sectoral composition, per cent, of self-employed in labour income distribution tails*

% of self-employed in highest/lowest decile and quartile groups of distribution of usual net monthly income (whole sample), by sector

	Lowest decile group (<£186.00)	Lowest quartile group (<£390.00)	Highest quartile group (>£931.00)	Highest decile group (>£1297.40)	Whole sample of self-employed
Agriculture, etc. (0)	8.0	7.8	5.5	1.1	6.7
Energy and water supply (1)	0.0	0.0	2.5	1.5	0.7
Chemicals, minerals, etc. (2)	2.8	3.7	0.7	0.0	1.8
Metal goods, engineering, vehicles (3)	3.5	3.1	5.5	6.5	4.0
Other manufacturing (4)	7.5	4.8	5.0	5.9	6.1
Construction (5)	5.0	9.5	22.4	16.7	20.2
Distribution, hotels, catering, etc. (6)	16.7	18.7	14.9	18.3	21.2
Transport and communication (7)	1.6	3.9	2.3	2.4	4.0
Banking, finance, business services (8)	6.5	8.5	32.1	35.9	15.1
Other services (9)	48.4	40.0	9.2	11.7	20.1
N (=100%)	61	132	131	75	784

Source: BHPS 1991 (weighted data).

comparison with all the self-employed. It shows that agriculture, other manufacturing and, in particular, 'other services' are the main sectors with an over-representation of the poorer self-employed relative to their share of all self-employment. At the other end of the scale is the banking, finance and business services sector, which is notably over-represented among the better-off. The 'other services' sector (which includes various household and personal services, including hairdressing and cleaning services) grew rapidly in the 1980s and its over-representation among the poor suggests that expansion of self-employment within it will tend to increase the number of poorer self-employed. The other category to grow rapidly in the past decade has been banking, finance and business services. Our results indicate that expansion here will have the opposite effect to that of 'other services' growth, contributing to higher incomes among the self-employed.

Multivariate analysis This descriptive analysis has begun to identify the extent to which self-employment *per se* is a factor in influencing an individual's location in the overall labour income distribution. It can, however, tell us only about the actual self-employment effect for particular categories of people – men and women, full-time and part-time workers, etc. – and does not allow the interaction between self-employment and a range of other factors to be analysed. To assess the effect of being self-employed *per se* on an individual's likelihood of being in the bottom and top decile groups of the overall labour income distribution requires multivariate analysis.

Taking low incomes first, we defined a dependent variable which takes the value one if an individual falls into the lowest decile group of the overall income distribution, and zero otherwise. Table 9.9 estimates a statistical model using logistical regression ('logit' techniques) and assesses the effect of changing one of the independent variables (e.g. shifting from self-employment to employee status) on the *odds* of an individual's being in the lowest decile group of the income distribution.[11] In the model, one category of each of the independent variables (the first category in each case) is chosen as the reference category. Thus, in the case of age, the reference category is the 16–24 age group, in the case of gender it is men, in the case of employment status it is employees, etc. The coefficient for this reference category is set to 1.00, and the coefficients for the other values of the variable are interpreted relative to this reference category. A coefficient of greater than 1.00 means that the value of the variable in question increases the odds of being in the low income group compared with the reference category; a coefficient of less than 1.00 means that the odds are reduced compared with the reference category.

Table 9.9 *Model 1: logit estimates of odds of being in lowest labour income decile group*

Dependent variable: odds of individual being in lowest decile group of overall labour income distribution

Independent variable	Coefficient: Exp (B)	Significance
Sex		
Male	(1.00)	—
Female	1.67	0.004[a]
Employment status		
Employee	(1.00)	—
Self-employed	3.66	0.000[a]
Age		
16–24	1.00	—
25–34	0.19	0.000[a]
35–44	0.17	0.000[a]
45–54	0.13	0.000[a]
55+	0.46	0.001[a]
Hours of work		
Full-time	(1.00)	—
Part-time	38.84	0.000[a]
Sector (SIC)		
Agriculture, etc. (0)	(1.00)	—
Production (1–4)	0.36	0.038
Construction (5)	1.24	0.695
Distribution, etc. (6)	0.61	0.300
Transport and communication (7)	0.35	0.069
Banking, etc. (8)	0.46	0.136
Other services (9)	0.66	0.387
Occupation		
Managerial and administrative	(1.00)	—
Professional and associate professional	0.60	0.176
Clerical and secretarial	0.55	0.101
Craft and related	1.29	0.528
Personal, protective and sales	2.10	0.029
Other	2.25	0.019
Qualifications		
Above 'A' level	(1.00)	—
'A' level or equivalent	0.98	0.949
GCSE or equivalent	1.84	0.031
None	1.50	0.167

Note:
[a] Indicates statistical significance at the 1% level.
Source: BHPS 1991 (weighted data).

As expected, compared with a man (and controlling for other variables), a woman has significantly greater odds of being in the lowest decile group. Likewise, a part-time worker has almost 39 times the odds of being in the lowest decile group compared to a full-time worker. The model also shows, as expected, that labour income is related to age. Relative to someone aged 16–24, those in all other age categories have lower odds of being in the bottom decile group of the distribution.

The employment status category is of most relevance to our current discussion. The results show that relative to an employee (and controlling for other variables in the model), a self-employed person has over three times the odds of being in the lowest decile group. This result is consistent with the findings detailed above, but since a group of other variables are controlled for, it allows us to be more confident about a distinct self-employment effect, not reducible to the personal and occupational/business activity characteristics of people who happen to be self-employed.

The other variables in the model (sector, occupation and qualification level) were not significant, although for the most part the values of the coefficients are not counter to what might be expected.

Table 9.10 repeats the analysis for the odds of being in the highest labour income decile group. For the most part the results are the obverse of those in model 1. Thus, relative to a man, a woman's odds of being in the highest decile group are low. The coefficient on the employment status category, while suggesting that the self-employed have slightly higher odds of being in the highest group than their employee counterparts, is not statistically significant. This indicates that while self-employment definitely increases an individual's odds of falling into the lowest income decile group, it has no significant effect on the odds of being in the highest decile group, once the other variables in the model have been controlled for. A further notable feature of this model is that the coefficients on the occupation and qualifications variables become statistically significant, indicating that occupation and qualifications affect significantly the odds of an individual falling into the highest decile group, but not the lowest decile group.

This analysis is based on actual reported labour incomes. There is considerable speculation about the extent to which the self-employed fully report their income, with under-reporting being estimated at between a sixth and a third of income (Baker, 1993), i.e. reported incomes need to be inflated by between 20 and 50 per cent in order to estimate the real income of the self-employed. Although we argued above that there are reasons to suggest lower levels of under-reporting in the BHPS than in some other survey datasets, we examined the impact of compensating for potential under-reporting on the odds of a self-employed person falling into the

Table 9.10 *Model 2: logit estimates of odds of being in highest labour income decile group*

Dependent variable: odds of individual being in highest decile group of overall labour income distribution

Independent variable	Coefficient: Exp (B)	Significance
Sex		
Male	(1.00)	—
Female	0.23	0.000[a]
Employment status		
Employee	(1.00)	—
Self-employed	1.07	0.690
Age		
16–24	(1.00)	—
25–34	5.10	0.000[a]
35–44	10.46	0.000[a]
45–54	10.07	0.000[a]
55+	5.72	0.000[a]
Hours of work		
Full-time	(1.00)	—
Part-time	0.33	0.000[a]
Sector (SIC)		
Agriculture, etc. (0)	(1.00)	—
Production (1–4)	6.54	0.020
Construction (5)	8.38	0.011
Distribution, etc. (6)	4.19	0.079
Transport and communication (7)	7.32	0.017
Banking, etc. (8)	12.69	0.002[a]
Other services (9)	4.69	0.057
Occupation		
Managerial and administrative	(1.00)	—
Professional and associate professional	0.47	0.000[a]
Clerical and secretarial	0.06	0.000[a]
Craft and related	0.14	0.000[a]
Personal, protective and sales	0.26	0.000[a]
Other	0.12	0.000[a]
Qualifications		
Above 'A' level	(1.00)	—
'A' level or equivalent	0.55	0.000[a]
GCSE or equivalent	0.39	0.000[a]
None	0.24	0.000[a]

Note:
[a] Indicates statistical significance at the 1% level.
Source: BHPS 1991 (weighted data).

lowest and highest decile groups by multiplying all self-employed incomes by a factor of 1.35 (the mid-point between 1.2 and 1.5). The analysis reported above was then repeated. The inflated incomes reduced the odds of a self-employed person being in the lowest income decile group to almost twice (1.99) those of an employee (with significance of 0.003). They also, as might be expected, raised the odds of such a person being in the highest decile group (3.2 times those of an employee) and made the coefficient statistically significant (0.000).

The key point here is that even once a reasonable estimate of under-reporting of self-employed incomes has been accounted for, the odds of a self-employed person falling into the lowest decile group remain higher than those of an equivalent employee. This provides additional evidence to suggest that, *ceteris paribus*, an increase in the proportion of self-employed people in the workforce will lead to increased income dispersal in the overall distribution of labour incomes.

9.5 Self-employment and incomes in later life

As discussed above, a key interest of our research was the relationship between self-employment and lifetime income prospects. More particularly, we were concerned with the effect that being self-employed at various times during one's working life may have on an individual's income levels not only during the period of self-employment, but subsequently, and after retirement in particular.

This question was explored in detail using a unique, and to date somewhat under-analysed data source, the survey of *Retirement and Retirement Plans* conducted in late 1988 on behalf of the Department of Social Security (see Bone *et al.*, 1992, for full details of the survey, which covered a sample of just over 3500 people between the ages of 55 and 69). This survey's particular value for our research stems from the fact that it included not only detailed information on these older individuals' financial and other circumstances, but also dated pension and work histories covering most respondents' entire working lives.

The results of our analysis of this survey are given in detail in Meager *et al.* (1994). For reasons of brevity, we simply summarise some of the main findings in this chapter. At a most general level, the analysis confirms some of the hypotheses outlined earlier: first that some key aspects of the income distribution of the self-employed relative to that of employees carry over into later life, with similar patterns being found in the income distribution of older people who have been self-employed in their working lives relative to that of people who have only been employees; and secondly that for some significant groups of people, self-employment experience during the working life appears to be associated with very low incomes in later life.

At a more detailed level, the findings show that groups who have had work histories including self-employment spells tend to have more dispersed income distributions (including income from all sources) in later life than do groups who have worked only as employees. Among men, in particular, this greater dispersion primarily reflects an over-representation of the ex-self-employed at the lower end of the distribution, and to a lesser extent at the upper end.

Multivariate analysis, moreover, reveals a very similar pattern to that undertaken above with BHPS data: namely that after controlling for other personal characteristics, having been self-employed significantly increases an individual's likelihood of falling into a very low income group (below the lowest decile of net incomes) in later life. It does not, however, appear to increase the likelihood of falling into the highest (upper decile) group (that is, although the ex-self-employed are over-represented in these groups, this is not associated with having been self-employed *per se*, but is associated with their other characteristics).

Many of the relationships which exist between income levels and the occupation or sector of self-employment and which were noted above with BHPS data appear also to carry over to the incomes in later life of those with previous self-employment experience. Thus, the ex-self-employed who have worked in certain sectors (especially distribution, hotels and catering, and some 'other services'), and in certain occupations (personal services, sales, transport) are over-represented among the lowest income decile group in later life, as are those who have spent longer than average periods in self-employment.

A key concern of the research was to examine not only the incomes in old age of the ex-self-employed, but their savings, asset and pension patterns. Although on average the ex-self-employed tend to have higher levels of savings and financial assets in old age than their ex-employee counterparts, the results show that there is a significant group with low savings (around a half of retired people with self-employment experience have savings below £3000). As far as pensions are concerned, among the sample as a whole, non-state pensions are the main source of relative prosperity in retirement. The ex-self-employed are generally worse off than ex-employees in this respect, and their relative lack of occupational pensions is only partly offset by a greater access to personal (private) pensions. There is, however, no clear evidence that the ex-self-employed have lower entitlement to state pensions and benefits than their ex-employee counterparts. It seems, rather, that they are more likely than average to be largely or wholly dependent on state sources.

Looking in particular at those people in the bottom tail of the overall income distribution of older people, the ex-self-employed in this low income group are much more likely than ex-employees to have low or negligible savings levels, and no (non-state) pension entitlement. Thus, for example, among retired people with self-employment experience nearly a third had net incomes less than £60 per week *and* financial assets of less than £3000 (the comparable proportion of ex-employees was less than a quarter). Similarly, among retired ex-self-employed, 22 per cent had incomes less than £60 per week *and* no occupational or private pension entitlement, compared to only 13 per cent of ex-employees.

Finally, previous research (see Meager, 1991) has noted the high proportion of people working beyond 'normal' retirement age who are self-employed. The existing evidence has not, however, been able to establish the extent to which this high self-employment rate in old age reflects the fact that the self-employed do not have to retire at any specified age, and that they may be reluctant to retire from an enterprise of their own creation, particularly if they have the opportunity to vary their hours of work and effort as they get older. Alternatively it may be argued that some of the self-employed, at least, continue working because they do not feel able to afford to retire (e.g. because of inadequate savings or pension provision). The new survey data do not enable us conclusively to resolve this question. They do confirm, however, that those with self-employment experience tend to retire on average up to two years later than their ex-employee counterparts, and there is some evidence that this is associated not only with a desire to continue working, but in many cases also with a financial need to do so.

9.6 Concluding remarks

Our new analysis of a number of secondary datasets has compared the labour incomes of the self-employed and employees and located the self-employed within the overall income distribution, as well as looking at the relationship between self-employment experience in an individual's work history and their income levels in later life.

We have shown that the labour income distributions of the self-employed and employees are different, with the self-employed having a more dispersed range of incomes. Self-employed women in particular have an especially dispersed income distribution and there is a group of self-employed women on very low incomes. It is clear also that the self-employed are over-represented in the tails of the overall income distribution, even once gender, hours of work, and industry have been taken into account. Our multivariate analysis, moreover, indicates that the self-employed have more than three times the odds of being in the lowest income decile group than an equivalent employee. Even once an estimate for under-reporting of self-employed incomes is included, the odds of a self-employed person falling into the lowest income decile group remain significantly higher than those of their employee counterparts.

Many of the groups among whom self-employment grew particularly strongly in the 1980s (women, young people, ex-unemployed, and self-employed in certain low income service sectors and occupations) are over-represented among the poor self-employed.

Self-employment experience is also associated with a more dispersed income distribution in later life than is a purely employee-based work history; the ex-self-employed are over-represented in the upper and lower tails of the income distribution of 55–69 year olds, and falling into the lowest income group, in particular, is significantly associated with having self-employment experience. It should be noted that these latter results relating to incomes in later life are revealed from data which do not yet pick up the rapid growth of 'new' self-employment in the 1980s, which can be expected to further accentuate these patterns.

These findings, despite the limitations of working with secondary data not designed to focus on the self-employed and the difficulties of dealing with under-reporting of incomes, raise a number of important policy issues, and point to the need for new in-depth survey work concentrating on the self-employed themselves and their personal and financial circumstances. They show that the self-employed are a very diverse group, with very diverse incomes, many of whom are far from the stereotypical 'entrepreneur' popularly associated with the 'enterprise culture' of the 1980s. It would appear that a significant group of the 'new' self-employed of that decade have very low incomes, and that their reported low incomes cannot be explained simply by under-reporting. Perhaps even more importantly in policy terms, it seems that many of the low income self-employed may also end up with low incomes and financial asset levels in later life, missing out on personal and occupational pensions, and ending up dependent on state benefits. It is not clear that the current pensions and National Insurance systems are well adapted to many of the new and growing categories of self-employment.

Notes

The research on which this chapter is based is reported in full in Meager et al. (1994). The British Household Panel Survey data used in the research were made available through the ESRC Data Archive, and were originally collected by the ESRC Research Centre on Micro-Social Change, both at the University of Essex.

The Retirement and Retirement Plans survey data collected on behalf of the Department of Social Security were also provided by the Archive. None of these bodies bears any responsibility for the analyses and interpretations presented here.

1. For a summary of recent trends in self-employment in the United Kingdom and in other European countries, see OECD (1992), and Meager (1993).

2. The existing research confirms the unusual position of the United Kingdom and suggests that no single factor can explain the growth in self-employment during the 1980s, and the unique experience of the United Kingdom in this respect. Rather it is clear that unemployment trends, the shift in employment structures from manufacturing and services, the 'contracting out' of service functions by large employers, and the regulatory and financial market conditions influencing business start-up all played a role (see Acs et al., 1992; Meager et al., 1992; Meager, 1992a, 1992b).

3. As documented in Meager (1993), EAS participants were not only unemployed (by definition), but more likely than other unemployed entrants to self-employment to be female, were much younger on average than the existing self-employed, and were over-represented in small-scale service sector activities.

4. Now renamed the Business Start Up Scheme, and administered locally by Training and Enterprise Councils (TECs).

5. See, in particular, Smith (1986), Curran et al. (1987), Hakim (1989), Pissarides and Weber (1989), OECD (1992), Rubery et al. (1993), Baker (1993), Jenkins (1994) and Goodman and Webb (1994).

6. The findings are reported in full in Meager et al. (1994).

7. See Taylor (1992) for more details of the survey.

8. Throughout this chapter, the figures for self-employed women are based on very small sample sizes and should be treated with some caution.

9. This difference is related to women's greater propensity to work part-time, as discussed below.

10. A slightly higher proportion of self-employed women work part-time than is the case among employees (42 per cent compared to 39 per cent). There is also a small difference between the two groups in terms of hours usually worked per week (including overtime for employees): women employees normally work 31.0 hours a week compared to 29.4 for self-employed women. Neither of these differences is, however, statistically significant using a chi-squared test and t-test respectively.

11. Odds in this context are just an alternative way of representing probabilities, so if the probability of being self-employed is 10 per cent, the odds are 9 to 1 against, or 0.11.

10 Fairer or Fowler? The effects of the 1986 Social Security Act on family incomes

Martin Evans

10.1 Introduction

This chapter summarises research into the changes to British means-tested benefits introduced by the 1986 Social Security Act. Greater detail of the research and other results can be found in Evans (1994) and Evans *et al.* (1994). First, I briefly outline the aims of the Act and the benefit regime it introduced. Second, I outline changing levels of government spending and the evidence of changing claimant income profiles. Last, I compare the preceding scheme to the one introduced by the Act, using the results from a micro-simulation model. The old system of means-tested benefits is modelled and brought forward and run alongside a similar model of the new scheme for the most recent year of the period studied, 1990–91. All discussion is focused on the four years between March 1987 and April 1991.

10.2 The policy changes

10.2.1 The old regime

The *Supplementary Benefit* (SB) system was a national means-tested assistance programme which had existed in some form since the mid-1930s.[1] The SB system in the 1960s and 1970s had been amended to reduce stigma and to provide greater legal rights to entitlement. However, these changes had not altered SB's individualised assessment of needs, and this level of detailed enquiry did not allow easy administration for the 4.9 million claimants who claimed it in 1987.

Family Income Supplement (FIS) was a means-tested benefit for families with children in low paid work introduced in 1971. This benefit was introduced to improve work incentives for those on the borderline of SB and waged or self-employment. It was seen as poorly taken-up by claimants.

Housing Benefits (HB) were a system of means-tested help with housing

236

costs for those who claimed SB (*certificated* cases), and others (*standard* cases). Rent for council tenants was reduced through *rent rebates* while *rent allowances* were paid to private tenants to assist in payment of rent. *Rate rebates* reduced local authority property taxes. HB and SB were poorly aligned which meant that additional HB (*housing benefit supplement*) had to be paid to those who did not claim SB but whose disposable income after paying housing costs fell below SB level.

These benefits existed alongside a system of non-means-tested National Insurance benefits (unemployment, sickness and maternity benefits; retirement, invalidity and widows' pensions), and contingency-related benefits (child benefit and a range of disability-based benefits). The social security system as a whole was far more complex than Beveridge's design of 40 years before. There was concern about its complexity, the interaction between different means tests, growing levels of expenditure, the effects of benefits on work incentives, and the balance of how much social security was targeted to those on low incomes.

Social security policy had already changed in the early 1980s:

- The basis of uprating most benefits changed in 1980 when the government moved away from increasing benefit levels in line with the greater of earnings or price rises. Uprating moved solely to reflect price increases. As earnings have risen faster than prices, the gap between those on benefits and those working has increased.
- The government's desire to contain public expenditure and to improve incentives to work gave rise to policy changes which affected the potential coverage of means-tested benefits. For instance, a reduction in the volume of national insurance unemployment benefit led to a growing proportion of the growing numbers of unemployed relying on SB.
- Spending on means-tested social security is demand-led, and hence directly influenced by other areas of social and economic policy. Increased unemployment and early retirement, in addition to demographic changes, increased spending. Other social policies, in particular the move towards higher rents in both private and public housing increased the number of potential claimants and the amounts of benefit paid.
- The reaction to increased spending was to make elements of the old means-tested scheme less generous. The HB system was so altered on several occasions for those not claiming SB.
- The aims of reduced spending and improved incentives were traded off as a result. As more people were drawn in to the web of means-tested provision, more faced incentive problems associated with them: high marginal tax and benefit withdrawal rates. The poverty and unemployment traps ensnared significant numbers of people, blunting the

improved incentives which were the supposed result of lower relative benefit levels. In addition, making schemes less generous as incomes rose worsened some such traps at the margins.

In 1984, Norman Fowler, the Secretary of State for Health and Social Security, announced a thorough examination of means-tested social security.

10.2.2 The aims of the Act

The Fowler reviews introduced legislation which sought to:
- Re-prioritise treatment within means-tested social security
- Meet genuine need
- Control spending
- Provide a simpler structure leading to reduced costs and greater claimant comprehension
- Target benefits more accurately
- Improve individual behaviour and incentives.

The new priority targets were families with children. Government analysis had shown them to be a growing proportion of the poorest families. The highest priority were working families with children on low income.

10.2.3 The new benefit regime: a common basis

Common rules for assessment of income and capital were introduced for all elements of the new scheme. Income Support (IS) replaced Supplementary Benefit. Family Credit (FC) replaced Family Income Support. The Social Fund replaced single payments of SB. HB kept its name but changed fundamentally in structure. All means-tested benefits moved to treat income as net after tax and National Insurance. Capital limits to eligibility were introduced for HB and FC and were originally the same as IS, £6000, quickly raised to £8000. The old limit for SB had been £3000. A capital limit for the new HB scheme produced many losers and proved to be politically controversial, and was eventually raised to £16,000 (see below). However, any capital between £3000 and £16,000 was taken as providing an income of £1 per week for each £250. This 'tariff income' was set at higher rates than normally obtainable from investments, and represented a direct incentive to draw from savings during a claim.

10.2.4 Family Credit

Family Credit replaced FIS for low paid families with children working full-time (24 hours per week or more, reduced to 16 in 1992). It was more generous than its predecessor and was designed to lift families out of dependence on weekly assistance benefits (Income Support), and into work by providing real increases in income. There was no longer an entitlement to free school meals and welfare foods previously a part of FIS. FC claimants with less than £500 in savings could also obtain Maternity and Funeral grants from the Social Fund, which were not available under FIS.

10.2.5 Income Support

Income Support replaced SB as a weekly minimum means-tested income. It was far simpler to calculate entitlement. Claimants' allowances were determined by age and family structure. Additional help, through *premiums*, was based either on presence of children, old age or on entitlement to disability benefits which had already been determined by other elements of the social security scheme. This clear and simple structure replaced the complexities of SB where needs were determined by householder status, whether the claimant had to 'sign on', and a large number of *additional requirements* (ARs) for extra needs. IS, like SB, also included some housing costs not covered by HB.

However, several elements of the change to IS pointed to potential inadequacies in the minimum safety net.

- Some elements of housing costs were not covered by the accompanying HB system and had to be paid from weekly rates of IS. Water rates, previously covered in full, were no longer included in the benefit. In addition, 20 per cent of rates, or community charge, was payable from weekly IS by all claimants.
- Weekly benefit would in the majority of cases bear the cost of large one-off needs previously paid for by way of grants; 'single payments' of SB were replaced by the Social Fund, a smaller system which provided the majority of one-off help though a system of interest-free loans repaid from weekly benefit. Grants were to be given in a minority of cases.
- The move to an assessment largely based on age meant that householders under the age of 25 would receive a reduced rate of benefit to meet the needs of running a home.

There were also groups of claimants who lost right to assistance. Young people who left school aged over 16 but under 18 were no longer entitled to IS. They would be offered training allowances not means-tested assistance. Such treatment therefore depended on the availability of training places and on young people remaining with their families in nearly all circumstances. The exclusion from IS was later relaxed and discretionary payments allowed where training was unavailable and in exceptional cases.

Later changes led to the majority of students in tertiary education being completely removed from entitlement to IS and HB.

10.2.6 The Social Fund

One-off assistance was available under the old system from two sources.

* Fixed-rate national insurance allowances of £25 for death and maternity which had lost any notion of a realistic contribution to the underlying needs of a funeral and the birth of a child.
* Single payments of SB for exceptional needs.

The Social Fund replaced this with:

* A small range of mandatory awards from a demand-led budget: fixed-rate maternity grants for claimants of IS and FC; funeral grants for claimants of IS, FC, and HB; grants of a fixed sum for additional heating costs during periods of exceptionally cold weather for IS claimants who were elderly and those with young children.
* A larger range of discretionary grants and loans from a fixed budget which would provide three forms of help:

  a *Community Care Grants*, in instances where the need arose from a need linked to ensuring care in the community (i.e. avoiding institutional care, or facilitating moves from it) and for 'families under stress'.

  b *Budgeting Loans* would provide loans for the majority of one-off needs but only for those who had been entitled to IS for six months or more.

  c *Crisis Loans* replaced weekly urgent needs payments of SB and other urgent or emergency help. Crisis loans also took over payments for urgent need previously part of weekly assessments in SB.

10.2.7 Housing Benefit

The new scheme harmonised the treatment of income, needs and capital with the new IS rules. IS claimants, and those with incomes equal to or less than IS levels, would receive maximum HB. While maximum HB was 100 per cent for rents, the government stipulated a maximum 80 per cent benefit for rates. The payment of the remainder of rate liability from weekly benefit, or its equivalent, was to encourage claimants to have greater interest in the financial management of their local authority. A contemporary review of local government finance and accountability proposed the Community Charge which would also attract a maximum 80 per cent rebate. In the government's original proposals no compensatory element was included in benefit rates; this was later partly conceded, as outlined below.

For those with incomes above IS levels, the new HB scheme withdrew benefit for rent and rates at tapers of 65 per cent and 20 per cent respectively. Thus with needs, income and capital calculated in the same manner as IS, and fewer, simpler tapers, the new HB scheme was clearer and avoided the old scheme's anomalies. A capital limit to eligibility was introduced. This limit at first matched IS but was then raised, first to £10,000 and then again to £16,000.

Overall the three major weekly benefits provided a more coherent and simpler structure of weekly means-tested assistance with common rules to assess income, capital and needs.

10.2.8 Implementation and amendment

Incremental changes brought about by political necessity altered the original design of the Act in several ways:

- During parliamentary discussion a new, higher, premium for severe disability was brought in, targeting a large amount of weekly help on a small tightly defined disabled population; and to reduce costs the HB rent taper was raised from an original level of 60p to 65p in the £1.
- A notional element for compensation of average 20 per cent rates contribution was included in weekly scale rates of IS, but the actual calculation of this was surrounded by confusion and contention (see Esam and Oppenheim, 1990).
- Losers under the new HB rules were compensated by a new transitional protection scheme introduced in May 1988.
- The harmonised structure between IS and HB was sacrificed and HB moved to a higher capital limit – at first £10,000.
- To attempt to ensure wider political acceptance of the Community Charge, the rebate scheme was made more generous through a change in the taper to 15p in the pound. At the same time, the capital limit to HB was raised to £16,000.
- Changes to the treatment of pensioners' benefits were made by increasing the rates paid to those aged between 75 and 80 in April 1990.
- A premium for Carers was introduced in October 1990.

Thus by 1990/91 the radical new design put forward by Fowler was largely intact, but several important incremental changes had taken place. More were to happen after 1990, outside the period studied here. Most significantly the government of John Major altered two fundamental elements of the Fowler changes. Child Benefit, previously left un-uprated in deference to greater spending on FC, began to be uprated again. In 1992 the definition of full-time work which determined entitlement to IS and FC was changed to 16 hours a week. The new Council Tax, which replaced

Table 10.1 *Spending on means-tested benefits, 1986–87 to 1990–91, at 1990–91 prices*

	Total spending*a* (1990–91 prices), £ million	Share of social security spending (%)	Share of all welfare spending (%)	Share of GDP (%)
1986–87	17163	29.3	15.2	3.3
1987–88	16530	28.7	14.5	3.1
1988–89	15256	28.0	13.4	2.8
1989–90	15086	27.9	13.4	2.7
1990–91	16642	29.6	14.7	3.0
% change 1986–87 to 1990–91	–3	+1	–3	–9

Note:
a Treasury GDP Deflator used for 1990–91 spending levels.
Sources: DSS (1993d), HM Treasury (1993).

the Community Charge, carried with it a rebate scheme which met 100 per cent for the poorest. Analysis of the effects of these new changes is left to future research.

10.3 The new Act in operation

10.3.1 Government spending and the new design

Table 10.1 shows government spending on means-tested social security between 1986–87 and 1990–91. Spending on means-tested benefits has declined by 3 per cent in real terms. End-year increases in spending in 1990–91 may be the combined effect of increased demand due to rising unemployment and the move to Community Charge rebates. There is no firm evidence of social security overall being 'better targeted' through any proportional increase in means-tested spending.

Figure 10.1 shows the proportion of families in receipt of means-tested benefits over the same period. Reduced spending coincided with reduced numbers of claimants, especially for housing benefits in 1988 and 1989. The increase in claimants due to the introduction of the Community Charge, together with an increase in claims for IS, raised the proportion of families relying on means-tested benefit in 1990 to 27.5 per cent of all fam-

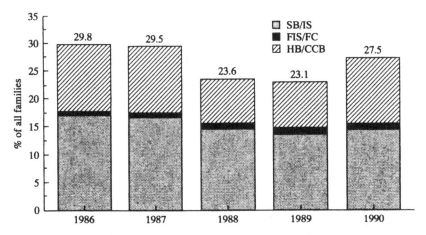

Figure 10.1   Families receiving means-tested benefits, proportion of all families,
1986–90

ilies, a fall of almost 8 per cent from 1986 levels. A large element of
reduced coverage and spending during 1988 and 1989 will be the impact of
the 1986 Act, but will also result from demographic and economic factors.

10.3.2 Spending on SB and IS

Government spending is shown in real terms in table 10.2. Payments of all
housing costs and charges and single payments have been deducted to estimate basic benefit payments for weekly living. In real terms, aggregate
spending has fallen between 1986–87 and 1990–91 by 24 per cent. But such
a headline figure is misleading, as falling unemployment and other factors
may have reduced underlying changes in numbers and composition of
claimants. Table 10.2 also deflates spending as a real *per capita* claimant
figure, and shows that allowing for changing caseload, spending has
remained flat in real terms. This *per capita* figure, however, does not allow
for any compositional change in claimant populations.

Table 10.2 therefore also shows the trends in claimants' underlying
incomes from social security benefits and other sources. There has been a
growth in the proportion of claimants who have original incomes from
non-social security sources, earnings and non-earned income excluding
social security benefits. In real terms the average income (after elements
are disregarded under the rules of SB and IS) has risen by 19 per cent. This
is partly due to more generous disregards in the new scheme. However, a
far bigger source of original income for claimants is other social security.

Table 10.2 *Government spending and claimant profiles, SB and IS, 1986–87 to 1990–91*

	Government spending[a]			Claimant's original income			
				From earnings and other income		From social security benefits	
	Total spending (1990–91 prices, £ million)	Share of social security spending (%)	Weekly per capita claimant (1990–91 prices, £)	Share of claimants with such income (%)	Average amount of income[b] (1990–91 prices, £)	Share of claimants with other benefits[c] (%)	Share of claimants with Child Benefit (%)
1986–87	8527	15	32	14	15	44	24
1987–88	7919	14	30	11	15	43	24
1988–89	7063	13	32	12	16	43	27
1989–90	6332	12	30	16	20	43	28
1990–91	6507	12	31	18	19	43	28
% change 1986–87 to 1990–91	−24	−23	—	+29	+19	—	+17

Notes:

[a] Excluding single payments, Social Fund, residential and nursing home and housing costs.

[b] Taken as income after disregards.

[c] Excluding benefits wholly disregarded.

Source: Author's calculations from DSS, *Annual Statistical Enquiry* and DSS (1993c).

Table 10.3 *Index of relative benefits rates, by family type and comparison of rates of SB and IS*

Model family type	Index of each scheme		% change in income (87 SB to 90 IS)
	SB	IS	
Householders			
Unemployed couple householder, no children	100	100	−6.1
Unemployed couple, two children (7 and 12)	109	115	+5.8
Unemployed single aged 25, no children	112	115	−3.9
Couple pensioner aged 60–74	131	134	−3.8
Couple pensioner aged 75–79	131	141	+1.2
Couple sick/disabled under 60	135	142	−1.6
Couple pensioner aged 80 and over	137	146	+0.6
Lone parent with single 6 year old	140	161	+7.8
Single pensioner aged 60–74	155	156	−5.7
Single pensioner aged 75–79	155	165	+0.2
Single sick/disabled under 60	162	167	−3.0
Single pensioner aged 80 and over	163	174	−0.4
Non-householders			
18 year old single unemployed	110	116	−1.1

Source: Author's calculations.

The proportion of claimants who receive SB and or IS in supplementation of a basic underlying entitlement to other benefits has remained constant at 43–44 per cent. However, the proportion who receive child benefit has increased by almost 17 per cent over the same period.

10.3.3 Changing relativities

Table 10.3 shows the relative treatment of family types by the two schemes using an index of weekly benefit set to 100 for an unemployed householder couple with no children. The index is produced by an equivalent comparison of benefits rates, including premiums, average Additional Requirements (ARs) awarded under the old scheme in real terms, and deductions for average Community Charge and water rates for each family type using the McClements after housing cost (AHC) equivalence scale.

There is very little difference between the two schemes in the ranking of the example family types. Both have rates for single pensioners and the sick and disabled ranked relatively the highest. However, IS has higher relative differences between the unemployed and others. The higher levels of personal allowances for children in IS also give rise to different ranking of lone parents as well as higher relative values for others with children.

But the greater relativities within the IS scheme have to be placed alongside the differences in levels of disposable income between schemes. In table 10.3 the right hand column shows these differences as a percentage rise or fall in income. These figures demonstrate that IS's greater relative generosity starts from an index point of 100 for an unemployed couple with no children who are 6 per cent worse off. And, even taking into account greater relative generosity within the new scheme, many family types remain worse off in this example. These results are very sensitive to the use of average figures for ARs, Community Charge and water rates.

A comparison of the IS and SB schemes confirms that the new regime is more selective in its approach. It ranks additional needs higher but has a lower base line of income for those who have no additional needs. However, any conclusions must be qualified by the fact that IS has replaced a system which could reflect very high individual needs with one which provides set rates of allowances at rates nearer to the average.

10.3.4 Disposable incomes of IS claimants

Table 10.4 shows the number, proportion and distribution of recipients of IS transitional protection[2] for the first three years of the new scheme. In 1988/89 over one third of all IS claimants were held at their old levels of SB; this represented about 40 per cent of continuing SB claimants. Over time such claimants decreased as benefit rates rose and with the outflow and inflow of claims. In May 1990 over 3 per cent of all IS claimants continued to receive transition protection. If this receipt is compared to the number and proportion of claimants who had been in receipt of benefits for over two years in 1990, then around 6 per cent of such long-term claimants had had no increase in benefit since April 1987. But transitional protection only provided an assurance against cash falls in benefit income. The disposable incomes of those on IS, both with protection and without, differed through the payment of housing costs. Maintenance and insurance costs of owner-occupiers, previously available in SB, were not longer covered by IS. But two other liabilities had a greater effect: 20 per cent of rates/Community Charge; and water rates. Three years of estimates of the effect of paying 20 per cent of rates and Community Charge suggest that between one third and one half of all IS claimants have a benefit income

Table 10.4 *Transitional protection, IS claimants, 1988–90*

	1988	1989	1990
All IS	4,352,000	4,161,000	4,180,000
TP claimants	1,585,400	497,300	134,300
% of all claimants	36%	12%	3%
Claimants over 60	710,300	241,400	51,800
% of all claimants over 60	46%	17%	4%
Disabled claimants	63,500	27,500	8,900
% of disabled claimants	26%	10%	3%
Claimants with children	284,900	47,300	10,400
% claimants with children	25%	4%	1%
Other claimants	531,400	132,100	63,300
% of other claimants	36%	10%	5%

Source: Author's calculations.

for non-housing needs below the weekly basic rates. In addition, high weekly levels of water rates of £2.50 and over were faced by over 25 per cent of IS households in 1990–91, while the highest proportion of claimants were paying between £2.00 and £2.50 in 1990–91 as opposed to £1–£1.50 in 1988.

There has been a recent commitment to uprate benefit scale rates in the future by an index which includes water charges. However, the losses already experienced will not be compensated, and water rates rose by 40.5 per cent between April 1987 and April 1990 (CSO, 1991).

10.3.5 The Social Fund for IS claimants

Table 10.5 shows spending on single payments and the Social Fund in real terms over the period 1986–87 to 1990–91 to have dropped by 68 per cent. However, 1986 was the year in which most was paid in the Single Payment system. The government labelled such high levels as partly arising from 'abuse'. The changes introduced in 1987 reduced spending by 42 per cent in a single year in advance of the majority of the new Social Fund.

The effect of this change on the incomes of IS claimants is estimated by a consistent definition of claimant populations and the value of grant and loan outputs (for details see Evans, 1994). Figure 10.2 shows such estimates in real terms. Pensioners, the group that had lowest *per capita* output from Single Payments, experienced a consequential smaller relative loss than other groups. Their loss is calculated as equivalent to 49p a week.

Table 10.5 *Real spending on single payments and the Social Fund,*
£ million, 1991–92 prices[a]

	Total spending (1991–92 prices, £ million)	Annual % difference	Share of all social security (%)	Share of SB/IS (%)
1986–87	516	—	0.9	4.6
1987–88	300	−42	0.4	2.6
1988–89	183	−39	0.3	2.0
1989–90	150	−18	0.3	1.7
1990–91	166	+11	0.3	1.7

Notes:
[a] 1991–92 prices from Adjusted GDP Deflator – Cm 2219 (1993).
Sources: Author's calculations from DSS (1989, T 34.97), and DSS (1993c) and equivalent for previous years.

The unemployed have had a larger weekly equivalent loss: around £1.55 in 1992 prices. Other claimants once received the highest *per capita* outputs from Single Payments and still receive the highest from the Social Fund. Even so, Figure 10.2 shows that they have lost most from the change – £2.20 in real terms. Discussion of the move to the Social Fund has highlighted the absence of any compensatory increase in weekly benefits. For a single pensioner aged 65–70, then, the change would require an approximate 2 per cent increase in benefit rates to compensate. Of course this simple average under-states actual losses in some instances and over-states them in others.

The change in levels of awards suggests that the Social Fund has provided less help to a claimant population with diminishing average capital resources. For the few claimants who receive them, the average levels of grant from the Fund are significantly greater than average grants from Single Payments. However, these small numbers of gainers are outweighed by those who receive a loan or nothing from the Fund.

10.3.6 Housing Benefit

Table 10.6 shows that spending on non-IS/SB rent rebates remained at 33–34 per cent of all rent rebate spending over the period. Rent rebates rose by almost 13 per cent in real terms. If average rebate is considered as a percentage of average local authority rents, then the value of rebates as such a percentage has also risen by 13 per cent. Yet this increased expendi-

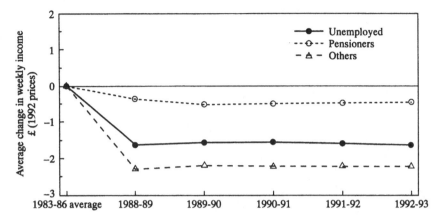

Figure 10.2 Single Payments and the Social Fund: change in average payment compared to 1983–86 average

ture appears to be more focused on the poorest local authority tenants who were not on IS, as real original incomes of rebate cases has fallen by 17 per cent; however no allowance has been made for changing composition of claimants in determining original incomes. Spending on non-IS/SB rent allowances has remained between 31 and 34 per cent of all spending on rent allowances, giving an overall fall of 3 per cent. However, the real value of rent allowances has increased by 28 per cent. This increased spending appears again to be more concentrated on poorer tenants, as claimants' real original incomes have fallen by 7 per cent. However, unknown changes in the composition of claimants mean that this conclusion must be qualified.

Spending on rate rebates and Community Charge rebates is more difficult to establish because of the change in volume of claimants with the introduction of an individual charge. Real levels of average non-SB/IS rate rebate rose each year up to 1989–90. The original incomes of claimants have fallen by almost 9 per cent in real terms over the whole period.

The real value of non-dependant deductions for rent has increased as shown in table 10.7. However, while the higher rate of deduction has neither increased or decreased in real terms overall, the lower deduction, presumably designed for the 'poorer' non-householder, has risen by 27 per cent in real terms. While a final conclusion requires more detailed consideration of the changes in definition of non-dependants, and access to administrative data on the number of deductions made at each level, on first sight this element of the scheme does not appear to support a targeting of help on the poorest.

Table 10.6 *Non-SB/IS Housing Benefits, by scheme, England and Wales, 1986–87 to 1990–91*

	Rent rebates				Rent allowance				Rate rebate and Community Charge rebates		
	Proportion of national spending, non-SB/IS (%)	Real average rebate	% of average rent	Real average claimant income[a] (1990–91 prices)	Proportion of national spending, non-SB/IS (%)	Real average allowance	% of average rent[b]	Real average claimant income[a] (1990–91 prices)	Proportion of national spending, non-SB/IS (%)	Real average rebate	Real average claimant income[a] (1990–91 prices)
1986–87	33.1	£14.29	60	—	34.9	£15.12	na	—	38.8	£5.56	—
1987–88 (FES sample)	31.9	£13.99	59	£93.23 (403)	31.2	£13.92	na	£83.85 (121)	36.7	£5.58	£97.72 (589)
1988–89 (FES sample)	31.8	£15.79	66	£83.31 (483)	32.6	£18.31	50	£73.71 (120)	36.8	£5.80	£91.50 (544)
1989–90 (FES sample)	33.2	£16.33	69	£81.29 (459)	31.8	£17.60	na	£72.57 (120)	36.1	£5.86	£93.20 (456)
1990–91 (FES sample)	33.8	£16.09	68	£77.42 (436)	33.7	£19.38	45	£77.83 (125)	47.6	£5.04	£89.17 (623)
% change	+2	+13	+13	−17	−3	+28	—	−7	+23	—[c]	−9

Notes:
[a] Income is net original after tax and NI contributions but *before* deduction of net (after HB) housing costs.
[b] Average private rents – England only.
[c] Not a consistent series.
Sources: Authors' calculations from *Social Security Statistics,* DoE (1993) and FES.

Table 10.7 *Real value of deductions for non-dependants, £, 1990–91 prices*

	Rent – high	Rent – low	Rates – high	Rates – low
1986–87	10.75	3.58	4.82	1.89
1987–88	10.60	3.56	4.62	1.83
1988–89	10.02	4.21	4.41	na
1989–90	10.21	4.30	4.49	na
1990–91	10.85	4.55	na	na
% change	—	+27	na	na

Notes:
— Not significant.
na Not available.
Source: Author's calculations.

10.3.7 Family Credit

Family Credit was introduced as a more generous benefit for low paid families with children in work in order to improve incentives to enter and remain in work. Family Credit, therefore, was intended to receive higher priority within social security in terms of absolute, real and relative spending. Table 10.8 shows real spending on FIS and FC between 1986 and 1990.

The introduction of FC, like the new HB scheme, involved great changes in the treatment of income and needs which, together with the absence of detailed administrative data, makes comparative analysis at this level difficult. However, table 10.8 shows a great increase in spending in real terms.

Real spending has grown by 138 per cent. As a proportion of all spending on social security, it has grown by 144 per cent. Claimant numbers grew by over 55 per cent, and by 57 per cent if such claimant families are taken as a proportion of all families with children. The benefits given are more generous and have been given to a claimant population with a rising real average income.

10.3.8 Income change

How have the claimants of means-tested benefits fared between 1987–88 and 1990–91? I have shown already that there were gainers and losers within a smaller overall claimant population. Among these gainers were those who were newly entitled after the changes. FES data suggest that

Table 10.8 *Government spending and claimant profiles, FIS and FC*

	Total spending (1990–91 prices, £ million)	Share of social security spending (%)	Claimants (000)	Claimants as % of families with children	Average award (1990–91 prices, £)	Average underlying income of claimants (1990–91 prices, £)
1986–87	208	0.36	202	3.0	17.58	na
1987–88	222	0.39	220	3.3	18.75	125.26
1988–89	453	0.83	285	4.3	na	112.22
1989–90	459	0.85	286	4.2	27.20	130.15
1990–91	494	0.88	313	4.7	27.40	138.60
% change	+138	+144	+55	+57	+56	+11

Notes:
na Not available.
FES sample for average incomes of claimants are 1987–88 (60); 1988–89 (65); 1989–90 (78) and 1990–91 (76).
Source: Author's calculations from *Social Security Statistics*, FES, DSS (1993c) and population estimates.

equivalent net incomes after housing costs for claimants of all means-tested benefits have fallen by about 10 per cent, against a general increase in incomes of 5 per cent for all.

Table 10.9 shows that mean real income rose by 5 per cent. The real incomes for recipients of all means-tested benefits fell in real terms by 9 per cent (a nominal rise of 8 per cent). The fall in the relative incomes of means-tested benefit claimants has been greater, a 13 per cent fall in the value of claimants' incomes relative to the average from 56 per cent to 49 per cent. However, this overall trend hides larger year-on-year losses in the first year of the new scheme when the average real incomes fell for all claimants, before rising over the next two years and then falling again in 1990–91. The first of these larger falls may be partly explained by the introduction of the requirement to pay 20 per cent of rates, the loss of higher income claimants due to changes in rules for eligibility, especially for housing benefits, and the transitional schemes which froze incomes in real terms for continuing claimants. The further drop in real income in 1990–91 is due in the main to the Community Charge.

However, within these claimant samples there are different income trends. Table 10.9 shows that incomes of claimants who received SB and IS

Table 10.9 *Mean real and relative incomes of means-tested benefit claimants, 1987–88 to 1990–91, 1990–91 prices*

	1987–88	1988–89	1989–90	1990–91	% change 1987–88 to 1990–91
*All – average income*ᵃ	£181.63	£186.12	£187.60	£189.82	+5
Sample	9257	9222	9260	8334	
All – means-tested claimants	£101.52	£94.79	£94.53	£92.61	–9
Income as % of all	56	51	50	49	–13
SB and IS claimants					
Average income	£93.31	£91.32	£89.40	£82.98	–11
% of all average	51	49	48	44	–15
Sample	1004	900	881	849	
Family Income Supplement and Family Credit					
Average income	£97.49	£105.25	£109.15	£106.46	+9
% of all average	45	47	58	56	+5
Sample	70	79	92	78	
Housing and Community Charge Benefits (no FIS/FC and no SB/IS)					
Average income	£109.20	£97.19	£97.92	£98.80	–10
% of all average	58	49	50	48	–13
Sample	1111	955	941	777	

Note:
ᵃ Income is equivalent income after housing costs deflated by financial year average ROSSI RPI index.
Source: Author's calculations from FES.

fell on average by 11 per cent in real terms, while their income as a proportion of average income fell by 15 per cent. In stark contrast to this, the incomes of low waged families with children who received FIS and FC rose. Targeting extra help to this group produced a 9 per cent real increase in income even with the changes in housing costs introduced by the introduction of Community Charge in the last year. However, the incomes of claimants of HB, defined as those who do not also receive FIS, FC or SB/IS, have fallen. The average incomes of these types of claimants have, through increased targeting, fallen. Their real AHC income has fallen by

10 per cent. Their relative position against average income has fallen by 13 per cent.

In broad terms, allowing for no change in claimant composition and economic activity, and within the overall policy of uprating benefits by prices rather than earnings, it can be seen that increased targeting may have occurred. Claimants of SB, IS, and HB are poorer in real terms and in relative terms, while the new priority group, FC claimants, have higher real and relative incomes against the overall trend. However, no firm conclusion can be made about the role that the changes to social security played in these changes. Other effects on income such as changing housing costs, tenure, levels of employment, and changing demographic make-up of the samples, all influence results.

In order to distinguish between the effects of the changes introduced by the Act from economic and compositional effects, further research was undertaken using micro-simulation models of both old and new schemes.

10.4 The old and new schemes compared

10.4.1 The models and their assumptions

The micro-simulation model applies the benefit rules to the FES sample population and calculates resulting net incomes. The model used calculates SB, FIS, HBS and old-style HB together with IS, FC and new-style HB. The sample population is the financial year of 1990–91 in FES. In summary these assumptions are:

- An assumed take-up of 100 per cent for all benefits
- The old rules for rate rebates under the 1987 scheme used for the Community Charge in 1990–91
- All elements of the old scheme uprated to equivalent benefit levels in 1990–91
- Income is net equivalent income after payment of tax, National Insurance and housing costs (incomes of FC claimants have been adjusted to remove payment for school meals)
- No modelling of the effects of the introduction of the Social Fund is attempted
- No allowance for the freezing of Child Benefit is made, nor for any changes in taxation between 1987–88 and 1990–91.

10.4.2 Transition between benefit regimes

Table 10.10 shows the modelled outcomes for all who would have been entitled to old-scheme benefits. Their new entitlement I call their 'benefit

Table 10.10 *Old system claimants, destination: new entrants to new system*

Old system – destinations	No change (<50p)	Losers	Gainers
SB claimants (941)			
IS (776)	(70)	£4.42 (340)	£5.53 (366)
Housing Benefit (103)	—	£13.67	—
Family Credit (7)*a*			
No entitlement (56)	—	£17.89	—
FIS claimants (71)			
IS (0)	—	—	—
Housing Benefit (0)	—	—	—
Family Credit (68)	—	£8.23 (16)*b*	£13.26 (52)
No entitlement (3)*a*			
HB claimants (1970)			
IS (244)	(9)	£3.76 (15)	£9.86 (221)
Housing Benefit (1279)	(306)	£3.66 (449)	£2.83 (524)
Family Credit (52)	(2)	£11.92 (9)	£13.80 (41)
No entitlement (394)	(35)	£3.92 (359)	—
New entrants to new system			
IS (4)	—	—	£9.34
New HB and CCB (78)	—	—	£2.50
Family Credit (10)	—	—	£10.06

Notes:
a Sample too small.
b FIS claimants who become losers on FC are mostly comprised of very low or zero income self-employed families in the sample.
Source: Author's calculation from FES.

destination'. Those claimants with a new-scheme entitlement but with no entitlement under the old scheme are called 'new entrants'. Those with an underlying entitlement to SB or IS are called claimants of these benefits, even though they are also receiving HB. Similarly, those who receive FIS or FC are identified by these entitlements. Thus those who have entitlement to HB under the old or new scheme and no underlying entitlement to SB, IS, FIS or FC are called HB claimants.

For modelled claimants of SB the majority, 82 per cent, have continued entitlement under the new system. Of these modelled IS claimants who used to have an entitlement to SB, a slim majority are losers and their average loss is £4.42. Those that gained had a slightly higher average gain of £5.53. Only a small number of old SB claimants have a modelled entitlement to new FC; the sample is too small to analyse, but they are all gainers. Those old SB claimants who lose entitlement to IS but remain entitled to CCB and HB have an average loss of £13.67. For those with no entitlement under the new benefit regime whatsoever there are losses of £17.89. However, these losers, the majority of whom are 16–18 year olds, appear to have no entitlement under the new scheme but may have an alternative of a training scheme place, or failing that, discretionary IS, which is not modelled.

The majority of FIS claimants are gainers under FC. Losers are created by the sample containing a small number of very low or zero income families (usually self-employed). I report such cases, but the effect of such cases on any general assessment of the Act should not be emphasised as it would be unlikely that such levels of income would be accepted in the determination of a real claim.

20 per cent of those modelled claimants of old-scheme HB have an entitlement to IS, and the majority are gainers and their average gain is £9.86. Claimants of HB under both schemes, 65 per cent of old-scheme HB modelled cases, were split as follows: 41 per cent were gainers with an average gain of £2.83, 35 per cent were losers with an average loss of £3.66, the remainder have changes of less than 50p.

The new scheme also drew in newly entitled claimants for IS through higher capital limits to entitlement. More generous treatment by HB, however, led to 78 new modelled new entitlements to HB with a small average gain of £2.50. New entrants to FC, though few in number, had large gains of £10.06 on average.

10.4.3 Better targeted on the poorest?

How did these changes fit the overall aim of targeting help on the poorest? The model was used to compare incomes according to the claimant's place in the income distribution.

The income distribution used for comparison was the ranked equivalent net income after housing costs produced by the modelling of the old scheme. However, the use of an equivalence scale which deflates the incomes of families with children will push such families down in the income distribution. As such families were a priority group for the Act, the effect of choice of equivalence scale could therefore affect the ranking of gainers and losers.

Figure 10.3 shows the distribution of gainers and losers by their position in the income distribution. The income distribution used as the basis

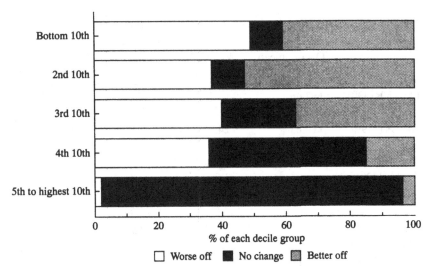

Figure 10.3 Gainers and losers, by decile group

for comparison is the one which results from modelling the old scheme. The changes were targeted on the bottom four decile groups of the income distribution, but the creation of losers and gainers was not solely distributed according to income. While there were equal numbers of gainers and losers in the bottom decile group, there was a greater concentration of better-off cases in the second decile group. For those made worse-off, there are higher proportions within the 4th and higher decile groups than there are of better-off cases. Churning the incomes of large proportions of the poorest may be a better description overall than targeting towards them.

While those either better-off or having no change form the bare majority of the bottom decile, 49 per cent of the very poorest lost. They also endured the highest average loss for any group. The fact that 41 per cent of their peers received marginally higher gains only averages out the losses. However, I must qualify this by again pointing out that some of these very high losers are likely to be 16–18 year olds who should, in theory, receive training allowances as an alternative. Many of the losers will also be paying 20 per cent of their Community Charge in the year when it was at its historically highest level. No allowance has been made to reflect levels of non-payment which may reduce the numbers of such losers. Since April 1993 such a requirement on the poorest has been discontinued.

But who were these modelled losers and gainers in the bottom decile groups?

Table 10.11 *Claimant types: modelled gainers and losers*

	Overall mean effect	Average loss % of group	Average gain % of group	No change % of group
Over 80s (330)	+£2.46	-£5.79	+£6.12	
		27.5	66.4	6.1
60–79s (1199)	+£0.63	-£4.25	+£4.03	
		32.4	49.4	18.2
Sick and disabled (201)	+£1.83	-£6.10	+£7.58	
		31.8	49.8	18.4
OPFs (314)	+£0.17	-£6.87	+£6.94	
		44.6	46.5	8.9
Couples with children (240)	+£2.18	-£8.00	+£8.95	
		37.1	57.5	5.4
Others (783)	-£3.43	-£5.71	+£5.64	
		73.4	13.5	13.0

Source: Author's calculations from FES.

10.4.4 Meeting new priorities?

Table 10.11 breaks down all entitled claimants under both schemes by family type. The aggregate gainers, as shown by positive mean outcomes, confirm the prioritisation of the very elderly, families with children and the sick and disabled. Pensioners aged 60–79 have an average gain only just above the 50p threshold. For those who are no longer a priority, the 'others', 73 per cent are losers, and the aggregate average loss is £3.43 a week. However, the strongest impression from the model is not the spread of gains and losses between the groups but the high incidence of losses and gains within family types which occurs at the same time. The average effects hide many significant changes.

10.4.5 Meeting poverty

I now assess the income profiles of both the old and new systems against a poverty threshold to assess how many families of all types have incomes below this level and the average income shortfall for those families. This measure, of poverty gaps, indicates the overall effectiveness of the systems in bringing families up to a minimum relative level.

Table 10.12 shows the population with incomes under two levels of rela-

Table 10.12 *Poverty gaps and the modelled schemes*[a]

	Old scheme	New scheme
Poverty line 1–50% of mean income		
% of families below 50% mean	27.5	27.6
Average gap	£5.89	£5.92
Poverty line 2–30% of mean income		
% of families below 30% mean	4.5	5.7
Average gap	£0.88	£1.08

Note:
[a] McClements After Housing Costs Equivalence Scale. Households ranked on basis of income in old scheme.
Source: Author's calculations from FES.

tive poverty: 50 per cent and 30 per cent of mean equivalent income. I use both these measures to assess the comparative effectiveness of both schemes. The 50 per cent level of mean income provides an indicator of general relative incomes, and is used by the European Union as an indicator of poverty. The 30 per cent line provides an estimate of the very poor – those most threatened by the move away from a guarantee of minimum adequacy in the new scheme.

There is no significant difference between the old- and new-scheme modelled incomes in the proportion of families below a poverty line of 50 per cent of average income. However, the most stringent of the poverty lines, 30 per cent of average income, does produce a difference, but of low statistical significance. The old scheme has a lower average gap than the new, and the proportion of families who are living below this line is larger under the new scheme. However, income data consistency for the very poorest in the FES suggests that this result may include significant numbers of problem cases where reported low income is accompanied by high expenditure.

10.5 Conclusions

This chapter has sought to identify and quantify the effects of the changes to social security introduced by the 1986 Social Security Act, described at the time as 'the most radical since Beveridge'. To do so I have used both micro-data and published tables to piece together a series of overlapping analyses.

The clear set of objectives set for the Act can be interpreted in a variety of ways. Some of the clarity was sacrificed to political expediency early on in the Act's history. Even so, the package of aims was one which would always require meeting some aims partly at others' expense. A harmonised, simpler system which improved incentives at no extra cost to the Treasury was largely a pipe-dream.

There is no doubt that the new system is simpler, more logically consistent in the treatment of claimants between means-tested schemes, and simpler to understand. However, this simplicity has had a price for the government. A single system of needs assessment means it is now less easy to allow one element to drop from annual uprating as happened before the Act, as this would jeopardise consistency. Thus, for example, HB scale rates have improved over time in harmony with IS and its premiums, a move away from uprating practice prior to 1988.

At the same time, the desire *to improve work incentives* and *remove very high marginal disincentives*, has been limited by the single combined taper for HB for rent and rates/Community Charge/Council Tax which is at a level which cannot easily be made much steeper without pushing all tenants into severe poverty and unemployment traps. The reality is that the new HB scheme for non-IS cases has reached a point where the opportunity for further cost containment is minimal. The new HB scheme is mostly a safety net payment of housing costs for those on IS, it hardly ensures affordability above that line. Unable to downrate help with housing costs, real rent and local tax rises have pushed spending higher in real terms and given less room to manoeuvre in response.

The aim to *control spending*, so prominent in 1985, provided real short-term lower spending levels, but in the medium term has become less effective due to the built-in tendencies of the new design to more comprehensive uprating and the additional spending caused by housing policy raising rents above inflation, and changes in local government finance. In addition, a recession has increased demand through increased unemployment. But the aim to control spending was also behind the changes to the Single Payments regime and its replacement by the Social Fund. The objective has been achieved, but the ability of the scheme to respond to genuine need, another objective of the changes, has been reduced.

Has the 1986 Act fulfilled its aim of targeting help more accurately? If means-testing is synonymous with targeting, then the Act has not helped to target all social security more. Spending on means-tested benefits has remained a constant proportion of all spending. In the modelling of the two schemes there was a high proportion of losers in the bottom quintile group, so targeting towards the poorest, has not happened unreservedly.

This is partly because targeting was not only about means-testing towards the poorest but also about reprioritisation and incentives. If targeting is like archery, then the definition of the target is as important as the skill and equipment of the archer. Despite an overall 'success' in reordering means-tested relativities of benefits, and hence changing the size of targets, there were significant losses incurred among supposedly high priority groups such as the sick and disabled, families with children and the elderly.

Changes in benefit relativities have taken away most areas of additional help from low priority groups. Some claimants are being pushed into work through a lowering of benefits, others enticed by supplementary earnings through higher benefits. As FC is a 'success' why should it not be extended to others or other alternatives found? There seems too sharp a divide. Without policies to attract people into work from benefits, training, or wider work-related incentives, a too heavy reliance on making the poorest of the unemployed relatively poorer may be unsustainable. Where the new scheme has made unemployed claimants poorer, what additional measures are necessary to achieve the greater aims of work, economic recovery, and prosperity?

Is a minimum safety net level of income still guaranteed? Recent policy changes have ended the requirement to pay 20 per cent of local taxation, and the indexation of benefits will now include an element for increases in water rates. But, even so, there are elements of the new design which consciously undermine such a safety net principle, especially the Social Fund.

Notes

Material from the Family Expenditure Survey, made available by the Central Statistical Office through the ESRC Data Archive at the University of Essex, has been used by permission of the Controller of Her Majesty's Stationery Office. Neither the CSO nor the Data Archive bears any responsibility for the analysis or interpretation of the data here.
1. For a detailed history of these changes see Hill (1990), Alcock (1987) and Walker (1993).
2. Such protection froze benefit entitlement in cash terms at the previous SB level.

Part III

Spatial aspects

11 Aspects of the changing geography of poverty and wealth

Anne E. Green

This chapter outlines why a geographical perspective on poverty and wealth is important and presents selected evidence on changes and continuities in poverty and wealth at the local level in Britain between 1981 and 1991.[1]

11.1 Introduction

11.1.1 Context

During the 1980s poverty emerged as an increasingly more significant issue for public debate in Britain, throughout Europe and in North America. While a substantial proportion of the population emerged as *winners* from the economic and social transformations of the 1980s – with rising living standards and incomes – concerns grew that the *losers* – particularly when *spatially concentrated* – may become 'dislocated' from mainstream social norms and values, and moreover pose a threat to public order.

Key features of the restructuring in the economic, social and political arenas during the 1980s include the shift in jobs from manufacturing to services, a new emphasis on 'individualism' as the 'enterprise culture' was actively promoted, and 'deformalisation' and 'deregularisation' of the economy – accompanied by a growth in the use of more 'flexible' employment relationships (Gregson and Robinson, 1989; Room, 1990; Cross, 1993; Green, 1993; Silver, 1993). These processes were instrumental in increasing *polarisation* in the structure of the labour market between the *privileged* on the one hand – mainly working in high wage non-manual jobs; and the *underprivileged* rest on the other – engaged in part-time, generally low wage jobs, or unemployed (Buck, 1992; Gaffikin and Morrisey, 1992).

An important feature of such developments is that they were *spatially uneven* in their *magnitude*, their *impact* upon different population sub-groups, and their *timing*. The areas which suffered least in the recession of

265

the early 1980s tended to gain most in the subsequent recovery; conversely the most depressed regions had not recovered the ground lost in the early 1980s. By the end of the decade, a 'North–South divide' in fortunes was evident (Champion and Green, 1988, 1990; Martin, 1988; Lewis and Townsend, 1989). Alongside these regional differentials in experience, an important *urban–rural dimension* of variation was also apparent (Townsend, 1993): during the 1980s the *large metropolitan areas* tended to fare relatively worse than other areas. However, those areas which gained most in the recovery were the first to feel the effects of rising unemployment as the economy entered the early 1990s' recession (Martin, 1993; Green *et al.*, 1994).

However, broad regional and urban size perspectives disguise pronounced *local* variations in poverty and wealth at intra-regional and intra-urban scales. Previous research shows that the *losers* from the processes of economic and social transformation are often spatially concentrated in particular localities and/or districts within cities. In North America – where spatial perspectives on poverty are most strongly developed – *ecological effects* have been implicated strongly in the growth of the 'underclass' in certain 'extreme poverty' areas in the inner city (Wilson, 1987; Hughes, 1989; Greene, 1991), and links have been made between processes of *spatial concentration*, structural transformation of urban economies and metropolitan deconcentration. It has been argued that if 'extreme poverty areas' are spatially concentrated rather than dispersed, the poor/disadvantaged within them may become isolated from the economic and social mainstream. The hypothesis that concentration and isolation are related is plausible in that a spatially concentrated or segregated group would be expected to have less contact with other groups than would one whose members were evenly distributed throughout a geographic area. The message emerging is that '*geography matters*'!

Despite indications that 'geography matters', a comprehensive spatial perspective on poverty and wealth in Britain is currently under-developed. This chapter is concerned with presenting selected evidence on the spatial *distribution* of poverty and wealth in Britain 1991 and 1981, and tracing the main *continuities* and *changes* in the spatial distribution and segregation of poverty and wealth between 1981 and 1991. (A more detailed insight into patterns of change in two particular local areas is presented by Noble and Smith, chapter 12 in this volume.)

11.1.2 Data sources: the Census of Population

The ideal data source for use in conducting spatial analyses of poverty and wealth would display comprehensive coverage, consistency between areas, accuracy, reliability, frequent updating, maximum possible detail/disaggregation and flexible spatial referencing. On the criterion of *comprehensive coverage* (notwithstanding debates about the scale and spatial and social patterns of under-enumeration in 1991 – OPCS, 1993; Simpson, 1993a) and *spatial disaggregation*, the Census of Population emerges as the best data source for use in a study concerned with issues of spatial distribution and segregation at the local scale: it is a detailed and flexible source of information on the demographic, social and economic characteristics of the British population (Norris and Ross, 1992; Dale and Marsh, 1993).

A *disadvantage* of the Census of Population as a data source for spatial analyses of poverty and wealth is the *lack* of direct measures of *income*. Hence, it is necessary to make use of proxy indicators, as outlined below. A second disadvantage of the Census of Population is that it is *infrequent* – providing only a decennial snapshot. Nevertheless, it remains a useful data source for examining change over the *medium term*.

In the detailed study on which this chapter is based (Green, 1994), three main *areal frameworks* are utilised for presentation of analyses. In ascending order of geographical size these are:

- Approximately 10,000 1981 Census wards:[2] in general, wards may be equated to the 'neighbourhood' scale
- 459 local authority districts (LADs): these are administrative areas
- 280 local labour market areas (LLMAs): these are relatively self-contained commuting areas.

These areal frameworks were defined in different ways for different purposes, and so use of more than one areal framework permits a variety of perspectives, and enables insights into confirmatory or contradictory patterns of spatial distribution at different geographical scales. In this chapter, however, analyses are restricted to the LAD and ward scales. In order to reduce the size and complexity of the data and summarise the main dimensions of the geographical patterns emerging, use is made of an 11-fold categorisation of LADs, based on urban size, regional location and selected socio-economic characteristics.

11.1.3 Identification of indicators of poverty and wealth

In the absence of direct income measures from the Census of Population, it is necessary to make use of *proxy indicators* of poverty and wealth. The identification, definition and operationalisation of indicators of poverty and deprivation are the subject of considerable debate (for example, Morris and Carstairs, 1991; Forrest and Gordon, 1993; Simpson, 1993; Hirschfield, 1994). Commonly used key indicators include unemployment, no car, rented housing, overcrowding, lack of basic amenities, households with elderly people, households with young children, large households, single person households, lone parent households and low social class/socio-economic group. However, there is no universal agreement about which indicators are most appropriate; rather, indicators tend to be selected to suit the specific purpose at hand in the light of data availability constraints. Debates about proxy indicators for wealth are much less well developed, although 'low' values on poverty indicators are often interpreted as such.

Recent research by Davies *et al.* (1993) has attempted to examine the validity of commonly used Census indicators as predictors of income using Family Expenditure Survey (FES) and General Household Survey (GHS) datasets in which income is also available. This research confirms the importance of car access and tenure as indicators of poverty: people with the lowest incomes are much less likely to have use of a car, and are much more likely to live in rented accommodation. Moreover, car access has become a more significant indicator of low income over the period 1983–90, while the income gap between renters and others has widened over the period 1983–90. Unemployment and economic inactivity are also important indicators of low income: the economically active in employment have higher incomes that their non-employed counterparts. The poor are also much more likely to live alone, or be lone parents. Skill level is significant – the presumption that the 'lower social orders' have low income and the 'higher social orders' have high income is supported. It should be borne in mind that any proxy indicator of poverty/wealth will exclude some of the poor/wealthy, while including others who are not amongst the poorest/wealthiest. Nevertheless, it may be concluded that many Census-based proxies do provide viable indicators of poverty/wealth.

It is useful to have indicators which measure slightly different dimensions of poverty and wealth, since experiences of poverty and wealth are themselves multi-dimensional. In this chapter analyses are restricted to three poverty indicators:

- Proportion of households with *no car*
- *Unemployment rate*
- *Inactivity rate* – 20–59 year olds

and two wealth indicators

- Proportion of households with *two or more cars*
- Proportion of households from *social classes 1 and 2*.

(For analyses across a wider range of proxy indicators – including renter households, proportions of highly qualified adults, and broad measures of occupational structure – see Green, 1994.)

11.2 Spatial distribution of poverty and wealth

11.2.1 Measures of degree

The most straightforward measure of spatial distribution is the value for an area on each specific indicator. This value may be thought of as a measure of *degree*.

Poverty

The 'top 15' LADs heading the rankings in 1991 and 1981 on each of the three *poverty indicators* are listed in the first and second data panels of tables 11.1 (no-car households), 11.2 (unemployment rate) and 11.3 (inactivity rate for persons aged 20–59). All of the 'top 15' LADs on the *no-car* indicator in both 1991 and 1981 (table 11.1) are metropolitan areas: Glasgow, Liverpool, Manchester and Newcastle upon Tyne are included in the lists for both years, and of the remainder (in each year) eight are inner London boroughs – seven of which are common to both the 1991 and 1981 list. Clearly, areas with the highest proportions of households with no car tend to be concentrated disproportionately in inner London, and in the large metropolitan areas of northern Britain: a clear urban–rural dimension of variation is apparent, with little change in relative position between 1981 and 1991.

On the *unemployment rate* indicator (table 11.2) there is a similar, although not identical, pattern: Liverpool, Glasgow and Manchester are again included in the lists for both years. Other representatives of regions characterised by long-term decline are also included: for example, Knowsley (Merseyside); Middlesbrough, Hartlepool, Sunderland and South Tyneside (north-east England – the latter three in 1981 only); and Rhondda, Afan and Blaenau Gwent (in South Wales – each in one year only). Alongside these elements of continuity, key features of change are first, the incorporation of seven inner London boroughs among the 'top 15' in 1991 (all were ranked lower in 1981), and secondly, the disappearance of many steel-closure districts (Corby, Derwentside (Consett), Scunthorpe, Middlesbrough, Afan (Port Talbot) and Blaenau Gwent (Ebbw Vale)) from the top of the rankings over the decade.

Turning to the *inactivity rate* indicator (table 11.3), the changes between 1981 and 1991 are more pronounced than the continuities. Over the 1980s there was a pronounced fall in inactivity rates for women and an increase in such rates for men. In 1981 the majority of the 'top 15' LADs were remote rural areas of the 'Celtic fringe'. In 1991 the remote rural areas are absent from the 'top 15'. Five of the 'top 6' LADs are in the South Wales Valleys, and other areas characterised by the demise of coal-mining (such

Table 11.1 *Households with no car: rankings of LADs on degree, extent and intensity measures, 1991*

'Top 15' LADs, 1991 (1981 rank in parentheses)

LAD	Degree		Extent		Intensity	
	score	rank	score	rank	score	rank
Glasgow City	65.56	1 (001)	70.73	9 (007)	91.34	1 (001)
Hackney	61.73	2 (003)	100.00	1 (002)	69.76	21 (025)
Tower Hamlets	61.55	3 (002)	94.74	3 (001)	70.30	20 (018)
Islington	59.91	4 (004)	100.00	2 (003)	66.79	29 (037)
Clydebank	58.74	5 (010)	55.56	21 (018)	65.90	33 (046)
Southwark	57.98	6 (007)	76.00	5 (004)	70.48	19 (033)
Westminster	57.74	7 (005)	78.26	4 (008)	69.28	23 (019)
Liverpool	56.95	8 (006)	75.76	6 (006)	84.55	3 (002)
Manchester	56.58	9 (011)	75.76	7 (011)	81.13	5 (004)
Camden	55.81	10 (008)	69.23	11 (009)	73.89	12 (013)
Lambeth	55.43	11 (013)	68.18	12 (014)	68.27	26 (029)
Newcastle upon Tyne	54.43	12 (014)	57.69	19 (015)	82.12	4 (003)
South Tyneside	53.62	13 (012)	68.18	13 (010)	69.67	22 (020)
Newham	53.52	14 (028)	75.00	8 (047)	65.43	34 (069)
Inverclyde	52.82	15 (015)	60.00	16 (027)	75.67	9 (010)
Haringey	49.94	23 (039)	69.57	10 (052)	60.85	54 (099)
Knowsley	51.92	17 (021)	64.29	14 (016)	70.55	18 (024)
Kingston upon Hull	51.14	21 (017)	61.90	15 (013)	70.60	17 (016)

'Top 15' LADs, 1981 (1991 rank in parentheses)

LAD	Degree		Extent		Intensity	
	score	rank	score	rank	score	rank
Glasgow City	70.63	1 (001)	74.80	7 (009)	95.44	1 (001)
Tower Hamlets	67.40	2 (003)	100.00	1 (003)	75.15	18 (020)
Hackney	65.60	3 (002)	100.00	2 (001)	71.91	25 (021)
Islington	64.89	4 (004)	100.00	3 (002)	70.03	37 (029)
Westminster	63.82	5 (007)	73.91	8 (004)	74.95	19 (023)
Liverpool	61.77	6 (008)	75.76	6 (006)	88.64	2 (003)
Southwark	61.37	7 (006)	80.00	4 (005)	70.89	33 (019)
Camden	61.09	8 (010)	73.08	9 (011)	77.22	13 (012)
Hammersmith and Fulham	60.84	9 (016)	65.22	12 (020)	71.35	30 (040)
Clydebank	60.64	10 (005)	55.56	18 (021)	67.49	46 (033)
Manchester	60.44	11 (009)	66.67	11 (007)	83.52	4 (005)
South Tyneside	59.48	12 (013)	68.18	10 (013)	74.91	20 (022)
Lambeth	59.05	13 (011)	59.09	14 (012)	71.50	29 (026)
Newcastle upon Tyne	58.75	14 (012)	57.69	15 (019)	83.54	3 (004)
Inverclyde	57.78	15 (015)	46.67	27 (016)	79.49	10 (009)
Isles of Scilly	54.63	25 (020)	80.00	5 (017)	80.85	7 (002)
Kingston upon Hull	57.39	17 (021)	61.90	13 (015)	76.79	16 (017)

Table 11.2 *Unemployment rate: rankings of LADs on degree, extent and intensity measures, 1991*

'Top 15' LADs, 1991 (1981 rank in parentheses)

LAD	Degree		Extent		Intensity	
	score	rank	score	rank	score	rank
Hackney	22.49	1 (032)	100.00	1 (023)	27.52	15 (081)
Knowsley	22.06	2 (002)	85.71	5 (004)	34.87	4 (003)
Tower Hamlets	21.80	3 (026)	100.00	2 (033)	28.52	10 (070)
Liverpool	21.14	4 (005)	81.82	6 (006)	43.07	2 (002)
Newham	19.33	5 (077)	87.50	4 (106)	25.34	26 (086)
Glasgow City	19.08	6 (007)	58.54	13 (020)	47.35	1 (001)
Manchester	18.72	7 (016)	78.79	7 (026)	37.92	3 (009)
Southwark	18.16	8 (075)	76.00	8 (113)	27.06	16 (113)
Haringey	17.68	9 (129)	69.57	9 (221)	23.49	32 (203)
Lambeth	17.10	10 (067)	68.18	10 (066)	22.88	36 (101)
Islington	17.06	11 (069)	90.00	3 (180)	20.56	57 (166)
Cumnock and Doon Valley	16.83	12 (020)	33.33	47 (070)	20.55	58 (095)
Middlesbrough	16.67	13 (006)	64.00	11 (010)	32.01	7 (005)
Rhondda	16.21	14 (030)	54.55	14 (017)	21.75	41 (071)
Nottingham	15.38	15 (059)	37.04	33 (061)	27.83	14 (032)
South Tyneside	15.35	17 (014)	59.09	12 (008)	23.03	35 (041)
Kingston upon Hull	15.27	19 (018)	52.38	15 (009)	26.90	18 (024)

'Top 15' LADs, 1981 (1991 rank in parentheses)

LAD	Degree		Extent		Intensity	
	score	rank	score	rank	score	rank
Corby	22.16	1 (091)	91.67	1 (099)	29.24	6 (159)
Knowsley	20.87	2 (002)	78.57	4 (005)	31.78	3 (004)
Derwentside	20.24	3 (064)	86.96	2 (059)	31.35	4 (093)
Scunthorpe	18.29	4 (044)	81.25	3 (049)	24.69	13 (078)
Liverpool	18.15	5 (004)	72.73	6 (006)	33.28	2 (002)
Middlesbrough	18.13	6 (013)	64.00	10 (011)	30.31	5 (007)
Glasgow City	16.63	7 (006)	53.66	20 (013)	40.34	1 (001)
Hartlepool	16.37	8 (020)	52.94	21 (039)	25.47	11 (017)
Cunninghame	15.48	9 (049)	51.43	24 (061)	22.37	29 (080)
Afan	15.38	10 (077)	54.55	16 (037)	20.96	38 (101)
Monklands	15.33	11 (018)	45.00	30 (041)	18.06	74 (100)
Blaenau Gwent	15.25	12 (052)	75.00	5 (108)	19.29	55 (105)
Sunderland	15.15	13 (025)	57.69	12 (017)	26.76	10 (012)
South Tyneside	14.96	14 (017)	68.18	8 (012)	20.81	41 (035)
Manchester	14.93	15 (007)	48.48	26 (007)	27.24	9 (003)
Western Isles	12.80	37 (083)	70.00	7 (053)	20.87	40 (122)
Kingston upon Hull	14.63	18 (019)	66.67	9 (015)	23.28	24 (018)
Wolverhampton	14.93	16 (028)	60.00	11 (029)	23.17	26 (022)
Clydebank	14.84	17 (027)	55.56	13 (021)	16.82	89 (111)
Coventry	14.10	23 (055)	55.56	14 (073)	21.20	36 (044)
Wear Valley	13.90	27 (059)	55.00	15 (081)	19.23	58 (074)

Table 11.3 *Inactivity rate, persons aged 20–59: rankings of LADs on degree, extent and intensity measures, 1991*

'Top 15' LADs, 1991 (1981 rank in parentheses)

LAD	Degree		Extent		Intensity	
	score	rank	score	rank	score	rank
Rhondda	32.29	1 (006)	100.0	1 (035)	37.40	11 (076)
Easington	31.22	2 (025)	76.92	4 (065)	41.01	2 (062)
Merthyr Tydfil	30.41	3 (034)	100.0	2 (042)	35.77	17 (125)
Afan	30.22	4 (017)	72.73	6 (021)	40.77	3 (032)
Rhymney Valley	29.30	5 (018)	71.43	8 (010)	38.80	5 (050)
Blaenau Gwent	29.26	6 (012)	75.00	5 (032)	35.35	20 (084)
Cynon Valley	29.24	7 (009)	71.43	9 (012)	35.17	21 (154)
Knowsley	28.21	8 (167)	64.29	12 (111)	36.23	14 (232)
Cumnock and Doon Valley	28.03	9 (033)	41.67	30 (034)	31.16	56 (035)
Glasgow City	27.82	10 (208)	56.91	17 (131)	47.33	1 (003)
Llanelli	27.62	11 (037)	72.73	7 (048)	31.55	53 (167)
Monklands	27.56	12 (136)	40.00	34 (100)	33.00	38 (128)
Manchester	27.46	13 (233)	66.67	11 (152)	39.30	4 (019)
Tower Hamlets	27.30	14 (282)	78.95	3 (335)	34.09	27 (387)
Motherwell	27.01	15 (103)	52.38	20 (109)	32.24	44 (093)
Neath	26.26	20 (047)	68.75	10 (078)	33.21	35 (103)
Liverpool	26.87	16 (239)	63.64	13 (153)	38.41	6 (151)
Middlesbrough	26.74	17 (067)	60.00	14 (061)	38.24	7 (108)
Newham	26.27	19 (226)	58.33	15 (307)	32.94	39 (301)

'Top 15' LADs, 1981 (1991 rank in parentheses)

LAD	Degree		Extent		Intensity	
	score	rank	score	rank	score	rank
Dwyfor	29.95	1 (044)	70.83	4 (022)	36.96	10 (066)
West Devon	29.06	2 (138)	71.43	3 (140)	41.19	5 (105)
Penwith	28.83	3 (058)	68.75	7 (244)	31.66	57 (182)
Ynys Mon	28.72	4 (024)	59.09	11 (018)	33.76	20 (057)
Kerrier	28.64	5 (053)	77.27	1 (069)	33.13	27 (116)
Rhondda	28.50	6 (001)	54.55	13 (001)	31.07	76 (011)
South Pembrokeshire	28.47	7 (021)	70.00	5 (025)	31.11	74 (071)
North Cornwall	28.42	8 (080)	74.07	2 (102)	34.58	15 (128)
Cynon Valley	27.70	9 (007)	57.14	12 (009)	31.81	54 (021)
Restormel	27.40	10 (098)	50.00	15 (159)	29.21	132 (203)
Skye and Lochalsh	27.39	11 (146)	26.32	50 (248)	30.07	99 (274)
Blaenau Gwent	27.27	12 (006)	35.00	32 (005)	30.61	84 (020)
Caradon	27.21	13 (127)	69.23	6 (218)	33.21	26 (149)
Ross and Cromarty	27.11	14 (070)	50.00	16 (109)	32.81	31 (143)
Preseli	26.96	15 (038)	41.94	25 (081)	31.35	64 (102)
Orkney Islands	25.58	43 (197)	66.67	8 (265)	25.80	299 (423)
Banff and Buchan	26.06	32 (100)	64.71	9 (120)	38.68	8 (174)
Rhymney Valley	26.90	18 (005)	61.90	10 (008)	31.86	50 (005)
Torridge	26.09	31 (121)	51.85	14 (157)	32.70	33 (166)

as Easington) and major industrial closures (such as Knowsley) are included in the 'top 15'.

Obviously, tables 11.1–11.3 focus only on continuity and change over the period 1981–91 in the very poorest areas. Further insights into the changing spatial distribution of the *degree* of poverty may be obtained by analysis of an 11-fold categorisation of LADs. Table 11.4 shows the mean value on each of the three poverty indicators by LAD category for 1991 and 1981, and change over the inter-censual period.

Across Great Britain as a whole the proportion of households with *no car* decreased from nearly two fifths to approximately a third. In 1991, as in 1981, the proportion of households with no car was highest in inner London, the principal cities and the large non-metropolitan cities (these are, by and large, the areas with the most well-developed public transport systems, so lack of a car in such areas may not indicate a level of disadvantage as acute as in a remote rural area with little, if any, public transport provision). In inner London and the principal cities the decline in the proportion of households with no car over the period 1981–91 was less pronounced than the national average; indeed, in 1991 all inner London boroughs and all except one of the principal cities were in the 'top' decile group of LADs on this indicator. By contrast, the proportion of households with no car was lowest in the mixed urban–rural and remoter rural areas. However, it was the LADs in the middle portion of the urban hierarchy which saw the largest decreases in proportions of households without cars over the inter-censual period.

The *unemployment rate* was higher in principal cities in both 1991 and 1981 than in any other category. All other metropolitan categories (with the exception of outer London), along with the industrial areas, recorded higher than average unemployment rates in both Census years. In terms of unemployment change, however, the most striking feature is the increase in unemployment rates in London – particularly inner London. In part, this reflects the timing of the 1991 Census snapshot – capturing the earlier upturn in unemployment in southern England than in other parts of Britain – but it also reflects the tendency for higher unemployment rates to become more pronounced in large metropolitan areas over the decade. By contrast, the mixed urban–rural areas and remoter rural areas recorded the lowest unemployment rates in 1991.

Similarly, increases in *inactivity rates* between 1981 and 1991 were most pronounced in the principal cities and inner London. These areas had lower than average inactivity rates in 1981 (so the scope for further reduction may have been less than in the more rural areas). However, they are also characterised by higher than average concentrations of minority ethnic groups, and – particularly in areas with markedly higher than

Table 11.4 *Change in poverty indicators, by LAD category, 1981–91*

LAD category	1991	1981	1981–91 change
Inner London			
% households with no car	53.67	58.34	–4.67
unemployment rate	15.44	10.38	5.06
inactivity rate – 20–59 years	21.43	19.15	2.28
Outer London			
% households with no car	32.05	36.18	–4.13
unemployment rate	8.97	6.05	2.92
inactivity rate – 20–59 years	18.30	19.39	–1.09
Principal cities			
% households with no car	52.12	57.26	–5.14
unemployment rate	15.68	13.68	2.00
inactivity rate – 20–59 years	23.78	21.30	2.48
Other metropolitan districts			
% households with no car	39.59	45.51	–5.92
unemployment rate	11.28	11.12	0.16
inactivity rate – 20–59 years	21.41	21.23	0.18
Large non-metropolitan cities			
% households with no car	41.35	47.87	–6.52
unemployment rate	11.08	10.18	0.90
inactivity rate – 20–59 years	20.81	21.13	–0.32
Small non-metropolitan cities			
% households with no car	35.58	42.58	–7.00
unemployment rate	9.35	8.93	0.42
inactivity rate – 20–59 years	19.59	21.23	–1.64
Industrial areas			
% households with no car	33.20	39.87	–6.67
unemployment rate	9.46	9.80	–0.34
inactivity rate – 20–59 years	20.95	22.59	–1.64
Districts with New Towns			
% households with no car	31.12	36.41	–5.29
unemployment rate	8.93	9.75	–0.82
inactivity rate – 20–59 years	19.01	21.26	–2.25
Resort and retirement areas			
% households with no car	29.62	36.55	–6.93
unemployment rate	8.13	7.79	0.34
inactivity rate – 20–59 years	19.72	23.41	–3.69

Table 11.4 (*contd.*)

LAD category	1991	1981	1981–91 change
Mixed urban–rural areas			
% households with no car	20.77	25.79	–5.02
unemployment rate	5.81	5.36	0.45
inactivity rate – 20–59 years	17.06	21.47	–4.41
Remoter rural areas			
% households with no car	24.54	30.11	–5.57
unemployment rate	6.88	7.38	–0.50
inactivity rate – 20–59 years	19.38	24.36	–4.98
GREAT BRITAIN			
% households with no car	33.35	39.47	–6.12
unemployment rate	9.28	8.83	0.45
inactivity rate – 20–59 years	19.74	21.60	–1.86

average proportions of South Asian females (for whom inactivity rates tend to be lower than average) – this may be a factor in rising rates of inactivity, alongside the severe decline in manufacturing jobs in such areas. Reductions in inactivity were most pronounced in rural areas, where female inactivity rates were initially higher than the national average.

Wealth

Turning to the two *wealth indicators*, the first and second data panels of tables 11.5 (two or more-car households) and 11.6 (households from social classes 1 and 2) list the 'top 15' LADs heading the rankings. A clear continuing southern and ex-large urban bias in the concentration of wealth emerges. There is also some evidence for increasing wealth in rural parts of northern England and north-east Scotland.

All of the 'top 15' LADs on the *two or more cars* indicator in both 1991 and 1981 (table 11.5) are in the Home Counties (or on the fringes of immediately adjoining areas): 12 are included in the 'top 15' in both years, with over 30 per cent of households having two or more cars in 1981 and rising to over 40 per cent in 1991 – these include representatives from Surrey, Buckinghamshire, Berkshire, Hampshire and Essex. This is indicative of relative stability in the geographical patterns over the decade (as on the 'no-car' poverty indicator).

Some of these same LADs appear in the 'top 15' on the proportion of *households from social classes 1 and 2* indicator (table 11.6). Alongside the

Table 11.5 *Households with two or more cars: rankings of LADs on degree, extent and intensity measures, 1991*

'Top 15' LADs, 1991 (1981 rank in parentheses)

LAD	Degree		Extent		Intensity	
	score	rank	score	rank	score	rank
Surrey Heath	50.99	1 (002)	62.50	2 (009)	67.84	1 (001)
Hart	50.49	2 (004)	81.25	1 (001)	59.86	19 (051)
Wokingham	48.54	3 (005)	58.33	4 (007)	62.37	9 (014)
Chiltern	47.66	4 (003)	60.00	3 (004)	67.67	2 (002)
South Bucks	47.26	5 (001)	50.00	10 (003)	59.25	24 (007)
Uttlesford	44.44	6 (006)	54.84	6 (005)	60.02	16 (025)
Tandridge	43.11	7 (010)	42.86	15 (015)	61.57	10 (009)
Wycombe	42.75	8 (009)	54.17	8 (008)	65.36	4 (010)
Mole Valley	42.71	9 (008)	34.78	29 (011)	56.75	40 (036)
East Hampshire	42.26	10 (024)	48.39	12 (027)	58.79	28 (041)
South Northampton-shire	42.14	11 (035)	37.50	25 (072)	53.74	73 (082)
Elmbridge	41.83	12 (007)	22.73	70 (016)	55.57	51 (038)
Windsor and Maidenhead	41.46	13 (011)	30.00	41 (029)	52.43	89 (077)
Waverley	41.43	14 (013)	40.00	18 (018)	58.21	31 (028)
East Hertfordshire	40.82	15 (022)	40.00	19 (024)	57.60	33 (027)
Harborough	39.64	23 (025)	56.52	5 (002)	59.25	23 (024)
Winchester	39.22	28 (040)	54.84	7 (022)	58.47	29 (048)
Malvern Hills	36.95	53 (028)	51.52	9 (006)	54.70	65 (054)
Daventry	39.51	24 (038)	50.00	11 (010)	56.26	42 (035)
Lichfield	39.23	27 (042)	44.44	13 (017)	63.39	7 (003)
Test Valley	37.80	43 (056)	43.38	14 (043)	55.93	46 (070)

'Top 15' LADs, 1981 (1991 rank in parentheses)

LAD	Degree		Extent		Intensity	
	score	rank	score	rank	score	rank
South Bucks	39.01	1 (005)	61.11	3 (010)	52.60	7 (024)
Surrey Heath	38.89	2 (001)	50.00	9 (002)	57.28	1 (001)
Chiltern	36.77	3 (004)	56.67	4 (003)	56.14	2 (002)
Hart	35.90	4 (002)	68.75	1 (001)	44.26	51 (019)
Wokingham	35.29	5 (003)	54.17	7 (004)	50.49	14 (009)
Uttlesford	32.62	6 (006)	54.84	5 (006)	46.64	25 (016)
Elmbridge	32.56	7 (012)	40.91	16 (070)	45.36	38 (051)
Mole Valley	32.45	8 (009)	47.83	11 (029)	45.52	36 (040)

Table 11.5 (contd.)
'Top 15' LADs, 1991 (1981 rank in parentheses)

LAD	Degree		Extent		Intensity	
	score	rank	score	rank	score	rank
Wycombe	32.33	9 (008)	54.17	8 (008)	51.53	10 (004)
Tandridge	32.25	10 (007)	42.86	15 (015)	52.10	9 (010)
Windsor and						
Maidenhead	31.73	11 (013)	35.00	29 (041)	41.27	77 (089)
Runnymede	29.99	12 (020)	35.71	26 (049)	43.21	57 (090)
Waverley	29.85	13 (014)	40.00	18 (018)	46.29	28 (031)
Eastwood	29.57	14 (050)	9.09	145 (137)	38.64	118 (192)
Epping Forest	29.26	15 (046)	43.33	14 (043)	47.58	21 (037)
Harborough	28.75	25 (023)	65.22	2 (005)	46.70	24 (023)
Malvern Hills	28.52	28 (053)	54.55	6 (009)	43.99	54 (065)
Daventry	27.58	38 (024)	50.00	10 (011)	45.56	35 (042)
Brentwood	29.20	18 (052)	44.44	12 (030)	49.46	16 (013)
Macclesfield	28.21	29 (051)	44.12	13 (035)	52.94	6 (014)

majority of representatives from the Home Counties are certain London boroughs (for example, Richmond-upon-Thames) and districts within other large metropolitan areas (for example, Bearsden and Milngavie in Glasgow). 11 and 13 LADs, respectively, are common to the 'top 15' in 1991 and 1981.

A broader insight into the changing spatial distribution of the *degree* of wealth is possible by analysing patterns of change across the 11-fold categorisation of LADs. Table 11.7 shows that all LAD categories shared in the increase in the proportion of *two or more-car households*. The percentage point increase was most marked in the mixed urban–rural areas which started from the highest initial base. At the opposite extreme, increases were least marked in inner London and the principal cities which had the lowest proportions of such households in 1981. By contrast, inner London and the principal cities showed the largest percentage point increases in the proportion of households from *social classes 1 and 2*. Alongside the relatively high values on the poverty indicators described above, this perhaps indicates increasing professionalisation and relative polarisation in the socio-economic structure in inner London and the principal cities. All LAD categories shared in the increase in such households, and although displaying a smaller than average percentage point increase over the decade, the mixed urban–rural areas maintained a higher proportion of households from social classes 1 and 2 than any other LAD category over the period 1981–91.

Table 11.6 *Households from social classes 1 and 2: rankings of LADs on* degree, extent *and* intensity *measures, 1991*

'Top 15' LADs, 1991 (1981 rank in parentheses)

LAD	Degree		Extent		Intensity	
	score	rank	score	rank	score	rank
City of London	71.43	1 (001)	16.00	99 (036)	86.96	5 (006)
Richmond upon Thames	63.31	2 (011)	57.89	3 (016)	74.93	23 (111)
Bearsden and Milngavie	63.01	3 (002)	55.56	4 (001)	76.95	16 (030)
Eastwood	62.32	4 (003)	45.45	12 (007)	71.48	53 (032)
Elmbridge	60.47	5 (006)	63.64	1 (003)	77.48	13 (042)
Kensington and Chelsea	60.30	6 (023)	61.90	2 (013)	76.73	17 (104)
Wokingham	59.81	7 (005)	54.17	5 (002)	74.02	33 (055)
Chiltern	59.65	8 (004)	50.00	10 (005)	80.11	9 (009)
St Albans	59.49	9 (008)	50.00	8 (010)	76.14	19 (024)
Mole Valley	57.28	10 (010)	43.48	15 (011)	70.69	66 (087)
South Bucks	57.16	11 (007)	50.00	9 (025)	74.57	27 (017)
Macclesfield	56.24	12 (017)	50.00	7 (012)	81.31	6 (016)
Waverley	56.21	13 (014)	48.00	11 (017)	71.54	50 (086)
Surrey Heath	55.86	14 (012)	31.25	28 (028)	74.66	26 (043)
Epsom and Ewell	55.61	15 (016)	23.08	50 (029)	70.62	67 (081)
Cambridge	49.56	40 (115)	50.00	6 (063)	69.52	80 (119)
Hart	55.35	16 (013)	43.75	13 (015)	66.00	125 (108)

'Top 15' LADs, 1981 (1991 rank in parentheses)

LAD	Degree		Extent		Intensity	
	score	rank	score	rank	score	rank
City of London	66.87	1 (001)	28.00	36 (099)	92.16	6 (005)
Bearsden and Milngavie	59.52	2 (003)	55.56	1 (004)	71.56	30 (006)
Eastwood	58.96	3 (004)	45.45	7 (012)	70.76	32 (053)
Chiltern	55.41	4 (008)	46.67	5 (010)	80.94	9 (009)
Wokingham	53.99	5 (007)	54.17	2 (005)	67.86	55 (033)
Elmbridge	53.92	6 (005)	50.00	3 (001)	69.69	42 (013)
South Bucks	52.77	7 (011)	33.33	25 (009)	76.07	17 (027)
St Albans	52.39	8 (009)	40.00	10 (008)	73.28	24 (019)
Tandridge	51.38	9 (019)	47.62	4 (017)	72.59	25 (012)
Mole Valley	50.95	10 (010)	39.13	11 (015)	64.46	87 (066)
Richmond upon Thames	50.86	11 (002)	36.84	16 (003)	62.76	111 (023)
Surrey Heath	50.45	12 (014)	31.25	28 (028)	69.49	43 (026)
Hart	50.26	13 (016)	37.50	15 (013)	62.86	108 (125)
Waverley	49.87	14 (013)	36.00	17 (011)	64.61	86 (050)
Mid-Sussex	49.59	15 (025)	23.33	54 (068)	64.00	93 (062)
Radnor	44.26	36 (172)	45.83	6 (090)	81.21	8 (020)
Ribble Valley	43.78	39 (044)	43.48	8 (014)	70.28	38 (024)
Isles of Scilly	40.82	67 (169)	40.00	9 (061)	72.22	26 (327)
Macclesfield	49.20	17 (012)	38.24	12 (007)	76.09	16 (006)
Kensington and Chelsea	46.49	23 (006)	38.10	13 (002)	63.21	104 (017)
Woking	48.49	18 (026)	37.50	14 (018)	70.27	39 (055)

Table 11.7 *Change in wealth indicators, by LAD category, 1981–91*

LAD category	1991	1981	1981–91 change
Inner London			
% households with 2 or more cars	9.81	7.39	2.42
% social class 1 and 2 households	44.30	31.56	12.74
Outer London			
% households with 2 or more cars	23.42	17.22	6.22
% social class 1 and 2 households	41.74	34.98	6.76
Principal cities			
% households with 2 or more cars	12.18	8.13	4.05
% social class 1 and 2 households	30.52	23.18	7.34
Other metropolitan districts			
% households with 2 or more cars	18.99	12.54	6.45
% social class 1 and 2 households	32.37	26.42	5.95
Large non-metropolitan cities			
% households with 2 or more cars	15.93	10.28	5.65
% social class 1 and 2 households	31.70	24.53	7.17
Small non-metropolitan cities			
% households with 2 or more cars	18.39	12.41	5.98
% social class 1 and 2 households	37.64	29.71	7.93
Industrial areas			
% households with 2 or more cars	21.79	13.56	8.23
% social class 1 and 2 households	30.64	24.87	5.77
Districts with New Towns			
% households with 2 or more cars	23.67	15.16	8.51
% social class 1 and 2 households	33.70	27.48	6.22
Resort and retirement areas			
% households with 2 or more cars	23.63	15.73	7.90
% social class 1 and 2 households	38.11	33.79	4.38
Mixed urban–rural areas			
% households with 2 or more cars	35.01	24.56	10.46
% social class 1 and 2 households	45.13	39.38	5.75
Remoter rural areas			
% households with 2 or more cars	27.22	19.19	8.03
% social class 1 and 2 households	37.20	33.72	3.48
GREAT BRITAIN			
% households with 2 or more cars	23.13	15.46	7.67
% social class 1 and 2 households	37.21	30.46	6.75

11.2.2 Classifying areas on experience of change in the degree of poverty and wealth, 1981–91

In order to gain a more comprehensive picture of experiences of continuity and change on the poverty and wealth indicators at a different level of geographical disaggregation, a series of matrices were constructed at the ward scale showing '1991 decile group' by '1981 decile group' for each indicator. On the basis of experience of relative change over the decade, wards were then allocated into one of seven classes: 'extreme loser', 'losing', 'worsening', 'stable', 'improving', 'gaining', 'extreme gainer' (for further details see Green, 1994). Having been allocated to the seven-fold 'experience of change' classification, the wards were then coded to the 11-fold categorisation of LADs.

Considering the poverty indicators first, the picture is one of continuity at the national scale on the *no-car households* indicator. Over 50 per cent of wards in Great Britain were in the same decile group in 1981 and 1991 on this indicator. This picture of 'stability' is replicated for most LAD categories: and is most apparent in the cases of inner London and the principal cities. Relative deterioration was greatest in outer London and the new towns, while improvement was most apparent in resorts and retirement areas, remoter rural areas and industrial districts. A *variety of experience* at the ward level within LAD categories is apparent. The trend towards greater concentration in metropolitan areas is also evident on the *unemployment rate* indicator (figure 11.1). Deterioration over the decade is most marked in London, while in the remoter rural areas category nearly half the wards are categorised as 'improving' or 'gaining'. The urban–rural dimension of variation is even more apparent on the *inactivity rate* indicator (figure 11.2). At least a third of the wards in inner London and the principal cities are categorised as 'extreme losers', and more than a further third as 'losers'. By contrast, over two fifths of wards in remoter rural areas and mixed urban–rural areas are 'gainers' or 'extreme gainers'. However, even in these two LAD categories between a fifth and a tenth of wards experienced relative deterioration over the decade.

Turning to the wealth indicators, as for no-car households, so for *two-car households* (figure 11.3), the main picture emerging is one of stability. On the *social class 1 and 2* indicator, inner London easily experienced the largest relative gains, with the small non-metropolitan cities in second place. In the principal cities and outer London there were fewer instances of 'improvement' than elsewhere.

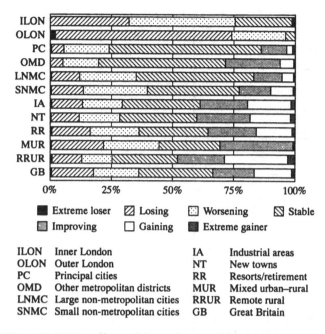

Figure 11.1 'Experience of change': unemployment rate

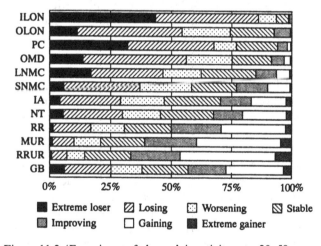

Figure 11.2 'Experience of change': inactivity rate, 20–59 year olds

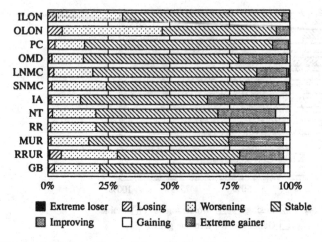

Figure 11.3 'Experience of change': households with two or more cars
Key as for figure 11.1

11.2.3 Measures of extent

Since the *degree* measure represents the 'average' across what might be a wide range of experience at the intra-LAD scale, a measure of *extent* was calculated as the percentage of all wards within a LAD ranked in the 'top' decile group (an arbitrarily chosen cut-off) of the national distribution of wards on each indicator, in order to provide an insight into the 'extensiveness' of poverty/wealth at the intra-urban scale.

Poverty

The third and fourth data panels of tables 11.1, 11.2 and 11.3 show the 'top 15' LADs on the measure of *extent* for the three poverty indicators. On the proportion of households with *no-car* indicator (table 11.1), all of the wards in Hackney and Islington fall in the top decile group of the national distribution in both 1981 and 1991. In six further LADs – Tower Hamlets, Westminster, Southwark, Liverpool, Manchester and Newham – at least three quarters of all wards were in the top decile group of the national distribution. On the *unemployment rate* indicator (table 11.2), all wards in Hackney and Tower Hamlets were included in the top decile group of the national distribution in 1991. In Islington, Newham, Knowsley and Liverpool the proportion exceeded four fifths. A comparison with the 'top 15' on the *extent* measure in 1981 reveals a clear tendency for high unemployment rates to become more extensive over the 1980s in inner London, as well as in large northern metropolitan areas such as Manchester, Merseyside (Liverpool and Knowsley) and Glasgow. By contrast, in many of the steel-closure areas, unemployment became less extensive over the 1980s (in these areas the 1981 Census snapshot coincided with localised very high unemployment rates around steel works which had been shut down/witnessed massive redundancies). It is in the South Wales Valleys that the *extent* of *inactivity* (table 11.3) is most pronounced: in 1991 all wards in both Rhondda and Merthyr Tydfil were in the top decile group of the national distribution. Already more extensive than in all except some of the remotest rural areas in 1981, high inactivity rates became even more extensive in the South Wales Valleys over the decade to 1991. While declining in remoter rural areas, the *extent* of inactivity – like the *extent* of unemployment – also became more pronounced than in inner London and the large metropolitan areas of northern Britain.

Wealth

Turning to the two wealth indicators, the third and fourth data panels of tables 11.5 and 11.6 list the 'top 15' ranked LADs on the *extent* measure. Approximately, 10 LADs in both 1981 and 1991 have at least half of their constituent wards in the top decile group on the households with *two or more-cars* indicator (table 11.5). The 'top 15' LADs on the *extent* measure are somewhat less concentrated in south-east England than is the case for the measure of *degree*: LADs such as Harborough (Leicestershire), Daventry (Northamptonshire) and Malvern Hills (Hereford and Worcester) display extensive high levels of two-car ownership. Ten LADs had at least half of their wards in the top decile group of the national distribution on the *households from social classes 1 and 2* indicator in 1991, compared with only three (Bearsden and Milngavie, Wokingham and Elmbridge) in 1981 (table 11.6). Again, strong continuities are evident between 1981 and 1991 with 'exclusive' residential areas in large cities (such as Bearsden and Milngavie), towns and cities in the Home Counties (for example, St Albans and Wokingham), as well as Macclesfield (in north-west England) included in both years.

11.2.4 Continuity and change in the extent of poverty and wealth, 1981–91

An overall impression of continuity and change in the *extent* of poverty may be gleaned by comparing the number of LADs with one or more constituent wards represented in the 'top' decile group of the national distribution of wards in 1991 and 1981 on an indicator. Table 11.8 provides an example of this approach for selected indicators at the LAD scale. The number of wards in the 'bottom' decile group as well as in the 'top' decile group in each year is tabulated.

On all indicators, fewer LADs were represented in the 'top' decile group

Table 11.8 *Number of LADs[a] with wards in the 'top' and 'bottom' decile groups of the national distribution of wards, on selected poverty and wealth measures, 1981–91*

Indicator	1991	1981	1981–91 change
Poverty			
% households with no car			
top decile group	192	193	–1
bottom decile group	267	281	–14
unemployment rate			
top decile group	208	217	–9
bottom decile group	235	245	–10
inactivity rate – 20–59 years			
top decile group	243	276	–33
bottom decile group	266	252	14
Wealth			
% households with 2 or more cars			
top decile group	231	241	–10
bottom decile group	189	215	–26
% social class 1 and 2 households			
top decile group	286	301	–15
bottom decile group	278	273	5

Note:
[a] 459 LADs in Great Britain.

in 1991 than in 1981 – indicating a somewhat greater spatial concentration of poverty and wealth over the decade (at the LAD scale). The pattern is less clear-cut for the 'bottom' decile group: with more LADs being represented in the 'bottom' decile group in 1991 than in 1981 on the *inactivity rate* and *households from social classes 1 and 2* indicators. Comparison of the absolute numbers of LADs represented in the 'top' and 'bottom' decile groups in both instances reveals that neighbourhoods characterised by extreme poverty are concentrated in a smaller number of LADs than are neighbourhoods of extreme wealth.

11.2.5 Measures of intensity

To ascertain the localised severity of poverty or wealth within an area, a measure of *intensity* was calculated as the mean of the 'highest three' ranked wards (an arbitrarily chosen cut-off) on the selected indicators.

Poverty
The fifth and sixth data panels on tables 11.1–11.3 show the 'top 15' LÁDs on each of the poverty indicators. A key feature of the highest ranked LADs on the *intensity* measure on each of the three indicators is the inclusion of large cities: for example, on the *no-car* and *unemployment* indicators the 'top 5' LADs include Glasgow, Liverpool, Newcastle upon Tyne and Manchester (tables 11.1 and 11.2). Clearly, many of the pockets of the most intense poverty are in the largest cities.

Wealth
Approximately half of the 'top 15' LADs on the *two or more-car households* indicator (table 11.5) are located in the South East. Outwith the Home Counties, pockets of intense wealth are evident in some parts of Scotland (where relatively small wards mean that high values on the *intensity* measure are relatively more easily achieved), in parts of the Midlands (for example, Stratford-on-Avon, Lichfield and South Staffordshire) and in the North West (for example, Macclesfield). There is a more overtly urban bias on the *households from social classes 1 and 2* indicator, but once again LADs from the South East and Scotland are well represented.

11.2.6 Comparisons of degree, extent and intensity

Tables 11.1–11.3 and 11.5–11.6 enable a preliminary comparison of the rankings of LADs on the *degree*, *extent* and *intensity* measures for each of the selected poverty and wealth indicators for 1991 and 1981. Some areas achieve high rankings on all three measures of spatial distribution: one of the foremost examples on the three poverty measures is Liverpool, while on the wealth measures Chiltern has a similar profile. In other instances there is much greater variation in the rankings on the *degree*, *extent* and *intensity* measures: for example, Cumnock and Doon Valley on the unemployment and inactivity rate indicators, and Mole Valley on the wealth indicators, are examples where the *extent* and *intensity* is less marked than the *degree* of poverty/wealth. On the unemployment indicators, some of the South Wales Valleys LADs provide good examples of areas where it is the *extent* of poverty that is even more apparent than the overall *degree* or the localised *intensity*, whereas Harborough (on the households with two or more-cars variable) and Cambridge (on the proportion of households from social classes 1 and 2) may be categorised similarly on the wealth indicators. By contrast, in many of the largest cities it is the localised *intensity* of poverty/wealth that is more marked than the overall *degree* or *extent*.

11.2.7 Synthesis: identification of 'concentrated poverty' and 'concentrated wealth' areas

In order to summarise the main spatial contours across the different dimensions of poverty and wealth, an attempt was made to categorise those areas displaying 'concentrated poverty/wealth'. A simple methodology (adapted from Simpson, 1993b) was employed, in which a wider range of poverty indicators (than discussed in this chapter) were assigned to five broad categories encompassing car ownership, unemployment, inactivity, housing and social class. Similarly, a wider range of wealth indicators were assigned to four broad categories: car ownership, economic activity, qualifications and social class. 'Concentrated poverty' areas were identified as those with values in the 'top' decile group of the national distribution on indicators in three or more of the five broad 'poverty' categories, while areas with values in the 'top' decile group on indicators in two or more of the four broad 'wealth' categories were labelled 'concentrated wealth' areas (for further details, see Green, 1994). Thus 'concentrated poverty/wealth' areas exhibit multiple aspects of poverty/wealth (i.e. they are 'poor'/'wealthy' on several different dimensions).

All LAD categories contain wards identified as 'concentrated poverty' areas. In 1991 74 per cent of 'concentrated poverty' wards were in northern Britain, compared with 80 per cent in 1981. The relative (and absolute) increase in 'concentrated poverty' wards in southern Britain is accounted for solely by the increased representation of such neighbourhoods in the large urban areas – mainly inner London: in 1991 55 per cent of wards in inner London were categorised as 'concentrated poverty' areas, compared with 32 per cent in 1981. From a higher base, the proportion of 'concentrated poverty' wards in principal cities increased from 46 per cent to 51 per cent. Together these two OPCS categories accounted for 36 per cent of all 'concentrated poverty' wards in 1991. Figure 11.4 underlines the disproportionate representation of 'concentrated poverty' wards in large urban centres and the older industrial areas.

As in the case of 'concentrated poverty' wards, so there were representatives of 'concentrated wealth' wards in all LAD categories. In 1991 60 per cent of 'concentrated wealth' wards were in southern Britain, compared with 56 per cent in 1981. About half of all 'concentrated wealth' wards are located in mixed urban–rural LADs, and a further fifth in remoter rural LADs. This rural/suburban/small and medium-size town bias in the distribution of 'concentrated wealth' wards (see figure 11.5) contrasts starkly with that of 'concentrated poverty' wards (shown in figure 11.4). Relative to the national distribution of wards, 'concentrated wealth' wards remain particularly under-represented in the principal cities,

Key: 'Concentrated poverty' ward
× 1981 only
○ 1991 only
✻ 1981 and 1991

Figure 11.4 'Concentrated poverty' wards in Britain, 1981 and 1991

Key: 'Concentrated wealth' ward
× 1981 only
○ 1991 only
＊ 1981 and 1991

Figure 11.5 'Concentrated wealth' wards in Britain, 1981 and 1991

other metropolitan districts, industrial areas and resort and retirement areas.

11.3 Conclusions

In this chapter selected evidence has been presented on the changing spatial distribution of poverty and wealth using selected proxy indicators from the 1991 and 1981 Censuses of Population. The analyses have outlined the spatially uneven *degree, extent* and *intensity* of poverty and wealth across Britain. Important regional 'North–South' and urban–rural patterns of variation are identifiable. Despite the fact that use of different indicators reveals rather different patterns in detail, at a crude level of generalisation the *degree* of poverty tends to be greater (in both 1981 and 1991) in northern than in southern Britain, and in large cities rather than in medium-sized/small towns and rural areas. There is evidence that the *extent* of poverty is most marked in areas (formerly) characterised by a relatively narrow industrial base – notably coal-mining, heavy manufacturing and port-related activities – in long-term decline. Amongst the clearest of the spatial patterns to emerge is that the *intensity* of poverty is most marked in the large metropolitan areas of northern Britain and in inner London. In some areas – notably Merseyside – a high *degree, extent* and *intensity* of poverty interact to produce severe economic and social problems in 'concentrated poverty' areas. In other areas – notably the South Wales Valleys – it is the 'extensive' nature of poverty which is particularly apparent, affecting the vast majority of the area rather than a few highly disadvantaged wards.

By contrast, the Home Counties immediately surrounding London, along with other areas on the fringes of the South East region, emerge as the main area of concentration of wealth in Britain. Of course, some 'outliers' from this 'ring' around London are evident in most other regions of Britain. Many of these areas of 'concentrated wealth' have a mixed urban–rural character.

While a great deal of *continuity* is revealed in the spatial patterns of poverty and wealth between 1981 and 1991, there is also some evidence for *change* (often very significant change) at the margins. Of the changes, perhaps the most significant is the increase in the *degree, extent* and *intensity* of poverty in inner London and the largest metropolitan centres outside the capital. However, in London there is also evidence for increases in the *degree* of wealth. Hence, it would seem that important changes are occurring at the intra-urban scale – leading to a *polarisation* of the social structure and increasing segregation of different population sub-groups in many large cities (with such processes being furthest advanced in London).

While inner London and parts of other large metropolitan centres emerge as the main *losers* from the processes of economic, social and political change in the 1980s, it is important also not to lose sight of other losers. Many of the (former) coal-mining areas may be placed in a category of 'poor areas, getting worse', while many resort and retirement areas – which are particularly vulnerable in the face of restructuring of the welfare state – may be labelled 'formerly richer areas, getting worse'. Although still dominant in the geography of wealth in 1991 (as in 1981), there is some evidence to suggest that the sub-dominant towns and cities around London were loosening their near-exclusive grip on 'extreme' wealth (although some of this 'loosening' may be attributable to the fact that such areas were amongst the first to suffer the economic downturn in the early 1990s' recession, and this is captured by the 1991 Census snapshot). The main *winners* from the processes of economic and social change were not so much these traditional 'Home Counties' areas as those somewhat more distant from London on the fringes of a 'Greater South East' region and some of the mixed urban–rural areas of northern England and north-eastern Scotland. Nevertheless, the continuities in the spatial distribution and segregation of wealth are much more apparent than the changes.

Such continuities and changes in the patterns of spatial distribution and segregation of poverty and wealth are indicative of the importance of *labour market policy* in links between income and wealth distribution and the productive economy. Various studies have highlighted observable long-term changes in the structure of the labour market in Britain which tend to increase the polarisation captured by the *underclass* idea: notably, an increase in the salience of educational qualifications as a determinant of employment prospects, and a decline in the opportunities available to those without skills or qualifications. The decline in the number of non-precarious job opportunities for those at the lower end of the occupational spectrum, in many instances exacerbated by problems of spatial mismatch (of residences and workplaces for the most disadvantaged sub-groups), would appear to be leading to a growth in 'no-earner' households (as outlined by Gregg and Wadsworth, chapter 8 in this volume), neighbourhoods and labour markets, in conjunction with a growth in 'dual-career' neighbourhoods and labour markets in other locations within the urban and regional system.

Notes

1. This chapter draws upon a study of the changing spatial distribution and segregation of poverty and wealth, reported in *The Geography of Poverty and*

Wealth by Anne E. Green (available from the Institute for Employment Research, University of Warwick). The study was supported by the Joseph Rowntree Foundation as part of its Programme on Income and Wealth. The facts presented and views expressed, however, are those of the author and not necessarily those of the Foundation. The support of Ruth Mahon and David Owen with regard to computing, and of John Hills (LSE), Derek Williams (the Joseph Rowntree Foundation) and members of the project Advisory Group is acknowledged. The chapter includes data derived from the 1981 and 1991 Censuses of Population, which are Crown Copyright. The 1991 Census of Population statistics are made available to the academic community via the ESRC. The assistance of Daniel Dorling in arranging early access to software used to handle 1991 Census of Population data for 1981 wards is acknowledged.

2. Analyses of inter-censual change between 1981 and 1991 are complicated by changes in the geographical base: in some parts of Britain the definitions of wards changed over the decade. Here the problem of 'changing areas' between 1981 and 1991 has been overcome by 'connecting' the 1981 and 1991 Censuses onto a common spatial base – 1981 wards – by allocating 1991 enumeration districts (EDs) to 1981 wards (Atkins *et al.*, 1993).

12 Two nations? Changing patterns of income and wealth in two contrasting areas

Michael Noble and George Smith

12.1 Background: the national pattern

12.1.1 Spatial

The 1980s and early 1990s have been marked by some of the sharpest changes in recent years in the relative position of different areas and regions within Britain in social and economic terms. Rapidly rising unemployment in the early 1980s most seriously affected regions linked to traditional manufacturing industries – the North West, the North East and the Midlands – that had also declined during the 1970s. Within such regions heavily industrialised urban areas typically declined more rapidly. However there were other parts of the country that remained relatively buoyant. The ESRC urban studies of the mid-1980s (Hausner, 1986, 1987) recorded that the fastest growing areas were in the urban south-east, particularly the London periphery, in towns such as Milton Keynes, Basingstoke, and Basildon. Though such areas were not immune from the recession of the early 1980s, unemployment fell sharply in the latter part of the decade to reach very low levels. Recovery was far less rapid and delayed in the more traditional industrial urban areas. Typically the pattern of the 1980s was reasonably described in terms of a 'growing divide' essentially between north and south (actually between south-east with the east against the rest of the country).

However, during the early 1990s the position altered dramatically. Rising unemployment and economic decline has been most rapid in those very regions that experienced the most rapid growth in the late 1980s. Indeed *within* such regions it is those areas that had prospered most that tended to fall back most rapidly. Typically this pattern has been seen as a convergence between areas and regions that until recently had apparently very different social and economic profiles.

292

12.1.2 Individual

Recent data (e.g. Goodman and Webb, 1994; DSS, 1994; and Cowell *et al.*, chapter 3 in this volume) have shown a widening gap between those on the lowest and those on the highest incomes during the 1980s – inequality in income distribution as measured by the Gini coefficient and other measures has increased. The top and bottom deciles in the income distribution have diverged sharply.

12.2 Scope and purpose

In chapter 11, Anne Green has shown the unevenness of the degree, extent and intensity of poverty and wealth across Britain with North/Inner London–South variations apparent. This has been the national pattern, but how has it worked out at the local level? How closely are the spatial and individual patterns of inequality linked? It is against this background of a decade or more of apparently growing inequality that we set out to examine in detail the changing pattern of income and wealth, and related sets of advantage/disadvantage at the local level in two contrasting areas – Oxford and Oldham.

The main purpose of the study was to chart the relative changes over time and space, to compare the way the two areas have fared over the 1980s and early 1990s; and also to examine changes *within* each of the towns.[1] Evidence over time allows us to explore how far the 'polarisation' found at the national level is reflected in this local data. By 'polarisation' we mean the process by which proportionately more of the overall distribution is found at the extremes. Much of our data is spatial (to a very local level); but we also have individual data on low income, thus allowing some insight into the spatial concentration of such low income households. This chapter concentrates on low income rather than wealth.

12.3 Data and methods

12.3.1 Data

The data analysed are from two main sources. To present the position of the two areas at the end of 1993 and to look at changes in patterns of low income since 1991 we have used data extracted from the housing benefit/council tax benefit (HB/CTB) systems of the two towns. The extract we obtain is at an individual claimant level; it contains all 'live' records at the date of extraction in an anonymised form. The data enable us to distinguish claimants who are in receipt of Income Support (IS cases) from those who are otherwise on a low income and receive HB/CTB ('NS' or non-income support cases). The dataset contains details of family/household structure and, in NS cases, income data. These data are post-coded and we have used this attribute to link cases to Census enumeration district (ED) level. We should make very clear that our definition of 'low income' is confined to those in households in receipt of IS.

To chart changes from 1981 to 1991 we have used the Censuses of Population 1981 and 1991 Small Area Statistics, generally at the ED level, that is areas with about 190–200 households. This itself gave considerable problems as ED boundaries changed between 1981 and 1991. In Oldham there are virtually no identical ED boundaries between the 1981 and 1991 Censuses. In Oxford the picture is better with some 102 (out of 295) having identical boundaries. The technique used to equate 1981 and 1991 ED boundaries is described in more detail elsewhere;[2] basically we have identified the physical 'urban space' that is common between the 1981 and 1991 ED areas and redistributed the data according to these overlaps on a *pro rata* basis. We have done this by redistributing the 1981 data to the 1991 boundaries, though the reverse is equally possible. We have also included EDs in the two additional wards added to Oxford City *after* the 1981 Census. Thus 'Oxford' in this chapter represents the enlarged 1991 city boundaries. There were no changes to Oldham's overall boundaries between the two Censuses.

12.3.2 Constructing an index of low income from Census data

The Census contains no *direct* information about income. Use is therefore made of proxies such as unemployment, car-ownership, housing tenure, numbers of earners in the household, etc. that are recorded. Some independent evidence is available about the links between these factors and income, for example from analysis of the General Household Survey (Davies *et al.*, 1993). We could therefore simply present information on these variables as proxies. However as we had direct information about low income households for both areas in 1993, we were able to link this directly to Census data at the ED level. The question was to find the combination of Census variables that best 'explained' (in the statistical sense) variations in the proportions dependent on low incomes in each ED. The procedure adopted[3] was to run a multiple regression with a set of 1991 Census variables selected for their *prima facie* association with low income. The resulting regression equation provided both the basis for the final selection of Census variables and more importantly their *relative weights*. Using this information allowed us to create an *index of low income*, based on the weighted combination of seven Census variables. This combined index correlates highly with our low income measure. In principle it was then possible to construct an identical index for the 1981 Census data and compare the positions in 1981, 1991 and 1993.

We have also made some use of the *index of dissimilarity*, a measure developed to assess the degree of residential segregation in the United States (Massey and Denton, 1988, 281; Wong, 1993, 559). This measure indicates how evenly a characteristic is distributed across the parts of a larger area. Basically if every part has the same distribution as the whole, then the index will be zero. If the area is completely segregated (e.g. some parts all white and others all black) then the index will be 1.00.

12.3.3 Cluster analysis

One problem with the information presented at ED level is that EDs themselves represent very small populations. There is a risk that detailed 'eye-balling' of the data at this level may detect patterns, continuities or discontinuities that may represent small fluctuations in actual numbers of cases or pick out EDs that contain special populations, for example that part of a council estate containing sheltered housing for the elderly or other special needs housing. This may particularly be a problem with only two observations (1981 and 1991), where it is not possible to be confident of trends. Also the adjustment of 1981 ED data to 1991 boundaries must inevitably have an element of 'rough justice', particularly in Oldham where almost all the ED boundaries changed.

However we can have more confidence in data for larger areas. For this reason we have used various methods to combine areas and group the data to make comparisons both within and between the two areas for the period 1981–91, particularly the clustering of EDs into different area types along the lines pioneered by Webber in Liverpool (Webber, 1975).

We have used a clustering procedure based on the Census data from the two areas, rather than a national classification such as ACORN (Craig, 1985). Oxford presents a number of problems here, particularly the presence of high levels of private rented accommodation in areas such as North Oxford also marked by high status owner-occupation. Nevertheless the procedure adopted provides a way of regrouping EDs into different types that makes sense on the ground, especially when combined with an analysis based on actual neighbourhoods.

Classification of areas
Five areas emerge from the cluster analysis.
- **Cluster 1: owner-occupied areas with significant private renting**
  EDs in this cluster are predominantly an Oxford phenomenon, and

dominate the central part of Oxford. Only one ED in Oldham falls into this category and has been excluded from the tables.
- **Cluster 2: mixed status owner-occupation**
  EDs in this type of area are predominantly found in Oldham. They are characterised by significantly higher unemployment rates, lower car-ownership, higher proportions from ethnic minorities, and higher proportions of households with partly skilled and unskilled heads than the more settled owner-occupation areas (cluster 5).
- **Cluster 3: council estates**
  The 105 EDs in this cluster are marked by higher levels of unemployment, particularly among males, low proportions of ethnic minorities, high proportions of single parents and single pensioners, higher levels of overcrowding and low car-ownership in 1981.
- **Cluster 4: mixed tenure areas (both council and owner-occupied)**
  These are rather like the EDs in cluster 2 but have significant levels of council tenure, high levels of economic activity and lower proportions of ethnic minorities, but also few lone parents and low levels of female unemployment.
- **Cluster 5: settled owner-occupied areas**
  This type of area predominates in Oldham, perhaps reflecting the way that the Oxford district boundary cuts off similar areas in the Oxford periphery. These EDs are marked by low levels of unemployment, high economic activity rates, high car-ownership and very few ethnic minorities or single parent households.

12.3.4 Neighbourhoods

To 'ground' the local area analysis, we identified five case study neighbourhoods in each town for further examination. Unlike EDs which are simply lines on a map, 'neighbourhoods' are areas that residents would broadly recognise as where they live. They are built up from their component EDs. In selecting neighbourhoods we were guided by the wish to have some which were typical of 'poor' areas and some typical of 'rich' areas in each town.[4]

The neighbourhoods
- In Oxford, **Barton (pop. 4137)** is a council estate built in a green field site beyond the ring road. It has a large proportion of 'systems built' housing. **Cutteslowe (pop. 2014)** contains both council housing built in the early 1930s and 'up market' private housing – initially for rent but now owner-occupied. **Blackbird Leys (pop. 7649)** is a large council estate build in the 1960s close to the Cowley car factory. The housing stock is

largely conventionally built. **St Clements (pop. 3396)** is a neighbourhood of Victorian terraces east of the city centre. It was and is a traditional working class area although some gentrification is evident.
Summertown (pop. 5273) is an area of North Oxford generally thought
of as one of the wealthiest areas in Oxford.

• In Oldham, **Grasscroft (pop. 1108)** is a village on the outskirts of metropolitan Oldham. It consists largely of substantial detached houses with
large gardens. **Holts (pop. 1938)** is a post-war council estate built on a
green field site on the outskirts of metropolitan Oldham close to the
moors. **Coppice (pop. 5711)** is a mixed 'inner city' community. Its houses
range from 'two up two down' Victorian terraces to more substantial
terraces and even detached properties. **Westwood (pop. 5701)** is almost
entirely composed of small Victorian terraces with modest housing
association and council house developments. It is the centre of
Oldham's Bangladeshi community. Finally, **Firwood Park (pop. 3577)** is
a new estate built in the 1970s and early 1980s within the Oldham urban
area.

12.4 Oxford and Oldham in 1993 and 1994

To set the scene for this chapter we begin our story at the end. What is the
distribution of low income in Oxford and Oldham in 1993/94? To answer
these questions we are using data extracted from the local authority
Housing Benefit/Council Tax Benefit (HB/CTB) data in the two towns.

One important feature of the data is that it is dynamic. Extracts can be
obtained at any time points, enabling close monitoring of changes in the
claimant population between and within the towns. We have decided to
take extracts at six-monthly intervals and, although some earlier data are
available for Oxford, most of the analysis in this chapter is based on the
first systematic extracts, one taken in June/July 1993 – the 'Summer 1993
sweep', and the other in December 1993/January 1994 – the 'Winter
1993/94 sweep'.

12.4.1 The overall picture

At first sight Oxford and Oldham appear to be contrasting towns – one
located in what is still thought of as the prosperous south-east and the
other in the depressed north-west. In 1994, however, both areas have very
similar poverty profiles when measured by the numbers living in families
dependent on means-tested benefits.

In the Winter 1993/94 sweep there were 15,312 claimants of HB/CTB in
Oxford and 28,839 in Oldham. These claimants may have partners or

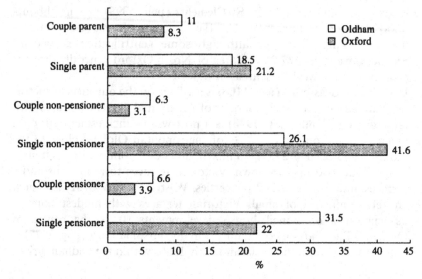

Figure 12.1 Claimants on IS, by household type as a percentage of all IS claimants, Winter 1993/94

dependent children. If we take 'dependants' into account there are 26,053 people in Oxford and 52,521 people in Oldham living in families receiving HB/CTB. Using the 1991 Census of Population counts as denominators[5] this represents just under 24.5 per cent of the total Oxford population and 24.7 per cent of the Oldham population.

Of the 15,312 Oxford claimants, 8776 were receiving income support. Taking their families into account 15,358 people in Oxford were dependent on IS – 14.4 per cent of the population. In Oldham 16,229 HB/CTB claimants were receiving income support – representing 30,985 people or 14.6 per cent dependent on the benefit.

Thus, the first striking finding is that taking size of population into account Oldham and Oxford have very similar 'poverty profiles' as defined by dependency on social security benefits. However, if we look more closely at the claimant population in the two towns, we find substantial differences. Figure 12.1 shows the percentage of IS claimants in the various household types – single pensioners, pensioner couples, single non-pensioners, childless non-pensioner couples, couples with children and single parents.

In Oxford 'single non-pensioners' are the biggest group at nearly 42 per cent. In Oldham this group accounts for only 26 per cent – less than single pensioners. As we will see later, it is the single non-pensioner group where most of the growth since 1991 in the income support population in Oxford has occurred and is almost certainly due to the rapid rise in unemployment in the area.

If we look at the mean age of IS claimant groups we find close similarity between Oxford and Oldham – thus the mean age of single pensioners is 76.8 years in Oxford, 76.5 in Oldham; the mean age of single parents is 31.8 in Oxford, 32.4 in Oldham. Perhaps the only case where there is a significant gap is single non-pensioners where the average age in Oxford is 32.8 as compared to 37.4 in Oldham.

12.4.2 Intra-town distributions

While the overall proportions on benefit are similar, the geographical distributions within the two towns are quite different. The maps in figures 12.2 and 12.3 show the distribution of income support claimants in the two towns. In Oxford the highest proportions of IS claimants are mainly located in the peripheral council estates; in Oldham there is also a concentration of IS claimants around the city centre.

If we now examine the proportions of IS claimants in the case study neighbourhoods of Oxford and Oldham in June 1993,[6] we find some striking differences in the spatial segregation of claimants in the two areas (figure 12.4).

In Oxford, Barton and Blackbird Leys have the highest percentages of people living in families dependent on income support; one in four people in Barton/Blackbird Leys lives in families dependent on income support. By contrast, Summertown has by far the lowest concentrations of people living in families dependent on income support (5 per cent).

In Oldham, Holts and Westwood have the highest percentages of people dependent on income support. Noticeably, although the overall means for Oxford and Oldham are very similar, there is far greater contrast between the case study neighbourhoods in Oldham than in Oxford. In Holts and Westwood, over 40 per cent of people live in families dependent on IS, whereas in Grasscroft and Firwood Park less than 3 per cent are in such families.

If we focus on dependent children and look at the extent to which they are living in low income families, we see that in Oxford overall, one in four children (24.3 per cent) lives in a household dependent on IS. This is slightly higher than in Oldham, where the figure is one in five (20.9 per cent). In both towns there are some very sharp geographical contrasts. In Oxford, 40 per cent of dependent children in Barton live in families on IS and just 6 per cent in Summertown. The difference is even more stark in Oldham, with 57 per cent of Holts' children dependent on IS, as against 4 per cent in Firwood Park and just 1 per cent in Grasscroft. In both Oxford

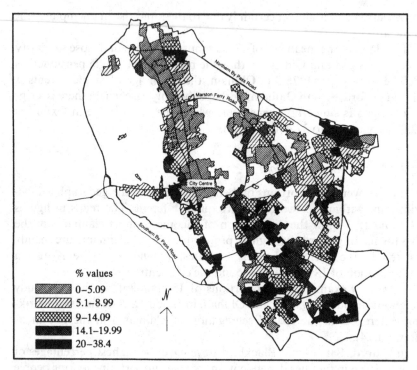

Figure 12.2 Oxford: persons on HB/CTB receiving IS, Winter 1993/94
Produced by the Department of Applied Social Studies, Oxford, September 1994
Source: Oxford City Council Housing Benefit database, 1991 Census boundaries
and base population counts.

and Oldham there is powerful evidence of the way low income is concentrated among single parent households. A majority of these households
were families dependent on IS; in the most disadvantaged neighbourhoods
in Oxford, almost all were.

12.4.3 The changes in the claimant population

Since the study began we have two sweeps of data for the two towns, the
first taken in the Summer of 1993 and the next in Winter 1993/94. These
will form part of a long-term time series which will yield considerable
information on the changing nature of the claimant population in the two
areas.

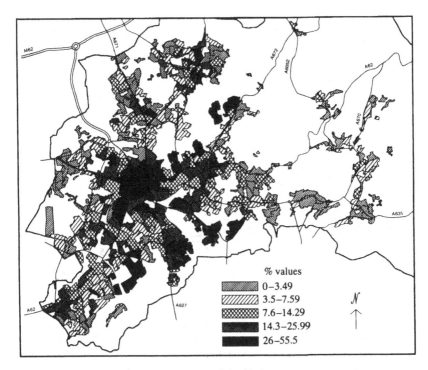

% values

▨ 0–3.49

▨ 3.5–7.59

▨ 7.6–14.29

■ 14.3–25.99

■ 26–55.5

N

↑

Figure 12.3 Oldham: persons on HB/CTB receiving IS, Winter 1993/94
Produced by the Department of Applied Social Studies, Oxford, September 1994
Source: OMBC Housing Benefit database, 1991 Census boundaries and base
population counts.

Oxford

Table 12.1 shows the number of housing benefit and council tax
benefit cases in Oxford at mid-summer 1993 and mid-winter 1993/94.
The striking feature of the two sweeps is the similarity of the claimant
distributions. There is a modest 1.7 per cent fall in the total number of
claimants and a similar fall in the number of people living in families
dependent on benefits. Non-pensioner couples – both childless and
parents – show the biggest drops in IS claims (10 per cent and 5 per cent
respectively). Single non-pensioners show a marginal increase.

However this apparent stability in the claimant population from two
'snapshots' disguises the dynamics of the situation. Because we have
unique identifiers we are able to trace through individual claimant benefit
careers. The stability is illusory. By the Winter sweep 236 IS claimants have
become non-claimants of IS, but claimed HB/CTB and a further 1633

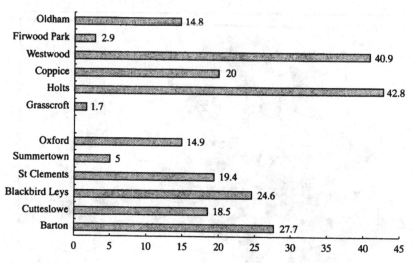

Figure 12.4 IS cases in Oxford and Oldham: Summer 1993 as a percentage of 1991 population

have left the dataset altogether. However, at the second time point there are 1717 new IS claimants, 1472 of whom are new to the dataset. It is amongst single non-pensioners where 'turnover' is at its highest. Around 30 per cent left and a further 30 per cent joined during the six months between the sweeps. Put another way, around 68 per cent of single non-pensioner IS claimants in the Summer 1993 sweep were still claimants of the same category by the Winter 1993/94 sweep. Of the *outflows*, small numbers had migrated into different 'household types' with the majority ceasing to be IS claimants.[7] The most stable group from Summer 1993 through to Winter 1993/94 was single pensioners – 93.7 per cent remaining in the dataset in the same category.

Oldham

In Oldham we see an even smaller change in the number of IS claimants between Summer and Winter sweeps – an increase of less than 1 per cent. The biggest increase – 5.7 per cent – is among single non-pensioners. Single and couple parent claimants both fall by nearly 4 per cent. There are similar changes in the population dependent on benefit.

As with Oxford, it is instructive to look at 'claimant careers' between the two time periods. Again these show a considerably more dynamic picture than the two snapshots. In fact if we compare the two areas (table 12.2) there is, perhaps surprisingly, less stability among Oldham claimants.

Table 12.1 *Oxford IS cases, Summer 1993 sweep and Winter 1993/94 sweep*

	Claimants		Individuals	
	S 1993	W 1993/94	S 1993	W 1993/94
Single pensioner	1985	1927	2018	1954
Couple pensioner	342	342	759	744
Single non-pensioner	3603	3642	3635	3645
Couple non-pensioner	302	267	598	536
Single parent	1912	1858	5309	5235
Couple parent	776	732	3380	3244
Totals	8920	8768	15699	15358

Table 12.2 *Percentage of each claimant group on IS in dataset in Summer 1993 also present and on IS in Winter sweep: inflows and outflows*

	% stability Oxford	% stability Oldham	% outflow Oxford	% outflow Oldham	% inflow Oxford	% inflow Oldham
Single pensioner	93.7	90.5	6.3	9.4	1.7	5.7
Couple pensioner	92.0	86.6	4.1	11.2	2.3	10
Single non-pensioner	68.6	66.8	29.6	27.2	30.8	34.3
Couple non-pensioner	71.0	55.7	17.2	32.9	11.8	41.9
Single parent	86.0	75.3	11.7	22.4	8.7	18.4
Couple parent	79.3	72.7	12.9	24.8	10.7	21.9

Some groups such as non-pensioner couples are small in Oxford (n = 268) and comparisons should be made with caution. However, with some groups such as single parents turnover in Oldham is double that in Oxford.

This section, using HB data, shows clearly the distribution of low income households within the two towns in 1993/94. While there are some overall similarities, the data show the very significant differences *within* the two towns. Thus low income households are spread very unevenly across the two towns, with Oldham showing this pattern much more markedly. Here in some better-off neighbourhoods there are virtually no families on IS, while in the poorest areas more than half the families are dependent on this benefit.

The next question to ask is whether this pattern of low income households has always been the case. Has the situation improved or deteriorated over the last decade or so? Is there evidence of polarisation in either area? We do not have IS data to make direct comparisons prior to 1991. However, we can use the 1981 and 1991 Census data, and particularly the 'index of low income' which links Census data to proportions dependent on IS.

12.5 Oxford and Oldham, 1981–91

So what has happened in the two towns between 1981 and 1991? As we have already seen, data at the district level may be misleading. If we drop down to the next level – the local ward level – there are 17 wards in Oxford in 1991 with populations ranging from 5000–8000, and 20 in Oldham with populations ranging from 8500 to 12,500 – the picture can still be misleading, as ward boundaries do not necessarily overlap with social or economic divisions. In Oldham particularly, ward boundaries can cut across these divisions. To provide real insight into what is happening we have to drop down to the enumeration district (ED) level.

12.5.1 Enumeration District analysis

There are some 440 EDs in Oldham and 295 in Oxford. However, a significant proportion of Oxford EDs cover colleges and other institutions in various parts of the city and have therefore been excluded from the analysis, giving a maximum usable 235 EDs for Oxford.[8]

We have looked at the *overall* distribution of EDs within each area at the two time points and particularly at the extremes, where we have used the cut-off points for the highest and lowest 20 per cent (or 'quintiles') of EDs.[9] We have also provided data on *location* to indicate the extent of physical clustering. Here we have made use of 'urban area' maps rather than full ED boundaries as these latter include an enormous amount of 'green field' space, particularly on the city periphery. This technique reduces, though does not fully eliminate, the problem of the eye being drawn to the largest (and therefore least densely populated) EDs. We have also drawn on comparisons between the two time points to gain some measure of *stability* or change over time.

In selecting Census variables we have focused on those that relate most closely to low income, defined in terms of those dependent on IS. To identify these we made use of the association between the ED-level data in 1991 and the 1993 extract from the Housing Benefit/Council Tax benefit system in both towns distributed according to 1991 Census ED bound-

Table 12.3 *Male unemployment: economically active population 16+, 1981–91, ED level, per cent*

	% rate	Lowest quintile	Highest quintile	SD[a]	Index of dissimilarity
Oldham 1981	11.9	5.7	18.1	7.2	0.28
Oldham 1991	12.7	5.7	23.2	11.1	0.35
Oxford 1981	10.5	6.1	13.9	5.7	0.20
Oxford 1991	11.3	5.7	16.7	6.5	0.24

Note:
[a] This is the unweighted Standard Deviation for the EDs.

aries. This not only allows us to select key variables, but also allows us to develop an overall Census predictor of low income for both the 1981 and 1991 Census.

Male unemployment and access to a car are examples of variables which are good predictors of low income,[10] and these are analysed before looking at changes in the overall index of low income.

Male unemployment

Male unemployment is a strong predictor of numbers dependent on IS. In both towns male unemployment rose slightly between 1981 and 1991, though this of course ignores the very different pattern of change during the decade. But as table 12.3 shows clearly, this change in the overall rate was associated with a widening gap between the highest and lowest 20 per cent of EDs in each area. Table 12.3 gives the highest and lowest quintiles, and shows the stable and low rates in both areas for the lowest quintile (approximately 6 per cent in 1981 and 1991), but an increase in the top quintile, particularly in Oldham (up from 18.1 per cent in 1981 to 23.2 per cent in 1991). If we look at spatial distribution, Oldham shows strong clustering of EDs with high levels of male unemployment, but in Oxford too, there is an increasing concentration of EDs with high levels of unemployment in the quadrant south east of the city centre (the St Clements' triangle).

There is rather more *stability* in Oldham with a rank correlation of 0.79 between the same EDs at the two time points; that for Oxford EDs is 0.59 – that is EDs in Oldham were likely to be in the same rank position in both 1981 and 1991. The index of dissimilarity, a measure of how unevenly male unemployment is distributed among EDs, widened in both towns.

Table 12.4 *Households without access to a car, 1981 and 1991, per cent*

	% rate	Lowest quintile	Highest quintile	SD	Index of dissimilarity
Oldham 1981	50.1	30.7	68.4	19.3	0.33
Oldham 1991	42.6	19.9	64.8	21.8	0.38
Oxford 1981	42.4	32.9	52.7	11.9	0.19
Oxford 1991	37.6	28.2	48.4	11.8	0.21

Households without access to a car

In line with national trends, the proportion of households without access to a car declined in both towns over the decade. However the range actually widens in Oldham with areas with already *high* levels of car-ownership falling more than those with low levels in 1981, as the comparison between the highest and lowest quintiles in table 12.4 shows. The index of dissimilarity for this variable also rises in Oldham suggesting a more uneven distribution of households without access to a car. On this variable of course the 'lowest' quintile represents the 'better-off' areas. Special factors are likely to be at work in Oxford affecting car-ownership both in terms of no-car ownership and two-car ownership. Correlation between proportions of households in low income and no-car ownership is much higher in Oldham than Oxford, suggesting a difference in both opportunity and preference.

Again there is very high stability in Oldham from 1981 to 1991 in the ranking on this variable (rank correlation 0.91) and fairly stable in Oxford (rank correlation 0.80).

Households with access to two or more cars

Table 12.5 shows a very sharp increase in two-car households at the top end of the Oldham distribution where the highest quintile rises sharply. Indeed the top 38 per cent of Oldham EDs have by 1991 the same or higher proportions of two-car households as the top 20 per cent of EDs in 1981. The increases in the standard deviation and index of dissimilarity indicate this uneven pattern. There is very little change at the bottom end. While Oxford displays a similar pattern it is much less marked and the index of dissimilarity hardly changes from 1981 to 1991. Again there is very considerable stability in Oldham with a rank correlation of 0.89 between the 1981 and 1991 EDs on this variable.

Table 12.5 *Households with access to two or more cars, 1981 and 1991, per cent*

	% rate	Lowest quintile	Highest quintile	SD	Index of dissimilarity
Oldham 1981	10.4	3.6	16.9	8.6	0.37
Oldham 1991	16.8	4.7	29.6	13.9	0.41
Oxford 1981	11.6	7.0	14.7	5.9	0.19
Oxford 1991	17.4	10.7	23.2	7.5	0.20

Index of low income
So far we have presented the information about the two towns variable by variable. Information obtained from the multiple correlation between the 1981 Census values at ED level and the outcome measures of low income based on the HB data for both towns was used to construct a composite and weighted *index of low income*. This made use of equivalent variables from the 1981 and 1991 Census for both areas. As the Census data were standardised in the process, the overall index of low income has a mean for the combined 1981 and 1991 data (and both areas) of zero, with *positive* values relating to the greater presence of factors linked to low income, and *negative* values the reverse. The intention was to make it easier to pick out significant changes over the decade.

Table 12.6 indicates the overall distribution on this composite measure (based on seven variables from the Census). The lowest quintiles represent areas with low proportions with low income and the highest quintiles the reverse.

The overall score for Oldham is higher than for Oxford at both time points and the two towns are on a diverging track. By 1991 the difference amounted to 1 point on the composite measure or about a quarter of a standard deviation. However rather more significant than this overall divergence is the different pattern of change *within* the two towns. This is particularly marked in Oldham, where the 'cut point' for the 20 per cent poorest areas increases from 2.31 to 3.40 index points. Conversely the better-off areas move in the other direction, from −2.68 to −3.52. Thus the actual gap widened from 4.99 to 6.92 points, effectively an increase of half a standard deviation in what was already a very wide gap. While there is some increase in divergence between the two ends of the distribution in Oxford, it is less marked – something under 20 per cent of a standard deviation.

Table 12.6 *Index of low income, 1981 and 1991*

	Mean	SD	Lowest quintile	Highest quintile
Oldham 1981	0.15	3.4	−2.68	2.31
Oldham 1991	0.42	5.12	−3.52	3.40
Oxford 1981	−0.37	2.64	−2.58	1.48
Oxford 1991	−0.60	2.85	−3.07	1.67
Overall 1981 and 1991 (both areas)	0.00	3.92	−3.01	2.35

The maps in figures 12.5–12.8 which use the 1981 top and bottom quintile 'cut points' as the benchmark show the location of EDs at the two time points and the way that both low and high areas tend to cluster geographically. For Oldham in 1991 there are now 112 EDs with index scores equal to or greater than the 80th percentile in 1981 and 158 with scores at or below the 20th percentile in 1981 (compared with 88 at each point in 1981). The map also shows the very strong spatial clustering of these EDs in Oldham. Though there is some change in the same direction in Oxford, it is much less marked.

This presentation of ED-level data for Oxford and Oldham using a set of values drawn from those that were closely associated with low income (measured by HB data on IS) suggests a clear pattern of results in the two towns. Oldham in 1981 is in general already more uneven than Oxford in the distribution of these characteristics across EDs, shown by a much wider spread of values, higher indices of dissimilarity and standard deviations. By 1991 these differences have increased, with higher indices of dissimilarity and greater ranges of values within Oldham. Finally the overall index of low income suggests increasing polarisation, particularly in Oldham, that is there are significantly more EDs at the two extremes of the distribution than in 1981.

Overall there is a high degree of stability in the EDs in the top and lowest quintiles at the two time points. The maps for 1981 and 1991 show that these are not random or chance features but that the two ends of the spectrum are quite tightly clustered in specific areas.

12.5.2 Cluster analysis

So far we have looked simply at the overall distribution of EDs in 1981 and 1991 and particularly at those at the top and bottom of the distribu-

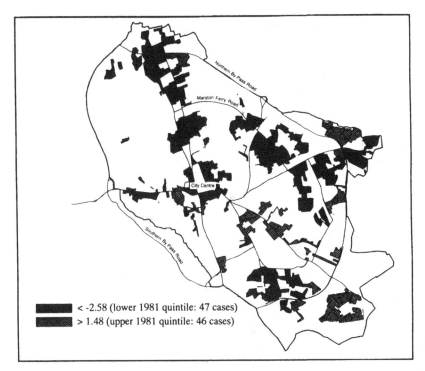

Figure 12.5 Oxford, 1981: index of low income
Produced by the Department of Applied Social Studies, Oxford, September 1994
Source: 1981 Census data redistributed to 1991 Census boundaries.

tion. But it is important to know what types of area these EDs might represent. In this section we have analysed Census variables by reference to the five area 'types' identified in the cluster analysis. EDs were classified on the basis of their 1981 data. We also include some data from the case study neighbourhoods to illustrate how the actual communities have fared over the decade.

Male unemployment
As table 12.7 shows, male unemployment in the Oldham council estates cluster increased from 22 per cent in 1981 to 29 per cent in 1991; that for males from the higher status owner-occupied areas from 6.1 per cent to 6.6 per cent over the same period. In Oxford the most significant rise was in the 'mixed status' owner-occupied area, with a 3 per cent rise over the decade.
If we look at the case study neighbourhoods, we see that in as much as

Table 12.7 *Male unemployment, 1981–91, per cent*

	O/O[a] and private rented[b]	Mixed status O/O	Council estates	Mixed tenure areas	Settled O/O
Oxford 1981	10.2	8.3	14.9	10.8	6.7
Oxford 1991	12.1	11.3	16.6	12.5	7.2
Oldham 1981	—	13.6	22.1	14.2	6.1
Oldham 1991	—	14.9	28.7	14.3	6.6

Notes:
[a] O/O owner-occupied.
[b] Only one ED of the 'private rented' cluster type appears in Oldham and analysis is therefore restricted to Oxford.

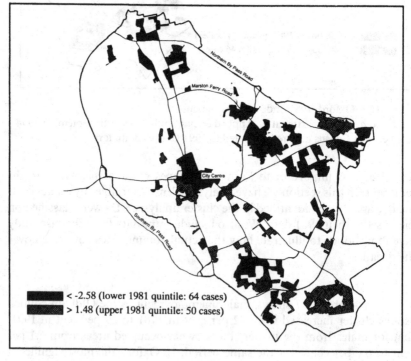

< -2.58 (lower 1981 quintile: 64 cases)
> 1.48 (upper 1981 quintile: 50 cases)

Figure 12.6 Oxford, 1991: index of low income
Produced by the Department of Applied Social Studies, Oxford, September 1994
Source: 1991 Census data and boundaries.

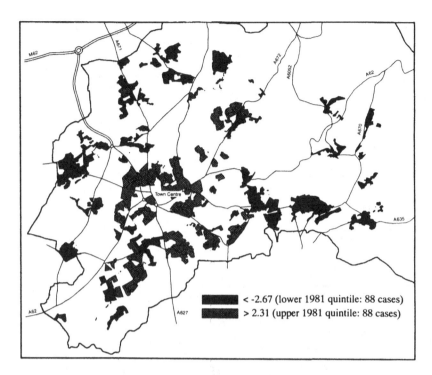

Figure 12.7 Oldham, 1981: index of low income
Produced by the Department of Applied Social Studies, Oxford, September 1994
Source: 1981 Census data redistributed to 1991 Census boundaries.

there was change in Oxford across the decade it was fairly even. The picture in Oldham is rather different. In Westwood the unemployment rate rose from 17.3 per cent in 1981 to 27.3 per cent in 1991. In Holts it rose from 19.8 per cent to 33.5 per cent. On the other hand, in Firwood Park there was actually a decrease. This, again, suggested polarisation between the more and less prosperous neighbourhoods of Oldham, which is not evident in Oxford.

Car ownership
All areas experienced a fall in the proportion of households without access to a car, but the drop is very small in the two council estate clusters, and thus the absolute gap widens (see table 12.8). Again Oldham is characterised by greater extremes between the council estate areas and the settled owner-occupation areas (cluster 5). Note the relatively similar levels of 'no access to a car' in all but the settled owner-occupied cluster in

Table 12.8 *Households without access to a car, 1981 and 1991, per cent*

	O/O[a] and private rented	Mixed status O/O	Council estates	Mixed tenure areas	Settled O/O
Oxford 1981	49.6	48.1	48.9	44.0	30.4
Oxford 1991	43.7	39.0	47.0	40.5	25.7
Oldham 1981	—	57.4	72.9	61.0	29.0
Oldham 1991		48.5	70.6	53.4	22.1

Note:
[a] O/O owner-occupied.

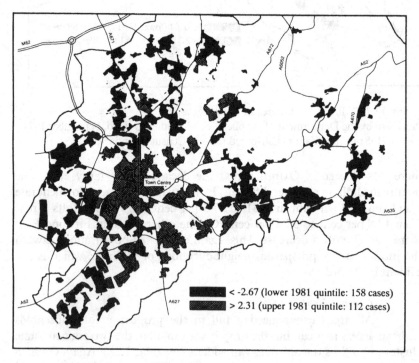

< -2.67 (lower 1981 quintile: 158 cases)
> 2.31 (upper 1981 quintile: 112 cases)

Figure 12.8 Oldham, 1991: index of low income
Produced by the Department of Applied Social Studies, Oxford, September 1994
Source: 1991 Census data and boundaries.

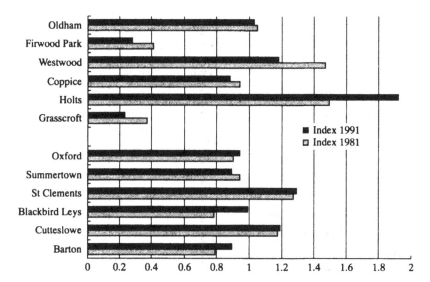

Figure 12.9 Index of representation of population without access to a car in study neighbourhoods: Oxford and Oldham, 1981–91

Oxford in 1981. The bulk of council housing in Oxford tends to be on the city periphery.

To give some handle on the extent of over- or under-representation of access to cars both within and between Oxford and Oldham, we use an index (the Index of Representation) based on a comparison of observed and expected values. A score of 1 would indicate that the proportion of the subgroup in the neighbourhood is as would be expected, given the distribution of the total population. A score below 1 suggests under-representation of the sub-group – above 1 indicates over-representation.

Figure 12.9 shows the picture on this index of representation for households without access to a car in the different neighbourhoods. In Oxford people without access to a car are over-represented in St Clements and Cutteslowe at both 1981 and 1991. However, perhaps surprisingly, in Blackbird Leys and Barton there is slight under-representation at both time points.[11]

In Oldham, on the other hand, we see a more predictable picture with the relatively prosperous areas of Grasscroft and Firwood Park having marked under-representation, with Westwood and Holts marked over-representation. Although by 1991 most areas have improved their position, the situation in Holts has significantly deteriorated.

If we look at access to two or more cars (table 12.9) we find that all areas show an increase in two-car households over the decade, but the gap

Table 12.9 *Households with access to two or
more cars, 1981 and 1991, per cent*

	Oxford %	Oldham %
Council estates 1981	9	3
Council estates 1991	12	4
Settled owner-occupied 1981	16	19
Settled owner-occupied 1991	25	30

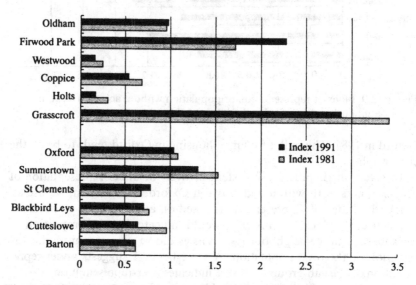

Figure 12.10 Index of representation of population with access to two or more
cars in study neighbourhoods: Oxford and Oldham, 1981–91

widens between the council estate areas (cluster 3) and the more settled
owner-occupied areas (cluster 5) where nearly 30 per cent of households
have access to two cars in Oldham.

Clearly the location of these latter areas in Oldham, predominantly on
the city periphery, and the high proportions of two-earner families may
make two cars a necessary part of household expenditure.

If we look at access to two or more cars, the Oldham study neighbourhoods again show much more extreme variations than the Oxford
neighbourhoods in both 1981 and 1991 (figure 12.10).

Table 12.10 *Index of low income, 1981–91*

	O/O[a] and private rented	Mixed status O/O	Council estates	Mixed tenure areas	Settled O/O
Oxford 1981	−0.59	−1.28	3.59	0.29	−2.35
Oxford 1991	−0.63	−1.26	2.81	0.21	−2.73
Oldham 1981	—	0.43[b]	4.90	1.10	−2.50
Oldham 1991	—	1.26	7.07	0.80	−3.14

Notes:
[a] O/O owner-occupied.
[b] Positive numbers indicate disadvantage, negative numbers indicate advantage.

Index of low income

Finally using the overall Census-based index of low income, what is at first sight striking in Oxford is the relative stability of the measure between 1981 and 1991 in three of the five cluster areas (table 12.10). The council estates experience a relative improvement in their overall positions though they are still highly disadvantaged. The more settled areas show a small increase in their advantage over the 1981–91 decade. But in Oldham the picture is subject to greater change. The already very disadvantaged council estates become substantially much worse than they were in 1981, while the more settled owner-occupation areas (cluster 5) become more advantaged. The mixed status owner-occupied areas which in Oldham clearly contain a more disadvantaged population than the apparent equivalent in Oxford, again deteriorate over the decade. Thus in Oldham the gap widens significantly between the council estate and settled owner-occupation areas.

This analysis by type of area and neighbourhood underlines the extent to which the distribution of low income is structured in social and spatial terms, and is not some randomly distributed 'misfortune' that could happen equally to anyone. What is striking about Oldham is that the areas in the lowest quintile group in 1981 were actually doing worse overall by 1991. The changes in Oxford from 1981 to 1991 were much less clear-cut. Thus the answer to the question posed at the beginning of this section is that the inequalities observed in 1993/94 had existed in 1981 but had significantly increased in Oldham.

12.6 From 1991 to 1993

To take us back to our starting point at the beginning of the chapter we are faced with one small 'missing link' – the period between the Census in April 1991 and our first systematic sweep of benefit information in the Summer of 1993. From the evidence presented so far this might well turn out to be a crucial period – particularly for Oxford. By 1993/94, as we have shown, the overall poverty profiles of the two towns were, perhaps surprisingly, very similar. However, in April 1991 it is clear on all the predictors of low income we examined as well as on the overall index of low income that Oxford was doing rather better than Oldham.

We do have some HB data for this period, but only at the district level and only for Oxford. We conveniently have HB data for Census night 1991 and for some other intervening periods. However, discontinuity between Community Charge Benefit (in force until April 1993) and Council Tax Benefit means that our analysis of IS claimants in this interim period must be limited to tenants. However, even the limited data available show the very substantial rise in IS claimants in the city in the two years following the 1991 Census.

There were 5793 IS claimant tenants in April 1991 and 7560 in June 1993 – a rise of over 30 per cent. Which claimant group accounts for most of the change? The most dramatic increase is in single non-pensioners. Non-pensioner couples also show significant increases. It is these groups who would have borne the brunt of the dramatic rise in unemployment between 1991 and 1993.

12.7 Discussion and conclusion

Data on low income and Census data for two apparently contrasting towns, covering the period 1981–93/94, were analysed to see how the growing inequalities in income and wealth found in national-level data since the early 1980s worked out at this local level. In this chapter we have concentrated on the changing distribution of low income as measured by those dependent on IS. The absence or low levels of such low income should not be taken to represent 'wealth'. However we have reasonably used the term 'better-off' to describe those areas that contained very few such households. Much of the analysis has necessarily been on aggregate spatial level data, but at the ED level, with populations of around 190 households. The low income data, however, relate to individual claimants and their families, but are held in a way that allows aggregation to ED level.

We conclude by summarising the main findings under five key questions.
1 Have overall proportions of low income increased in the two areas?
In 1994 both Oxford and Oldham have similar proportions of their

population living in families with low incomes measured by receipt of means-tested benefits. In Oxford the proportion receiving IS has increased by 30 per cent since 1991. Evidence from proxy measures for low income from the Census indicates that both areas experienced an increase over the 1980s but this was much more marked in Oldham. Overall measures for the two areas mask this pattern of change because the increase was concentrated among particular groups and areas within each town. At the other end of the scale 'better-off' areas improved, particularly in Oldham.

2 Is there increased spatial concentration of low income?
The answer for Oldham is particularly clear. There is little doubt that there were already concentrations of low income households in particular areas in 1981, but these have become much more marked in the 1990s. Many areas in Oldham failed to improve or even fell back over the 1980s, while others improved rapidly. The result is increased spatial concentration of social and economic disadvantage linked to low income. The picture in Oxford is less clear-cut. While there is increased concentration of low income households in some council estates, in other areas mixed tenure patterns, for example private rented households in prosperous owner-occupied areas, ensure a level of diversity across different areas.

3 Is there stability over time in poor and better-off areas?
Comparison of 1981 and 1991 Census data at the ED level suggests a high level of stability in rank position within each area, but particularly in Oldham; that is, areas doing particularly well or badly in 1981 were very likely to be in the same position in 1991.

4 Are there particular groups at increasing disadvantage?
In both areas lone parents are increasingly dependent on IS and may be concentrated in peripheral estates. However single parent claimants tend to be over 30 years old and even over short periods of time there is a great deal of movement in and out of benefit. Minority ethnic groups are concentrated in a very few areas of Oldham and these tend to be the most disadvantaged parts of the town. This concentration has increased over the decade.

The evidence from Oldham particularly might be used to support the thesis of a growing 'underclass', that is a group outside the labour market, dependent on welfare benefits over a long period. While we would avoid using the term for the series of moral overtones it carries, some of the data may appear to point in this direction. However it is important to keep in mind the evidence on the quite rapid turnover within Oldham of people on benefit. In what is a stable area, such mobility is most likely to be explained by movement on and off benefit.

5 Is there evidence of polarisation in income and wealth?

We defined 'polarisation' as an increase at both ends of the distribution. Again the consistent message from Oldham is that from an already more extreme distribution than Oxford in 1981 there was a clear increase in polarisation in spatial terms over the decade. This is seen most clearly in the overall index of low income, where there are both more EDs doing much better in 1991 *and* more doing worse. Oxford shows some evidence of a similar trend, but much less so. However Oxford may well have become more polarised since 1991 with the sharp increase in unemployment. This polarisation is socially and spatially structured. Thus Oldham council estates fall back sharply over the decade; the settled owner-occupied areas in the same town improve. More fine grain analysis from the neighbourhood case studies suggests that this may vary, with some council estates doing better than others; these latter may be taking on an increasingly 'residual' role with a growing proportion of their population on benefit, unable to move elsewhere and in types of property that may not for several reasons be attractive to owner-occupiers.

Notes

We would like to thank both Oxford City Council and Oldham Metropolitan Borough Council for their support and co-operation and for providing the housing benefit data.

1. For a full report of the study see Noble *et al.* (1994).
2. Noble *et al.*, p. 110.
3. Noble *et al.*, p. 113.
4. The selection procedure was guided by their ranking on income support dependency measures.
5. There is no more accurate population estimate available at district level. The population count used is 'Residents 1991 to 1981 Base' (from SAS table 1).
6. Although we have a more recent extract of HB/CTB data, the changes do not merit a revision of these figures.
7. Some, of course, may have continued to claim IS but simply moved out of Oxford.
8. Five EDs covering institutions or other special circumstances were also dropped from the Oldham data.
9. The procedure is to use the values for the EDs at the 20th and 80th percentiles as 'cut points'. This procedure cuts out the potentially 'rogue' observations at the extreme ends of the distribution.
10. See Noble *et al.* (1994, appendix A).
11. We show elsewhere (Noble *et al.*, 1994) that no access to a car is not a very good predictor of low income in the city (cf. Davies *et al.*, 1993).

Part IV

Income and wealth

13 Patterns of financial wealth-holding in the United Kingdom

James Banks, Andrew Dilnot and Hamish Low

13.1 Introduction

There are three broad reasons why households might want to accumulate wealth. First, asset stocks are partly a provision for predictable future periods of low income (such as retirement) or high consumption costs (such as those associated with children). Secondly, holding assets can be a precaution against periods of unpredictably low income (such as unemployment) or high consumption costs (such as illness). The third reason is that most forms of saving earn a positive real return which might outweigh the costs of forgoing current consumption for some households. These three motives for saving lead us to expect very different patterns of asset-holding both across and within household types. These differences will be exacerbated by the fact that asset balances are integrally related to past shocks to the households' income or consumption, as well as future plans. In addition, different asset types will play very different roles in household saving plans – high pension saving, for example, is of very little benefit if an individual becomes unemployed. The pattern and level of household saving, which we expect to be highly diverse, will be affected by government policies (particularly tax policies), and will in turn determine the nature of any desirable intervention by government. Yet there is almost no empirical evidence concerning the distribution of wealth at the household or individual level in the United Kingdom, and even less about how portfolios vary by household type and income.[1]

There is a number of reasons why economists concern themselves with the level of household saving and advocate government policies towards household saving. Paternalism – the idea that individuals might not adequately provide for their retirement or might choose to rely on social security payments thus unnecessarily increasing government expenditure – often figures in these. Other arguments concern economic growth. One apparent suggestion is that motivation and economic performance will be enhanced by increasing the number of individuals with a direct stake in the performance of the economy through the holding of assets. Alternatively insufficient saving is argued to put a brake on the level of the capital stock, and thus on the rate of economic growth.[2] Whilst this chapter presents indirect evidence on the level of household saving we do not address these arguments. We simply present a disaggregate analysis of the distribution and composition of household wealth stocks for the first time.

Until now, most work on wealth in the United Kingdom has relied on data produced by the Inland Revenue, which collects data to calculate inheritance duties. More specifically, the Inland Revenue takes data from estates and weights these amounts according to age-specific mortality rates. The three obvious problems with such an approach are the very small sample sizes for younger groups, *inter vivos* transfers, and the possibility that the tax system encourages the wealthy to divest themselves of their wealth before death. Added to these problems at the aggregate level, the lack of disaggregated data, and the absence of income and demographic information means that the Inland Revenue data can tell us relatively little about the process of wealth accumulation or the extent of correlation between the two distributions of greatest interest to us – the distribution of wealth and income. In contrast, studies of saving at the household level have tended to concentrate on analyses of consumption growth and addressed saving only as the residual between income and consumption.

The empirical analysis of household savings is also complicated by measurement and definitional problems. Private pension contributions are quite clearly saving but difficult to measure – particularly that part of contributions made by employers. State social security contributions are saving insofar as they confer clear rights to future benefits. Mortgage expenditure has elements of both saving (insofar as it will provide future consumption of housing) and current consumption but most people would regard much of it as saving. This is probably not the case for expenditure on durable goods – which actually has similar properties. This chapter concerns itself primarily with presenting the distribution and composition of *financial* wealth in 1991–92 using a new dataset – that is, we do not consider housing wealth or accrued pension wealth for the majority of the analysis. Having said this, we draw on some evidence on pension wealth and compute some estimates of net housing wealth for our sample numbers to put this analysis of financial wealth into a broad perspective of total saving. In addition we use an earlier year of data to analyse how some of these figures have changed since 1987 – a period of enormous variation in financial conditions also characterised by significant reform to the taxation of personal saving.

The data we use are drawn from the Financial Research Survey (FRS), compiled privately by National Opinion Polls (NOP). We have access to this data from 1987 to 1992, but have used data for the financial years at either end of this period – 1987–88 and 1991–92. This dataset allows us to analyse the relationship between financial wealth and a range of other characteristics such as income, age and demographic structure, in a way that has not previously been possible in the United Kingdom. The detailed information available on the form in which wealth is held enables us to form views about the distributional consequences of government action in the capital market. We present detailed analysis of each cross-section without attempting to control for cohort (or date-of-birth) effects. This requires an important qualification when we present patterns of saving by age. Whilst the age structure of saving in any particular year is an important statistic in itself it cannot, in general, be used to infer savings patterns for a young household in the future from those of an older household now. This is particularly true in the current economic and demographic climate of the United Kingdom. Households that retire in 1991 are different from those that will retire in, say, 2021 in two very important ways. First, young cohorts will usually be richer than their predecessors as a result of economic growth and this will presumably affect the level and composition of their saving. Secondly, however, the choices older cohorts have faced during their work histories are very different to those faced by working households today – not only is there a very different range of savings vehicles available but it is already clear that the retirement income provided by the state pension will be worth very little and private provision for retirement will be much more important for younger cohorts.[3] For both these reasons we would expect personal wealth of households currently retired to be less than that of retired households in the future. For these reasons, then, the age profiles presented here cannot be separately identified from cohort or even time effects. A truly dynamic analysis of household saving and wealth accumulation is left as a topic for a significant future research programme.[4]

The layout of the chapter is as follows. In section 13.2 we discuss the data used in some detail. In particular, we pay attention to how the demographic composition of the FRS compares to the distribution of the population as a whole and to the Family Expenditure Survey (FES) – the foremost household level dataset in the United Kingdom. In section 13.3 we describe the distribution of wealth in the United Kingdom. This analysis is most detailed for the distribution of non-housing, non-pension financial wealth in 1991/92. In addition, however, we consider the size of pension rights and housing wealth. Further, we consider some measures of how this might have changed since 1987 – the earliest year we have available. In section 13.4 we summarise our findings and draw conclusions.

13.2 The Financial Research Survey

The data used in this study come from the FRS, which is carried out by NOP in six-month spells. Respondents are chosen by random selection of adults aged 16+, covering both electors and non-electors. Respondents are then interviewed in their homes and asked about the type but not the amount of assets and liabilities that they hold. Approximately 40,000 people are interviewed at this stage in a rolling survey over the six-month period. A random selection of a tenth of these are then reinterviewed by telephone to construct 'value data'. At this second interview respondents are asked the value of the assets and liabilities they hold, but values are given within bands and not as exact amounts. This second interview takes place within three weeks of the initial interview. In this chapter, we make use of the value data from four of these surveys, covering April 1987–March 1988 and April 1991–March 1992.[5] This gives us a total sample size of 6622 individuals in 1991–92 and, due to a different sampling process, almost twice as many observations as in the 1987–88 period.[6] For these households we have banded information of values on holdings of 53 assets and liabilities. Banks, Dilnot and Low (1994) present summary statistics for the number of households holding each disaggregate asset type in the 1991–92 sample along with the numbers of households in the top value band. We talk more about the analysis of banded data later in this section.

13.2.1 Testing the robustness of FRS data

The data have been tested in two ways. First, the demographics of the sample have been compared to the demographics of the sample in the FES; and second, asset-holdings have been compared to holdings in data from the Inland Revenue and the Central Statistical Office (CSO). Before making these comparisons, however, it is necessary to discuss the grossing up of the sample to match population statistics.

Below where we compare wealth-holdings in our sample to aggregate statistics, the data have been multiplied up in order to match the demographic structure of the population as a whole. If the spread of people in the FRS sample exactly matched the spread in the population at a national level, then the grossing up factor would simply be the total population size divided by the sample size. Since it does not, different grossing up factors are needed for different types of people in the population. A higher than average grossing up factor for a particular group indicates that the group is under-represented in the sample. The grossing up factors hence give an indication of the demographic bias of the sample.

Table 13.1 *Grossing up factors, FRS to 1991 Census*

		1991–92		1987–88	
Group	Age	(1)^a	(2)^a	(1)	(2)
Single male	20–35	6927	7440	5308	5765
Single female	20–35	6156	6968	4915	5468
Married male	20–35	5382	5355	2780	2997
Married female	20–35	4531	4494	2143	2238
Single male	36–65	8583	9812	7240	8803
Single female	36–60	5649	5923	3728	3933
Married male	36–65	6265	5904	3194	2955
Married female	36–60	5198	4870	2633	2439
Single male	65+	11805	13998	7181	9377
Single female	60+	14855	14660	7043	7252
Married male	65+	8773	8317	4278	4050
Married female	60+	10636	10078	4620	4320
All		6634	—	3625	—

Note:
^{a} Column (1) presents grossing up factors without adjustment for the presence of phones, Column (2) presents phone-adjusted grossing up factors.

Table 13.1 shows the differential grossing up factors calculated. We show figures for 1987–88 and for 1991–92, and for each year grossing up factors are given with and without adjustment for the presence of a telephone. The FRS value survey is conducted by telephone; those without a telephone are therefore automatically excluded. Adjustment for the presence of telephones is simply done by computing the proportion of individuals in the FES in each group with access to a phone. These proportions are used to weight the unadjusted grossing up factors which are then rescaled to sum to the correct Census aggregate. The demographic characteristics of respondents are broadly similar in the two years, although the absolute level of the grossing up factors is lower in 1987–88, reflecting the larger sample size discussed earlier. The most apparent pattern is the under-sampling of the retired; this problem is worst for single females over age 60 – each observation in this group needs to be multiplied by over 14,000 to aggregate to Census totals, whereas the average grossing up factor is only 6634 in 1992.

In this section we compare the 1991–92 FRS dataset with FES data. The FES data used cover the last nine months of 1991. The sample size is 5306

Table 13.2 *Percentage of sample in income bands, household (FES), tax unit (FES) and 'family' (FRS)*

Income (£)	FES household	FES tax unit	FRS 'family'
<2500	0.68	5.73	2.83
2501–4500	7.50	13.00	8.14
4501–6500	8.89	10.77	8.64
6501–7500	3.14	4.42	4.40
7501–9500	6.22	8.11	5.27
9501–11500	5.71	7.15	7.57
11501–13500	5.96	6.55	7.78
13501–15500	6.22	6.16	7.57
15501–17500	6.01	5.20	7.48
17501–25000	19.26	15.45	19.86
25000+	30.40	17.46	20.46
Total	100.00	100.00	100.00

households, but both FRS and FES data are displayed as proportions of the sample size to allow comparability. These proportions, however, are not weighted to reflect the under- and over-sampling of different groups in either the FRS or FES data. Table 13.2 shows the spread of income in each dataset. The first FES income statistics are for household gross income, not including income in kind. The second FES statistics are for tax unit gross income. The difference between the two is that the tax unit includes only the 'nuclear' family, that is the head of the household, spouse and children, whereas the household includes anyone living in the house. A grandmother living with her child's family forms a separate tax unit, but is part of the same household.

The FRS asks about 'gross family income' which seems to allow a definition of the family which would include relatives living in the house even where they are technically separate tax units, but would exclude unrelated household members. The FRS data correspondingly lie between the income ranges for the tax unit and those for the household. This is consistent with a definitional problem which led to grandparents being classed as family, while lodgers and fellow students, for example, were not. The income for FES tax units is lower than for the FRS family unit, but the income for FES households is higher than for the FRS.

Table 13.3 again highlights the under-representation of retired people in the FRS sample, relative to the FES. The obvious corollary of this is that

Table 13.3 *Work status*

Work status	% of FES	% of FRS
Full-time	37.64	47.58
Part-time	10.33	14.67
Self-employed	7.37	3.53
Retired	21.24	12.13
Not working	23.42	22.08

the FRS has a disproportionately large number of working individuals. Table 13.3 also shows that there is under-sampling of self-employed individuals.

The aim of comparing the FRS and FES data without correcting for known under-sampling is to give an idea of the type of person that is in the FRS sample. There are several notable characteristics which all stem from the lack of retired individuals and couples: first, the high proportion of full-time and part-time workers; second, the high proportion of mortgage-holders; and third, the low number of households with income between £2500 and £6500. In the comparison of wealth-holdings to aggregate statistics below these characteristics are corrected for by giving extra weight to those who are under-sampled, as described on p. 325 concerning grossing up.

Table 13.4 presents information on the numbers holding particular assets in our data and compares these figures with aggregate holdings numbers from official statistics. As we have already mentioned, aggregate data are very sparse so our holdings comparisons have to be limited to assets which have special tax status. Table 13.4 presents grossed up FRS totals for the incidence of share-holding, Tax Exempt Special Savings Accounts (TESSAs), Personal Equity Plans (PEPs) and Personal Pension Plans (PPPs). For these assets we are able to use Inland Revenue information on personal asset-holdings. We concentrate on 1991–92, but we also give figures from aggregate statistics and grossed up FRS in 1987–88 where possible.

The comparison of share-holdings shows that for those holding shares in only a few companies, who represent the great bulk of individual shareholders, the FRS sample is fairly accurate. For those with more diversified equity portfolios the FRS data do far less well, as we would expect. The overall figures for TESSA-holdings match reasonably well with the aggregate holding data, although they mask a divergence between holdings of

Table 13.4 *Comparison with National Accounts and Inland Revenue statistics, asset-holdings, by number, 000*

	Aggregate statistic end 1987–88	FRS[a] 1987–88	FRS as % of aggregate	Aggregate statistic end 1991–92	FRS 1991–92	FRS as % of aggregate
Share ownership						
No. of Comp: 1	na	5246	—	5940	6041	101.70
No. of Comp: 2	na	1215	—	2200	1683	76.50
No. of Comp: 3	na	541	—	990	808	81.62
No. of Comp: 4+	na	273	—	1870	512	27.38
Total	8600	7275	84.59	11000	9044	82.22
TESSA						
Bank	na	na	—	906	375	41.39
Building Soc.	na	na	—	1745	1482	84.92
Total	na	na	—	2651	1857	70.05
PEP	300	264	88.00	2110	1239	58.72
PPP (if working)						
Male	na	na	—	2461	2262	91.91
Female	na	na	—	1156	1332	115.22
Total PPP	na	na	—	3617	3595	99.39

Notes:
[a] All FRS values grossed up using differential grossing up factors accounting for phone ownership.
Aggregate figures unavailable in 1987–88 for disaggregated share holdings, TESSAs and PPPs.
Sources: FRS, Inland Revenue Statistics, Financial Statistics.

Building Society TESSAs, which are well represented and bank TESSAs which are under-represented. PEP-holdings are under-represented, but like multiple share holdings are concentrated towards the top of the wealth distribution. Holdings of Personal Pension Plans (PPPs) by women are over-stated in the FRS data. Our suspicion is that this reflects mis-labelling of non-PPP contracts, such as Additional Voluntary Contributions (AVCs); much of the over-representation reflects a large number of the over 50 age group claiming to have PPPs.

In table 13.5 we report comparisons of asset values, which are consistent with the holdings data in table 13.4, and in particular with the fact that the FRS data miss the very wealthy. Once again there is less information to use for the 1987 comparison, but we can at least use National Accounts data from the personal sector balance sheet for widely-held assets which do not have special tax status, such as Interest-Bearing Accounts (IBAs) and National Savings. Accurate data on the value of PEP holdings are not available in the FRS for 1987–88.

A number of points are worth bearing in mind when making these comparisons. First, as in most OECD countries, the National Accounts include unincorporated businesses in the personal sector balance sheet, so we would never expect to capture all of 'aggregate' personal sector wealth in the form of shares, National Savings or IBAs from our survey alone. Secondly, the FRS data on bank account saving do not include balances in current accounts. More importantly, however, the under-sampling of the extremely wealthy will have more implications for the levels of holdings of assets rather than the number of holdings, since this group will presumably hold significantly more in each asset type, rather than just many more types of asset (although wealthy portfolios will also be more diversified). It is worth noting that the Inland Revenue wealth distribution statistics suggest that for the broad categories of wealth identified here, the least wealthy 87 per cent hold only 37 per cent of the total, while the least wealthy 96 per cent hold only 57 per cent of the total. It is no surprise that the FRS identifies only around 40 per cent of aggregate financial wealth, given the highly skewed nature of the wealth distribution and the volun-tary nature of the survey. The results we report in this chapter clearly provide little insight into the very wealthiest group of the population, but for the least wealthy 90 per cent we believe the data we are using to be rea-sonably reliable.

13.2.2 Aggregating the value data

The main difficulty posed by the value data is that the reported values are not exact amounts, instead they are given within value bands. This causes

Table 13.5 *Comparison of asset values, end 1987 and end 1991, £ million*

	Aggregate statistic end 1987	FRS[c] 1987/88	FRS as % of aggregate	Aggregate statistic end 1991	FRS[c] 1991/92	FRS as % of aggregate
Wealth	389700	153549	39.4	400474	147733	36.9
Shares[a]	149120	23748	15.9	137200	30719	22.4
National savings[a]	45813	15689	34.2	39000	19015	48.8
IBA[a]	146670	91049	62.1	179084	75657	42.2
PEP	578	—	—	6970	4404	63.2
Bank TESSA[b]	na	na	—	2189	875	40.0
Building Soc. TESSA[b]	na	na	—	4634	4118	88.9
Total TESSA[b]	na	na	—	6823	4993	73.2
Other	47519	22505	47.4	31670	12945	40.9

Notes:
[a] Aggregate figures include holdings by unincorporated businesses.
[b] Aggregate statistic is for mid-period.
[c] All FRS values grossed up using differential grossing up factors accounting for phone ownership.
Sources: FRS, Inland Revenue Statistics, Financial Statistics.

two problems: first, the distribution within each band is not known, and second there is no upper limit for the top band. In what follows, we have ignored the first problem by assigning a value to each asset equal to the mid-point of the corresponding value band. This would clearly be a reasonable simplification if the distribution within each band was close to uniform. If, however, the distribution across the whole value range were peaked, taking the mid-point for any band covering an area below (above) the peak under-estimates (over-estimates) the average value within that value band. Although it is unlikely that the distribution is uniform, assigning mid-points does serve as a first approximation.

The second problem remains because it is obviously not possible to assign a mid-point if the upper limit is not known. Again we have had to make a first approximation by simply assigning the minimum of the value band for the upper band. Although this might in theory be a problem, appendix 1 of Banks, Dilnot and Low (1994) shows that the implications in this case are not too severe. In only two asset groups (premium bonds and 'other' shares) do we have more than three truncated observations. Different assets are coded with different band widths such that the number of truncated observations is low. Whilst this would still be a problem in an econometric model, for the purpose of this descriptive study we can reasonably say that medians will be unaffected and means may only move slightly according to the top-coding assumptions described above.

There is a further question about how to deal with answers of 'Refused' or 'Not known', and what it means if no answer is recorded at all. It seems reasonable to assume that no answer at all indicates that the respondent does not hold any savings in that asset. In the other two cases, however, there are two ways of dealing with the answer. The first is to assign a value of zero to that asset, while the second is to leave the value for that asset out of the data calculations. The advantage of the second method is that median values will not be distorted by having extra numbers of zeros included and hence details for individual asset-holdings will be more accurate. The disadvantage is that aggregate values will be under-counted. This happens because, for any one respondent, a missing value on any asset means that *total* wealth cannot be counted. In other words, aggregate values only include values for individuals who have neither refused nor answered 'Not known' to any question. The corollary of this is that the first method is less accurate for details on particular assets, but more accurate for aggregate statistics. In section 13.3 below, we use the first method to give a better indication of total values.

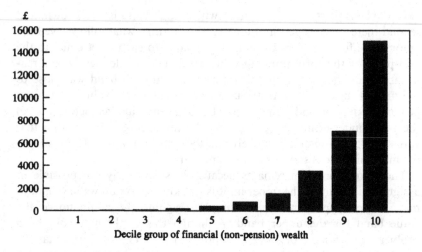

Figure 13.1 Median financial (non-pension) wealth, by decile group of financial wealth

13.3 The distribution of wealth

In this section we move on to analyse the distribution of holdings of different assets, the relationship between this distribution and income, wealth and age, and finally the way in which portfolio structures vary across age, income and wealth groups. To begin with we concentrate on describing the most recent year of our data in detail and use an aggregate definition of financial wealth.[7] This definition does not include estimates of either accrued pension wealth or net housing wealth. We turn to these later in this section.

Figure 13.1 presents this financial wealth variable by decile group medians (i.e. the 5th to 95th percentile points). This demonstrates the concentration of financial wealth at the top of the distribution. Half the sample have less than £455 and the median of the fifth decile group is £350. Median wealth in the top 10 per cent of the wealth distribution is over twice that of those households between the 80th and 90th percentiles.

One of the most important uses of the micro-data in this study is to analyse how this distribution varies conditional on household-level variables – particularly age and income. First we present the distribution by income band. Figure 13.2 graphs the median financial wealth by income band. We concentrate on medians because of the high degree of skewness in the positive wealth values and also the large numbers with zero wealth. (Not only is the mean over six times the size of the median, but the 90/10 ratio, for example, is not defined as the 10th percentile is zero.) The distrib-

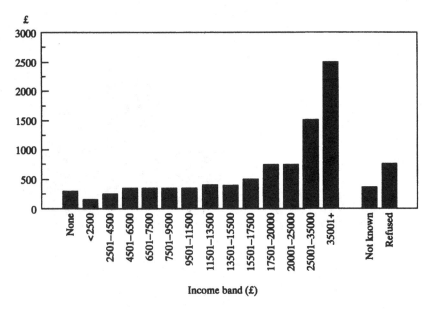

Figure 13.2 Median financial (non-pension) wealth, by income band

ution is reasonably flat over most of its range. It is not until the £25,000+
income bands (20.4 per cent of the sample) that the conditional median
rises substantially. It is worth noting that the financial wealth of those
households that did not (or could not) answer the income question is not
out of line with that of the survey as a whole.

Figure 13.3 presents a similar analysis by age band. Unsurprisingly,
there is a striking pattern of asset-holding by age. Median and mean financial wealth rise with age until retirement. However, given our discussion in
section 13.1 we would caution that the observed low levels of asset-
holding for retired households in 1991/92 might just as much be due to the
currently retired generation being worse off as a whole, rather than due to
older households spending down their assets in retirement. The fact that
most retired households have more than the median level of wealth means
that, given the under-representation of the elderly described in section
13.2, our survey median of £455 might be slightly low as an estimate of the
population median.

Using the household level data on wealth-holdings we can split our
sample by age and income simultaneously to analyse the joint distribution
of income, age and financial wealth. In Figure 13.4 we allocate each
household in the FRS sample into one of six age bands and one of five
income bands. We can then compute median financial wealth in each of

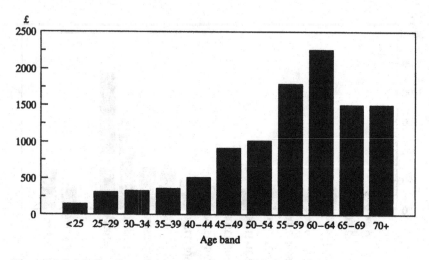

Figure 13.3 Median financial (non-pension) wealth, by age band

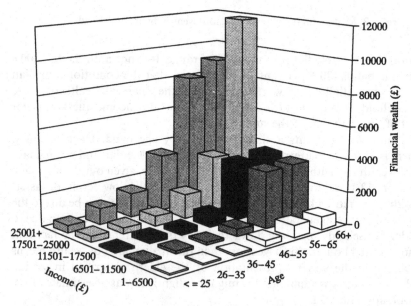

Figure 13.4 Median financial (non-pension) wealth, by age and income

Table 13.6 *Median financial wealth, £, by income and age band*

	1–6500	6501–11500	11501–17500	17501–25000	25000+	Not known /Refused	None
<25	50	55	100	350	428	53	150
26–35	50	150	300	400	1000	185	350
36–45	50	110	325	605	1500	355	450
46–55	330	403	753	1500	3505	683	200
56–65	750	3390	3503	3463	8150	1500	1500
65+	750	3530	3713	11850	9053	750	1500

the thirty cells[8] and this forms the vertical axis in the three-dimensional figure 13.4 – the numbers for which are in table 13.6. Interesting patterns emerge. In most cases, wealth rises by age at each income level and by income within each age band. Therefore there is a large concentration amongst high income older households, as predicted by economic intuition and economic theory. It is worth noting that the distinction between income and wealth is blurred for retired households since the presence of very high income for non-working households reveals a prior choice to annuitise past holdings of wealth stocks. This may well explain the fact that the highest income retired households have slightly less stocks of (unannuitised) wealth than those in the income band below them.

In table 13.7 we break this analysis down by asset group. Since the incidence of holdings is very low for all asset groups except two, tabulation of percentiles such as the median or quartiles is uninformative. Therefore we simply report the proportion of our sample we observe holding the asset and the mean value held for those with positive holdings by each conditioning variable. In addition to splitting by income and age we also disaggregate this analysis by band of total financial wealth. Assets are aggregated as follows. The two most commonly held asset groups are interest-bearing accounts (all interest-bearing bank and building society accounts (non-TESSAs) and savings clubs) and National Savings. We then consider TESSAs and PEPs as separate items in the portfolio since the take-up of these recently introduced tax-privileged assets is interesting in itself. Finally we split remaining wealth into groups – equities and 'Other'. The 'Other' category comprises primarily unit trusts, investment trusts and government securities.

There are many trends apparent in these distributions of asset-holdings. This is particularly the case with PEPs, shares and 'other' assets, holdings of which are only prevalent amongst high income, high wealth households.

Table 13.7 Percentage of non-zero asset-holdings and mean of non-zero asset-holdings, by income, wealth and age, FRS 1991–92

	N	TESSAs		Interest Accounts		PEPs		Shares		Nat. Savings		Other	
		%>0	Mean (>0)	%>0	Mean (>0)	%>0	Mean (>0)	%>0	Mean (>0)	%>0	Mean (>0)	%>0	Mean (>0)
By income band													
1–2500	125	0.80	3500	76.00	965	0.80	3500	4.80	3833	30.40	1374	0.80	7500
2501–4500	359	1.67	1150	67.69	1595	0.00	—	7.52	1009	42.06	1660	1.11	8562
4501–6500	380	3.16	3341	71.05	1871	1.05	2500	10.53	1593	36.58	1090	2.11	2812
6501–7500	195	2.56	2700	71.28	2443	0.51	7500	13.33	3038	34.36	1385	2.56	4050
7501–9500	231	3.46	3462	75.76	2404	2.16	3750	15.15	3278	33.33	1195	5.63	8134
9501–11500	335	3.28	4772	75.52	2410	1.19	7375	16.42	2463	29.85	1498	2.39	2062
11501–13500	346	4.91	2458	76.59	1950	1.16	4000	15.61	2171	29.48	1446	4.91	6808
13501–15500	334	5.39	1875	74.55	2304	2.69	3944	17.96	3762	31.74	354	4.79	10406
15501–17500	328	4.57	2413	78.96	1740	1.83	3375	17.07	2754	29.88	362	4.27	6500
17501–25000	880	3.86	2591	80.23	2295	2.27	4312	21.36	4918	32.95	996	5.34	8005
25001+	900	7.22	2953	78.78	3187	5.44	4770	29.22	5589	38.22	801	8.00	6281
By wealth band													
1–49	457	0.00	0	42.89	12	0.00	0	0.00	0	61.71	16	0.00	0
50–100	884	0.68	50	91.29	55	0.00	0	0.00	0	21.04	38	0.00	0
101–305	596	0.84	110	81.21	143	0.00	0	17.11	250	36.24	70	0.34	250
306–575	647	0.93	350	90.42	343	0.31	250	8.35	296	32.30	138	0.15	250
576–1000	650	1.54	640	91.38	664	0.62	625	15.85	471	31.69	211	2.00	654
1001–1850	661	3.63	873	90.92	1222	0.76	1100	21.33	766	36.01	342	3.33	1091
1851–3850	627	6.06	2159	91.39	2645	2.39	2150	23.44	1226	34.61	599	5.58	2029
3851–8250	632	10.13	2909	94.78	5027	4.59	3379	30.22	2000	43.67	810	8.07	2877

8251–15000	313	14.06	3770	95.53	7358	6.39	3550	48.24	2738	48.88	1779	9.90	3750
15001+	332	15.06	4702	87.95	8911	17.77	7352	61.45	15212	62.95	6802	32.53	13023
By age band												
21–30	1866	1.50	1600	77.22	1001	0.91	4220	9.59	1818	22.24	440	2.20	2798
31–34	648	2.62	2702	74.54	1421	1.23	4687	12.65	3411	27.31	273	3.55	4032
35–39	776	2.84	1956	76.03	1845	1.29	7600	16.62	2563	31.31	645	2.06	3125
40–44	772	4.40	2377	72.67	2087	1.81	3160	17.88	3494	33.94	279	3.76	5594
45–49	621	5.31	3071	77.78	2591	2.90	3375	20.45	4899	38.81	430	4.51	6223
50–54	436	5.96	3194	72.48	3163	4.59	6987	22.02	4562	36.01	868	6.42	8508
55–59	388	8.51	4224	77.06	3539	5.41	4678	25.00	5453	40.21	1291	8.51	10287
60–64	363	7.16	2446	80.17	3754	3.31	4729	23.14	4592	46.28	2158	6.06	9943
65–69	342	3.51	2875	79.24	3592	1.75	3166	23.68	3154	47.66	2452	7.02	7781
70+	410	3.90	3934	71.95	3425	1.95	4937	19.51	7853	51.22	2677	4.63	10342
All	6622	3.73	2831	75.96	2142	2.02	4802	16.51	3913	33.10	1016	3.97	6744

Average balances for those households holding these assets also increase markedly with income and wealth as we might expect. In fact, the trends are significantly stronger by wealth level than by income. This reflects the fact that many high income households may still be quite young (a more appropriate measure of 'lifetime' living standards might be total expenditure about which we have no information for our data) and therefore have not accumulated large stocks of assets despite saving significantly.

The probability of holding a TESSA increases with income, albeit weakly, and even in the highest income band only 7 per cent of individuals hold TESSAs. There is little discernible relationship between the mean of non-zero holdings and income. The probability of holding a TESSA is quite strongly related to aggregate financial wealth, as is the mean value of non-zero holdings. The probability of holding a TESSA by age peaks in the years running up to retirement age. In this case, once again, we should stress that on the basis of this cross-sectional data we cannot say anything about life-cycle behaviour. While it is tempting to deduce (from the fall in the frequency of TESSA-holding in the 65+ age group) that TESSAs are less attractive to the retired than to the pre-retired, this pattern in the data could simply reflect a cohort effect.

Interest-bearing accounts (IBAs) are fairly evenly distributed by income, with only a slight tendency for mean holdings to increase with income. Those in the lowest band of wealth have a far lower probability of holding an IBA, while mean holdings do rise quite rapidly with aggregate wealth. Holding of IBAs is fairly constant by age, with mean holdings rising slowly.

PEP-holding is concentrated in higher income and wealth bands, particularly higher wealth bands. The mean value rises with aggregate wealth, possibly suggesting that those with greater wealth first invested in PEPs sooner after their introduction in 1987. PEP-holding by age peaks, as with TESSAs, before retirement. The direct holding of shares is still much more common in 1991–92 than the holding of PEPs, but follows a broadly similar pattern, with concentration of holding at higher income and especially higher wealth levels. The mean level of holding increases particularly quickly with wealth.

National Savings products are widely held, with some tendency for increased frequency of holding and mean non-zero holding at higher wealth levels. There is also a clear tendency for frequency and mean level of holding to increase with age. This may be because National Savings-type products appeal to older individuals, or it may be a simple generational effect that will become less prevalent as new households or individuals retire.

Before moving on to consider housing and pension wealth we briefly

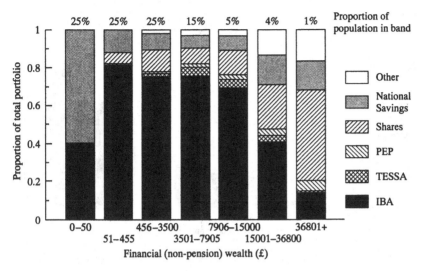

Figure 13.5 Mean portfolios, by financial wealth band

describe the structure of portfolios by wealth level. This analysis is pursued further when we compare the 1987–88 and 1991–92 distributions below. Figure 13.5 presents mean portfolios for different bands of the wealth distribution. Figure 13.5 demonstrates the striking differences in diversity of portfolios across the population. The portfolios of households in the bottom half of the wealth distribution are heavily concentrated in IBAs and National Savings.

The average portfolio for the whole sample is heavily concentrated in IBAs and National Savings. Other forms of saving account for only 15 per cent of wealth on average. The numbers are very different for the top 10, and particularly for the top 5, per cent of the sample population ranked by wealth. It is worth noting that IBAs are the most heavily taxed of all forms of wealth. On the other hand it is the tax treatment of assets held by high wealth individuals that most approximates an expenditure tax.[9]

13.3.1 Housing wealth

To get an idea of how the levels of wealth described above compare to some notion of total wealth that includes saving in the form of housing and pensions we have to impute some information for our sample. In this section we add a reasonably ad hoc approximation to housing wealth onto total financial wealth for our sample to assess how the distributions might change. The imputation of net housing wealth from the information in our

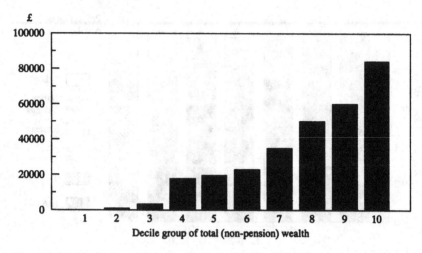

Figure 13.6 Median total (non-pension) wealth, by decile group of total wealth

dataset is described fully in Banks, Dilnot and Low (1994). As the FRS is a survey of financial products rather than financial or physical wealth we know information on mortgage values for mortgage-holders but do not know house values for owner-occupiers. For this group we impute housing wealth from the 1991 British Household Panel Survey (BHPS) conditional on household income band. The procedure for mortgage-holders is, briefly, to uprate the purchase value of the individual's house (which we know from our dataset) and then to subtract an estimate of the outstanding mortgage. The first figure we present (figure 13.6) is simply the distribution of wealth by decile group of wealth (where both definitions include housing). This corresponds to figure 13.1, and demonstrates both the significantly increased orders of magnitude generated by the inclusion of net housing wealth and the equalising effect housing wealth has on the overall distributional shape.

Great care must be taken in interpreting figures that relate to housing wealth. While housing was widely seen in the 1970s and 1980s as an investment good, it is also a consumption good, and indeed a consumption good which is an absolute necessity. If rents are closely linked to house prices the extent to which an increase in house prices increases the lifetime consumption possibilities for a homeowner is quite limited. It is mainly to the extent that individuals can trade down or bequeath their houses that increasing house prices genuinely increase wealth.

Figure 13.7 and table 13.8 present medians of total wealth including housing by age and income. Although the concentration of wealth

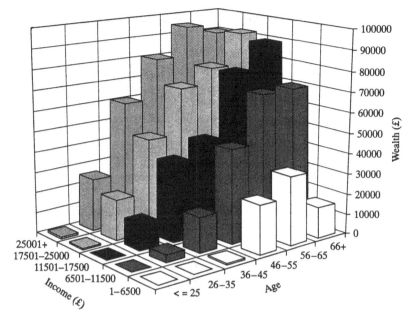

Figure 13.7 Median total (non-pension) wealth, by age and income

amongst high income, high age households is still apparent, the distribution now rises more uniformly with both age and income as households who own their own homes (about three quarters of our 1991 sample) begin to pay off their mortgage debt and accumulate capital gains on their house. Again the only non-uniformity in the wealth–income relationship is for the very high income retired households who will have already annuitised some of their wealth.

13.3.2 Pension wealth

The FRS data we have used in earlier sections of this chapter do not provide enough information to attempt individual-level estimates of pension status, for which a great deal of detailed information is necessary.[10] Pensions are often treated as wealth, and quite reasonably, since they confer the ability to consume, in retirement, without earning. If future pension entitlements and longevity are known, a flow of pension income can be translated into a measure of wealth. Unfortunately, future pension entitlements are rarely known with any certainty, since future job tenure, earnings growth, capital market performance, inflation, and changes in government policy can all have an effect. We cannot therefore

Table 13.8 *Median non-pension wealth, by income and age band*

	1–6500	6501–11500	11501–17500	17501–25000	25000+	Not known /Refused	None
<25	53	55	118	365	859	53	185
26–35	150	3596	13032	19943	25644	13008	4050
36–45	700	17244	38379	46192	60739	53287	49800
46–55	23944	45913	45798	68797	80536	61275	49825
56–65	33662	69452	76792	76643	94908	70819	50550
65+	15237	69743	89121	92110	90231	70379	50550

Table 13.9 *Impact of pensions on the distribution of wealth, 1991*

Percentage of wealth owned by:		Marketable	Marketable+ occupational	Marketable+occupational+state
Most wealthy (%)	1	18	14	11
	2	25	19	15
	5	37	30	25
	10	50	43	36
	25	71	66	58
	50	92	88	82

Source: Inland Revenue Statistics (1994).

make any estimates of individual pension wealth comparable with our estimates of financial wealth. The Inland Revenue, however, does estimate the value of both occupational and state pension rights (see Inland Revenue, 1994, for details). The Inland Revenue estimates for 1991 are of occupational pension wealth of £605 billion, and state pension wealth of £698 billion. Each of these is thus of a similar size to estimated housing wealth. It is important to note that the assumptions necessary to arrive at such figures, in particular future uprating of state pensions, make them necessarily subject to a wide margin of error.

To give some idea of the distribution of this pension wealth we present in table 13.9 the Inland Revenue estimates of the distribution of marketable, occupational pension and state pension wealth. We would expect the state pension, which is a basically flat rate benefit, to have a significant equalising effect, but occupational pensions also reduce wealth inequality, being received or expected by some 50 per cent of the population.

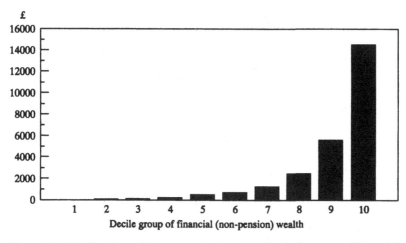

Figure 13.8 Median financial (non-pension) wealth, by decile group of financial wealth, 1987–88

Table 13.9 demonstrates that pension wealth has a significant equalising effect in the overall distribution of wealth.

13.3.3 Changes since 1987

To illustrate the changes in the level and composition of wealth between 1987–88 and 1991–92 we first present the comparable breakdown to that in figure 13.1. We then describe the portfolio structure of the population by age and wealth, for each dataset.

Figure 13.8 presents median financial (non-pension) wealth by wealth decile group for the 1987–88 FRS data. This dataset does not permit the imputation of housing wealth since the survey did not ask questions regarding the purchase price of owner-occupied accommodation. Therefore we can only compare non-housing distributions. The shape of the distribution of wealth looks very similar across the two years, although there is some evidence that the wealth of the top three decile groups increased.

Tables 13.10 and 13.11 show how the portfolio structure of the population by age and wealth has changed. In these tables we have changed the structure of the bands where possible to facilitate comparison between the different years' data. In 1987/88 TESSAs were not available and PEPs were still very new so we cannot include them in the earlier portfolios. This obviously creates a problem in comparing the two datasets because the range of portfolio choice in 1991–92 is wider than in 1987/88. However, it is possible to see some broad patterns. It is

Table 13.10 *Mean portfolios, by age group, 1987–88 and 1991–92*

Asset type	Age										All
	30	30–34	35–39	40–44	45–49	50–54	55–59	60–64	65–69	70+	
1987–88											
IBAs	0.831	0.792	0.778	0.747	0.728	0.732	0.725	0.714	0.681	0.671	0.761
Shares	0.039	0.063	0.073	0.074	0.080	0.083	0.072	0.066	0.066	0.046	0.062
National Savings	0.110	0.119	0.123	0.136	0.151	0.134	0.161	0.185	0.219	0.256	0.146
Other	0.010	0.019	0.019	0.033	0.032	0.041	0.035	0.030	0.029	0.022	0.023
1991–92											
IBAs	0.789	0.769	0.754	0.705	0.680	0.660	0.632	0.665	0.655	0.599	0.718
Shares	0.063	0.081	0.102	0.104	0.122	0.110	0.110	0.093	0.096	0.100	0.091
National Savings	0.118	0.108	0.105	0.131	0.130	0.134	0.142	0.167	0.186	0.269	0.137
Other	0.014	0.022	0.016	0.025	0.025	0.035	0.049	0.030	0.038	0.015	0.023
PEPs	0.006	0.007	0.005	0.009	0.013	0.023	0.023	0.008	0.006	0.004	0.009
TESSAs	0.010	0.013	0.018	0.026	0.031	0.030	0.044	0.038	0.018	0.013	0.021

Table 13.11 *Mean portfolios, by wealth group, 1987–88 and 1991–92*

Asset type	Band of financial wealth £										
	1–49	50–100	101–305	306–575	576–1000	1001–1850	1851–3850	3851–8200	8201–15000	15000+	All
1987–88											
IBAs	0.502	0.883	0.825	0.779	0.813	0.745	0.799	0.774	0.814	0.469	0.761
Shares	0.0	0.0	0.0	0.101	0.070	0.128	0.086	0.083	0.069	0.207	0.062
National Savings	0.463	0.109	0.171	0.110	0.102	0.104	0.092	0.094	0.065	0.113	0.146
Other	0.0	0.0	0.0	0.009	0.009	0.015	0.019	0.043	0.049	0.202	0.023
1991–92											
IBAs	0.404	0.884	0.685	0.817	0.786	0.752	0.746	0.724	0.686	0.349	0.718
Shares	0.0	0.0	0.162	0.059	0.096	0.113	0.098	0.102	0.124	0.282	0.091
National Savings	0.596	0.110	0.145	0.114	0.085	0.084	0.064	0.062	0.082	0.157	0.137
Other	0.0	0.0	0.003	0.001	0.015	0.024	0.036	0.036	0.037	0.143	0.023
PEPs	0.0	0.0	0.0	0.002	0.005	0.006	0.015	0.024	0.022	0.039	0.009
TESSAs	0.0	0.005	0.005	0.009	0.012	0.022	0.041	0.051	0.049	0.030	0.021

also possible to see how the introduction of PEPs and TESSAs affected portfolio composition.

By age, portfolio structure seems relatively stable: the share of wealth accounted for by IBAs falls slowly with age, that in National Savings products tends to rise. This may partly reflect the lack of wealth of the young, but may also reflect a need for greater liquidity. National Savings seem particularly popular with the very old, due primarily to 'Granny' bonds. The proportion of wealth accounted for by shares is relatively low for both the very young and the very old. This may also reflect a need for greater liquidity at those points in the life-cycle.

By wealth, we see the more striking variations in portfolio structure observed in section 13.1. Across time, the more wealthy have shifted much of their wealth out of IBAs and into shares and National Savings. The least wealthy still concentrate their wealth in National Savings and IBAs, though there has been a noticeable shift towards National Savings. In contrast, savings of the average wealth-holders have shifted away from National Savings, partly to take out PEPs and partly to take out TESSAs. The most striking change in portfolio composition between the two periods is the rise in share ownership, both directly and indirectly through PEPs, and the fall in holdings in IBAs.

13.4 Conclusions

This chapter presents the first detailed results from a newly available survey of income, household characteristics and financial assets and liabilities. It is clear that the very wealthiest group of the population is under-represented, but for the great bulk of the population the data seem representative. The relationships we show seem consistent with intuition and economic theory. Financial wealth is unequally distributed, and varies predictably with both age and income. The distribution of wealth within age and income groups is unequal to an extent similar to that for the overall distribution of wealth. Portfolio compositions vary with wealth, age and income, with a particularly marked shift from IBAs as the dominant asset for those with low wealth and income into equity-based assets dominating for the wealthy. The shift from IBAs to equity-based and more favourably taxed assets that we observe as wealth and income increase is also evident for the whole distribution as we move from 1987–88 to 1991–92. We would stress again that these cross-sectional results cannot be interpreted as relevant for the experience of given households as they age through their life-cycle. Although the focus of this chapter is on financial wealth, we show that housing wealth and pension wealth are more equally distributed, and larger, than financial wealth.

Notes

Research for this project was carried out at the ESRC Research Centre for the Microeconomic Analysis of Fiscal Policy at IFS. Thanks are due to Richard Blundell and Edward Whitehouse for many useful comments and to Marysia Walsh for assistance on an earlier draft of this chapter. We are very grateful to NOP Corporate and Financial for providing the FRS data used in this study, and to Midge Clayton at NOP for extensive assistance. We are also grateful to the ESRC-funded British Household Panel Study at the University of Essex for the BHPS data. Material from the Family Expenditure Survey, made available by the Central Statistical Office through the ESRC Data Archive at the University of Essex, has been used by permission of the Controller of Her Majesty's Stationery Office. NOP, the CSO and the ESRC Data Archive bear no responsibility for the analysis or interpretation of the data reported here. Any errors are entirely our own.

1. Some examples are *Inland Revenue Statistics* (1993), Atkinson and Harrison (1978).
2. It is worth noting that while the level of national saving is often said to determine the return on investment and therefore the capital stock in a closed economy, its role in a small, increasingly open economy like the United Kingdom is far less clear.
3. See Dilnot *et al.* (1994).
4. Some papers have addressed this problem, but not directly on wealth or savings data. Banks and Blundell (1994b) consider a cohort-based analysis of saving and consumption using FES data and King and Leape (1989) estimate a life-cycle model of asset holding behaviour using Canadian data.
5. An early six-month period of this data was analysed in two previous studies – see Lee and Saunders (1988) and Saunders and Webb (1988).
6. The 1987–88 survey was undertaken very differently to later years and NOP do not have much information to supplement the data itself. Indeed some asset types currently available were not yet in existence (e.g. TESSAs and PPPs). Consequently we present analysis of the 1987/88 data as evidence of some broad time-series trends and concentrate on using the 1991/92 data to describe the wealth distribution.
7. Throughout this section we will refer to financial non-pension wealth as simply 'financial' wealth for brevity. Again, see Banks, Dilnot and Low (1994).
8. When computing joint distributions the cell size can collapse to quite small numbers relatively quickly – hence we have to use broader income and age bands than those in the univariate distributions used elsewhere in the chapter.
9. See Banks and Blundell (1994a).
10. See Dilnot *et al.* (1994, chapter 4).

14 Home-ownership, housing wealth and wealth distribution in Britain

Chris Hamnett and Jenny Seavers

14.1 Introduction

The level of home-ownership in Britain has increased rapidly during the last 40 years. In 1950 there were some 4 million owner-occupied dwellings, 29 per cent of the total. By 1990, there were 15 million owner-occupied dwellings, 67 per cent of total dwellings (Department of the Environment, 1993; CML, 1994). The 30 years from 1960 to 1989 also saw rapid house price inflation over and above the general level of inflation. National average house prices rose from £2500 in 1960 to £5000 in 1970 and £65,000 in 1990 (CML, 1994). This represents an increase of 1200 per cent in nominal terms in just 20 years, and in real terms the value of housing has risen about three-fold (Holmans, 1990). These trends, the growth of home-ownership and house-price inflation have, between them, led to major changes in the importance of property ownership in personal wealth and in inheritance. Not only do many home-owners now own a substantial asset, but a large proportion of both wealth and inheritance now consists of housing (Forrest and Murie, 1989; Hamnett, 1993).

14.1.1 Housing and the distribution of wealth

The Royal Commission on the Distribution of Income and Wealth (1977) estimated that the value of dwellings as a proportion of net personal wealth increased from 18 per cent in 1960 to 37 per cent in 1975, and this had risen to just over 53 per cent by 1990. The proportion has subsequently fallen back as a result of the sharp slump in the home-ownership market – prices in London and the South East fell by 25 per cent in cash terms between 1989 and early 1994, and by far more in real terms. In addition, the period from mid-1992 to early 1994 saw a sharp rise in share prices which will have increased the relative importance of shares in net personal wealth. Thus, in 1991, the Inland Revenue showed that residential buildings accounted for 48.1 per cent of identified personal wealth.

Table 14.1 *Importance of various assets in personal wealth as percentage of total gross assets, 1990*

UK residential buildings	48.1
Insurance policies	15.3
Cash, including bank and interest bearing accounts	12.1
Stocks and shares	8.5
Loans and mortgages	3.3
UK land and buildings	3.3
Household goods	2.9
Trade assets and partnerships	2.3
Other personalty	2.2
Government securities	1.6
Foreign immovables	0.4
Total	100

Source: Inland Revenue Statistics (1992, table 11.3)

This is the first significant fall for many years, and it is likely that data for 1992 and 1993 will also show smaller falls. Nonetheless, ownership of residential property now accounts for almost half of all net personal wealth in Britain, far above other assets such as stocks and shares (table 14.1). The figures are based on the Inland Revenue's 'series C' marketable wealth and exclude pension rights. Because they are based on estates data, insurance policies figure strongly. This would not be the case if the figures were based on the living population.

Work by Good (1990) suggests that the degree of inequality has risen since 1987, possibly as a result of Thatcherite fiscal and economic policies in the 1980s. Nonetheless, the degree of wealth inequality has fallen since the war, particularly among the top 10 per cent and raises the question of why this has occurred. Atkinson (1983) suggests four possible causes. First, he points to the role of higher tax rates on large estates and the incentive to tax avoidance, particularly gifts *inter vivos*. Second, he identifies the increase in wealth-holding among women, helped by the tendency for married couples to hold wealth jointly. Third, there is the role of changes in the price of different assets which tend to be held by different wealth groups. Atkinson singles out the role of share prices on the grounds that three quarters of personally-held shares are held by the top 5 per cent of wealth-holders. A decline in the price of shares relative to the price of other assets would therefore lead to a fall in the wealth share of the top 5 per cent. The converse is true of a rise in the price of houses, which are owned much more widely, and the final factor identified by Atkinson is that of owner-occupation. As he puts it:

One of the most striking social changes since the beginning of this century has been the increase in owner occupation. Between 1900 and 1970, the proportion of owner occupied dwellings rose from around 10 per cent to 50 per cent. Coupled with the rise in house prices, this must have had a profound effect on the distribution. (1983, p. 171)

Atkinson is correct to point to the importance of rising owner-occupation and rising house prices as significant influences on the distribution of wealth. Conversely, the sharp decline in private landlordism has also reduced the concentration of property ownership. In 1914, 90 per cent of all dwellings were privately rented but by 1991 the figure had fallen to 8 per cent. As Revell (1967) noted:

when one individual owned several houses which he let out as an investment, he had a good chance of appearing in the top 1 per cent, whereas the houses now appear in a number of smaller estates. (p. 381)

14.1.2 The distribution of housing within wealth holdings

Housing wealth is not evenly distributed across wealth bands. It is most important in the middle wealth bands, from £25–200,000 where it accounts for well over 60 per cent of identified net personal wealth, rising to ·almost 70 per cent in the £40–50,000 band in 1990. Even in the £100–300,000 band it still accounted for 46 per cent of net personal wealth (table 14.2; figure 14.1 shows asset composition of *gross* wealth).

Cumulative proportionate distribution curves for each of the major asset types show that housing is the most equally distributed asset in identified personal wealth, ahead of cash and government securities, and far ahead of stocks and shares. This suggests that an increase in the proportion of housing in personal wealth-holdings should be associated with a reduction in the degree of wealth inequality. For many people the house is their only major asset and the major importance of housing within personal wealth merits careful study.

14.2 The distribution of housing wealth: bridging the data gap

One of the most important questions concerning housing wealth is that of its distribution among different groups in the population and, in particular, its links to income. Do high income groups tend to possess more housing wealth or is housing wealth distributed independently of income, and labour market position as Saunders (1984, 1991) has argued? Forrest

Table 14.2 *Residential property as percentage of total net identified personal wealth, year of account basis, 1990 and 1991*

Size band (lower limit of net wealth, £)	1990	1991
0	53.6	28.4
10,000	44.6	46.0
25,000	65.2	63.1
40,000	69.9	70.1
50,000	65.7	60.8
60,000	62.5	63.2
80,000	66.8	59.9
100,000	53.1	48.5
200,000	46.6	42.8
300,000	46.2	34.4
500,000	36.3	27.6
1 million	26.1	20.0
2 million	24.3	28.8
Total	53.7	49.4

Source: Inland Revenue Statistics (1992, 1993)

and Murie (1989) and Hamnett (1991) have argued for the continuing importance of class in housing wealth, although they also recognise the importance of age, length of time in the housing market, timing of purchase and region.

The Inland Revenue statistics on estates passing at death and on personal wealth-holdings provide the best data on overall personal wealth distribution currently available. But not only do the wealth figures have the disadvantage of being derived from a sample of the dying population, with the potential biases that that entails, they also contain no information on the breakdown of wealth-holdings by age, household type, region or income. Conversely, most of the existing data sources on income contain no information on wealth (but see Banks *et al.*, chapter 13 this volume). In order to try to get a detailed picture of the current distribution of housing wealth in Britain and its relationship to incomes we needed a source of survey data which contained both housing wealth and income data.

A partial solution was provided by the British Household Panel Study (BHPS). This is an annual survey of 5500 households in Great Britain organised by the University of Essex and begun in 1991. It contains a major section on housing and housing tenure and, for home-owners,

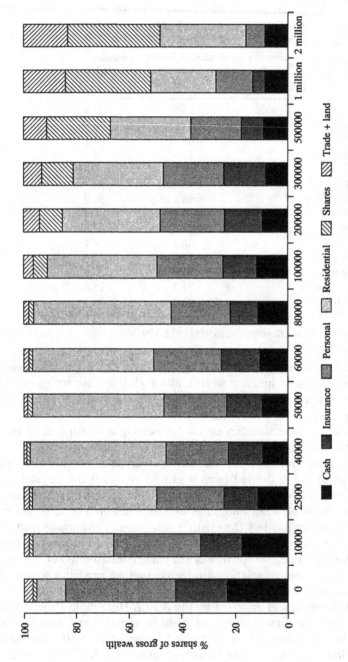

Figure 14.1 Identified personal wealth, asset distribution by wealth bands, 1990
Source: *Inland Revenue Statistics* (1992).

original price paid, mortgage, estimated current value and other information as well as individual and household income. Inevitably, as it is not purpose-designed, it presents some problems but it offered the best available current source of information for our purposes. In the remainder of the chapter we first outline the structure of the home-ownership dataset and the comparability of the BHPS to other datasets. We then discuss the problems of estimating housing wealth using the BHPS, before examining the distribution of housing wealth by income, class, region, age and gender. Buck *et al.* (1994) provide preliminary information from the BHPS.

14.2.1 The structure of the BHPS home ownership dataset

The BHPS first wave has a total sample of 5511 households in Great Britain. It includes 1822 (33.1 per cent) tenants and 3672 (66.6 per cent) owners. Of the owners some 1278 (34.8 per cent) own outright and 2394 (65.2 per cent) are buying with a mortgage. These figures closely match other data sources such as the 1991 Census and the General Household Survey (GHS). 13 per cent of owners had bought as sitting tenants: 10 per cent from councils and New Towns, 3 per cent from other landlords. The response rate for different questions varied slightly: 96 per cent of mortgaged owners gave the amount they paid for the property, as did 91 per cent of the outright owners. Where current estimated value was concerned, 94 per cent of mortgaged owners responded compared to 87 per cent of outright owners. This may reflect greater awareness of current value among mortgaged owners who bought more recently. In the analyses which follow, the distribution of housing wealth is restricted to these particular sub-samples. No attempt has been made to impute wealth to households with missing data but we believe the figures are robust and the response rates are generally quite high.

14.2.2 Comparability of BHPS income data with other datasets

How does the income distribution of the BHPS sample match up against the established official datasets? The income distribution of the BHPS sample closely matches the GHS, but has a somewhat higher proportion of incomes between £5200 and £13,000 and a lower proportion over £26,000. Compared to the FES (figure 14.2), BHPS data over-represent the proportion of low income households and considerably under-represent high income households. The difference is small for mortgaged owners but is particularly marked for outright owners (figure 14.3). The differences may reflect the fact that the GHS and the FES are official surveys and obtain a

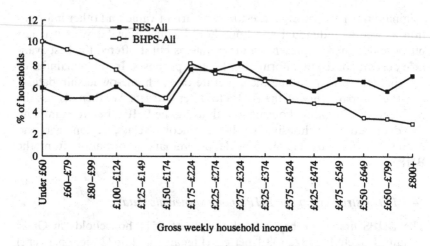

Figure 14.2 Comparative graph, FES and BHPS: household income distribution, 1991

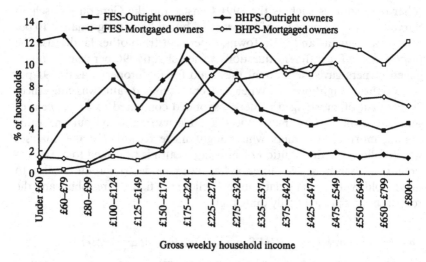

Figure 14.3 Comparative graph, FES and BHPS: outright/mortgaged owners' household income, 1991

higher response rate for higher income groups than the BHPS which may have a bias towards lower income groups. This should be borne in mind where housing wealth and income are examined. No attempt has been made to gross up or reweight to correct for these biases.

Annual household income data were initially only available for 70 per cent of outright owners and 53 per cent of mortgaged owners. Checks showed, however, that the response rate was higher for weekly than annual income, and that the low response rate reflected missing data for some household members. A new household income variable based on the incomes of the head of household and spouse (if applicable) was created, which gave income data for 88 per cent of outright and 80 per cent of mortgaged owners. These non-response rates may under-state the proportion of incomes at the top end of the income distribution.

14.3 Estimates of current house prices

The best definition of net housing wealth is the current market value of all house property owned by the household *less* any outstanding mortgage debt or other loans secured on the home. Unfortunately, sale values or valuations are rarely available, and the BHPS asked respondent owners to estimate the current market value of 'this' home. This has the dual deficiency of relying on home-owners' perceptions of the current market value of their home (which may be prone to over- or under-estimation) and it excludes other property owned either as second homes or for investment. This will result in some under-statement of the amount of housing wealth, particularly for wealthier households who are more likely to own second homes or rented houses.

14.3.1 Estimated and adjusted values

The reliance on *estimated current value* may be somewhat problematic in that some households may not have a clear or accurate idea of the value of their house, and others may have over-estimated the value of their home given the sharp fall in house prices between 1989 and 1991, particularly in southern England where, according to the Halifax and Nationwide Building Societies, average price of homes mortgaged fell by approximately 25 per cent over this period. Thus an alternative method of assessing current house prices was also used. This calculated the *adjusted* purchase price (APP) by inflating the original purchase price to a 1991 price using the BSA/DoE mix-adjusted regional house-price series. This method, which was primarily used as a check on estimated values, has three main deficiencies. First, it does not take improvements, extensions or dilapidations into account. Second, it makes no allowance for changes in the value of different types of property over time. Third, it takes no account of cases where the buyer was a sitting tenant and may have bought the property at a discount. All such cases were eliminated from the analysis. Finally, it takes no account of the small number of households who paid a nominal amount for the property. In such cases the inflation-

Table 14.3 *Comparison of estimated current values and adjusted purchase prices, per cent in range*

£000	Estimated current value	APP
<2	0.1	0.1
2–13	0.7	1.0
14–25	2.1	3.9
26–37	9.0	10.9
38–49	15.7	15.3
50–61	20.4	17.2
62–73	14.1	12.1
74–85	11.5	10.3
86–97	6.1	7.6
98–109	4.0	5.1
110–121	4.0	3.5
122–133	1.9	2.8
134–145	1.3	2.2
146–157	2.3	1.9
158–169	0.8	1.3
>170	6.1	4.9
Valid cases	2822	3371

adjusted value is very low (under £14,000) and they were also excluded from the APP data.

The two sets of value distributions bear a close resemblance to one another (table 14.3), although household estimated values had a higher concentration in the middle bands (£50–73,999) than adjusted prices. Mean estimated value was £79,312 and the mean adjusted purchase price was £80,903. The values for both estimates looked normally distributed with a slight negative skew. Thus, 62 per cent of households live in properties with an *estimated value* of between £38,000 and £86,000 with 6 per cent in properties valued over £170,000. At the other end of the spectrum, 12 per cent live in homes with an *estimated value* of less than £38,000. The equivalent *APP* figures are 55 per cent, 5 per cent, and 16 per cent respectively.

Although the overall distributions are very close, the match between individual household figures is not always as close. Table 14.4 shows estimated price as a percentage of the adjusted purchase price. Although the tails of the distribution are quite small (estimated value was 25 per cent or more below APP in only 7 per cent of cases and higher than APP by over

Table 14.4 *Distribution of household estimated values as percentage of APP estimates, per cent in range*

Estimated as per cent of APP	
0–49	2.0
50–74	5.0
75–99	32.8
100–124	36.2
125–149	13.7
150–199	7.5
200–249	1.7
>250	1.2
Valid cases	2690

50 per cent in 10.5 per cent of cases), the distribution is skewed with 39.7 per cent of estimated valuations below APP and 60.3 per cent above APP.

It must be stressed that these differences do not show that the household estimates are necessarily wrong. What they show are differences between two estimation methods. The average difference (measured as the over-estimation of households' estimates compared to adjusted purchase prices) was £3056 or 7 per cent. However, this percentage varies between mortgaged and outright owners. The difference between the mortgaged owners' estimates and the adjusted figure was 3 per cent, whereas for outright owners it was *minus* 31 per cent. This may be the result of two very different factors. First, that outright owners do in fact considerably under-estimate the value of their property and second, because outright owners have generally owned for longer, the APPs are less accurate. We have no way of determining the validity of these interpretations. It should be noted, however, that there is a strong positive relationship between the scale of 'under-estimation' by outright owners and purchase date. The longer they had owned, the greater the degree of under-estimation compared to APP. In the case of mortgaged owners the pattern was less distinct, although there is a consistent over-estimation for those who bought post-1976.

As a consequence of these differences, the degree of over- and under-estimation varies by household income and amount of equity. The estimated values for households with low incomes were well below those produced by the APP method. Where housing equity is concerned, the degree of 'under-estimation' was strongly negative for those with estimated equity of under £2000. At the other end of the spectrum, the degree of 'over-estimation' varied from 12 per cent to 18 per cent for those with equity of between £122–169,999.

The difference in estimated house prices between the two methods has considerable implications for the assessment of housing equity, particularly where outright owners on low incomes are concerned. It may be that their housing equity is larger than their own estimates suggest. So too it may be that the smaller degree of 'over-estimation' by mortgagors has the effect of reducing the proportion with negative equity. Thus, in the subsequent analyses we have used both the household valuation and the APP method as a basis for calculation, and we have also made analyses which deflate mortgagors' equity by 3 per cent across the board to assess the impact on the distribution of negative equity.

As we are concerned with current housing wealth and not with capital gains, we have not examined the absolute size, or the rate of gains based on price paid for the property, although this is a subject of some interest. Analysis is restricted to net housing wealth after the subtraction of any outstanding mortgage debt. Unfortunately, as section 14.3.2 outlines, the problems associated with estimation of outstanding mortgage debt using the BHPS data were not inconsiderable.

14.3.2 Problems with the BHPS data in estimating housing wealth

The estimate of current housing wealth is quite simple in the case of outright owners, who have no mortgage debt on their property. We simply take the current estimated sale value or the original purchase price inflated by the DoE/BSA house-price index as a measure of housing wealth. Tenants are assumed to have no housing wealth and they are excluded from the analysis. Some respondents may rent the home where they were interviewed and own another, but the probability of this occurring is extremely small.

In the case of mortgaged owners the situation is more difficult. Ideally, all outstanding mortgage debt would be subtracted from current estimated value or APP to give a measure of housing equity. But the BHPS did not ask a question on outstanding mortgage debt and we had to estimate it. Where repayment mortgages were concerned, we used data on the year the household started paying the mortgage on the current property and the number of years it had left to run to calculate the original term. No information was given on interest rates or on whether the rate was fixed or variable and it was necessary to make various assumptions regarding annual UK mortgage rates. We were then able to calculate repayments to date and thus the proportion of the mortgage paid off using a formula supplied by the Halifax Building Society (further details available from the authors on request).

The second major problem concerns additional mortgages, which 34 per cent of mortgagors had taken out. The BHPS asked if the household had taken out additional mortgages or loans on the home, and the total size, but they did not ask when they were taken out, the duration or the number of years left to run. There are various ways of estimating the size of additional mortgage outstanding. The first is to assume that the additional mortgages (there may be more than one of them) were taken out on initial purchase. The second is to assume that they were all taken out immediately prior to the BHPS survey in 1991. Both assumptions are unlikely but set the boundary limits. The method used here was to assume that additional mortgages were taken out mid-way between the date of purchase and the time of survey.

The third major problem concerns endowment mortgages, where the capital outstanding is only repaid at the end of the mortgage using the income from the endowment policy. This might not matter if the number of endowment mortgages was small. But, given the rapid growth of endowment mortgages in the 1980s, no fewer than 67 per cent of respondents said they had an endowment mortgage compared to 28 per cent with repayment mortgages. This presents us with considerable problems in estimating housing wealth as endowment mortgages have a limited surrender value in the first few years and only acquire a substantial value as they near maturity. There were two main options open to us. The first was to try to estimate the current surrender values of endowments. This was fraught with difficulties, not the least of which was that insurance companies were unwilling to provide us with a formula for calculating surrender values. Second, there is a problem of separating the 'with-profits' elements of endowments from the mortgage repayment element. As this is paid for by a higher level of premium than is necessary to repay the mortgage on the property, this seemed to us to be wealth which is not directly housing-related.

The second option was to treat endowment mortgages as repayment mortgages. This may seem rather drastic, and it may over-state the amount of mortgage assumed to have been paid off, but it appeared to be the most sensible course of action. There is some estimation error in all cases, but the estimates are considered robust although there may be some under-estimation of the size of mortgage outstanding where a mortgage is redeemed within the first few years.

Table 14.5 *Distribution of all home-owners' equity, per cent in range*

Range of equity (£000)	Owners' estimated value-based	APP-based	'Corrected' estimates
<0	1.5	1.8	2.4
0–2	1.3	2.7	1.5
2–13	8.3	10.6	8.1
14–25	11.3	12.8	12.0
26–37	14.4	13.0	14.2
38–49	13.7	11.6	14.2
50–61	14.6	12.5	14.0
62–73	9.0	8.3	8.6
74–85	7.5	6.6	7.7
86–97	4.3	5.6	3.8
98–109	3.0	3.7	2.8
110–121	2.3	1.9	2.4
122–133	1.4	1.9	1.1
134–145	0.9	1.3	1.1
146–157	1.8	1.1	1.6
158–169	0.5	0.8	0.4
>170	4.1	3.7	4.0
Valid cases	3,121	2,650	3,121

14.4 The distribution of housing wealth among all home-owners

The distribution of housing wealth among home-owners in 1991 is shown in table 14.5 and figure 14.4. Mean estimated housing wealth was £60,900 but there is a broadly spread negatively skewed distribution, with 11 per cent of owners having under £14,000, 26 per cent having £14–38,000, 28 per cent having £38–61,000 and 17 per cent having £62–85,000. There is then a long tail with the remaining 18 per cent widely spread, 11 per cent having over £110,000 and 4 per cent over £170,000. Tenants are assumed to have no housing wealth. If they are included, the mean household housing wealth in Britain across all tenures in 1991 was £40,200. This figure closely approximates the estimate made by Banks *et al.* (chapter 13 in this volume).

Not all owners had positive housing wealth, of course. Estimated values suggested that 2.3 per cent of mortgagors (1.5 per cent of all owners) had negative equity, with a mean of £8000 and a median of £4500. This gives a grossed up national total of 253,000 mortgagors with negative equity – well below other estimates which suggest a figure of between 1 and 1.4

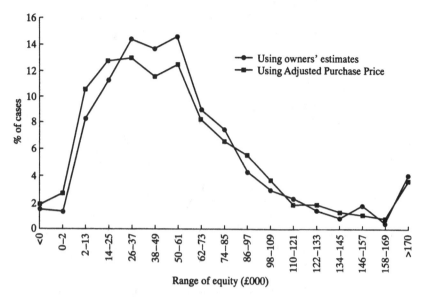

Figure 14.4 Distribution of owners' equity, BHPS and DoE (all owners), 1991

million owners in 1991 (Bank of England, 1992; Wrigglesworth, 1992; Gentle *et al.*, 1994).

This may indicate either that many mortgagors are over-estimating the value of their homes, thus leading to an under-estimation of negative equity, or that assumptions regarding endowment mortgages are over-generous, or that all the other estimates are wide of the mark, which seems unlikely. The APP figure gives a total of 1.8 per cent of owners with negative equity, little more than the BHPS estimate, but it has been argued (Hamnett, 1993) that the DoE/BSA's mix-adjusted index under-estimates price falls since 1989 relative to building society figures. As most estimates of the number of mortgagors with negative equity are based on building society figures this would explain a significant part of the difference between our figures and other national estimates.

One solution to the problem of household over-estimation by mortgagors relative to the APP figures is to deflate their estimated equity by 3 per cent to bring it into line with the adjusted estimates. This is done in table 14.5 and gives a figure of 2.4 per cent of owners with 'corrected' negative equity: a grossed up national total of 370,000.

Not surprisingly, given the spatial and temporal character of the slump, 59 per cent of those with corrected negative equity were found in London and the South East, 89 per cent had bought since 1988 and 57 per cent

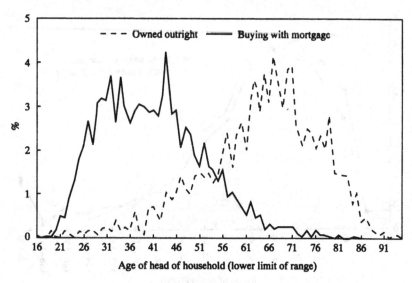

Figure 14.5 Age distribution of head of household: outright and mortgaged owners

were aged 20–29. Negative equity seems to be concentrated among recent, young, southern buyers.

14.5 Outright and mortgaged owners: a comparative analysis

The discussion of housing wealth outlined above embraced both outright and mortgaged owners. But these two groups are very different in a number of major respects, and they have very different patterns of housing wealth-holdings.

Outright owners are, on average, considerably older than those buying on a mortgage. The mean age of the head of household for outright owners was 64.4 years compared to 40.9 years for mortgaged owners. The age distribution of the two groups is shown in figure 14.5.

Outright owners also own property which they estimated as worth marginally more (£82,200) than did mortgaged owners (£77,900). The mean value for all owners was £79,300. These figures were cross-checked using the APP and the difference was more marked – £92,570 for outright owners compared to £75,800 for mortgaged owners.

Table 14.6 shows the distribution of current estimated value for outright and mortgaged owners. It should be noted that a small proportion of outright (4.7 per cent) and mortgaged owners (2 per cent) own property which they estimate as being worth under £25,000. It is difficult to determine the

Table 14.6 *Housing equity of outright and mortgaged owners, per cent in*
range

| Range of equity (£000) | Estimated equity | | APP-based equity all owners |
	outright owners	mortgaged owners	
<0	0	2.3	1.8
0–2	0.2	1.9	2.7
2–13	1.3	12.3	10.6
14–25	3.2	15.8	12.8
26–37	7.8	18.1	13.0
38–49	13.3	14.0	11.6
50–61	20.7	11.3	12.5
62–73	13.6	6.4	8.3
74–85	12.2	4.9	6.6
86–97	6.0	3.3	5.6
98–109	4.9	2.0	3.7
110–121	3.6	1.5	1.9
122–133	1.3	1.4	1.9
134–145	1.0	0.9	1.3
146–157	3.1	1.0	1.1
158–169	0.5	0.5	0.8
>170	7.3	2.3	3.7

nature of these owners and their properties. There are few shared owners
in the sample and they are not concentrated in the under £25,000 price
range. These low value owners may be living in terraced houses or small
flats in northern Britain.

The income distributions of the two groups are completely different,
however, largely a result of the different age distribution and the fact that
many outright owners have retired. The mean household income of outright owners was £10,485 compared to £22,000 for mortgaged owners.

The graph of annual household income by ownership status (figure
14.6) shows that two thirds of outright owners had annual household
incomes of under £11,000 compared to 14.7 per cent of mortgaged
owners. Conversely, 62.3 per cent of mortgaged owners had incomes of
over £17,000 compared to 17 per cent of all outright owners. This discrepancy continues up the income scale. Some 45.4 per cent of mortgaged
owners had incomes of over £21,000 compared to just 10.1 per cent of
outright owners. This difference reflects age and economic activity status.

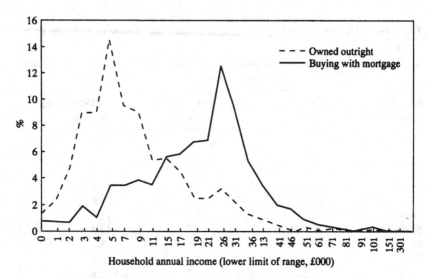

Household annual income (lower limit of range, £000)

Figure 14.6 Income distribution of outright and mortgaged owners

14.6 The net housing wealth of outright and mortgaged owners

The difference in the age and mortgage debt of outright and mortgaged owners is reflected in sharp differences in estimated equity between the two groups. Whereas outright owners have a mean estimated equity of £82,000, mortgaged owners have a mean estimated equity of £49,000. The difference of £33,000 largely reflects outstanding mortgage debt. The mean outstanding mortgage of mortgaged owners is £27,368. The equivalent APP equity estimates are £92,437 for outright and £44,576 for mortgaged owners.

The distribution of housing equity over the two groups is shown in figure 14.7. Where outright owners are concerned, the modal category (20.7 per cent) was £50–62,000, with a further 26.9 per cent between £28,000 and £74,000. Just over two thirds (67.6 per cent) of all outright owners had housing wealth between £26,000 and £86,000. Of the remainder, 28 per cent had housing wealth of over £86,000, and 7 per cent had housing wealth of over £170,000. At the other extreme, there is a tiny proportion (4.7 per cent) of outright owners with equity of under £26,000 and 1.4 per cent with equity of under £14,000. The distribution for mortgagors was very different with the modal category of £26–37,000 (18 per cent) and 46 per cent having equity between £2,000–37,000 and 71 per cent with between £2,000 and £61,000. Only 25 per cent had equity over £62,000 and

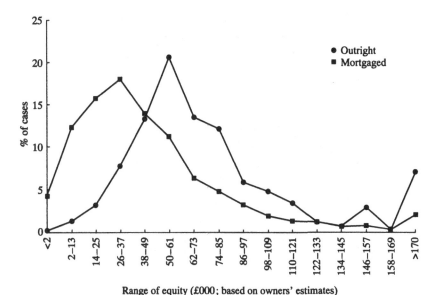

Figure 14.7 Housing equity of outright and mortgaged owners

only 6 per cent had equity of over £122,000 compared to 15 per cent of outright owners (table 14.6).

14.7 Variations in mean home-owners' equity

The distribution of home-owners' equity differs across a number of important variables. Not surprisingly, there is a strong positive relationship between current estimated house price and equity. In the case of outright owners the two are identical. Given the regional variations in house prices there is a marked *regional* difference with average estimated equity in London, the rest of the South East (ROSE) and the South West of £75,000, falling to £57,000 in the East and West Midlands, £49,000 in Yorkshire and a low of £33,000 in Scotland. Mean APP equity ranged from £87,600 in East Anglia and £78,000 in London to £56,000 in the Midlands and £28,900 in Scotland (table 14.7). Table 14.7 also shows the variation in APP mean equity by region for outright and mortgaged owners. These range from £107,000 for outright owners in London and £121,000 in ROSE to £59,000 in Scotland. For mortgaged owners the range was from £66,000 in London to £20,700 in Scotland. The differences between the two are sometimes considerable but the regional ranking is broadly stable. Mean equity in London and the rest of the South East is

Table 14.7 *Variation in mean equity, by region, £*

| | Owners' estimated value-based | | | APP-based | | |
	All owners	Outright	Mortgaged	All owners	Outright	Mortgaged
London	75,400	102,200	61,700	78,300	107,100	66,600
ROSE	76,700	102,400	64,400	79,000	121,100	61,100
South West	75,200	106,200	50,300	67,200	97,700	46,200
East Anglia	69,900	91,900	52,600	87,600	139,900	51,900
East Midlands	56,900	69,200	49,600	55,300	75,000	44,400
West Midlands	56,800	80,800	45,100	56,400	94,300	38,800
North West	54,400	65,200	48,300	47,100	66,200	38,000
Yorks and Humb	49,200	59,500	42,800	49,000	74,800	35,300
North	44,200	63,500	34,700	35,200	57,300	26,400
Wales	51,500	72,400	34,100	49,500	83,200	28,800
Scotland	33,400	50,900	27,200	28,900	58,900	20,700
All regions	61,000	82,200	49,100	60,300	92,600	44,900

Table 14.8 *Mean equity, by grouped SEG, £*

| | Owners' estimated value-based | | | APP-based |
	All	Outright owners	Mortgagors	All
Professional	71,200	122,200	63,400	66,500
Managerial	72,500	134,800	63,900	67,700
Other non-manual	50,800	86,500	43,300	46,100
Skilled manual	47,400	80,200	39,800	42,700
Partly skilled	42,400	64,200	34,700	32,300
Unskilled	46,700	63,900	40,100	44,600
Other	51,400	******	******	50,100
All SEGs	55,800	90,600	48,600	51,500

two to three times that in Scotland and about 50 per cent higher than in the Midlands and the North.

There was also a sharp variation in mean estimated equity by *grouped socio-economic group* (SEG) of head of household, ranging from £72,000 for professionals and managers to £50,000 for other non-manual workers, £47,000 for skilled manual and unskilled and £42,000 for partly skilled (table 14.8). These variations parallel the differences in estimated current value of property by SEG. These varied from the £103,000 for professionals and managers to £75,000 for other non-manual and £58,000 for the partly skilled. The mean APP-based equity was consistently below estimated value-based equity, largely because of the lower estimate of outright owners' equity, but the SEG differentials were similar. Professionals and managers had about 80 per cent more home equity than unskilled workers on average.

Not surprisingly, there was also considerable variation according to the *age of the head of household*, with mean estimated equity rising from £17,000 for 20–29 year olds to £41,000 for 30–39 year olds and £67,000 for 40–49 year olds to a peak of £80,000 for 50–59 year olds. This figure remains roughly constant up to age 79, falling slightly to £66,000 for those aged 80 or over. Mean APP-based equity is slightly lower for the younger age groups but considerably higher for the 60 year olds and above as this method produces higher estimates for outright owners and lower estimates for mortgaged owners (table 14.9). For mortgagors, estimated equity rises with age from an average of £16,000 for 20–29 year olds to £77,000 for 50–59 year olds, then dips to £56,000 for the 60–69 age group before peaking at £83,700 for 70–79 year olds. The variations reflect the predict-

Table 14.9 *Mean equity, by age of head of household, £*

| | Owners' estimated value-based | | | APP-based |
	All	Outright owners	Mortgagors	All
20–29 years	16,900	50,600	15,900	14,300
30–39 years	41,200	84,200	39,400	37,200
40–49 years	66,600	89,900	62,500	60,100
50–59 years	80,400	85,200	77,100	83,000
60–69 years	79,800	84,400	55,900	90,900
70–79 years	78,500	78,200	83,700	97,600
80 years +	66,200	66,600	******	82,000

able rise in equity with age as the mortgage is paid off and owners move to more expensive property. For outright owners the pattern is rather different. Equity rises from £51,000 for 20–29 year olds to £84,000 for 30–39 year olds and remains at over £80,000 until age 60–69. The age differentials in equity are the most strongly marked of all variations and exceed those of region, socio-economic group or income.

The distribution of mean equity by the *year respondents bought their current home* is much less clear-cut, with no clear pattern in estimated or in APP equity for outright owners. The reason is that the BHPS only asked for year of purchase of the current home, not the previous home. The mean for any period includes both first time buyers and those who have owned several homes. For mortgaged owners, the proportion of first time buyers steadily increases with date of purchase, reducing mean equity (table 14.10).

The distribution of equity by *annual household income* is less clear-cut than the distribution by region, class or age. Mean equity based on estimated values varies from £68,000 for all owners with incomes under £3000, falling slowly to a low of £48,000 for those with incomes of £15–20,000 and rising to a peak of £76,300 for those with incomes of over £30,000. The reason for this U-shaped distribution is that the figures include both retired home-owners on lower incomes and mortgaged owners with higher incomes. When the two categories of owner are disaggregated, the variations in equity become clearer (table 14.11). Although the mean estimated equity of outright owners rises with household income, from a low of £65,000 in the £3000–6999 income band to a high of £125,000 in the over £30,000 income band, the mean estimated equity of mortgaged owners has a U-shaped distribution, falling to a low of £33,000

Table 14.10 *Mean equity, by year of purchase, by owner type, £*

Year of purchase	Owners' estimated value-based		APP-based	
	Outright owners	Mortgagors	Outright owners	Mortgagors
Pre 1950	70,000	******	112,600	*****
1950–59	66,100	******	83,900	*****
1960–64	76,200	68,900	85,800	103,500
1965–69	92,700	65,500	96,800	75,000
1970–71	83,000	80,300	117,700	65,900
1972–73	76,000	65,100	91,300	84,100
1974–75	104,400	65,800	101,700	67,200
1976–77	109,700	95,200	70,500	67,300
1978–79	73,500	73,700	90,600	67,000
1980–81	72,200	61,800	94,300	58,000
1982–83	85,500	62,500	90,800	53,700
1984–85	88,100	56,400	127,800	51,700
1986–87	97,200	47,800	85,200	44,700
1988–89	77,700	33,700	76,700	28,400
1990–91	76,600	24,400	75,900	22,700

Table 14.11 *Mean equity, by gross household income, £: outright and mortgaged owners*

Household income band (lower limit, £000)	Owners' estimated value-based			APP-based	
	All	outright owners	mortgagors	outright owners	mortgagors
0	68,000	79,000	43,300	85,900	44,700
3	62,900	65,000	55,300	76,200	38,400
5	59,900	65,600	45,000	104,000	46,000
7	62,300	74,900	41,900	76,700	40,400
11	53,700	85,200	32,800	83,100	30,600
15	47,500	88,800	36,100	98,300	33,300
21	50,400	111,900	42,600	92,300	38,500
25	51,200	94,200	45,300	106,000	41,300
30	76,300	125,200	69,900	123,000	62,300
All	58,300	58,300	46,100	89,100	42,500

Table 14.12 *Mean equity, by household type, £*

Household type	Estimated value-based equity	(cases)	APP-based
Single non-elderly	41,200	(282)	37,600
Single elderly	66,700	(300)	92,900
Couple: no children	64,100	(1020)	62,900
Couple: dependent children	57,800	(951)	51,300
Couple: non-dependent children	74,000	(297)	81,200
Lone parent: dependent children	53,100	(102)	49,000
Lone parent: non-dependent children	67,300	(94)	75,400
2+ unrelated adults	65,100	(34)	34,500
Other households	56,100	(41)	51,600
All households	61,000	(3121)	60,300

in the £11–14,999 income band and rising to £70,000 in the over £30,000 band. This pattern is also found in the APP-based equity figures and reflects the lower incomes of some retired mortgaged owners. There is therefore no clear-cut relationship between high incomes and high equity, although higher income groups are likely to have accumulated higher equity as they age.

There is also a considerable variation in mean equity by *household type*. As table 14.12 shows, this varies from a low of £41,000 for single non-elderly households to a high of £74,000 for couples with non-dependent children. The other low equity household type are lone parents with dependent children (£53,000) and couples with dependent children (£58,000). The groups with the highest equity are couples with no children (£64,000), single elderly (£70,000) and lone parent with no dependent children (£67,000).

These differences partly reflect the age of household heads. The mean age of household heads was 50 years, but for couples with non-dependent children it was 54 and for couples with no children 53. Lone parents with dependent children averaged 35 years and unrelated adults 36 years. Rather surprisingly, there were no differences in housing equity by the *gender of the head of household*. Male heads accounted for 78.5 per cent of heads and females for 21.5 per cent, but mean equity was identical at £60,500 for men and £60,800 for women despite the very sharp differences in household income (£18,300 for male headed households and £8000 for female headed households). It is, however, worth noting that the proportion of male and female headed households in the BHPS sample as a whole was 70/30. Female heads are thus under-represented in home-ownership compared to all tenures, which has implications for the distribution of housing wealth. It might be thought because of the much lower income of female headed households that they would be more likely to be mortgaged owners until quite late in their lives, but a comparison of the age and mortgage status of male and female heads revealed no major differences apart from an over-representation of female mortgagors in the 70–79 age group (4.6 per cent of female mortgagors and 0.8 per cent of males) and the predictable over-representation of female outright owners in the over 70 age groups (the males having died early).

14.8 Market and non-market buyers

One of the most important changes in the home ownership market in the last 15 years has been the rapid growth in the number of ex-council tenants who have bought their own home. There are now over 1.5 million such owners and in the BHPS sample, 10 per cent of home owners had bought from a council or New Town. In addition, 3.2 per cent had bought from other landlords. These two groups constitute a distinctive sub-sample and merit analysis, particularly given the debate as to whether council tenant buyers have done as well as other owners or whether many of them have bought an asset which will not appreciate much in value.

There is a marked difference between Right to Buy (RTB) tenant buyers and those who bought from other landlords. RTB buyers are far more likely to have bought more recently and to be mortgagors than those who bought from private landlords. In addition, RTB buyers generally bought at a considerable discount to market value, often 50 per cent or more. Finally, RTB buyers are likely to have purchased cheaper property than open market buyers.

The mean year of purchase of the current property for all buyers was 1980. This compares to 1984 for those buying from a local authority or council, 1986 for those buying from a New Town or development agency and 1970 for those buying from private landlords. The mean purchase price of the current property was £37,000 for non-sitting tenant buyers, but for council tenant buyers it was £16,400 and for those buying from other landlords £11,600. Current estimated value was £57,000 for sitting tenant buyers but £79,000 for non-sitting tenant buyers.

These differences in the date of purchase and purchase price result in major differentials in housing equity for different types of owner. The mean equity of non-sitting tenant outright owners was £85,200, but the mean for local authority buyers was £45,200 and the mean for buyers from private landlords was £79,300. For mortgaged owners, mean equity for

Table 14.13 *Mean equity, by market/non-market buyers, £: estimated value-based*

	Mortgagors	Outright owners
Local authority sitting tenant	41,000	45,200
Private landlord sitting tenant	35,300	79,300
Non-sitting tenant	50,600	85,200

non-sitting tenant purchasers was £50,600 compared to £41,000 for council tenant buyers and £35,300 for those who had bought from private landlords.

The mean equity for both outright and mortgaged ex-council tenant buyers is substantially lower than that of market purchasers and suggests that the high discounts have not outweighed the lower original property value (table 14.13).

14.9 Conclusions

We have attempted to calculate the value and distribution of housing wealth in Britain using data from the BHPS. We examined the comparability of BHPS data on housing tenure and income with data from the GHS and FES and we outlined the problems of producing estimates of housing equity. We used two methods, the estimated and the adjusted purchase price (APP) method, and compared the equity distributions they produced. Although there is considerable comparability in the aggregate distributions, there are marked variations at the individual level, especially where outright owners are concerned. There is, however, considerable stability in the mean equity rankings produced using both methods across a range of variables. For example, professionals and managers both have higher mean equity than other non-manual groups on both sets of rankings.

We have seen that the distribution of housing equity varies considerably according to a wide range of factors including social class, age, household type, region, etc. Crucially, it also varies according to whether the owner is outright or mortgaged. There is no simple determinant of housing equity. It is the outcome of a complex set of interactions, the most important of which are the date when buyers first entered the housing market (best proxied by age of the head of household), the initial price of the property, its region and whether the property is owned outright or mortgaged. Grouped SEG also captures a significant level of variation. In general, more expensive properties in the South East, bought some years ago, will yield the highest equity. Rather paradoxically, the lowest levels of equity are linked to recent buyers in London and the South East.

The relationship between equity and income is complex and reflects variations in initial house price, region, year purchased, age and mortgage status. Mean equity is higher for outright owners than mortgaged owners at all income levels, though equity does generally rise with income. The equity of mortgaged owners is higher in the lower and highest income brackets than it is in the middle brackets (£11–21,000), reflecting a combination of both the lower income of some retired mortgagors and the more expensive property owned by mortgagors with incomes of over £25,000. There is no simple and direct relationship between income and housing equity.

Note

We would like to thank the ESRC Centre on Micro-Social Change at the University of Essex for making the first wave British Household Panel Study data available to us.

Bibliography

Acs, Z., Audretsch, D. and Evans, D. 1992. *The Determinants of Variations in Self-employment Rates Across Countries and Over Time*, Wissenschaftszentrum Berlin, *WZB Discussion Paper* FSIV 92–3. Berlin: Wissenschaftszentrum Berlin für Sozialforschung

Akerlof, G. A. and Yellen, J. L. (eds.) 1986. *Efficiency Wage Models of the Labor Market*. Cambridge: Cambridge University Press

Alcock, P. 1987. *Poverty and State Support*. London: Longman

Allen, R. G. D. 1958. 'Movements in retail prices since 1953', *Economica* 25: 14–25

Ashworth, J. and Ulph, D. 1981. 'Household models', in Brown, C. (ed.), *Taxation and Labour Supply*. London: George Allen & Unwin

Atkins, D., Charlton, M., Dorling, D. and Wymer, C. 1993. 'Connecting the 1981 and 1991 Censuses', NE.RRL, *Research Report* 93/9. Newcastle upon Tyne: University of Newcastle upon Tyne

Atkinson, A. B. 1983. *The Economics of Inequality*, 2nd edn. Oxford: Clarendon Press

1990. 'Income maintenance for the unemployed in Britain and the response to high unemployment', *Ethics* 100: 569–85

1993a. 'What is happening to the distribution of income in the UK?', *Proceedings of the British Academy* 82: 317–51

1993b. 'Have social security benefits seriously damaged work incentives in Britain?', in Atkinson, A. B. and Mogensen, G. (eds.), *Welfare and Work Incentives*. Oxford: Clarendon Press

Atkinson, A. B. and Harrison, A. J. 1978. *The Distribution of Personal Wealth in Britain*. Cambridge: Cambridge University Press

Atkinson, A. B. and Micklewright, J. 1989. 'Turning the screw: Benefits for the unemployed 1979–1988', in Dilnot, A. and Walker, I. (eds.), *The Economics of Social Security*. Oxford: Oxford University Press

1992. *Economic Transformation in Eastern Europe and the Distribution of Income*. Cambridge: Cambridge University Press

Atkinson, A. B., Gordon, J. P. and Harrison, A. 1989. 'Trends in the shares of top wealth holders in Britain, 1923–1981', *Oxford Bulletin of Economics and Statistics* 51(3): 315–32

Atkinson, A. B., Rainwater, L. and Smeeding, T. 1995. *Income Distribution in*

OECD Countries: The evidence from the Luxembourg Income Study (LIS). Paris: Organisation for Economic Co-operation and Development

Baker, P. 1993. 'Taxpayer compliance of the self-employed: estimates from household spending data', IFS, *Working Paper* no. W93/14. London: Institute of Fiscal Studies

Baker, P. and Crawford, I. 1993. 'The distributional aspects of environmental taxation', *Scottish Economic Bulletin* 46: 35–44

Bank of England 1992. 'Negative equity in the housing market', *Bank of England Quarterly Review* (August): 266–8

1993. 'Inflation report', *Quarterly Bulletin* 33(1): 3–45

Banks, J. and Blundell, R. 1994a. 'Taxation and personal savings incentives in the UK', in Poterba, J. (ed.), *Public Policies and Household Saving*. Chicago: University of Chicago Press

1994b. 'Household saving behaviour in the UK', forthcoming in Poterba, J. (ed.), *International Comparisons of Household Saving*. Chicago: University of Chicago Press

Banks, J., Blundell, R. and Dilnot, A. 1994. 'Tax-based savings incentives in the UK', NBER/OECD Conference on International Comparisons of Household Saving. Paris: OECD, June

Banks, J., Blundell, R. and Lewbel, A. 1994. 'Quadratic Engel curves, indirect tax reform and welfare measurement', University College, *Discussion Paper* no. 94–04. London: University College

Banks, J., Dilnot, A. and Low, H. 1994. *The Distribution of Wealth in the UK, IFS Commentary* no. 45. London: Institute for Fiscal Studies

Barr, N. and Coulter, F. A. E. 1991. 'Social security: solution or problem?', in Hills, J. (ed.), *The State of Welfare*. Oxford: Oxford University Press

Bean, C. R. and Pissarides, C. A. 1991. 'Skill shortages and structural unemployment in Britain: a (mis)matching approach', in Padoa Schioppa, F. (ed.), *Mismatch and Labour Mobility*. Cambridge: Cambridge University Press

Becker, G. 1975. *Human Capital*. New York: Basic Books

Berman, E., Bound, J. and Griliches, Z. 1994. 'Changes in the relative demand for skilled labour within US manufacturing industries: Evidence from the Annual Survey of Manufacturing', *Quarterly Journal of Economics* 109: 367–98

Blanchard, O. 1993. 'Movements in the equity premium', *Brookings Papers on Economic Activity* 2: 75–118

Blundell, R., Pashardes, P. and Weber, G. 1994. 'What do we learn about consumer demand patterns from micro-data?', *American Economic Review* 83: 570–83

Bone, M., Gregory, J., Gill, B. and Lader, D. 1992. *Retirement and Retirement Plans*. London: HMSO

Boroah, V. K., McGregor, P. P. L. and McKee, P. M. 1991. *Regional Income Inequality and Poverty in the United Kingdom*. Aldershot: Dartmouth

Boroah, V. K., McGregor, P. P. L., McKee, P. M. and Collins, G. 1994. *Cost-of-living Differences Between the Regions of the United Kingdom*, University of

Ulster, *Papers in Public Policy and Management* no. 34. Newtownabbey: University of Ulster

Boskin, M. and Nold, F. 1975. 'A Markov model of turnover in aid to families with dependent children', *Journal of Human Resources* (Fall): 467–87

Boston, J. 1993. 'Reshaping social policy in New Zealand', *Fiscal Studies* 14: 64–85

Bound, J. and Johnson, G. 1992. 'Changes in the structure of wages in the 1980s: An evaluation of alternative explanations', *American Economic Review* 82: 371–92

Bradshaw, J. and Godfrey, C. 1983. 'Inflation and the poor', *New Society* 65: 247–8

Bradshaw, J. and Millar, J. 1991. *Lone Parent Families in the UK*. London: HMSO

Brandolini, A. 1992. *Nonlinear Dynamics, Entitlement Rules, and the Cyclical Behaviour of the Personal Income Distribution*, Centre for Economic Performance, *Discussion Paper* no. 84. London: London School of Economics

Brandolini, A. and Sestito, P. 1993. 'La distribuzione dei redditi familiari in Italia, 1977–1991', *Servizio Studi*. Rome: Banca d'Italia

Brittain, J. A. 1960. 'Some neglected features of Britain's income levelling', *American Economic Review*, Papers and Proceedings 50: 335–44

Brown, J., 1992. *A Policy Vacuum: Social security for the self-employed*. York: Joseph Rowntree Foundation

Buck, N. 1992. 'Labour market inactivity and polarisation: a household perspective on the idea of an underclass', in Smith, D. J. (ed.), *Understanding the Underclass*. London: Policy Studies Institute

Buck, N., Gershuny, J., Rose, D. and Scott, J. 1994. *Changing Households*, ESRC Research Centre for Micro-Social Change. Colchester: University of Essex

Burrows, R. 1991. 'Who are the contemporary British *petit bourgeoisie*?', *International Small Business Journal* 9(2): 12–25

Bushinsky, M. 1994. 'Changes in the US Wage structure 1963 to 1987: An application of quantile regressions', *Econometrica* 62(2): 405–58

Callan, T. and Nolan, B. 1993. *Income Inequality and Poverty in Ireland in the 1970s and 1980s*, ESRI, *Working Paper* no. 43. Dublin: ESRI

Canceill, G. and Villeneuve, A. 1990. 'Les inégalités de revenus: quasi statu quo entre 1979 et 1984 pour les salariés et les inactifs', *Economie et Statistique* 230: 65–74

Cancian, M., Danziger, S. and Gottschalk, P. 1993a. 'Working wives and family income inequality among married couples', in Danziger, S. and Gottschalk, P. (eds.), *Uneven Tides: Rising Inequality in America*. New York: Russell Sage Foundation

1993b. 'The changing contributions of men and women to the level and distribution of family income, 1968–88', in Papadimitriou, D. and Wolff, E. (eds.), *Poverty and Prosperity in the USA in the Late Twentieth Century*. New York: St Martin's Press

Cannan, E. 1905. 'The division of income', *Quarterly Journal of Economics* 19: 341–69

Cantillon, B., Marx, I., Proost, D. and Van Dam, R. 1994. *Indicateurs sociaux: 1985–1992*, Centrum voor Sociaal Beleid. Antwerp: University of Antwerp

Capital Taxes Group 1994. *Setting Savings Free*. London: Institute for Fiscal Studies

Card, D. 1989. *Deregulation and Labor Earnings in the Airline Industry*, Princeton University Industrial Relations Section, *Working Paper* no. 247. Princeton: Princeton University

1991. 'The effect of unions on the distribution of wages: Redistribution or relabelling?', Princeton University Industrial Relations Section, *Discussion Paper* 287

Central Statistical Office [CSO] 1987. 'The distribution of income in the United Kingdom 1984/85', *Economic Trends* 409: 94–104

1991. *Retail Prices 1914–1990*. London: HMSO

1993. *National Income and Expenditure 1993*. London: HMSO

1994. 'The effects of taxes and benefits on household income, 1993', *Economic Trends* 491: 35–73

Champion, A. G. and Green, A. E. 1988. *Local Prosperity and the North–South Divide: Winners and losers in 1980s Britain*. Gosforth and Kenilworth: Booming Towns

1990. *The Spread of Prosperity and the North–South Divide: Local economic performance in Britain during the late eighties*. Gosforth and Kenilworth: Booming Towns

Chennells, L. and Van Reenen, J. 1994. 'The rising price of skill: Investigating British skill premia in the 1980s using complementary data sets'. London: Institute for Fiscal Studies, mimeo

Christensen, A. G., Jorgenson, D. W. and Lau, L. J. 1975. 'Transcendental logarithmic utility functions', *American Economic Review* 65: 367–83

Clark, A. and Oswald, A. 1994. 'Unhappiness and unemployment', *Economic Journal* 104 (May): 648–59

Clegg, H. 1979. *The Changing System of Industrial Relations in Britain*. Oxford: Basil Blackwell

Cornish, J. W. P. and Waterson, M. J. 1992. 'The UK Retail Prices Index: A suitable case for treatment', *NTC Research, Economic Research Paper* no 1 (February)

Coulter, F. A. E., Cowell, F. A. and Jenkins, S. P. 1994. 'Family fortunes in the 1980s', in Blundell, R., Preston, I. and Walker, I. (eds.), *The Distribution of Household Welfare*. Cambridge: Cambridge University Press

Council of Economic Advisers 1994. *Economic Report of the President 1994*. Washington, DC: US Government Printing Office

Council of Mortgage Lenders [CML] 1994. *Housing Finance* no. 22 (May)

Cowell, F., 1995. *Measuring Inequality*, 2nd ed. Hemel Hempstead: Harvester Wheatsheaf

Craig, J. 1985. *A 1981 Socio Economic Classification of Local and Health Authorities in Great Britain, Studies on medical and population projects* 48. London: OPCS

Craven, J. 1979. *The Distribution of the Product*. London: Allen & Unwin

Crawford, I. 1994. *UK Household Cost-of-living Indices: 1979–1992, Commentary* no. 44. London: Institute for Fiscal Studies

Crawford, I., Smith, S. and Webb, S. 1993. *VAT on Domestic Energy*, Commentary no. 39. London: Institute for Fiscal Studies

Cross, M. 1993. 'Generating the "new poverty": A European comparison', in Simpson, R. and Walker, R. (eds.), *Europe: For richer for poorer*. London: Child Poverty Action Group

Curran, J., Burrows, R. and Evandrou, M., 1987. *Small Business Owners and the Self-employed in Britain: An analysis of General Household Survey data*. London: Small Business Research Trust

Dale, A. and Marsh, C. (eds.) 1993. *The 1991 Census User's Guide*. London: HMSO

Davies, H., Joshi, H. and Clarke, L. 1993. 'Is it cash the deprived are short of?' paper presented to the 'Research on the 1991 Census' Conference, University of Newcastle upon Tyne (September)

Davies, R., Elias, P. and Penn, R. 1992. 'The relationship between a husband's unemployment and his wife's participation in the labour force', *Oxford Bulletin of Economic and Statistics* 54(2): 145–71

Davis, S. J. and Haltiwanger, J. 1991. 'Wage dispersion between and within US manufacturing plants, 1963–86', *Brookings Papers on Economic Activity*, Special Issue: 115–80

Deaton, A. and Muellbauer, J. 1980a. 'An almost ideal demand system', *American Economic Review* 70: 312–36

1980b. *Economics and Consumer Behaviour*. Cambridge: Cambridge University Press

Department of the Environment [DoE] 1993. *Housing and Construction Statistics*. London: HMSO

Department of Health 1991. *Children's Day Care Facilities at 31 March 1990, 1991*. London: HMSO

Department of Social Security [DSS] 1989. *Social Security Statistics*, London: HMSO

1992. *Households Below Average Income: A statistical analysis 1979–1988/89*. London: HMSO

1993a. *Households Below Average Income: A statistical analysis 1979–1990/91*. London: HMSO

1993b. *Social Security Statistics*. London: HMSO

1993c. *Social Security Departmental Report: The Government's expenditure plans 1993–94 to 1995–96*, Cm 2213. London: HMSO

1993d. *The Growth of Social Security*. London: HMSO

1994. *Households Below Average Income: A statistical analysis 1979–1991/92*. London: HMSO

Diewert, W. E. 1976. 'Exact and superlative index numbers', *Journal of Econometrics* 4: 115–45

1978. 'The economic theory of index numbers: A survey', in Deaton, A. (ed.), *The Theory and Measurement of Consumer Behaviour: Essays in honour of Sir Richard Stone*. Cambridge: Cambridge University Press

1990. 'The theory of the cost-of-living index and the measurement of welfare change', in Diewert, W. E. (ed.), *Price Level Measurement*. Amsterdam: North-Holland

Dilnot, A. and Kell, M. 1989. 'Male unemployment and women's work', in Dilnot, A. and Walker, I. (eds.), *The Economics of Social Security*. Oxford: Oxford University Press

Dilnot, A., Disney, R., Johnson, P. and Whitehouse, E. 1994. *Pensions Policy in the UK: An Economic Analysis*. London: Institute for Fiscal Studies

Disney, R., Gosling, A. and Machin, S. 1995. 'British unions in decline: an examination of the 1980s fall in trade union recognition', *Industrial and Labor Relations Review* forthcoming

Dougherty, A. and Van Order, R. 1982. 'Inflation, housing costs, and the consumer price index', *American Economic Review* 72(1): 154–64

Engel, E. 1895. 'Die Lebenskosten Belgischer Arbeiter-Familien früher und jetzt', *International Statistical Institute Bulletin* 9: 171–80

Epland, J. 1992. 'Inntektsfordelingen i 80-årene', *Økonomiske analyser* 2: 17–26

Esam, P. and Oppenheim, C. 1990. *A Charge on the Community*. London: Child Poverty Action Group/Local Government Information Unit

Evans, M. 1994. *Not Granted? An assessment of the change from single payments to the Social Fund*, STICERD Welfare State Programme, *Discussion Paper* WSP/101. London: London School of Economics

Evans, M., Piachaud, D. and Sutherland, H. 1994. *Designed for the Poor – Poorer by Design? The effects of the 1986 Social Security Act on family incomes*, STICERD Welfare State Programme, *Discussion Paper* WSP/105. London: London School of Economics

Fallon, P. R. and Layard, P. R. G. 1975. 'Capital–skill complementarity, income distribution, and output accounting', *Journal of Political Economy* 83: 279–301

Feinstein, C. H. 1988. 'The rise and fall of the Williamson Curve', *Journal of Economic History* 48: 699–729

Finegold, D. and Soskice, D. 1988. 'The failure of training in Britain: Analysis and prescription', *Oxford Review of Economic Policy* 4: 21–53

Forrest, R. and Gordon, D. 1993. *People and Places: A 1991 Census atlas of England*. Bristol: School for Advanced Urban Studies

Forrest, R. and Murie, A. 1989. 'Differential accumulation wealth, inheritance and housing policy reconsidered', *Policy and Politics* 17(1): 25–39

Forsyth, F. G. and Fowler, R. F. 1981. 'The theory and practice of chain price index numbers', *Journal of the Royal Statistical Society*, series A 144(2): 224–46

Fox, J. 1990. 'Describing univariate distributions', in Fox, J. and Long, J. S. (eds.), *Modern Methods of Data Analysis*. Newbury Park, CA: Sage

Freeman, R. 1980. 'Unionism and the dispersion of wages', *Industrial and Labor Relations Review* 34: 3–24

  1982. 'Union wage practices and wage dispersion within establishments', *Industrial and Labor Relations Review* 36: 3–21

  1993. 'How much has de-unionization contributed to the rise in male earnings inequality?', in Danziger, S. and Gottschalk, P. (eds.), *Uneven Tides: Rising inequality in America.* New York: Russell Sage Foundation

Freeman, R. and Katz, L. 1994. 'Rising wage inequality: United States vs. other advanced countries', in Freeman, R. (ed.), *Working Under Different Rules.* New York: Russell Sage Foundation

Fry, V. and Pashardes, P. 1985. 'Constructing true cost-of-living indices from Engel curves', Institute for Fiscal Studies, *Working Paper* no. 65. London: Institute for Fiscal Studies

1986. *The Retail Prices Index and the Cost of Living, Report Series* no 22. London: Institute for Fiscal Studies

Gaffikin, F. and Morrisey, M. 1992. *The New Unemployed.* London: Zed Books

Gardiner, K. 1993. *A Survey of Income Inequality Over the Last Twenty Years – how does the UK compare?*, STICERD Welfare State Programme, *Discussion Paper* WSP/100. London: London School of Economics

1994. 'The scale of injustice', *New Economy* 1(1): 62–5

Gentle, C., Dorling, D. F. L. and Cornford, J. 1994. 'Negative equity and British housing in the 1990s: Cause and effect', *Urban Studies* 31(2): 181–200

Giles, C. and Johnson, P. 1994. 'Tax reform in the UK and changes in the progressivity of the tax system, 1985–95', *Fiscal Studies* 15(3): 64–86

Good, F. J. 1990. 'Estimates of the distribution of personal wealth: 1. marketable wealth of individuals 1976–88', *Economic Trends* 444 (October): 137–57

Goodman, A. and Webb, S. 1994. *For Richer, for Poorer: The changing distribution of income in the United Kingdom, 1961–91,* Commentary no. 42. London: Institute for Fiscal Studies

Gosling, A. and Machin, S. 1993. *Trade Unions and the Dispersion of Earnings in UK Establishments, 1980–90, Discussion Paper* 93–05. London: University College

1995. 'Trade unions and the dispersion of earnings in British establishments, 1980–90', *Oxford Bulletin of Economics and Statistics* forthcoming

Gosling, A., Machin, S. and Meghir, C. 1994a. *What Has Happened to Wages?*, Commentary no. 43. London: Institute for Fiscal Studies

1994b. 'The changing distribution of male wages in the UK 1966 to 1992'. London: Institute for Fiscal Studies, mimeo

Green, A. E. 1993. 'Employment and unemployment in the "enterprise decade"', *Town and Country Planning* 62(3): 50–3

1994. *The Geography of Poverty and Wealth.* Coventry: Institute for Employment Research, University of Warwick

Green, A. E., Owen, D. W. and Winnett, C. M. 1994. 'The changing geography of recession: analyses of local unemployment time series', *Institute of British Geographers Transactions* NS 19: 142–62

Greene, R. 1991. 'Poverty concentration measures and the urban underclass', *Economic Geography* 67: 240–52

Gregg, P. and Machin, S. 1994. 'Is the UK rise in inequality different?', in Barrell, R. (ed.), *The UK Labour Market.* Cambridge: Cambridge University Press

Gregg, P. and Wadsworth, J. 1994a. 'How effective are state employment agencies?

Job centre use and job matching in Britain', NIESR, *Discussion Paper* no. 135. London: National Institute for Economic and Social Research

1994b. 'Opportunity knocks: Labour market transitions and unemployment'. London: NIESR, mimeo

Gregson, N. and Robinson, F. 1989. 'The casualties of Thatcherism', CURDS, *Discussion Paper* 93. Newcastle upon Tyne: CURDS, University of Newcastle upon Tyne

Gustafsson, B. and Palmer, E. E. 1993. 'Changes in Swedish inequality: a study of equivalent income 1975–1991', University of Gothenburg

Hakim, C. 1989. 'Workforce restructuring, social insurance coverage and the black economy', *Journal of Social Policy* 18(4): 471–503

Hamnett, C. 1991. 'A nation of inheritors? Housing inheritance, wealth and inequality in Britain', *Journal of Social Policy* 20(4): 509–36

1992. 'The geography of housing wealth and inheritance in Britain', *The Geographical Journal* 158(3): 307–21

1993. 'Measuring house price changes', *Housing Review* 42: 65–6

Hansen, F. K. 1993. 'Social exclusion in Denmark', Center for Alternativ Samfundsanalyse Copenhagen

Harkness, S., Machin, S. and Waldfogel, J. 1994. *Evaluating the Pin-money Hypothesis*, STICERD Welfare State Programme, *Discussion Paper* WSP/108. London: London School of Economics

Hauser, R. and Becker, I. 1993. 'The development of the income distribution in the Federal Republic of Germany during the seventies and eighties'. University of Frankfurt

Hausner, V. A. (ed.) 1986. *Critical Issues in Urban Economic Development*, vol. 1. Oxford: Clarendon Press

(ed.) 1987. *Critical Issues in Urban Economic Development*, vol. 2. Oxford: Clarendon Press

Hill, M. 1990. *Social Security Policy in Britain*, Aldershot: Edward Elgar

Hills, J. 1984. *Savings and Fiscal Privilege, Report Series no. 9*. London: Institute for Fiscal Studies

1989. 'Counting the family silver: the public sector's balance sheet 1957 to 1987', *Fiscal Studies* 10: 66–85

1993. *The Future of Welfare: A guide to the debate*. York: Joseph Rowntree Foundation

Hirschfield, A. 1994. 'Using the 1991 Population Census to study deprivation', *Planning Practice and Research* 9(1): 43–54

HM Treasury 1993. *Public Expenditure Analysis to 1995–96*, Cm 2219. London: HMSO

Hofmann, E. and Lambert, S. 1993. 'The 1993 Share Register survey', *Economic Trends* 480: 124–9

Holmans, A. 1990. *House Prices: changes through time at national and sub-national level*, Government Economic Service, *Working Paper* no. 110. London: Department of the Environment

1991. *Estimates of Housing Equity Withdrawal by Owner Occupiers in the United*

Kingdom 1970 to 1990, Government Economic Service, *Working Paper* 116. London: Department of the Environment

Hughes, M. A. 1989. 'Misspeaking truth to power: a geographical perspective on the "underclass" fallacy', *Economic Geography* 65(3): 189–207

Inland Revenue 1993. *Inland Revenue Statistics*. London: HMSO

1994. *Inland Revenue Statistics*. London: HMSO

Jenkins, S. P. 1994. *Winners and Losers: A portrait of the UK income distribution during the 1980s* (Report to the Joseph Rowntree Foundation), *Economics Discussion Paper* 94–07. Swansea: University of Swansea

1995. 'Accounting for inequality trends: decomposition analyses for the UK 1971–86', *Economica* 62: 29–63

Jenkins, S. P. and Cowell, F. A. 1993. *Dwarfs and Giants in the 1980s: The UK income distribution and how it changed*, *Economics Discussion Paper* 93–03. Swansea: University of Swansea

1994. 'Dwarfs and giants in the 1980s: Trends in the UK income distribution', *Fiscal Studies* 15: 99–118

Jenkins, S. P. and Millar, J. 1989. 'Income risk and income maintenance: Implications for incentives to work', in Dilnot, A. and Walker. I. (eds.), *The Economics of Social Security*. Oxford: Oxford University Press

Johnson, P. and Webb, S. 1992. 'The treatment of housing in official low income statistics', *Journal of the Royal Statistical Society A* 155: 273–90

1993. 'Explaining the growth in UK income inequality', *Economic Journal* 103: 429–43

Juhn, C., Murphy, K. and Pierce, B. 1993. 'Wage inequality and the rise in returns to skill', *Journal of Political Economy* 108: 410–42

Katz, L. and Murphy, L. 1992. 'Changes in relative wages 1963–1987: Supply and demand factors', *Quarterly Journal of Economics* 107: 35–78

Kay, J. A. and King, M. A. 1990. *The British Tax System*, 5th edn. Oxford: Oxford University Press

Kemsley, W. F. F., Redpath, R. U. and Holmes, M. 1980. *Family Expenditure Survey Handbook*. London: HMSO

King, M., and Leape, J. 1989. 'Asset accumulation, information and the life-cycle', Financial Markets Group, *Discussion Paper* no. 14. London: London School of Economics

Kuznets, S. 1955. 'Economic growth and income inequality', *American Economic Review* 45: 1–28

Lambert, P. J. 1993. *The Distribution and Redistribution of Income*, 2nd edn. Manchester: Manchester University Press

Layard, R. and Zabalza, A. 1979. 'Family income distribution: explanation and policy evaluation', *Journal of Political Economy* 87, Supplement: S133–61

Lee, C. and Saunders, M. 1988. 'Personal equity plans: success or failure?', *Fiscal Studies* 9: 36–50

Levy, F. and Murnane, R. J. 1992. 'US earnings levels and earnings inequality: A review of recent trends and proposed explanations', *Journal of Economic Literature* 30: 1333–81

Lewis, J. and Townsend, A. 1989. *The North–South Divide: Regional change in Britain in the 1980s.* London: Paul Chapman

Lucas, R. E. 1988. 'On the mechanics of economic development', *Journal of Monetary Economics* 22: 3–42

Lundberg, S. 1985. 'The added worker effect', *Journal of Labour Economics* 3(1): 11–37

Machin, S. 1994. 'Changes in the relative demand for skills in the UK labour market', in Booth, A. and Snower, D. (eds.), *Acquiring Skills: Market failures, their symptoms and policy responses.* Cambridge: Cambridge University Press

Machin, S. and Manning, A. 1994. 'Minimum wages, wage dispersion and employment: Evidence from UK wages councils', *Industrial and Labor Relations Review* 47(2): 319–29

Machin, S. and Waldfogel, J. 1994a. *The Decline of the Male Breadwinner: changing shares of the earnings of husbands and wives in family income in the UK,* STICERD Welfare State Programme, *Discussion Paper* WSP/103. London: London School of Economics

1994b. 'What has happened to the income shares of male and female earnings in American families since the 1960s?'. London: University College, mimeo

Marron, J. S. and Schmitz, H.-P. 1992. 'Simultaneous density estimation of several income distributions', *Journal of Econometric Theory* 8: 476–88

Martin, J. and Roberts, C. 1984. *Women and Employment: A lifetime perspective.* London: HMSO

Martin, R. 1988. 'The political economy of Britain's North–South divide?', *Institute of British Geographers Transactions* NS 13: 389–418

1993. 'Remapping British regional policy: the end of the North–South divide?', *Regional Studies* 27(8): 797–805

Massey, D. S. and Denton, N. A. 1988. 'The dimensions of residential segregation', *Social Forces* 67(2): 281–315

Mayhew, K. 1977. 'Earnings dispersion in local labour markets: implications for search behaviour', *Oxford Bulletin of Economics and Statistics* 39: 93–107

McGregor, P. P. L. and Borooah, V. K. 1992. 'Is low spending or low income a better indicator of whether or not a household is poor?: Some results from the 1985 Family Expenditure Survey', *Journal of Social Policy* 21: 53–69

McKee, L. and Bell, C. 1985. 'Marital and family relations in times of male unemployment', in Roberts, B., Finnegan, R. and Gallie, D. (eds.), *New Approaches to Economic Life.* Manchester: Manchester University Press

Meager, N., 1991. *Self-employment in the UK, IMS Report* no. 205. Brighton: Institute of Manpower Studies

1992a. 'Does unemployment lead to self-employment?', *Small Business Economics* 4: 87–103

1992b. 'The fall and rise of self-employment (again): A comment on Bögenhold and Staber', *Work, Employment and Society* 6(1): 127–34

1993. *Self-employment and Labour Market Policy in the EC,* a report to the European Commission (DGV) under the MISEP programme. Berlin: Wissen-

384   Bibliography

schaftszentrum Berlin für Sozialforschung (Published as *WZB Discussion Paper* FSI 93–2010)

Meager, N., Court, G. and Moralee, J. 1994. *Self-employment and the Distribution of Income*, IMS Report no. 270. Brighton: Institute of Manpower Studies

Meager, N., Kaiser, M. and Dietrich, H. 1992. *Self-employment in the United Kingdom and Germany*. London/Bonn: Anglo–German Foundation for the Study of Industrial Society

Millward, N., Stevens, M., Smart, D. and Hawes, W. R. 1992. *Workplace Industrial Relations in Transition*. Aldershot: Dartmouth

Mincer, J. 1974. *Schooling, Experience and Earnings*. New York: Columbia University Press

Mookherjee, D. and Shorrocks, A. F. 1982. 'A decomposition analysis of the trend in UK income inequality', *Economic Journal* 92: 886–92

Morris, R. and Carstairs, V. 1991. 'Which deprivation? A comparison of selected deprivation indexes', *Journal of Public Health Medicine* 13(4): 318–26

Muellbauer, J. 1977. 'The cost-of-living', *Social Security Research*, papers presented at a series of Social Security seminars, Sunningdale, 1976. London: HMSO

Murphy, K. and Welch, F. 1992. 'The structure of wages', *Quarterly Journal of Economics* 107: 285–326

Musgrave, R. A. 1959. *The Theory of Public Finance*. New York: McGraw-Hill

National Audit Office 1990. *The Retail Prices Index*. London: HMSO

Noble, M., Smith, G., Avenell, D., Smith, T. and Sharland, E. 1994. *Changing Patterns of Income and Wealth in Oxford and Oldham*. Oxford: University of Oxford Department of Applied Social Studies and Social Research

Nolan, B. 1987. *Income Distribution and the Macroeconomy*. Cambridge: Cambridge University Press

Norris, P. and Ross, C. 1992. *Working with the Census*. London: Local Government Management Board

OECD 1992. 'Recent developments in self-employment', in *OECD Economic Outlook, July 1992*. Paris: Organisation for Economic Co-operation and Development

1993. 'Earnings inequality: changes in the 1980s', chapter 5, *Employment Outlook, July 1993*. Paris: Organisation for Economic Co-operation and Development

OPCS 1993. 'How complete was the 1991 Census?', *Population Trends* 71: 22–5

Owens, A. 1989. *Enterprise Allowance Scheme Evaluation: Sixth 6-month national survey*. Sheffield: Employment Service: Research and Evaluation Branch

Pen, J. 1971. *Income Distribution*. Harmondsworth: Penguin Books

Piachaud, D. 1978. 'Prices and the distribution of incomes', in Lord Diamond (Chairman), Royal Commission on the Distribution of Income and Wealth, *Selected Evidence for Report 6*. London: HMSO

Pissarides, C. 1986. 'Unemployment and vacancies in Britain', *Economic Policy* 3: 500–59

Pissarides, C. and Weber, G. 1989. 'An expenditure-based estimate of Britain's black economy', *Journal of Public Economics* 39: 17–32

Pratten, C. 1993. *The Stock Market.* Cambridge: Cambridge University Press
Pudney, S. and Thomas, J. 1993. 'Unemployment benefits, incentives and the labour supply of wives of unemployed men: Econometric estimates'. Cambridge: University of Cambridge, Department of Applied Economics, mimeo
Redmond, G. and Sutherland, H. forthcoming. *How has Tax and Social Security Policy Changed since 1978? A distributional analysis,* Micro-simulation Unit, *Discussion Paper.* Cambridge: University of Cambridge, Department of Applied Economics
Retail Prices Index Advisory Committee 1986. *Methodological Issues Affecting the Retail Price Index,* Cmnd 9848. London: HMSO
Revell, J. B. S. 1967. *The Wealth of the Nation.* Cambridge: Cambridge University Press
Ricardo, D. 1951. *The Works and Correspondence of David Ricardo,* P. Sraffa (ed.), vol. VIII. Cambridge: Cambridge University Press
Robinson, W. and Skinner, T. 1989. *Reforming the RPI: A better treatment of housing costs?, Commentary* no. 15. London: Institute for Fiscal Studies
Rodrigues, C. 1993. *The Measurement and Decomposition of Inequality in Portugal, 1980/81–1989/90,* Micro-simulation Unit, *Discussion Paper* 9302. Cambridge: University of Cambridge, Department of Applied Economics
Room, G. 1990. *'New poverty' in the European Community.* London: Macmillan
Royal Commission on the Distribution of Income and Wealth 1977. *Third Report on the Standing Reference,* Report no. 5, Cmnd 6999. London: HMSO
Rubery, J., Earnshaw, J. and Burchell, B. 1993. *New Forms and Patterns of Employment: the role of self-employment in Britain.* Baden Baden: Nomos Verlagsgesellschaft
Ruggles, P. 1990. *Drawing the Line: alternative poverty measures and their implications for public policy.* Washington, DC: The Urban Institute
Salgado-Ugarte, I. H., Shimizu, M. and Taniuchi, T. 1993. 'Exploring the shape of univariate data using kernel density estimators', *STATA Technical Bulletin* 16: 8–19
Samuelson, P. A. and Nordhaus, W. D. 1989. *Economics,* 13th edn. New York: McGraw-Hill
Saunders, M. and Webb, S. 1988. 'Fiscal privilege and financial assets: some distributive effects', *Fiscal Studies* 9: 51–66
Saunders, P. 1984. 'Beyond housing classes. The sociological significance of private property rights in means of consumption', *International Journal of Urban and Regional Research* 8(2): 202–27
1991. *A Nation of Home Owners.* London: Unwin Hyman
Saunders, P. 1994. *Rising on the Tasman tide: Income inequality in Australia and New Zealand in the 1980s,* SPRC, *Discussion Paper* no. 49. Kensington, NSW: University of New South Wales
Schmitt, J. 1994. 'The changing structure of male earnings in Britain, 1974–88', in Freeman, R. and Katz, L. (eds.), *Differences and Changes in Wage Structures.* Chicago: University of Chicago Press forthcoming
Schmitt, J. and Wadsworth, J. 1993. *Why are Two Million Men Inactive? The decline*

in male labour force participation in Britain, Centre for Economic Performance, *Working Paper* no. 336. London: Centre for Economic Performance

Sen, A. 1985. 'The standard of living: Lecture I – concepts and critiques', in Hawthorn, G. (ed.), *The Standard of Living*. Cambridge: Cambridge University Press

Silver, H. 1993. 'National conceptions of the new urban poverty: social structural change in Britain, France and the United States', *International Journal of Urban and Regional Research* 17(3): 336–54

Silverman, B. W. 1981. 'Using kernel density estimates to investigate multimodality', *Journal of the Royal Statistical Society B* 43: 97–9

1986. *Density Estimation for Statistics and Data Analysis*. London: Chapman Hall

Simpson, S. 1993a. 'Local analysis of the Census undercount', *BURISA Newsletter* 108: 11–14

1993b. *Areas of Stress Within Bradford district*. Bradford: City of Bradford Metropolitan Council

(ed.) 1993c. *Census Indicators of Local Poverty and Deprivation*. Newcastle upon Tyne: LARIA

Smith, A. 1776. *The Wealth of Nations*

Smith, J. 1979. 'The distribution of family earnings', *Journal of Political Economy* 87, Supplement: S163–93

Smith, S. 1986. *Britain's Shadow Economy*. Oxford: Oxford University Press

Stoker, T. 1986. 'The distributional welfare effects of rising prices in the United States', *American Economic Review* 76: 335–49

Taylor, M. (ed.) 1992. *British Household Panel Survey User Manual, Volume A: Introduction, technical report and appendices*. Colchester: University of Essex

Tipping, D. G. 1970. 'Price changes and income distribution', *Applied Statistics* 19: 1–17

Törnqvist, L. 1936. 'The Bank of Finland's consumption price index', *Bank of Finland Monthly Bulletin* 10: 1–8

Townsend, A. 1993. 'The urban–rural cycle in the Thatcher growth years', *Institute of British Geographers Transactions* NS 18: 207–21

US Department of Commerce 1993. *Money Income of Households, Families, and Persons in the United States: 1992*, *Current Population Reports*, Series P-60, no. 184, Washington DC: US Government Printing Office

Uusitalo, H. 1989. *Income Distribution in Finland*. Helsinki: Central Statistical Office of Finland

Van Reenen, J. 1993. 'Getting a fair share of the plunder? Technological change and the wage structure', Institute for Fiscal Studies, *Working Paper* no. 93/3. London: Institute for Fiscal Studies

von Weizsäcker, R. 1993. *A Theory of Earnings Distribution*. Cambridge: Cambridge University Press

Waddington, J. 1992. 'Trade union membership in Britain 1980–87: Unemployment and restructuring', *British Journal of Industrial Relations* 30: 282–324

Waldfogel, J. 1994. *Women Working for Less: Family status and women's pay in the US and UK.* Harvard University, Ph.D. thesis

Walker, C. 1993. *Managing Poverty: The limits of social assistance.* London: Routledge

Webber, R. J. 1975. *Liverpool Social Area Study: 1971 data: final report.* London: Centre for Environmental Studies

Williamson, J. G. 1985. *Did British Capitalism Breed Inequality?* Boston: Allen & Unwin

1991. *Inequality, Poverty, and History.* Oxford: Basil Blackwell

Wilson, W. J. 1987. *The Truly Disadvantaged.* Chicago: University of Chicago Press

Wolfson, M. 1986. 'Stasis amid change – income inequality in Canada 1965–1983', *Review of Income and Wealth* 32: 337–69

1994. 'When inequalities diverge', *American Economic Review* 84, Papers and Proceedings: 353–8

Wong, D. W. S. 1993. 'Spatial indices of segregation', *Urban Studies* 30(3): 559–72

Wood, A. 1994. *North–south trade, employment and inequality.* Oxford: Clarendon Press

Wrigglesworth, J. 1992. *The Housing Market Debt Trap.* London: UBS Phillips & Drew

Index

Printed in the United States
By Bookmasters